Expert Testimony on the Psychology of Eyewitness Identification

American Psychology-Law Society Series

Books in the Series

Trial Consulting
Amy J. Posey and Lawrence S. Wrightsman

Death by Design
Craig Haney

Psychological Injuries
William J. Koch, Kevin S. Douglas, Tonia L. Nicholls, and Melanie L. O'Neill

Emergency Department Treatment of the Psychiatric Patient
Susan Stefan

The Psychology of the Supreme Court
Lawrence S. Wrightsman

Proving the Unprovable
Christopher Slobogin

Adolescents, Media, and the Law
Roger J.R. Levesque

Oral Arguments Before the Supreme Court
Lawrence S. Wrightsman

God in the Courtroom
Brian H. Bornstein and Monica K. Miller

Expert Testimony on the Psychology of Eyewitness Identification
Edited by Brian L. Cutler

Expert Testimony on the Psychology of Eyewitness Identification

Edited by

Brian L. Cutler

OXFORD
UNIVERSITY PRESS
2009

OXFORD
UNIVERSITY PRESS

Oxford University Press, Inc., publishes works that further
Oxford University's objective of excellence
in research, scholarship, and education.

Oxford New York
Auckland   Cape Town   Dar es   Salaam   Hong Kong   Karachi
Kuala Lumpur   Madrid   Melbourne   Mexico City   Nairobi
New Delhi   Shanghai   Taipei   Toronto

With offices in
Argentina   Austria   Brazil   Chile   Czech   Republic   France   Greece
Guatemala   Hungary   Italy   Japan   Poland   Portugal   Singapore
South Korea   Switzerland   Thailand   Turkey   Ukraine   Vietnam

Published by Oxford University Press, Inc.
198 Madison Avenue, New York, New York 10016
www.oup.com

Library of Congress Cataloging-in-Publication Data

Expert testimony on the psychology of eyewitness identification /
edited by Brian L. Cutler.
   p. cm. – (American psychology-law society series)
Includes bibliographical references and index.
ISBN 978–0–19–533197–4
1. Eyewitness identification–United States–Psychological aspects.
2. Forensic psychology–United States. I. Cutler, Brian L.
KF9672.E936 2009
345.73'066–dc22
                                                        2009018809

9 8 7 6 5 4 3 2 1

Printed in the United States of America

on acid-free paper

Series Foreword

This book series is sponsored by the American Psychology-Law Society (APLS). APLS is an interdisciplinary organization devoted to scholarship, practice, and public service in psychology and law. Its goals include advancing the contributions of psychology to the understanding of law and legal institutions through basic and applied research; promoting the education of psychologists in matters of law and the education of legal personnel in matters of psychology; and informing the psychological and legal communities and the general public of current research, educational, and service activities in the field of psychology and law. APLS membership includes psychologists from the academic research and clinical practice communities, as well as members of the legal community. Research and practice is represented in both the civil and criminal legal arenas. APLS has chosen Oxford University Press as a strategic partner because of its commitment to scholarship, quality, and the international dissemination of ideas. These strengths will help APLS reach its goal of educating the psychology and legal professions and the general public about important developments in psychology and law. The focus of the book series reflects the diversity of the field of psychology and law, as we continue to publish books on a broad range of topics.

Over 20 years ago, a special issue of the journal *Law and Human Behavior* was devoted to the topic of expert psychological testimony about eyewitness memory. At the time, research on this topic was in its infancy, but it is clear from the chapters in Brian Cutler's book that the research has grown, both in sheer amount and also, importantly, in methodological sophistication. Eyewitness research in the past two decades had led to major changes in police practices, and expert testimony about this research has gradually become more accepted in American courts.

Eyewitness testimony is highly compelling in a criminal trial. When a witness identifies a defendant in court, the impact on jurors can be substantial. We now know that eyewitnesses are sometimes wrong, even when they are highly confident that they are making correct identifications. Cutler notes that investigations by The Innocence Project have led to the exoneration of well over 200 cases in which DNA evidence has proven the innocence of convicted persons, the vast majority of whom were identified by eyewitnesses to be perpetrators of crimes they clearly did not commit.

The purpose of Cutler's book is to both update and expand on the topics covered in that special issue of *Law and Human Behavior*. Cutler is well-positioned to take on this task, as he is now the editor of *Law and Human Behavior* and has long been one of the key researchers on eyewitness testimony. Cutler chose to limit the chapter topics to expert psychological testimony in cases that focus on eyewitness identification of perpetrators by adult eyewitnesses. I think this was a wise choice, because it allowed him to provide an in-depth analysis of the many aspects of this issue. He has brought together an impressive group of researchers and practicing attorneys to provide current overviews and critiques of key topics. They address the ethics and practice of expert testimony, its admissibility in court, and how such testimony might impact jury decisions. Importantly, many of the chapters identify the strengths and limitations of current research, particularly the key issue of the external validity of laboratory-based studies. As Cutler notes in his Afterword, the issue of external validity ultimately must be addressed in order to clearly establish the appropriateness of expert testimony.

A primary audience for this book are psychologists who are involved in eyewitness research and/or expert testimony. But interest in the book should reach beyond this audience to the legal community, including defense attorneys, prosecutors, and judges. It is notable that Cutler has invited contributors who represent both the prosecution and defense in criminal cases, and they provide practical advice for lawyers about how to select and make the most effective use of experts, including ways to maximize the likelihood that such testimony will be admitted at trial, as well as how to rigorously challenge the admissibility of expert testimony and ensure that the science of eyewitness identification is not misrepresented.

Ronald Roesch
Series Editor

Preface

The June, 1986 issue of *Law and Human Behavior* was devoted to the topic of expert psychological testimony about eyewitness memory, a relatively new phenomenon at the time. Topics of the articles in the special issue included historical and legal perspectives on expert testimony, the role of the expert, the ethics of expert testimony, the effects of expert testimony on jurors, and the external validity of the research upon which the expert testimony is based. It has been over 20 years since that special issue was published, and much has happened in the interim, including the following:

- Investigations by members of the Innocence Project, using DNA testimony, have led to the exoneration of over 235 felons, many of whom spent significant time in prison. Mistaken identification has been established as the single most common precursor to conviction of the innocent.
- Hundreds of new empirical studies of eyewitness identification have been published in refereed journals. This research examines factors affecting eyewitness identification, methods of improving identification accuracy and reducing identification errors, and the relation between eyewitness confidence and identification accuracy. This research includes more than a dozen new meta-analyses. The methodological sophistication of the research and reporting standards have increased substantially. The number of laboratories conducting eyewitness research has grown dramatically. In addition, there are many new research articles about expert testimony, including studies of expert

consensus, lay and expert knowledge about eyewitness factors, the effects of traditional safeguards against wrongful conviction in eyewitness cases, and the effects of expert testimony on jury decision-making.

- Guided by the psychological research on eyewitness identification, the United States Department of Justice, two states (New Jersey, North Carolina), and many police departments in the United States have adopted guidelines for improving identification procedures. Other states are in the process of reforming their identification procedures or are considering the possibility.
- Courts in many states have become more receptive to expert testimony about eyewitness memory. The number of eyewitness experts, the number of attorneys who are knowledgeable about eyewitness research, and the incidences of proffers of expert testimony and admitted expert testimony have all increased substantially.

The confluence of these events supports the need for a fresh look at issues surrounding expert testimony on eyewitness identification. The aim of this volume, therefore, is to provide a thorough update and expansion of the topics addressed in the 1986 special issue of *Law and Human Behavior*. This volume well-exceeds the special issue in breadth and depth. The cast of authors has changed by nearly 100%. Indeed, only one author (Ebbe Ebbesen) will have served as an author in both the special issue and this volume. The current authors include well-established eyewitness scholars, many of whom also have considerable experience as expert witnesses. Some of the authors were active in research at the time of the 1986 special issue. The authors also include seasoned practicing attorneys who have had very significant experience with eyewitnesses and expert witnesses. Some of the authors are credentialed in both Psychology and Law. And some of the authors are from the newest generation of scholars, who can provide future leadership in research on these and other important topics and phenomena. In sum, we bring a wide range of perspectives to this volume.

This volume is very focused. The chapter topics are limited to expert psychological testimony in cases that focus on eyewitness identification of perpetrators by adult eyewitnesses. The volume does not contain a lengthy review of the research on eyewitness identification accuracy (although this research will be referenced in various chapters) and does not address expert testimony in other areas involving eyewitnesses (e.g., children's suggestibility, child sexual abuse, repressed and recovered memories). For more broad-based coverage of the research on eyewitness memory, readers may consult the recently published, two-volume *Handbook of Eyewitness Testimony* (Lindsay, Ross, Read, & Toglia, 2007; Toglia, Read, Ross, & Lindsay, 2007) or the *Encyclopedia of Psychology and Law* (Cutler, 2008).

I now turn to the topics that *are* covered in this volume. Malpass, Meissner, Ross, and Marcon lead off with an overview of the link between mistaken identification and wrongful conviction, and the research base that serves as the foundation for expert testimony. Their chapter also places expert testimony on eyewitness memory into a broader context of psychological science and the application of knowledge to societal problems. Pezdek provides an analysis of the content and form of expert testimony—topics that have received relatively little previous attention in the published literature. Pezdek also reviews ethical issues associated with expert testimony. Devenport, Kimbrough, and I review the research on the effectiveness of traditional safeguards (e.g., pretrial procedures and cross-examination) in place to protect innocent defendants who have been mistakenly identified by eyewitnesses from becoming wrongfully convicted.

Expert testimony on eyewitness memory requires a series of decisions. Practicing attorneys must decide whether expert testimony is appropriate and whether it would be helpful in a specific case. Eyewitness researchers who are willing to serve as expert witnesses must likewise decide whether it is appropriate to testify about eyewitness research in general and in specific cases. Judges must decide whether or not to admit expert testimony. These decisions may depend on a variety of factors. One factor is legal precedence. How have the courts viewed expert testimony on eyewitness memory? Two chapters examine this question. Epstein reviews the current status of admissibility in U.S. state and federal courts, whereas Groscup and Penrod examine how appellate courts have responded to appeals based on lower court admissibility decisions. There are other considerations. Will the testimony inform the jury; that is, does the testimony go beyond what the jury is already likely to know? Read and Desmarais provide a review of the research on lay understanding of eyewitness memory. Is the research on eyewitness memory commonly accepted within the expert's scientific community? Hosch, Jolly, Schmersal, and Smith review the research on expert consensus from a variety of data sources. Given the research methods that are typical of eyewitness research, will the research conclusions generalize to what occurs in actual crimes? Flowe, Finklea, and Ebbesen provide a review of eyewitness research and examine whether the research is sufficiently conclusive to justify expert testimony. What effect will expert testimony have on the jury? Will it confuse jurors, make them skeptical of eyewitness testimony, or help them make more informed evaluations of eyewitness testimony? Leippe and Eisenstadt review the research on the effects of expert testimony on jury decision making.

Our final two chapters provide unique perspectives on expert testimony. Seasoned practicing attorneys, each of whom has impressive experience in criminal cases, have contributed these chapters. As is typical in court procedures, the prosecutor gets the first word. In their chapter, attorneys Bailey and Mecklenburg provide a rigorous challenge to the admissibility and helpfulness of expert testimony from their unique perspectives. Attorneys Drouet and Kent were not asked to defend expert testimony, but rather to provide readers with an understanding of their considerations, needs, and advice with respect to expert testimony. For practicing attorneys and researchers who offer expert testimony or are considering offering expert testimony, these chapters provide extremely useful perspectives and insights that are not easily obtained from other sources.

This volume should be of use to a variety of audiences. Researchers of expert testimony can update their knowledge based on new summaries and perspectives. Practicing attorneys and judges will find this volume to be a useful and efficient resource for gaining an understanding of a wide variety of issues associated with this form of expert testimony. Expert witnesses will find many of these chapters helpful for sharpening their knowledge bases and skills and benchmarking their practice against the research. My largest hope is that this volume will inspire students to undertake careers in Psychology and Law and to affiliate with the American Psychology-Law Society. This career path has brought enormous professional fulfillment to me and to many others.

I am honored to be among the company of the impressive eyewitness scholars (at all levels) and seasoned attorneys who are contributors to this volume. Publication of scholarship is routine for eyewitness scholars, but they nevertheless make choices about where to direct their efforts. I thank them for their decisions to join this effort. Practicing attorneys are not given "release time" to contribute to volumes such as these, and so I am particularly indebted to Patrice Bailey, Suzanne Drouet, Patrick Kent, and Sheri Mecklenburg for making the time for this project. I wish to also acknowledge my former dean (Dr. Nancy Gutierrez, Dean, College of Arts & Sciences, University of North Carolina at Charlotte) and my current dean (Dr. Nawal Ammar, Dean, Faculty of Criminology, Justice & Policy Studies, University of Ontario Institute of Technology) for their support of my scholarship, without which this volume would not have been possible. I wish to thank Dr. Ronald Roesch, series editor, for his encouragement and expert assistance throughout this project. James Lant and Andrew Smith provided valuable research assistance for this project. Last, I thank my family, Karin, Penelope, Dennison, and Alison Cutler, for their support and encouragement throughout this project.

Brian L. Cutler

References

Cutler, B. L. (Ed.). (2007). *Encyclopedia of psychology & law* (Vols. 1, 2). Thousand Oaks, CA: Sage Publications.

Lindsay, R. C. L., Ross, D. F., Read, J. D., & Toglia, M. P. (Eds.). (2007). *The handbook of eyewitness psychology, Vol. II: Memory for people.* Mahwah, NJ: Lawrence Erlbaum.

Toglia, M. P., Read, J. D., Ross, D. F., & Lindsay, R. C. L. (Eds.). (2007). *The handbook of eyewitness psychology, Vol. I: Memory for events.* Mahwah, NJ: Lawrence Erlbaum.

Contents

Contributors

Patricia J. Bailey
Office of the New York County District Attorney
New York, NY

Brian L. Cutler
University of Ontario Institute of Technology
Oshawa, ON

Sarah L. Desmarais
University of British Columbia
Vancouver, BC

Jennifer L. Devenport
Western Washington University
Bellingham, WA

Suzanne K. Drouet
Maryland Office of the Public Defender
Baltimore, MD

Ebbe B. Ebbesen
University of California, San Diego
San Diego, CA

Donna Eisenstadt
Illinois State University
Normal, IL

Jules Epstein
Widener University School of Law
Wilmington, DE

Kristin M. Finklea
Univesity of California, San Diego
San Diego, CA

Heather D. Flowe
University of Leicester
Leicester, UK

Jennifer Groscup
Scripps College
Claremont, CA

Harmon M. Hosch
University of Texas at El Paso
El Paso, TX

Kevin W. Jolly
University of Texas at El Paso
El Paso, TX

Patrick E. Kent
Maryland Office of the Public Defender
Baltimore, MD

Christopher D. Kimbrough
Western Washington University
Bellingham, WA

Michael R. Leippe
Illinois State University
Normal, IL

Roy S. Malpass
University of Texas at El Paso
El Paso, TX

Jessica L. Marcon
University of Texas at El Paso
El Paso, TX

Christian A. Meissner
University of Texas at El Paso
El Paso, TX

Sheri H. Mecklenburg
Assistant United States Attorney
Northern District of Illinois
Chicago, IL

Steven Penrod
John Jay College of Criminal Justice, CUNY
New York, NY

Kathy Pezdek
Claremont Graduate University
Claremont, CA

J. Don Read
Simon Fraser University
Burnaby, BC

Stephen J. Ross
Florida International University
Miami, FL

Larissa A. Schmersal
University of Texas at El Paso
El Paso, TX

Brooke A. Smith
University of Texas at El Paso
El Paso, TX

1

The Need for Expert Psychological Testimony on Eyewitness Identification

Roy S. Malpass, Stephen J. Ross, Christian A. Meissner, and Jessica L. Marcon

The evidence requirements for eyewitness identification were improved in the middle of the 19th century by a Middlesex magistrates' court in the United Kingdom (Malpass, Tredoux, & McQuiston-Surrett, 2007), which established lineups as a means of protecting innocent suspects from false identification. Members of the many groups involved in the criminal justice system have recognized the fragility of eyewitness identification and a troublingly large possibility of error that sends innocent people to jail. Although the problem has appeared to be resistant to reduction, it has not been difficult to document.

Evidence of a need for diagnostic procedures for obtaining and evaluating eyewitness and other memory-based evidence has been apparent for many decades. Borchard (1932) reviewed 65 criminal cases involving persons known to be completely innocent. He began with this analysis: "Perhaps the major source of these tragic errors is an identification of the accused by the victim of a crime of violence. This mistake was practically alone responsible for twenty-nine of these convictions." He continues "How valueless are these identifications by the victim of a crime is indicated by the fact that in eight of these cases, the wrongfully accused person and the really guilty criminal bore not the slightest resemblance to each other, whereas in twelve other cases, the resemblance, while fair, was still not at all close. In only two cases can the resemblance be called striking" (p. xiii). Borchard made a series of recommendations, which had little detectable impact on the legal system.

Brandon and Davies (1973) similarly reviewed 70 cases from the United Kingdom. As to causes of wrongful convictions, they write: "Since eyewitness identification is a very common form of evidence in criminal cases, it is perhaps not surprising that a large proportion of the mistakes we have come across occur in this field. Nevertheless, a greater number of mistakes seem to occur in this field even than one would expect. Of the cases we have examined of people who have subsequently been pardoned, or whose convictions have been quashed, or sentences remitted, a remarkably high proportion have involved misidentification" (p. 24).

Almost 45 years after Borchard (1932) and shortly after Brandon and Davies (1973)—and again in the United Kingdom—Devlin (1976) was asked to lead an inquiry into eyewitness identification after two cases of wrongful conviction came to the attention of the public. Devlin made a detailed series of recommendations; however, there was little effect leading to immediate changes in the administration of investigations and the development of eyewitness evidence. Devlin's impact was subtle and took time; some of his impact may be seen in the U.K. National Court of Appeal decision in *R v. Turnbull* (1976), but substantial changes were not visible until the Police and Criminal Evidence (PACE) Act of 1984 and its subsequent updates. The organization of law enforcement and its administration into a highly centralized entity in the United Kingdom likely lends itself to more effective centralized research and development processes, compared with the highly fractionated criminal justice system in the United States.

Radelet, Bedau, and Putnam (1992) reviewed the magnitude of wrongful convictions in 400 capital cases in the United States. They assess the causes as follows: "As for the causes of the errors, our research has shown that the two most frequent are perjury by prosecution witnesses and mistaken eyewitness testimony" (p. 18). Shortly afterward, Huff, Ratner, and Sagarin (1996) reviewed more than 200 cases of wrongful conviction in the United States and articulated the distribution of errors contributing to such instances. Out of 205 cases in their database, the authors cite eyewitness misidentification as a major contributor to 100 of these—just under 50% of the cases. They write: "We believe that the single most important factor leading to wrongful conviction in the United States and England is eyewitness misidentification . . . This is shown not only in our database but in the responses to our questionnaire [sent to attorneys and judges], where nearly 8 out of 10 ranked witness error (primarily witness misidentification, but also including some less frequent types of witness error) as by far the most frequent type of error leading to false convictions."

At about the same time, events began to move forward on two fronts. The need for a focused response was broadly recognized among eyewitness researchers, and a policy paper was composed and published by the American

Psychology-Law Society in the Society's journal *Law and Human Behavior.* This paper (Wells et al., 1998) contained a focused set of recommendations based on a review of findings of well-established lines of scientific investigation. The second front was manifested in a report from a study commissioned by the National Institute of Justice on the exoneration of wrongfully convicted persons via the then-new technology of DNA analysis (Connors, Lundregan, Miller, & McEwen, 1996). The results of the Connors and colleagues' (1996) analysis was examined by Wells and associates (1998) to show that, of the many causes associated with wrongful conviction, faulty eyewitness identification was primary among them. This outcome was recognized by the National Institute of Justice, which subsequently convened the Technical Working Group on Eyewitness Evidence that completed their report in 1999. The Technical Working Group was composed of police investigators, prosecutors, defense attorneys, and scientists, and was tasked to develop a guide for law enforcement representing best practices in the development of eyewitness identification evidence and the administration of eyewitness identification procedures by law enforcement (Technical Working Group on Eyewitness Evidence, 1999).

The most intensive and effective review of wrongful convictions has been carried out by the Innocence Project, created by Barry C. Scheck and Peter J. Neufeld and affiliated with the Benjamin N. Cardozo School of Law at Yeshiva University, New York City. As of this writing, 225 persons have been exonerated through the efforts of the Innocence Project and released from incarceration as innocent persons. Their assessment of the causes of wrongful conviction contains the following statement: "Eyewitness misidentification is the single greatest cause of wrongful convictions nationwide, playing a role in more than 75% of convictions overturned through DNA testing." And "In case after case, DNA has proven what scientists already know— that eyewitness identification is frequently inaccurate. In the wrongful convictions caused by eyewitness misidentification, the circumstances varied, but judges and juries all relied on testimony that could have been more accurate if reforms proven by science had been implemented" (Innocence Project, 2008).

The point not to miss is this: Failures in the development of diagnostic procedures for obtaining eyewitness identification evidence, failures in the administration of eyewitness identification procedures, and failures in the evaluation of eyewitness testimony by police, attorneys, jurors, judges, the public, and the American criminal justice system, considered as a fact-finding entity, have been documented repeatedly over at least the last 75 years, with remarkably little effect (in the United States) on the routine operation of these systems of justice. Yet, a scientific approach to understanding the causes of eyewitness misidentification has been undertaken, and a body of knowledge and the means of expanding it to benefit society in general and the criminal justice system in particular is available to law enforcement entities. This chapter explores the underlying research base on eyewitness identification, including the scientific basis upon which expert testimony relies. We begin by considering conflicting knowledge systems employed in the criminal justice system.

Conflicting Knowledge Systems: Customary Versus Scientific Knowledge

Imagine that two societal institutions are concerned with the same domain of knowledge, but they do not share information about what they know, what they do not know, and how they use the knowledge they have.

Imagine that the first of these institutions makes judgments about whether people will lose their freedom, live, or die based in whole or in part on accusations made by other persons based on their memory, judgment, and response to various events in their cognitive and social environment. Participants in this process make laws governing the process, measure the process against constitutional requirements, administer the process of bringing accused persons into the process, develop evidence for and against their guilt, and judge the validity of the evidence. Imagine further that these participants in the process—through which life or death decisions are made—are informed primarily by customary knowledge and personal experience.

Imagine that the second of these institutions uses scientific techniques of investigation to study the processes through which persons come to have the knowledge—beliefs, perception, memory, etc.—that forms the basis of their accusations that a particular individual acted in a certain way or committed specific acts at a specific time and place. Additionally, this institution studies the ways in which events subsequent to observation of an event may change an individual's memory for events and/or persons. They further study the ways in which errors of memory and reports based on memory contribute to the judgment processes—and errors—of the first institution (including the ways in which memory is contaminated in the process of investigation and prosecution). These matters, known to the second institution through scientific study, are largely unaddressed in the procedural manuals, training, and oversight processes of the first institution.

We know that customary knowledge is commonly used in many areas of our society and in a number of domains of social life. For example, individuals treat themselves (and sometimes others) for various ailments using folk medicines that have never seen scientific evaluation, and modern governments (e.g., Canada and the United States) have made provision for certain indigenous groups to exercise customary legal and governance processes as part of their cultural and tribal autonomy. But we also know that folk medicines and treatment regimes have been supplanted and regulated in the light of science-based medicine and surgical practice, that modern building codes supplant customary principles of construction, and that modern property law has supplanted folk concepts of ownership (Malpass, 1999).

Science is a means of evaluating claims to knowledge based on open, public, explicit procedure. Customary practices are not amenable to such evaluations. Modern knowledge based on scientific analysis has made important contributions to many areas of society, and this process continues in many areas of criminal investigation and legal process—however, the degree of penetration has been quite modest. We will discuss the contrast between customary and scientific knowledge later, but for now it might be surprising that, in a time when scientific contributions to the improvement of life and knowledge have been strong in so many important areas of public and private life, there continues to be vigorous resistance to the contribution of science-based information to criminal justice processes and especially to the deliberations of those every-day people—lay jurors—who make life and death decisions about persons accused of crimes.

To some extent, this should not be surprising, since an adversarial approach is hard-wired into our system of justice, such that both prosecution and defense are devoted to making the best case possible (within certain broad limits) for their "side." It is expensive to replace customary knowledge and traditional approaches with scientifically based information and procedures. And a science-based approach requires knowledge beyond the ken of many practitioners in the legal system, from police and attorneys to judges and legislators. Progress on this front has been slow. It is in the adversarial interest of prosecutors in criminal cases (although not necessarily in the interest of justice) to keep modern scientific analysis—as contrasted with common sense–based "common knowledge"—out of the legal system. Although one can argue for many interpretations of evidence based on customary knowledge, interpretations based on a scientific footing are less easy to mold to the purposes of a particular case.

It is reasonable to inquire into the critical differences between customary knowledge and science. To start with, scientific knowledge is designed from the ground up to be questioned, challenged, evaluated as to its validity and reliability, and ultimately improved. Science provides criteria against which accuracy and adequacy can be evaluated. Apart from what people generally believe, the law has no way of applying validity tests to substantive knowledge other than by asking experts.

Science-based improvements can be monitored according to procedures and evaluative criteria that are open, accessible to anyone with the background to understand them, and which become part of the public domain and discourse. Customary knowledge, on the other hand, has merely the force of common belief and is a standard of society by default—rather than evaluated and improved by rational methods. Evaluation and development of customary knowledge and practice more often occur against criteria of general agreement or political popularity.

Customary knowledge has no explicit origins, it has no records of the conditions on which beliefs are based that might facilitate replication, and it provides no way for interested parties to test the reliability and generalizability of the resulting conclusions beyond specific forms of personal experience. Rather customary knowledge relies on the perceptions and memories of unknown people under unexamined conditions and in unknowable circumstances; thus it is for these reasons mostly incapable of being evaluated for validity in anything but an impressionistic way.

Science has made great advances specifically because the history of scientific findings is publicly available. The records of this history are explicit, quantitative, and tied to procedures that can be repeated for contemporary evaluation. Reliance on memory is minimized because the publication standards of academic journals and other sources in which scientific studies are published require records that can be produced for inspection. Detailed information is available about the individuals involved, their scientific history and credentials, their institutional location, and the methods and procedures on which observations are based. Records of the original observations frequently are available for scrutiny and reanalysis.

A scientific approach to the collection and evaluation of eyewitness evidence is far more likely to result in improved effectiveness, and it is more likely to benefit from both new science and the continuing experience of the criminal justice system with obtaining and evaluating evidence based on eyewitness testimony. A systematic eye to improving the quality of the information contributed to criminal investigation by eyewitnesses and the way it is used by the criminal justice system can bring important benefits. Application of a scientific approach is likely to provide greater benefits the closer it is to the initial investigation. Placed within the investigation process in law enforcement organizations, science provides a powerful set of tools. Brought in after an investigation has run its course and a prosecution is under way, its power and scope is greatly reduced. In lieu of its presence in the initial investigation and the framing of the prosecutions' case, scientifically based expert testimony is an important way to bring science into the process.

Arguments regarding expert testimony and its legitimacy for the courtroom are endemic to the adversarial system. Many debates have been undertaken over whether eyewitness researchers should testify as experts in criminal trials and the moral and ethical dilemmas that such testimony elicits (i.e., Clifford, 1997; Ebbesen & Konečni, 1996; Elliot, 1993; Loftus, 1983; McCloskey & Egeth, 1983; McCullough, 2002; Wells, 1993; Yarmey, 2001). It is not our goal to rehash these arguments and determine the answer to the question of whether we should be testifying. This issue is a topic for the courts to decide, and we feel that it should remain so. Instead, we focus on the arguments that arise from evaluating the utility of the research on eyewitness identification. Specifically, these arguments are related to whether the testimony is needed and whether the research on which the testimony is based is scientifically valid.

We have already documented that a need exists for understanding the factors that influence eyewitness identification errors, because these errors are a principal cause of wrongful convictions of innocent individuals.

However, even though overwhelming evidence suggests that eyewitness identifications are fallible, arguments have arisen as to whether it is necessary for social scientists to testify about these issues in the courts. A common argument against the admissibility of expert testimony is that jurors already know about the fallibility of eyewitness memory and, therefore, expert testimony on these issues is not needed. We offer the following as a contemporary illustration. From WJBC, AM1230, Radio Bloomington, the Voice of McLean County (Bloomington, Illinois) comes this news report, dated 04/24/2008:

> A McLean County judge will not let an expert about witness identification testify during next month's rape trial for former Bloomington Police Sergeant Jeff Pelo. Pelo is accused of sexually assaulting four women, dating back to 2002. Judge Bob Freitag says there's no compelling reason to allow an Ohio expert to testify about factors, such as memory, that can affect eyewitness identification. Prosecutor Mark Messman had argued putting such an expert on the stand to sort out what are *common sense* issues would only make for a "battle of experts." (WJBC, 2008; italics added)

Read and Desmarais (Chapter 6) dissect this "common sense" argument in detail, and therefore we will not take too much space to discuss their thesis. In short, they present evidence from multiple studies evaluating layperson knowledge of factors affecting eyewitness identifications that have shown that jurors do not understand many of the variables that influence eyewitness identifications. In the few situations in which jurors do understand, they do not know how to apply their understanding to the interpretation of evidence. Laymen may have some forms of knowledge about eyewitness matters (e.g., that certain instructions influence eyewitness identification), but they are much less likely to know what moderates that effect, such as not getting a good opportunity to view the face at the witnessing event, thus making a false identification more likely if an unbiased instruction is not used. In general, laymen (jurors) are unlikely to have discovered for themselves the fruits of the last 50 years of scientific research on eyewitness identification and memory.

In addition to the "common sense" approach, critics of expert testimony on eyewitness issues have argued that the legal system provides effective safeguards against erroneous eyewitness identifications leading to wrongful convictions. Expert testimony is therefore unnecessary. These safeguards include the presence of counsel during identification procedures, the use of voir dire to discover jurors who may be unwilling or unable to carefully evaluate eyewitness evidence, motions to suppress identifications, cross-examination of eyewitnesses and procedure administrators during trial, and judicial instructions. Devenport, Kimbrough, and Cutler (Chapter 3) present research that has evaluated the effectiveness of these safeguards and the defense of "common sense" criticism; we direct the reader to their chapter for a detailed evaluation of the validity of this argument. Briefly, their research suggests that these safeguards are relatively ineffective for preventing eyewitness errors from being presented at trial and influencing juror judgments. A closer examination of their research indicates that judges and attorneys (similar to jurors) are generally insensitive to the factors that influence eyewitness accuracy, thereby limiting the effectiveness of these safeguards. It is evident that layperson, attorney, and judicial insensitivity to the factors that influence eyewitness memory present a need for expert testimony to serve as a knowledge transfer approach.

What can be said, though, regarding the scientific merit of the research upon which expert eyewitness testimony is based? Other authors in this volume discuss the ecological validity and generalizability of eyewitness research in detail (Flowe, Finklea, & Ebbesen, in Chapter 9; Bailey & Mecklenburg, in Chapter 10). We, therefore, focus our efforts on evaluating the methodologies of the eyewitness research.

Is the Study of Eyewitness Memory and Identification a Field of Science?

The study of eyewitness identification emerged from basic research in experimental psychology, particularly with regard to the study of human memory, which was an active field of scientific study in the last half of the 19th century. At the beginning of the 20th century, the first laboratory containing a research program on eyewitness identification was established in the Psychology Department at Harvard University by Prof. Hugo Münsterberg. With the birth of what has become known as "cognitive psychology" in the 1960s, research on perception, memory, and decision-making processes has greatly accelerated. During this period, research specifically on the memory of eyewitnesses was vastly expanded, and it has been the subject of inquiry by psychologists from many diverse areas of psychological science, including cognitive, social, and developmental psychology.

Experimental psychology and the applied field of eyewitness identification and memory are widely recognized as fields of scientific study, embodying the techniques, methodologies, and standards that define science in relation to other forms of knowledge. The field is characterized by the development and evaluation of explicit theory and the use of controlled studies, with experimental methods and research designs capable of producing clearly interpretable results and theoretical advances. Further, researchers seek to generalize their findings to encompass the real-world constraints that witnesses may be exposed to.

In this section, we describe the organizational structure of scientific psychology, placing the study of eyewitness memory within this system. We then briefly describe the methodologies that make the study of eyewitness memory a scientific endeavor, and we discuss the concept of general agreement within the scientific community. Finally, we highlight the reliable phenomena that scientists have discovered with regard to eyewitness memory.

The Organizational Structure of Scientific Psychology

The International Congress of Scientific Unions (ICSU) is the umbrella international organization of all scientific fields in the world. Representing psychology in this world-wide scientific organization is the International Union of Psychological Sciences (IUPsyS). Members of IUPsyS are national psychological associations rather than individual scientists. Both the American Psychological Association (APA) and the Association for Psychological Science (APS) are members of IUPsyS, and many other specialty societies are affiliated. One of the oldest international organizations in which individual psychologists can be members is the International Association for Applied Psychology (IAAP), founded in the 1920s in Europe.

The major umbrella organization for the sciences in the United States is the American Association for the Advancement of Science (AAAS). Serving more than 10 million members, AAAS is the world's largest federation of scientific and engineering societies. The premiere scientific publication in the United States is *Science*, an official publication of the AAAS. Researchers studying both the basic and applied aspects of memory have published their findings in this journal (e.g., Loftus, 1979).

Among the 271 societies and academies of science affiliated with AAAS are the two most prominent associations in the field of scientific psychology, namely the APS and the APA. Researchers who conduct studies on eyewitness memory are members of these organizations, as well as of several specialized divisions or sections of the just-noted societies devoted to psychology and law, including the American Psychology-Law Society (AP-LS, Division 41 of APA) and the Division of Psychology and Law in the IAAP (Division 10). Many scientific specialty organizations in American psychology, including the Psychonomic Society, the Society for Research in Child Development (SRCD), the Society of Personality and Social Psychology (SPSP), and the Society for Applied Research in Memory and Cognition (SARMAC) include eyewitness scientists among their members and publish research on eyewitness identification and memory in their journals.

The Scientific Methodologies of Eyewitness Research

Science is generally characterized by a form of knowledge development based on empirical observation. Theories are tested and modified through observation of events in the environment that are intersubjective in nature—that is, different observers can agree on whether an event occurred and about the attributes of the event. Like all sciences (including the "hard sciences" such as engineering, physics, chemistry, and biology), psychologists rely upon basic principles of scientific inquiry that ensure the reliability and validity of their findings and that alleviate bias or error resulting from the intersubjective characteristics of observation. These methodological principles involve (a) strict adherence to the scientific method, with a focus on the concept of falsifiability; (b) experimental design that ensures both internal and external validity; (c) reliance upon statistical inference and the provision of error rates associated with each hypothesis test; and (d) a peer review process that provides quality control over studies that are ultimately published. An important publication (Hedges, 1987) favorably compares the reliability and replicability of findings in scientific psychology with the physical sciences. Specifically, Hedges (1987) evaluated the statistical consistency of research in particle physics with that of psychology and found that the results of research in particle physics were no more consistent than the results found in psychological research. In short, the results in psychology were just as reliable and replicable as those in the "hard science" of particle physics.

The Scientific Method

All scientific endeavors, regardless of discipline, must adhere to a common method in which theoretical inquiry allows one to generate specific hypotheses that are objective and clearly testable. Such hypotheses are tested based upon commonly accepted paradigms or measurement standards within a given field, and the results of these tests permit scientists to either support or refute a specific theoretical position. A critical requirement of this method of inquiry is commonly referred to as *falsification*—the notion that it must be possible to disprove any given theoretical proposition through reliable methods of assessment. Thus, the scientific method provides a manner in which scientists may test, or falsify, a given theoretical position.

Experimental Design That Ensures Both Internal and External Validity

Hypotheses may be tested in a number of ways via the scientific method, including direct observation of behavior (*observational designs*), assessing the relative association between two variables of interest (*correlational designs*), identifying groups of individuals that may differ in the hypothesized manner (*quasi-experimental designs*), or experimentally inducing the hypothesized differences in groups of individuals that have been randomly assigned to the relevant conditions (true *experimental designs*). Although each of these approaches is used across the various sub-disciplines of psychological science, it is important to note that these approaches differ in the extent to which causal inferences may be generated and strong internal validity may be established. Specifically, true experimental designs provide the most robust test regarding the direct effect of one variable on another. These designs involve the random assignment of participants to "conditions" (or groups) that systematically vary along a specified dimension relating to the proposed hypothesis. Such an experimental treatment of the hypothesis allows scientists to infer that any differences between conditions are the result of the proposed hypothesis (because other potential factors are controlled through aspects of the design). Although psychologists studying eyewitness memory have relied upon the variety of designs just described, the most robust findings stem from those studies employing a true experimental design that ensures strong internal validity.

One critique often sounded against the domain of eyewitness psychology is that the experiments conducted fail to simulate the reality of a crime or the "real world." In scientific terms, this critique centers on the degree of ecological validity demonstrated by the science—or the extent to which the findings of a given study can generalize to the population from which the sample was generated or the real-world conditions in which the phenomenon might be observed. For example, one might inquire whether university students who participate in experimental research differ from those individuals who might find themselves witnesses to a real crime, or whether a laboratory demonstration of a given effect might generalize to perception and memory in everyday life. As mentioned previously, other contributors address this ecological validity concern later in this volume (Flowe and colleagues, in Chapter 9; Bailey & Mecklenburg, in Chapter 10), therefore we will not go into great detail in discussing it. However, we are compelled to mention that there appear to be very few, if any, discontinuities in the processes that influence individuals in experimental research and the real world. Perception and memory processes do not work in one way under one circumstance and in quite another way in a different situation. Most events effecting memory and witness testimony are located on an ordered continuum, and the functional relationship is a monotonic function: As the causative factor increases, so does the result. With some well-known exceptions (e.g., stress and arousal, Deffenbacher, Bornstein, & Penrod, 2006), this appears to be true across a wide range of factors, and even what were thought to be exceptions recently have appeared to be less exceptional.

One approach taken by scientists to generalize their results involves systematically examining a phenomenon across a variety of conditions and methodological parameters. Although scientists may begin to explore a phenomenon by employing controlled laboratory experiments, they will often seek to generalize the observed phenomenon by taking their tests of the effect out of the laboratory and into the real world. Eyewitness researchers often utilize experimental paradigms that more appropriately replicate the conditions of a real-world event, such as unintentional encoding conditions and significant delays between the presentation of the event and the administration of a lineup. Researchers may also conduct archival analyses of real-world cases to determine if a given phenomenon has any effect on real witnesses.

One example of this approach can be seen in studies on the cross-race effect in memory for faces (i.e., the finding that memory for faces of one's own race is superior to memory for faces of another, less familiar race). The first studies examining the cross-race effect involved a laboratory experiment in which White and Black university participants viewed a sequence of slides depicting photographs of same- and other-race faces (Malpass & Kravitz, 1969).

Although this phenomenon has been replicated in the laboratory many times over the past 40 years (see Meissner & Brigham, 2001), researchers have also demonstrated that the effect is not unique to individuals of certain racial or ethnic backgrounds (or to university participants), and that the phenomenon is observed both in "eyewitness" paradigms that capture many real-world elements and archival analyses of true witness identifications.

Statistical Inference and Error Rates

As described earlier, the process of scientific inquiry involves the assessment of relationships between variables and the testing of differences between groups of individuals who are randomly assigned to experimentally differentiated conditions. The process of scientific work and the evaluation of theories and hypotheses inherently involve the calculation of error rates associated with the work. In fact, most areas of psychological science use inferential statistical analysis, in which the calculation of error rates is a basic part of the analysis and interpretation of research findings. Generally, to be considered statistically reliable and reported in scientific journals, observed findings must rise above levels of error by specific amounts calculated from data and dictated by quantitative analytic techniques developed and accepted by researchers over a period of more than a century.

The Process of Peer Review

The International Union (IUPsyS), IAAP, APA, APS, and various specialty organizations (such as the Psychonomic Society, SARMAC, and AP-LS) publish scientific journals in psychology, many of which include scientific work on memory and eyewitness identification. All of these journals engage in a process of peer review that is devoted to evaluating the validity of those scientific studies submitted for consideration. The peer review process is a method of quality control that ensures the validity and reliability of experimental research. Papers submitted for publication are reviewed by leading scientists (experts) in the relevant area. These experts provide their critique of the studies in an anonymous fashion, including such aspects as the quality of theoretical contribution, the validity and appropriateness of the scientific methods and procedures employed, and the appropriateness of the data analysis and interpretations. The editor who solicits these reviews is then responsible for permitting revisions to the work by the authors (if such revisions would promote the scientific value of the study) or rejecting the manuscript for publication (if fatal flaws in the study are apparent to the reviewers, such that the study contributes no scientific value to knowledge development). Journals using the peer review system generally accept only a small percentage of the manuscripts that have been submitted for publication—thus, studies published in these outlets have passed a rigorous test and are generally considered worthy of consideration by the greater scientific community.

Determining General Acceptance Within the Scientific Community

As with other scientific communities, there is general agreement about the scientific findings of the eyewitness community (see Hosch, Jolly, Schmersal, & Smith, Chapter 7). General agreement can be evidenced objectively in many ways, including qualitative and quantitative (meta-analytic) reviews of the literature, representation in primary texts representing the science, through documents that chronicle the findings of consensus panels of scientific experts, or more directly through surveys of scientific experts. A review of these areas suggests that it would be very difficult to sustain the position that many of the findings in research on eyewitness memory lack general agreement within the scientific community.

Qualitative and Quantitative (Meta-analytic) Reviews of the Literature

Comprehensive reviews of the nature, content, and contemporary achievements of scientific fields are important indicators of their maturation and standing. Examples are the recent article on eyewitness testimony in the *Annual Review of Psychology*[1] (Wells & Olson, 2003) and the Psychology and Law section in the *Encyclopedia of Applied Psychology*: 13 articles on psychology and law in general and two on eyewitness memory and identification in particular (Spielberg, 2004). More recent publications, the *Encyclopedia of Psychology & Law* (Cutler, 2007) and the two-volume *Handbook of Eyewitness Psychology* (Toglia, Read, Ross, & Lindsay, 2006; Lindsay, Ross, Read, & Toglia, 2007) provide up-to-date treatments of many facets of the field.

In many areas of eyewitness identification, general agreement on a given phenomenon is bolstered via the findings of meta-analytic reviews of the research literature. A meta-analysis is a synthesis of all obtainable data collected in a specified topical area. The benefits of a meta-analysis are that greater statistical power can be obtained by combining data from many studies. Hypotheses not originally specified in the research, such as publication bias or gender effects, can be examined. And finally, directions for future research can be reported when applicable. Like most scientific research, meta-analyses are subject to peer review prior to publication. Important examples of such analyses include topics such as the cross-race effect (Meissner & Brigham, 2001), the confidence–accuracy relationship (Bothwell, Deffenbacher, & Brigham, 1987; Cutler & Penrod, 1989; Sporer, Penrod, Read, & Cutler, 1995), factors influencing face identification (Shapiro & Penrod, 1986), the description–identification relationship (Meissner & Brigham, 2001; Meissner, Sporer, & Susa, 2008), the effects of sequential versus simultaneous lineups and showups (Steblay, Dysart, Fulero, & Lindsay, 2001; McQuiston-Surrett, Malpass, & Tredoux, 2006), the influence of lineup instructions (Steblay, 1997; Clark, 2005), the mug-shot exposure effect

(Deffenbacher, Bornstein, & Penrod, 2006), the weapon-focus effect (Steblay, 1992), the influence of emotion/anxiety (Deffenbacher, Bornstein, Penrod, & McGorty, 2004), the effects of hypnosis on recall (Steblay & Bothwell, 1994), and post-identification feedback (Douglass & Steblay, 2006).

Representation in Introductory Textbooks

Introductory textbooks are the most concise and authoritative presentations of the core concepts and findings of a field. They are aggressively peer-reviewed and represent a range of professionally acceptable emphases or versions of the nature of the field. Eyewitness research concepts are represented in psychology textbooks at a high rate. Hosch and associates (Chapter 7) provide a thorough evaluation of the extent to which phenomena related to eyewitness processes are presented in commonly adopted textbooks across various areas of psychology. In short, they found that almost every textbook contained a presentation of research related to eyewitness issues, with some devoting entire chapters to the discussion of these issues.

Consensus Panels of Scientific Experts

Groups of experts are frequently brought together to assess the foundations of a given area of scientific inquiry. Such consensus panels have been assembled in the field of eyewitness psychology over the past decade. For example, the AP-LS sponsored a review of the scientific work on eyewitness identification with the purpose of proposing changes in law enforcement policy. This "white paper," entitled *Eyewitness Identification Procedures: Recommendations for Lineups and Photospreads*, was authored by Wells and colleagues (1998). It represented the study of eyewitness identification as a stable body of research as of that date, and was authored by six prominent scientists in the field.

A second consensus panel document on eyewitness identification research involved the publication of *Eyewitness Evidence: A Guide for Law Enforcement* by the Technical Working Group on Eyewitness Evidence, under the direction of the Attorney General of the United States (see Wells et al., 2000). This Technical Working Group consisted of a select group of psychological researchers, attorneys, and representatives of law enforcement, and its findings and recommendations were published in 1999, with a training manual following in 2003. The guide and training manual were disseminated to all law enforcement agencies in the United States.

Surveys of Scientific Experts

Periodically, researchers and experts in the eyewitness field are administered questionnaires to determine their level of agreement on specific eyewitness topics. The results of these questionnaires indicate that a high level of consensus exists regarding those issues relevant to the field (Kassin, Ellsworth, &

Smith, 1989; Kassin, Tubb, Hosch, & Memon, 2001). For example, the most recent survey conducted by Kassin and colleagues indicated significant agreement (over 90% of experts surveyed) on the effects of cross-racial identification, alcohol intoxication, hypnotic suggestibility, attitudes and expectations, child suggestibility, post-event information, mug-shot exposure, confidence malleability, lineup instructions, and leading interview questions. This matter is reviewed at length by Hosch and colleagues later in this volume.

What Can Research Tell Us About the Factors That Influence Eyewitness Identification?

As described earlier, psychologists have developed a scientific understanding of factors that influence human perception, memory, and judgment that are relevant to the evaluation of eyewitness evidence. Numerous reviews are available to the interested reader that document, in detail, the specific findings and scientific studies that serve as the scientific basis of this literature (see Brewer & Williams, 2005; Lindsay et al., 2007; Neuschatz & Cutler, 2008; Toglia et al., 2006). This corpus of research has been published in many of the most highly regarded, peer-reviewed journals in the fields of experimental, cognitive, social, developmental, and applied psychology. Although it is not our charge to systematically review the scientific research on eyewitness identification, we review more generally the basic scientific knowledge evidenced by these studies.

Following a timeline beginning with a criminal event, and leading to the investigation of this crime and, ultimately, to the trial of an accused perpetrator, accurate or inaccurate identifications derive principally from the following:

- *The cognitive structures (encoding capabilities), fears, or values that a witness brings to the witnessing situation.* Witnesses who are cognitively impaired through their affective response to a situation, or those distracted from observing relevant information via a focus on other salient aspects of the event (e.g., the weapon used to threaten them), are less likely to render an accurate identification. Certain individuals who are cognitively impaired or those with limited cognitive capability either through alcohol/drug inducement or more natural developmental processes are similarly less accurate in their identifications.
- *The opportunities and constraints afforded the witness at the witnessing situation.* The greater the opportunity a witness has to observe an event or a perpetrator, and the clearer the resolution and acuity associated with this observation, the more accurate the witness's memory is likely to be. Factors such as distance, lighting, and time to view have all been shown to influence the accuracy of witness identification.

- *The information a witness encodes about the offender from the initial viewing of the event.* As we've noted earlier, the constraints on the information a witness encodes into memory depend upon both attributes of the person and attributes of the environment. But whatever the constraints on encoding, the information obtained at the original event is the base from which all subsequent memory (recall, recognition, identification) processes work. If the initial encoding is weak, then subsequent memory-contaminating events are likely to have greater effects than if the original memory is strong.

- *The history of the encoded information from the initial viewing to the time of the identification request.* Witnesses are susceptible to the influence of both suggestive questioning by investigators, as well as to social information that may be shared by other witnesses. They may be exposed to images of other persons or faces represented as being the offender in the media or as part of the investigation process. In addition, witnesses may forget information as the time between their viewing of the event and their attempt at an identification increases.

- *The circumstances surrounding the identification (including the identification procedures, the quality of the lineup that is presented, the witness's social motives and values, etc.).* Suggestive lineup identification procedures can lead to misidentification, including the exposure of a witness to multiple images of the same target person, poorly constructed lineups in which the target person is perceptually salient to the witness, and lineup instructions that induce choosing on the part of the witness.

- *The witness's expectations about testimony and the task of giving evidence, including information derived from interactions with law enforcement or other witnesses.* Witnesses may become overconfident in their testimony in the courtroom if they are provided positive feedback at the time of their identification or if they subsequently draw conclusions about their likely accuracy based on prosecution of the identified person.

The accuracy of a witness's identification(s) and identification testimony is a function of all these factors. Many of these are attributes of human perception, memory, and judgment processes, and these psychological processes have been subject to both general models of cognition (see Lane & Meissner, 2008; Turtle, Read, Lindsay, & Brimacombe, 2008) and more specific models of eyewitness identification performance (Clark, 2008). Although this corpus of research will continue to mature and expand its knowledge base, it is without controversy that our current scientific understanding of eyewitness memory is beyond the ken of lay and customary knowledge (see Read & Desmarais, Chapter 6). It is critical, then, that we seek to transfer this knowledge to those who rely upon eyewitness evidence and make decisions within our criminal justice system.

Knowledge Transfer

The transfer of scientific knowledge from research laboratories to criminal justice practitioners can be accomplished in many ways. Legislative action, as well as training for law enforcement investigators, attorneys (in law school and beyond), and judges are all mechanisms for changing the criminal justice system. But any training regimen has its problems. For example, for attorneys and judges, the path to the law is not often through the sciences, a fact that creates a training-readiness question. Similarly, for law enforcement investigators, educational standards are uneven, frequently low, and infrequently based in science. Legal reform, in the sense of requiring new standards of evidence and standards of oversight of investigation processes, are cumbersome and have low levels of probable success.

Training for law enforcement personnel has an effect more proximal to the source of errors leading to wrongful conviction, and this seems to be a promising knowledge transfer path. However, law enforcement as a societal institution is severely fractionated in the United States (thousands of individual and overlapping jurisdictions), as are training standards and facilities. Budgets for training are commonly thin, and professionalism and educational standards vary widely across individual law enforcement units. Law enforcement has very limited research and development capabilities, especially in the areas of the social and behavioral sciences that focus on such a large range of issues in investigation, use of witnesses, and other areas of legal decision making (Geller, 1997). The contributions of university-based research and educational programs, therefore, are correspondingly more important, and the few genuinely collaborative research programs between law enforcement and university-based researchers have unique value.

Expert testimony, provided to the finders of fact during trial, is another knowledge transfer point. It is particularistic in the sense that it is applied one case at a time. However, this volume and the cumulative base of scientific study of eyewitness identification exemplify the fact that, as in the laboratory, evidence gathered one instance at a time can be productively examined as a means of understanding a phenomenon. Expert testimony has become a field for scientific scrutiny while at the same time it confronts the problems associated with making a case for scientific knowledge to persons who overwhelmingly bring customary knowledge to the courthouse. The many questions of its importance and effectiveness, as well as the size and location of discrepancies between scientific and customary knowledge, are the subject of detailed treatment in the remaining chapters of this volume.

Conceptualizations of Expert Testimony

Ultimate Opinion Testimony

Offering an opinion about whether a witness is correct or incorrect in his identification of a defendant is a form of *ultimate opinion testimony*.

Ultimate opinion testimony is beyond our reach for a number of reasons, beginning with the fact that no one can retrieve precise information on the witnesses' personal state, attentional deployment, memory capability, and similar factors that were present at the time of the offense. The science, based on controlled studies, tells us that these factors have effects on the encoding of information into memory, but we cannot retrospectively measure the degree to which they were present at any particular time. We can advise the finders of fact about indicators of the strength of these factors, but we ourselves cannot form a science-based opinion of the degree of their presence in a given case. However, we can say that, for example, when a weapon was visible in a crime, controlled studies show that effects occur on person recognition and evidence suggests that these effects result from attention distraction resulting from the presence of the weapon. We cannot quantify the degree of attention distraction; we can, however, inform the finder of fact that the presence of a weapon is known to reduce identification accuracy, through the mechanism of attention deployment. This, of course, is only one of many factors that may potentially interfere with the process of acquiring information about the appearance of the offender at the crime scene, and this imposes a limit on the quality of the subsequent memory of the offender's image for use in other processes (e.g., judgment of whether a photograph is or is not the same person who is in their memory). Obviously, if his image is not well established in the witness' memory, the later identification task will be more difficult for the witness and the result will be less reliable as evidence. These are things we can share with the finders of fact.

Likewise, we may know what memory-contaminating events may have occurred in the witness' experience, such as making and subsequently studying a composite image intended to represent the offender. But we cannot quantify exactly the magnitude of the effect that this would have on the witness. We can come very close to specifying the average of a group of people exposed to a similar condition, but it is a characteristic of any science based in statistical analysis and statements of group averages that individual observations (in this case, responses of individual research participants) vary from the group average in a direction and to a degree that cannot be specified for an individual, whether they are in the laboratory or in the witness box. We know the average effect, and we can share that information with the finders of fact. But we stop short of ultimate opinion testimony because the specific quantity of events that we and the finders of fact are certain to have occurred cannot be quantitatively specified on an individual basis with great precision beyond that of the group average.

Similarly, we cannot know exactly what the witness brings to the identification task: what self instructions were present, how the witness values accurate identification of offenders in relation to avoidance of false identification of innocent persons (Malpass, 2006), how instructions were weighed, and with what retrieval and identification decision strategies the witness approached the task. What does the witness believe is her task in the identification procedure, apart from the instructions given, which may or may not be believed? From early studies (Malpass & Devine, 1981), we know that research participants mis-remember having been given biased lineup instructions more than four times as frequently than mis-remembering having been given unbiased instructions. Does the witness believe that arresting someone who has a reasonably high probability of being the offender is of primary importance? Does the witness consider the importance of not identifying an innocent person and its consequences (that an innocent person may be imprisoned, which results in the guilty person going unpunished and free to commit more crimes)? Does the witness believe it is almost certain that the police have caught the right person, and that the identification is confirmatory rather than independent information? We can determine, in many cases, for example, what instructions were given by law enforcement, and we have a very good idea of their effects (Clark, 2005; Steblay, 1997). We can often determine how the identification procedure was administered and whether the lineup, for example, was fair (Malpass et al., 2007; Eyewitness Identification Research Laboratory, 2008), and we can inform the finders of fact about what we know of the effects on identification of what was, in fact, done. But again, we can speak of the effects on research participants generally but not claim to know exactly (quantitatively) how these factors affected the accuracy of a specific witness' identification.

Expert As Educator

The evaluation of witness accuracy and the weight that eyewitness evidence is to be given in arriving at a verdict are within the task of the finder(s) of fact, and the responsibility of experts does not extend to offering conclusions. Doing so is widely thought of as invading the province of the jury. However, on the experts' side of that line is plenty of room for other functions. Although it is within the task of the finder of fact to make judgments on these matters, the contribution our science can make is to alert them to the existence of factors known to have effects on identification, and to indicate how strong those effects have been shown to be. In many cases, this will bring factors known to be important to the attention of the finders of fact. They may not have thought of these if not reminded of them, or they may not know of them at all. The extent to which the finders of fact know what scientists know about eyewitness identification is discussed by Read and Desmarais later in this volume (Chapter 6).

"Educator" is an obvious way to think about the role of an expert witness. This role can be expressed in a range of knowledge-transfer contexts, as discussed earlier. In the context of the ultimate opinion testimony discussion, the expert's role as educator is explicit. Clearly, there are bits of factual knowledge that it would be appropriate for the finders of fact to learn. These range from the very concrete (e.g., how long a look at a face is sufficient for a good memory image under good viewing conditions) to very abstract (e.g., that memory involves integrative processes that take place outside of awareness). These are part of an effort to educate the finders of fact and the court more generally about what psychological science knows, and how it might be applied to their evaluation of the eyewitness evidence in the case at hand. However, there are integrative functions that the expert witness can perform that are not simple transfers of knowledge about the effects of a list of factors.

Wagenaar (1988) suggests (p. 149) a Bayesian approach to the expert's role, and uncovers two quite different orientations to the expert's testimony. The first is the estimation of *the probability of guilt given the evidence.* This framing of expert testimony is perilously close to giving an ultimate opinion about guilt or innocence, given the evidence in the case. The second approach reveals a very different and interesting use of an eyewitness scientist's expertise: to provide an estimate of *the probability of the evidence given innocence.* This is based on the principle of *diagnosticity:* if the probability of the evidence given innocence is as high as the probability of the evidence given guilt then the evidence is not diagnostic either of guilt or of innocence, and guilt and innocence cannot be distinguished based on the evidence. The evidence is diagnostic of guilt only when its probability given innocence is substantially lower than its probability given guilt. For example, if, prior to making an identification, the witness who saw the offender briefly under poor conditions viewed the defendant on television as someone being sought in the case, saw the defendant in the police station prior to the identification procedure, saw the defendant's photo in a mug book, saw a lineup in which no other photos resembled either the description given of the offender or the defendant and, without further admonitions or instructions, was told that the police have caught the offender and need the witness to pick him out of a lineup, then one can argue that the witness would not need to have seen the defendant commit the crime in order to "remember" his face and choose to select him from a lineup. The probability of the lineup choice is as likely to result from the events prior to the identification procedure as it is from having seen the defendant commit the crime—perhaps even more likely because, as a result of those events, the witness is likely to have developed a strong memory image of the defendant. Thus, the suggestions in the administration of the identification process come perilously close to forcing an identification of *someone* from the lineup: the most familiar and distinctive person. This use of a scientist's expertise goes beyond a recitation of factors affecting identification, and allows for an integrative approach to informing the finders of fact about the scientific evaluation of the evidence without offering an ultimate opinion about the accuracy of the witness.

Conclusion

It is an extremely unusual law enforcement organization that has research and evaluation components that work on improving the process of evidence collection and preservation. The techniques used are to a large extent "customary" in that they have been developed over a period of time by law enforcement officers, without benefit of scientific consultation. This is less true of scientific procedures that are, without question, inaccessible to persons without specific training.

DNA is a good example. Biological materials are harvested by trained technicians and brought to other, more specifically trained and certified technicians who analyze the materials by procedures developed by scientists and approved by the courts. Eyewitness evidence, on the other hand, is collected by people who are not trained as technicians, and the material harvested is not delivered for evaluation to certified technicians who use techniques that have been developed by scientists and approved by the courts. In contrast, reports based on eyewitness evidence are not constructed by specialists qualified to evaluate the significance of the findings of the identification procedure, and they are not contributed to the evidence file, as they are for even the most troublesome areas of forensic evidence, such as bite marks or hair samples.

Procedures that are customary, and that have been developed by non-technicians, non-scientists, without a research base, and not calibrated to continuing scientific findings have not met the burden of showing that the procedures used to develop the evidence being offered to the court are valid. When a scientific field of study 100 years old develops theories and findings that have only rarely been used to inform evidence gathering, preservation, and interpretation processes in law enforcement, it is improper to grant implicit validity to customary procedures without consideration of the corpus of scientific work, or its absence.

Because of the great power of systematic study that it would bring, there is almost no rational way to argue that scientific approaches to the evaluation of eyewitness identification procedures used in investigations would not be helpful. And, in the face of decades of documentation of wrongful conviction based on erroneous eyewitness testimony, it is scandalous that law enforcement has not taken on this problem itself. Although some U.S. jurisdictions have attempted to implement modifications in identification procedures based on scientific evidence, the evidence on which such change was based was developed in academic research laboratories, not as the product of law enforcement agency studies of the effectiveness of their own procedures. We grant that the severe fractionation of law enforcement and legal jurisdictions in the United States works against the development of an effective research and development arm of law enforcement. When we look to nations where law enforcement is far more integrated and centralized, as in the United Kingdom, we find that law enforcement does in fact undertake research and development activities with regard to eyewitness identification (and many other topics), and they work closely with members of the academic community and with members of law enforcement who have scientific training. With fractionation in the United States, much of the research and development activity has fallen to academic researchers who attempt to fill the void.

It is unfortunate that so few collaborative projects exist. We acknowledge that since the advent of DNA exonerations more collaborative projects have sprung up, but these too are fractionated, and the projects are not integrated into the everyday practice of evidence collection on eyewitness identification and systematic evaluation as an ongoing activity. It would be beneficial if the task of doing the research could be placed inside the police station.

From our position outside of the customs and traditions of law enforcement and the courts, we are not bound to accept precedent as important. Our premise is that the legal system is wrong and wrong-headed about the role of scientific study of eyewitness identification in the criminal justice system. If eyewitness research is rightfully criticized for taking place outside of it, that is because law enforcement agencies and the courts have not done the work themselves. No effective research and development organization embedded within the fractionated criminal justice system in the United States has evaluated the questions addressed by academic research. The way in which law enforcement holds onto customary methods and procedures (i.e., eyewitness identification, interviewing and interrogation, detection of deception) is based on a commitment to customary knowledge and a rejection of scientific knowledge. Rather than bring scientific knowledge into the house and work with it to evaluate and improve techniques that are demonstrably flawed, the U.S. criminal justice system has abrogated this work to academic researchers instead.

Without these activities becoming a routine part of law enforcement, there remain other mechanisms for making the knowledge gained through psychological science, and administered from outside the criminal justice system, available to law enforcement and the courts. Expert testimony is but one of these, and it is the mechanism examined in this book.

References

Borchard, E. M. (1932). *Convicting the innocent*. New Haven: Yale University Press.

Bothwell, R. K., Deffenbacher, K. A., Brigham, J. C. (1987). Correlation of eyewitness accuracy and confidence: Optimality hypothesis revisited. *Journal of Applied Psychology*, *72*, 691–695.

Brandon, R., & Davies, C. (1973). Wrongful imprisonment: Mistaken convictions and their consequences. Hamden, CT: Archon.

Brewer, N., & Williams, K. D. (Eds.). (2005). *Psychology and law: An empirical perspective*. New York: The Guilford Press.

Clark, S. E. (2005). A re-examination of the effects of biased lineup instructions in eyewitness identification. *Law and Human Behavior*, *29*, 395–424.

Clark, S. E. (2008). The importance (and necessity) of computational modeling for eyewitness identification research. *Applied Cognitive Psychology*, *22*, 803–813.

Clifford, B.R. (1997). A commentary on Ebbesen and Konečni's "Eyewitness memory research: Probative v. prejudicial value." *Expert Evidence*, *5*, 140–143.

Connors, E., Lundregan, T., Miller, N., & McEwen, T. (1996). Convicted by juries, exonerated by science: Case studies in the use of DNA evidence to establish innocence after trial. Washington, DC: National Institute of Justice.

Cutler, B. L. (Ed.) (2007). *Encyclopedia of Psychology & Law*. Sage Publications.

Cutler, B. L., & Penrod, S. D. (1989). Forensically relevant moderators of the relation between eyewitness identification accuracy and confidence. *Journal of Applied Psychology, 74*, 650–652.

Deffenbacher, K. A., Bornstein, B. H., & Penrod, S. D. (2006). Mugshot exposure effects: Retroactive interference, mugshot commitment, source confusion, and unconscious transference. *Law and Human Behavior, 30*, 287–307.

Deffenbacher, K. A., Bornstein, B. H., Penrod, S. D., & McGorty, E. K. (2004). A meta-analytic review of the effects of high stress on eyewitness memory. *Law and Human Behavior, 28*, 687–706.

Devlin, Hon. Lord Patrick. (1976). Report to the Secretary of State for the *Home Department of the Departmental Committee on Evidence of Identification in Criminal Cases*. London: Her Majesty's Stationery Office.

Douglass, A. B., & Steblay, N. (2006). Memory distortion in eyewitnesses: A meta-analysis of the post-identification feedback effect. *Applied Cognitive Psychology, 20*, 859–869.

Ebbesen, E. B., & Konečni, V. J. (1996). Eyewitness memory research: Probative v. prejudicial value. *Expert Evidence: The International Digest of Human Behaviour Science and the Law, 5*, 2–28.

Elliott, R., (1993). Expert testimony about eyewitness identification: A critique. *Law and Human Behavior, 17*, 423–437.

Eyewitness Identification Research Laboratory (2008). *Consultation and expert testimony*. Retrieved from http://eyewitness.utep.edu/consult01.html.

Geller, W. A. (1997). Suppose we were really serious about police departments becoming "learning organizations"? *National Institute of Justice Journal*, 234, 2–8.

Hedges, L. V. (1987). How hard is hard science, how soft is soft science?: The empirical cumulativeness of research. *American Psychologist, 42(2)*, 443–455.

Huff, C. R., Rattner, A., & Sagarin, E. (1996). *Convicted but innocent: Wrongful conviction and public policy*. Thousand Oaks: Sage.

Innocence Project. (2008). *Understand the causes: Eyewitness misidentification*. Retrieved November 24, 2008 from http://www.innocenceproject.org/understand/Eyewitness-Misidentification.php.

Kassin, S. M., Ellsworth, P. C., & Smith, V. L. (1989). The "general acceptance" of psychological research on eyewitness testimony. *American Psychologist, 44*, 1089–1098.

Kassin, S. M., Tubb, V. A., Hosch, H. M., & Memon, A. (2001). On the "general acceptance" of eyewitness testimony research: A new survey of the experts. *American Psychologist, 56*, 405–416.

Lane, S. M., & Meissner, C. A. (2008). A 'middle road' approach to bridging the basic-applied gap in eyewitness identification research. *Applied Cognitive Psychology, 22*, 779–787.

Lindsay, R. C. L., Ross, D. F., Read, J. D., & Toglia, M. P. (Eds.). (2007). *The handbook of eyewitness psychology, Vol. II: Memory for people*. Mahwah, NJ: Lawrence Erlbaum.

Loftus, E. F. (1979). Eyewitness reliability. *Science, 205*, 386–387.

Loftus, E. F. (1983). Silence is not golden. *American Psychologist, 38*, 564–572.

Malpass, R.S. (1999). Subjective culture and the law. In J. Adamopoulos & Y. Kashima (Eds.) *Social Psychology and Cultural Context*. Newberry Park, CA: Sage Publications.

Malpass, R. S. (2006). A policy evaluation of simultaneous and sequential lineups. *Psychology, Public Policy and Law, 12(4)*, 394–418.

Malpass, R. S., & Devine, P. G. (1981). Eyewitness identification: Lineup instructions and the absence of the offender. *Journal of Applied Psychology, 66*, 482–489.

Malpass, R. S., & Kravitz, J. (1969). Recognition for faces of own and other race. *Journal of Personality and Social Psychology, 13*, 330–334.

Malpass, R. S., Tredoux, C. G., & McQuiston-Surrett, D. E. (2007). Lineup construction and lineup fairness. In R. C. L. Lindsay, D. F. Ross, J. D. Read, & M. P. Toglia (Eds.), *The handbook of eyewitness psychology, Vol. II: Memory for people*. (pp. 87–100). Mahwah, NJ: Lawrence Erlbaum.

McCloskey, M., & Egeth, H. E. (1983). Eyewitness identification: What can a psychologist tell a jury? *American Psychologist, 38*, 550–563.

McCullough, M. L. (2002). Do not discount lay opinion. *American Psychologist, 57*, 376–377.

McQuiston-Surrett, D., Malpass, R. S., & Tredoux, C. G. (2006). Sequential vs. simultaneous lineups: A review of methods, data, and theory. *Psychology, Public Policy, and Law, 12*, 137–169.

Meissner, C. A., Sporer, S. L., & Susa, K. J. (2008). A theoretical review and meta-analysis of the description-identification relationship in memory for faces. *European Journal of Cognitive Psychology, 20(3)*, 414–455.

Meissner, C. M., & Brigham, J. C. (2001). A meta-analysis of the verbal overshadowing effect in face identification. *Applied Cognitive Psychology, 15*, 603–616.

Neuschatz, J. S., & Cutler, B. L. (2008). Eyewitness identification. In H. L. Roediger, III (Ed.), *Cognitive psychology of memory (Vol. 2 of Learning and memory: A comprehensive reference*, J. Byrne, Series Ed., pp. 845–865). Oxford: Elsevier.

Police and Criminal Evidence Act 1984 (s.60(1)(a)) Code of Practice (D) on identification of persons. Section 2: Identification by witnesses. London: Home Office Directorate.

R v. *Turnbull*, 63 Cr. App. R. 132 (1976).

Radelet, M. L., Bedau, H. A., & Putnam, C. E. (1992). *In spite of innocence: Erroneous convictions in capital cases*. Boston: Northeastern University Press.

Shapiro, P., & Penrod, S. (1986). Meta-analysis of facial identification studies. *Psychological Bulletin, 100*, 139–156.

Spielberg, C. D. (Ed.). (2004). *Encyclopedia of applied psychology*. New York: Elsevier Academic Press.

Sporer, S. L., Penrod, S. D., Read, J. D., & Cutler, B. L. (1995). Choosing, confidence and accuracy: A meta-analysis of the confidence-accuracy relation in eyewitness identification studies. *Psychological Bulletin, 118*, 315–327.

Steblay, N. (1997). Social influence in eyewitness recall: A meta-analytic review of lineup instruction effects. *Law and Human Behavior, 21*, 283–298.

Steblay, N. Dysart, J., Fulero, S. Lindsay, R. C. L. (2003). Eyewitness accuracy rates in police showup and lineup presentations: A meta-analytic comparison. *Law and Human Behavior, 27*, 523–540.

Steblay, N., & Bothwell, R. K. (1994). Evidence for hypnotically refreshed testimony: The view from the laboratory. *Law and Human Behavior, 18,* 635–652.

Steblay, N., Dysart, J., Fulero, S., & Lindsay, R. C. L. (2001). Eyewitness accuracy rates in sequential and simultaneous lineup presentation: A meta-analytic comparison. *Law and Human Behavior, 25,* 459–473.

Steblay, N. M. (1992). A meta-analytic review of the weapon focus effect. *Law and Human Behavior, 16(4),* 413–424.

Technical Working Group on Eyewitness Evidence (1999). *Eyewitness evidence: A guide for law enforcement.* Washington, D.C.: National Institute of Justice (i-x, 1–44).

Toglia, M. P., Read, J. D., Ross, D. F., & Lindsay, R. C. L. (Eds.). (2007). *The handbook of eyewitness psychology, Vol. I: Memory for events.* Mahwah, NJ: Lawrence Erlbaum.

Turtle, J., Read, J. D., Lindsay, S., & Brimacombe, C. A. E. (2008). Toward a more informative psychological science of eyewitness evidence. *Applied Cognitive Psychology, 22,* 769–778.

Wagenaar, W. A. (1988). *Identifying Ivan: A case study in legal psychology.* Cambridge, MA: Harvard University Press.

Wells, G. L. (1993). What do we know about eyewitness identification? *American Psychologist, 48,* 553–571.

Wells, G. L., & Olson, E. A. (2003). Eyewitness testimony. *Annual Review of Psychology, 54,* 277–295.

Wells, G. L., Malpass, R. S., Lindsay, R. C. L., Fisher, R. P., Turtle, J. W., & Fulero, S. M. (2000). From the lab to the police station: A successful application of eyewitness research. *American Psychologist, 55(6),* 581–598.

Wells, G. L., Small, M., Penrod, S., Malpass, R. S., Fulero, S. M., & Brimacombe, C. A. E. (1998). Eyewitness identification procedures: Recommendations for lineups and photospreads. *Law and Human Behavior, 23(6),* 603–647.

WJBC (2008). *Eyewitness expert can't testify at Pelo's rape trial.* Retrieved April 27, 2008 from http://www.wjbc.com/wire2/news/06480_Pelo_final_pre-trialWEB_125804.htm.

Yarmey, A. D. (2001). Expert testimony: Does eyewitness memory research have probative value for the Courts? *Canadian Psychology, 42(2),* 92–100.

Notes

1. An independent scientific publisher not related to scientific societies, and therefore not a self-promotional arm of the profession.

2

Content, Form, and Ethical Issues Concerning Expert Psychological Testimony on Eyewitness Identification

Kathy Pezdek

Two concurrent forces have led to the increase in the admissibility of eyewitness expert testimony over the past two decades. First, to date nationwide, at least 209 men and one woman have been exonerated through DNA evidence. At least two dozen of these people were imprisoned as teenagers, and about 35% spent more than 15 years in jail before being exonerated. The majority were initially convicted based on eyewitness evidence, and more than a quarter of them had falsely confessed or made incriminating statements. The Innocence Project in New York maintains an up-to-date website that catalogues DNA exonerations in this country (www.innocenceproject. org), and there are innocence projects worldwide (http://forjustice.org/wc/ wrongful_conviction_websites.htm). Well-publicized stories of these exonerees (Santos, 2007; Scheck, Neufeld, & Dwyer, 2000) have aroused public compassion and motivated legal reforms regarding how best to secure accurate eyewitness identifications. The most sweeping of these reforms is included in the U.S. Department of Justice's national guidelines for how to collect eyewitness evidence in criminal cases (Technical Working Group for Eyewitness Evidence, 1999). The DNA exonerations have also helped to highlight the ineffectiveness of traditional safeguards designed to protect defendants from erroneous convictions resulting from mistaken identification (e.g., jury instructions from the judge, known as Telfaire instructions), thus promoting the admissibility of eyewitness expert testimony.

The second force that has led to the increase in the admissibility of eyewitness expert testimony is the significant increase in scientific research on factors that affect the accuracy of eyewitness identifications. This is true as well in many other areas of psychology in which psychologists testify in court (see Costanzo, Krauss, & Pezdek, 2007). Although research on eyewitness memory dates back at least 100 years (Munsterberg, 1908), the number of published scientific studies on eyewitness memory has increased exponentially over the past two decades. We now have a scientifically grounded understanding of not only the situational factors that affect the accuracy of eyewitness memory (estimator variables), but also the identification procedures that are more likely to be associated with accurate versus inaccurate identifications (system variables). This impressive body of scientific research has increased the credibility of the eyewitness expert testimony per se and increased the "general acceptance" of eyewitness memory research among psychologists (Kassin, Tubb, Hosch, & Memon, 2001). As discussed in Chapter 7 of this volume, the "general acceptance" of the explanatory theory presented by an expert has been one of the criteria for admitting expert testimony since the classic case of *Frye v. United States* (1923), commonly called the Frye Test. Together, these factors have fostered the increased rate of admissibility of eyewitness expert testimony in the courts.

The purpose of this chapter is to provide a realistic sense of the nature of eyewitness expert testimony—its content, form, and related ethical issues. As a caveat, I need to say up front that no one really knows how many individuals testify as eyewitness expert witnesses, what the range in their qualifications is, or what each does when he or she testifies. Individuals are not "credentialed" or "licensed" as eyewitness expert witnesses; rather, throughout this country, each trial judge decides on a case-by-case basis whether to admit a particular individual as an eyewitness expert witness or not. I frequently testify as an eyewitness expert witness. I know about 12 other psychologists who regularly testify as eyewitness expert witnesses, most of whom are academics with a Ph.D. in cognitive or social psychology and an impressive track record of published research on eyewitness memory and identification. Two are forensic psychologists who left academic positions to work full time as forensic consultants. I am generally familiar with the thrust of the testimony of these 12 individuals and will rely on this knowledge, as well as my own experiences, in discussing typical eyewitness expert testimony. A second caveat is that this chapter is most relevant to eyewitness expert testimony in the United States, simply because I am most familiar with the relevant legal restrictions and practices in this country.

The Content of Eyewitness Expert Testimony

When an eyewitness expert testifies, the bulk of his or her testimony is focused on psychological factors that affect the accuracy of eyewitness memory and the research that supports each of these factors. The eyewitness factors are generally divided into two classes of variables: estimator variables and system variables. *Estimator variables* are those that are not under control of the criminal justice system and include characteristics of the witness and characteristics of the observed event. *System variables* are those that are under the control of the criminal justices system and relate to how a witness was interviewed and the conditions under which an identification was made. There are excellent reviews of the research on the psychological factors that affect the accuracy of eyewitness memory. These include a meta-analysis of facial identification studies by Shapiro and Penrod (1986) and more recent articles by Wells, Memon, and Penrod (2006) and Wells and Olson (2003). In this chapter, I summarize these findings and focus on how eyewitness experts present this research to jurors.

Estimator Variables: Characteristics of the Witness

Witness Confidence

A case is more likely to go to trial if the eyewitnesses are confident in their identifications, because attorneys know that confident witnesses are perceived to be more compelling to jurors. However, is it true that more confident eyewitnesses are likely to be more accurate eyewitnesses? In a meta-analysis of the research on the confidence–accuracy relationship, Sporer, Penrod, Read, and Cutler (1995) found that across 30 studies on this topic (total sample size = 4036), the accuracy–confidence relationship was $r = .29$. Although this correlation is statistically significant, it accounts for only 8% of the variance. One way of thinking of this is to picture a pie chart representing all of the factors that affect eyewitness accuracy. Eyewitness confidence alone accounts for only 8% of this pie chart.

However, Sporer and colleagues (1995) reported a stronger accuracy–confidence relationship when they limited their analysis only to individuals who chose to make an identification. The accuracy–confidence rate for these individuals is more forensically relevant because the individuals who are more likely to testify in court are those who chose someone from a prior lineup, showup, or some other type of identification test. Among the choosers, the accuracy–confidence relationship was $r = .41$. How can an eyewitness expert help a jury understand what a .41 correlation means? Wells, Olson, and Charman (2002) suggested that one way to think about this correlation is to draw the comparison to a similar relationship for which the correlation is in this same range. Using U.S. Department of Health and Human Services data, they reported that the correlation between a person's height and gender is $r = .43$. Thus, if we assume that eyewitnesses make accurate identifications about 50% of the time, encountering a highly confident mistaken identification would be about as common as encountering a tall female or a short male. Presenting the accuracy–confidence relationship to a jury in these terms would help diminish the sanctity of a highly confident eyewitness.

It is also important to recognize that witness confidence is malleable. Typically, witness memory declines with the passage of time and, correspondingly, witness confidence decreases as well. However, occasionally witness confidence increases over time, for example, from an identification at a field showup ("He looks like the perpetrator") to the live lineup ("I think that's him; yes, that's him") to testimony at the trial ("I'm sure that's the man who robbed me at the ATM"). When this occurs, it is usually a red flag that something in addition to eyewitness memory is at play. For example, it has been reported that repeatedly questioning eyewitnesses inflates their confidence without affecting the accuracy of memory (Shaw, 1996). Also, if after making an identification (correct or incorrect), eyewitnesses are provided feedback that they are good witnesses, their subsequent confidence increases (Wells & Bradfield, 1999). By the time most witnesses testify in court, they have been questioned multiple times, and it would not be surprising to learn that, along the way, they have either inadvertently or directly received feedback that they "picked the right guy." This alone can explain why many eyewitnesses are so confident in their identification in front of the jury at the trial.

Cross-Race Identification

One of the strongest witness characteristics associated with identification accuracy is whether the race or ethnicity of the eyewitness and the perpetrator are the same or different. Meissner and Brigham (2001) recently reviewed 39 research studies on cross-race identification (also known as the own-race bias). In terms of correct identifications, across these 39 studies, eyewitnesses were 1.4 times more likely to correctly identify a previously viewed own-race face than a previously viewed other-race face. In terms of misidentifications, selection of the wrong suspect was 1.56 times more likely with other-race individuals than with same-race individuals. The cross-race effect has also been observed to be consistent across age. Pezdek, Blandon-Gitlin, and Moore (2003) compared kindergarten children, third graders, and young adults in their ability to identify a Black and a White individual from a six-person lineup after a one day delay. Similarly sized cross-race effects were reported at each age level.

Although the cross-race effect is somewhat reduced by exposure to other-race individuals, the effect of other-race contact on reducing the false alarm rate to other-race faces is modest. However, Meissner and Brigham (2001) reported that increased viewing time reduced the own-race bias; that is, when a witness has a shorter time to view a perpetrator, the false alarm rate to other-race faces increased. This finding is interesting because it suggests an interaction among eyewitness factors such that eyewitness identification accuracy would be expected to be especially unreliable when multiple deleterious eyewitness factors co-occur.

Eyewitness Stress

In presenting an eyewitness to a jury, the government's attorney frequently claims that certainly the eyewitness would be reliable, given the high rate of stress that focused her attention during the incident. Ironically, however, the research evidence clearly suggests that under high levels of stress, eyewitness memory is less—not more—reliable. This conclusion follows from a meta-analysis recently conducted by Deffenbacher, Bornstein, Penrod, and McGorty (2004). Included in the meta-analysis were 36 tests of the effects of stress on recall of crime-related details and 27 tests of stress on person identification. High levels of stress significantly impaired both types of memory, and the effect of stress was greater on (a) reducing correct identification rates than (b) increasing false alarm rates.

During cross-examination of an eyewitness expert, the government's attorney also frequently argues that findings of impaired memory under high levels of stress is restricted to laboratory tests of face recognition memory and have little bearing on high stress during real crimes. However, in the meta-analysis by Deffenbacher and colleagues (2004), the effects of stress were actually significantly higher in eyewitness identification studies that involved staged crimes than in those that involved laboratory face recognition tasks. One of the most impressive real-world studies of the effects of high stress on face recognition accuracy was recently reported by Morgan and associates (2004). In this study, more than 500 active duty military personnel were tested on their ability to recognize two individuals, each of whom had interrogated them for 40 minutes as part of a prisoner of war survival program. After 12 hours of confinement, each participant experienced both (a) a high-stress interrogation in which questioning was accompanied by physical confrontation, and (b) a low-stress interrogation without physical confrontation. A different individual had interrogated them in each condition. One day later, after recovering from sleep and food deprivation, each participant was tested on memory for the two interrogators using a live lineup or a photographic lineup. Correct identifications were significantly lower and incorrect identifications were significantly higher under the high- than the low-stress condition.

Other Estimator Variables That Are Characteristics of the Witness

In addition to the witness characteristics just described that affect the accuracy of eyewitness memory, additional factors can sometimes come into play. First, intoxicated eyewitnesses are less reliable that sober eyewitnesses, especially if they are intoxicated both at the time of observation and test. This would occur, for example, if an intoxicated eyewitness was presented a field showup shortly after observing an incident. Dysart, Lindsay, MacDonald, and Wicke (2002) reported that under these conditions, although blood-alcohol level was not significantly related to correct identification when the eyewitness was shown a target-present showup[1], when presented a target-absent showup, the false identification rate was vastly higher in the high (52%) than the low (22%) blood-alcohol level condition.

A few personality factors are also associated with eyewitness memory accuracy. Shapiro and Penrod (1986) discussed several of these factors in their meta-analysis of facial identification studies. However, it is not likely that an eyewitness expert would be able to testify about these personality factors because eyewitness experts rarely test or interview eyewitnesses and are not permitted by the court to comment directly on the reliability of any witness.

Estimator Variables: Characteristics of the Observed Event

Exposure Time, Distance, and Lighting

It is generally true that characteristics of the observed event have a greater impact on eyewitness memory than characteristics of the eyewitness. This is because even the best eyewitnesses are relatively more reliable under some conditions than under other conditions. It is thus important, at the most basic level, to examine how well each eyewitness actually observed the perpetrator to begin with. This issue involves an assessment of how long each eyewitness observed the perpetrator, at what distance, and what lighting was available. These are the major factors that determine how many of the details in the perpetrator's face are likely to have been encoded into memory. Most eyewitness identifications occur from a photographic lineup, and in a fair and unbiased photographic lineup, a photograph of a suspect is included along with photographs of five other individuals who all match the description given of the perpetrator. All six individuals in the lineup should have the same general characteristics in terms of gender, race or ethnicity, age, and physical stature. The differences among the six individuals in the lineup are more likely to be in terms of the more specific details of each face, and it is these more specific details that are less likely to have been encoded if the perpetrator was observed very quickly, from some distance away, and under poor lighting. Although few would disagree that an individual cannot be observed in detail when seen after dark from several hundred feet away, the effect of brief exposure time may be less obvious.

A wealth of research exists on the effects of exposure time on eyewitness memory. In their meta-analysis of facial identification studies, Shapiro and Penrod (1986) reported a linear trend between exposure time to a face and the probability of correctly identifying the face. Memon, Hope, and Bull (2003) conducted a study that demonstrated this effect under reasonably ecologically valid conditions. They had mock witnesses view a realistic videotape of a crime in which the perpetrator was visible for either 12 or 45 seconds. Tested only 40 minutes later, the probability of a correct identification in the target-present arrays was vastly higher in the 45-second than the 12-second condition (90% versus 32%), and the probability of an incorrect identification in the target-absent arrays was significantly higher in the 12-second than the 45-second condition (85% versus 41%).

Time Delay

Although most jurors realize that their memory for an event declines as the time since the event increases, they sometimes do not apply this same memory fact to eyewitness memory for the face of a perpetrator. Perhaps it is the over-confident eyewitness saying, "I remember him as clearly today as the night of the attack a year ago," that trumps the good sense of jurors. Nonetheless, it is clear from the results of Shapiro and Penrod's (1986) meta-analysis that longer delays led to fewer correct identifications and more false identifications.

System Variables

System variables are those that are under the control of the criminal justice system and relate to how the witnesses were interviewed and the conditions under which an identification was made. The testimony of an eyewitness expert can be especially helpful in educating a jury about the potential fallacies in eyewitness identification that can result from the police identification procedures themselves, because people are not generally aware of the substantial differences in outcomes that can result from subtle differences in police identification procedures. Several excellent reviews are available of the effects of system variables on eyewitness identification (Wells & Olson, 2003; Wells et al., 1998; Wells et al., 2006). All of this work will not be summarized here, but rather, the three rules for conducting lineups suggested by Wells and colleagues (1998) are discussed.

The first rule is, "The person who conducts the lineup or photo-spread should not be aware of which member of the lineup or photo-spread is the suspect" (p. 627). This is also referred to as a *double-blind procedure*. This is important because if the officer administering the lineup knows who the suspect is, this knowledge (a) can be communicated to the eyewitness via verbal or nonverbal cues, and (b) can influence the officer's interpretation of the eyewitness's comments during the lineup. Regarding the first point, a large body of research exists on experimenter expectancy effects. This refers to the fact that individuals who have expectations about the performance of others (e.g., researchers, teachers, parents, judges, police officers) can communicate these expectations to their subordinates (e.g., subjects, students, children, jurors, witnesses) using a wide range of cues, and these cues can actually affect the performance of these individuals (Rosenthal, 2002). The experimenter expectancy effect can be eliminated in eyewitness identification procedures by simply ensuring that the officer administering the lineup does not know who the suspect is.

The second point of the above-stated rule number one is that knowledge of who the suspect is in a lineup can influence the officer's interpretation of the eyewitness's comments during the lineup. For example, if the eyewitness points to one of the filler faces in a photographic lineup and says, "That looks kind of like the shooter," the officer might interpret this as an ambivalent remark and respond, "Well, is there anyone else in the lineup who looks like the shooter?" However, if the eyewitness points to the suspect and makes this same remark, the officer is more likely to interpret this response affirmatively and ask the eyewitness to circle that face and sign the identification card. This is especially problematic because photographic lineups are rarely recorded, and the defense attorney is rarely present to observe this procedure. Thus, all the jury is likely to hear is that "the eyewitness positively identified the defendant."

The second of Wells and colleagues' rules (1998) is, "Eyewitnesses should be told explicitly that the person in question might not be in the lineup or photo-spread and therefore should not feel that they must make an identification. They should also be told that the person administering the lineup does not know which person is the suspect in the case" (p. 629). This rule follows from the finding by Parker and Ryan (1993) that eyewitnesses are less likely to false alarm and identify an innocent suspect if they are told that the perpetrator may not be in the lineup. In reality, however, what is more important is whether the eyewitness believes that she will be shown a lineup including the perpetrator, rather than what she is told. If, after a crime, an eyewitness has no contact with the police for several months, and then suddenly the stolen property is returned and she is asked to attend a lineup, the eyewitness is likely to attend the lineup with the expectation that her job is to select someone. Under these conditions, the eyewitness is likely to select from the lineup that individual who looks most like the perpetrator, even if she does not actually recognize that individual from the scene of the crime. In other words, the eyewitness simply lowers her response criterion. The probability of a misidentification increases when the response criterion is lowered. The testimony of an eyewitness expert can be useful in educating the jury about how an eyewitness can sometimes select an individual from a lineup because of system variables such as these and not because she actually recognizes the individual.

The third rule (Wells et al., 1998) is, "A clear statement should be taken from the eyewitness at the time of the identification and prior to any feedback as to his or her confidence that the identified person is the actual culprit" (p. 635). Although, as mentioned previously, the correlation between witness confidence and witness accuracy is not strong, jurors often do rely on an eyewitness's expressed confidence in gauging the reliability of the witness. Thus, estimates of witness confidence obtained prior to any biasing feedback are less likely to be artificially inflated.

Estimator Variables and System Variables Together

Are the effects of estimator variables and system variables independent? No. When eyewitness memory is weak, system variables are more likely to have a stronger impact. Consider the situation in which two co-workers in a doctor's office are having lunch. The office is closed, so when they hear some noise in the adjacent room, they walk over to see who might be there. When they see an unfamiliar man packing up a box, they ask him what he is doing. He claims to be looking for the restroom and leaves when confronted. The co-workers call the police, who have a suspect apprehended within 30 minutes. Both co-workers, standing together, confidently identify the defendant at a field showup at which they are told, "We've got him." Under the conditions of observation in this situation, these eyewitnesses would be expected to have a strong memory for the perpetrator—they were close to him, the lighting was good, they were face-to-face talking to him for about 45 seconds, their attention was directed to the perpetrator by the witnesses' suspicion, and they identified him only 30 minutes later. The witnesses should have been tested independently, and they should not have been given the biased comment, "We've got him." Nonetheless, we have sufficient reason to believe that these witnesses have a strong and enduring memory for the perpetrator's face, and such a memory is less likely to be influenced by flawed system variables.

The Form of Eyewitness Expert Testimony

Generally, there are two aspects to the work done by an eyewitness expert witness: pretrial consultation and testimony. In many ways, these are two equally important roles. However, the extent to which an expert witness participates in pretrial consultation depends primarily on when he or she becomes involved in a case. The reality is that trial attorneys, especially public defenders, are pervasively overworked and are usually assigned a case only after the preliminary hearing. Consequently, they give their eyewitness expert witness about as much time as they have to prepare for a case—frequently only a couple of weeks.

Pretrial Consultation

How does an eyewitness expert get involved in a case? The first point of contact between an attorney and an eyewitness expert is normally a telephone conversation. At this point, the attorney has usually consulted with colleagues and identified an eyewitness expert who has the reputation that he thinks will work best with his case. In the initial telephone conversation with the eyewitness expert, the attorney describes the facts of the case relevant to the eyewitness identifications. The eyewitness expert takes careful notes and asks questions to fill in the relevant details. The purpose of this initial conversation, conducted for no fee, is (a) for the attorney to determine whether eyewitness expert testimony in general, and the testimony of this eyewitness expert specifically, is likely to work with his defense strategy for the case, and (b) for the eyewitness expert to determine whether a basis exists in the psychological research literature to question the reliability of the eyewitnesses in the case, and whether he or she wants to work with this attorney on this case. In other words, this is a two-way interview to assess fit, with each individual utilizing his or her own criteria. It is important to realize that this dynamic is operative because it has implications for some of the ethical issues discussed later in this chapter, specifically regarding what cases an eyewitness expert takes on and how this decision is made.

Once an eyewitness expert is retained on a case, he or she conducts the pretrial consultation. This involves reviewing all of the materials that present the facts of the case relevant to the eyewitness identifications. This usually includes the initial police reports, transcripts (and sometimes tapes) of interviews with each eyewitness, the investigating officer's report from the photographic or live lineup, and the transcript of the preliminary hearing. In reviewing this material, the eyewitness expert identifies factors that are likely to have affected the reliability of the eyewitness identifications. These would include the estimator variables and system variables that were discussed previously in this chapter.

At this point, the eyewitness expert can also identify factors about which additional information is needed. Perhaps it is necessary to have an investigator go to the scene of the crime and identify (a) the location of lights in the area, (b) how well the face of a man with a baseball cap could have been observed from a second-story window above the alley, or (c) the extent to which a tree in front of the eyewitness's living room window might have obscured the view of the perpetrator running down the street. Eyewitnesses' memory for details such as these can be as unreliable as their memory for the perpetrator's face. Independent corroboration of circumstantial details is often crucial, and an eyewitness expert can help identify important factors that need to be clarified.

The eyewitness expert also maps out the "identification history" of each witness. This is a timeline specifying what types of identification tests were presented to each eyewitness and the eyewitness's response to each. From this information, the eyewitness expert can determine whether there may have been suggestive or biasing influences on the identification of the defendant. For example, it is not uncommon for an eyewitness to be shown an apparently fair and unbiased photographic lineup that includes the defendant and make no identification, but later to be shown a second photographic or live lineup that includes the defendant and identify him—perhaps saying "this man looks familiar." One interpretation of this sequence of events is that the defendant's picture in the second lineup looked familiar because he *is* familiar, but only from the first lineup and not from the scene of the crime. A substantial body of research provides a scientific basis for this phenomenon (cf. Pezdek & Blandon-Gitlin, 2005). Also, as presented in the first section of this chapter, eyewitness confidence is also malleable and can increase over time if an eyewitness is repeatedly questioned or provided confirming feedback.

However, the point here is that this interpretation would not be possible without assessing exactly what transpired over time from the occurrence of the crime to the first identification by an eyewitness. Often, the case file does not include a report from the first photographic lineup that resulted in a "no identification" of the defendant; this can only be inferred from what the witness might have said subsequently in an interview or at the preliminary hearing. This is one reason why it is important for an eyewitness expert to be very familiar with the case file. I mention this because, in my experience, some judges try to limit payment for pretrial preparation and consultation. They contend that if an eyewitness expert knows her content area, all he or she has to do is come into court and testify. This view is inconsistent with the fact that the content of eyewitness expert testimony is not the same in every trial. The factors that are likely to have affected the accuracy of eyewitness memory and identification are not the same in every case. To identify what these factors are in each case, the eyewitness expert must be familiar with the case file.

There are several points at which the attorney might decide not to retain the eyewitness expert to testify in the trial. This decision is normally made based on whether the attorney thinks that the expert can advance his strategy for the case. The eyewitness expert can participate in this decision by offering her opinion regarding whether, on balance, she thinks that the eyewitness evidence is reliable. However, because the attorney, but not usually the eyewitness expert, knows the full scope of the evidence to be presented in a trial, he is usually in a better position to decide the extent to which eyewitness expert testimony is likely to facilitate his case strategy. In any particular case, the eyewitness evidence can vary along a continuum from very weak (the eyewitnesses really never saw the perpetrator very clearly and a misidentification is likely) to very strong (the eyewitnesses got a good look at the perpetrator and a correct identification is likely); generally, the utility of the testimony of the eyewitness expert would be expected to vary conversely along this same continuum. However, if the only evidence against a defendant is the eyewitness evidence, the attorney may feel that his best strategy is to have the eyewitness expert testify regardless of the strength of the eyewitness evidence. In this sense, the decision regarding whether an eyewitness expert should testify in a case or not is best made by the attorney. However, and relevant to the third section of this chapter, it is the ethical obligation of the eyewitness expert to testify similarly to the facts of a case regardless of whether her advice to the defense attorney was for or against proceeding with her testimony in the trial. It is the job of the defense attorney—not the eyewitness expert—to provide the best defense for the defendant.

On a related point, the attorney will often request a written report from the eyewitness expert after she has reviewed the case file. This report is to (a) offer the opinion of the eyewitness expert regarding the strength of the eyewitness evidence and (b) articulate the specific factors that led to this opinion.[2] Less than half of all cases on which I am retained to testify as an eyewitness expert actually go to trial, and this appears typical from my conversations with other eyewitness experts. The majority of these cases are settled prior to trial, and the written report of an eyewitness expert frequently plays a role in the pretrial resolution of these cases. In light of the potential importance of this report, it is the ethical obligation of the eyewitness expert to present in this report a balanced view of the reliability of the eyewitness evidence.

If the attorney decides to have the eyewitness expert testify in the trial, the next step is to prepare the testimony. Courtroom testimony is necessarily in a question-and-answer format; this is not an academic lecture by the expert. Thus, the attorney needs to be informed regarding those areas about which to question the expert and anticipate issues that are likely to arise during cross-examination. And, usually there is a best organization for presenting this information to make it clear and comprehensible to the jury. The pretrial work of the eyewitness expert can be very effective in preparing an attorney to present eyewitness evidence to the jury most effectively.

The eyewitness expert can also assist the attorney in preparing for the presentation of other aspects of the eyewitness case to the jury, specifically (a) introducing the eyewitness evidence in the opening and closing statements, (b) cross-examining the police officer, and (c) cross-examining the eyewitnesses. These and other suggestions for presenting eyewitness evidence to a jury have been discussed by Nettles, Nettles, and Wells (1996). It is appropriate for an eyewitness expert to assist the attorney with preparation of these other aspects of the case because this can help lay a foundation for the testimony of the expert and give the jury the proper frame of mind for the eyewitness expert testimony; thus, the eyewitness expert testimony is not processed in a vacuum, independently of other trial testimony.

Assisting in the Preparation of the Attorney's Opening and Closing Statements

In an eyewitness case, both attorneys can expect that during direct testimony, the eyewitness will point to the defendant and identify him as the perpetrator of the crime. In anticipation of this, and to "steal the thunder" from the government's case, the defense attorney should tell the jury during opening statement that this will occur. He should then present his interpretation for why this will occur by giving the jury another reason why the eyewitness will identify the defendant, a reason that has nothing to do with who committed the crime. The attorney should then tell the jury that an expert witness—a scientist with impeccable credentials—will testify to support this interpretation. During closing statement, the attorney should then summarize how the facts presented in the trial support his alternative interpretation of why the eyewitness identified the defendant, even though the defendant was not the perpetrator.

Assisting in the Preparation of the Attorney's Cross-Examination of the Police Officer

Often, the reason for questioning the reliability of the eyewitness evidence rests on the procedures utilized by police officers in eliciting the identification from the eyewitness. These are the system variables that were introduced in the first section of this chapter. The eyewitness expert can help the attorney lay the foundation for this aspect of the expert testimony by identifying procedures the police officer may have used that could have led to a misidentification. A number of sources present reviews of the scientific support for utilizing appropriate system variables (cf. Wells et al., 2006). However, rather than trying to convince the jury that the police may have followed procedures determined *by scientific studies* to be suggestive and associated with a high rate of false alarms, I think it is more effective to convince the jury that the police may have followed procedures determined *by their own state police guidelines* to be suggestive and associated with a high rate of false alarms.

In fact, the California Peace Officers Legal Sourcebook (2001) specifies, among other things, the following: (a) "You must avoid any conduct *prior to* the identification which might be ruled suggestive" (p. 8.1), and then a list of clarifying examples is provided; (b) "You must avoid any conduct *during* the identification which might be ruled suggestive"; and then a list of clarifying examples is provided (p. 8.2); (c) "You should not say or do anything during the lineup which would draw the attention of a witness to the suspect. To avoid any problems, try not to say or do *anything* during the identification" (p. 8.3); and (d) "If, prior to the lineup, the witness describes the suspect as having a particular or distinguishing characteristic. . . . , make sure that others in the lineup also have this characteristic, if at all possible" (*Adams*, 1982; p. 8.3). When the attorney cross-examines the police officer, it would be useful to ask him the extent to which each of the specified state police guidelines for conducting lineups and showups was followed in conducting the identification in the case.

Assisting in the Preparation of the Attorney's Cross-Examination of the Eyewitness

The most important thing for the attorney to keep in mind when cross-examining the eyewitness is to ally with the jury's perception that the eyewitness is an innocent bystander, and to treat the eyewitness accordingly. In other words, the proper frame of mind is that the eyewitness is mistaken in her identification; however, a witness can be incorrect without being dishonest. During the eyewitness expert testimony, the expert should also emphasis this point, that even well-intended eyewitnesses can be mistaken. The jury should never be in the position of having to find the eyewitness dishonest or otherwise malevolent in order to find the defendant not guilty.

Trial Testimony of an Eyewitness Expert Witness

When an eyewitness case does go to trial, most of the substance of the eyewitness expert testimony pertains to what is referred to in the landmark California eyewitness case of *People v. McDonald* (1984) as "certain psychological factors that may impair the accuracy of a typical eyewitness identification, . . . with supporting references to experimental studies of such phenomena (p. 246)."

Generally, this is done by presenting the estimator and system variables that the eyewitness expert identified as factors likely to have affected the reliability of the eyewitness identifications. However, a successful expert witness does not simply present the jury with a list of the relevant eyewitness factors and the experimental support for each. Rather, the task of the eyewitness expert is to persuade the jury to evaluate the eyewitness evidence more analytically, so that they can more accurately judge its reliability in light of the eyewitness circumstances in the specific case at hand.

The first step in this process is to provide jurors with an accurate schema for how eyewitness memory works. If jurors believe that memory works like a video-camera, and this schema is shared by many jurors, then eyewitness memory is simply the process of playing back the digitized recording that was laid down with relatively higher or lower resolution. Such a schema would lead to many inaccurate conclusions about the reliability of eyewitness evidence. An important part of getting jurors to evaluate eyewitness evidence more accurately is to dispel this myth.

One approach that serves this purpose is to show jurors fallacies in their own everyday memory. For example, the eyewitness expert can ask the jurors to recall the features on the front and back of a U.S. penny,[3] the features of the state seal (which is typically on the wall right over the judge's head), or the face of the security officer with whom they interacted when they entered the courthouse that morning. Lest they think, well, these are not salient or important things, ask them to recall the face of the minister who married them or the face of the delivery room nurse who delivered their first child. When jurors attempt any of these memory tasks, they quickly realize that what they remember, even about salient and important things, is not just a mental photograph of what they viewed. Expert testimony, like good teaching, involves not just dishing out information, but actually transforming the way people think about a domain. This should be the goal of an eyewitness expert as he or she prepares to testify.

Another challenge for an eyewitness expert in preparing to testify is to realize that although his or her testimony must be grounded in the scientific research literature on eyewitness memory and identification, most people find a good example more persuasive than a library full of good data. Thus, most jurors are going to find that a point made by providing a memorable illustrative example is going to be more persuasive than presenting the results of a scientific study. As of December 2008, more than 210 post-conviction DNA exoneration cases are available to serve as examples of cases in which highly confident eyewitnesses have been dead wrong, many under circumstances that may approximate the conditions of the case at hand. Another advantage for an eyewitness expert in structuring her testimony around illustrative examples rather than scientific studies is that it reduces the chance that cross-examination will consist of a long and boring sequence of questions about picayune details of experiments. Unlike a typical classroom lecture, when an expert witness testifies in court, he or she needs to contemplate the type of cross-examination that is likely to follow from the nature of the direct testimony provided. The form of the eyewitness expert testimony should take this into consideration.

What can be expected during cross-examination of an eyewitness expert? It is not uncommon for the district attorney to have in front of him several transcripts of previous testimony by the expert, against which to compare the expert's testimony in the current case. Remember, the job of the prosecutor is to present the strongest case possible for the government, in this case, by reducing the credibility of the eyewitness expert. During cross-examination, an expert witness should be prepared to defend his or her fee, professional record, and the basis for any points made during direct examination. Chapter 10 in this volume, by Bailey and Mecklenburg, presents a critique of the typical eyewitness expert testimony. In preparing for cross-examination, eyewitness experts should plan their responses to the issues raised in Chapter 11. During cross-examination, the expert should also be prepared to present a list of the factors that would *bolster* the accuracy of the eyewitness evidence, and the research support for these factors. After all, there are few cases for which all of the evidence suggests that the eyewitness identifications are faulty, and such cases are not those that are likely to be prosecuted. Additional suggestions for how to prepare for cross-examination are presented in the section that follows, on ethical issues.

Ethical Issues Concerning Eyewitness Expert Testimony

Every expert witness faces a host of ethical issues when she enters the legal arena, from the first point of contact in a telephone conversation to the trial testimony. The American Psychology-Law Society provides guidelines for forensic psychologists. These guidelines address some of the ethical principles that govern work in the courts (see http://www.ap-ls.org/links/SGFP%20 January%202006.pdf). However, the more subtle factors are more likely to challenge the ethics of an eyewitness expert witness.

To identify some of these more subtle factors, I contacted the 12 individuals whom I know throughout the United States who regularly testify as eyewitness expert witnesses. I asked each to specify the three major ethical concerns he or she encounters when serving as an eyewitness expert witness. I received responses from seven of these people; their comments, along with my own, provide the basis for this section of the chapter.

The most frequently raised ethical concern can be characterized as maintaining balance and objectivity. In California, where the courts have been more open to the testimony of eyewitness expert witnesses, the relevant evidence codes for appointing any court expert are California Evidence Code Sections 730 and 952 (see West's). When an eyewitness expert is first appointed, the conditions for the appointment are typically specified by these two evidence codes. Evidence Code 730 simply states:

> When it appears to the court, at any time before or during the trial of an action, that expert evidence is or may be required by the court or by any party to the action, the court on its own motion or on motion of any party may appoint one or more experts to investigate, to render a report as may be ordered by the court, and to testify as an expert at the trial.

However, Evidence Code 952 specifies that the communication between the expert and the lawyer is confidential. This means that information transmitted between the expert and the lawyer cannot be disclosed to a third person, other than those who are present to further the interest of the client.[4] The fact that an eyewitness expert is initially appointed under the umbrella of these two evidence codes makes it immediately salient that the legal system in the United States is an adversarial system. The job of the defense attorney is to provide his best defense for the defendant. The job of the government's attorney is to provide his best case against the defendant. An expert witness is retained by one side, usually the defense, but the expert witness is expected to be an objective, unbiased participant in the process. *So, what does it mean to be objective if retained by a defense attorney in the context of an adversarial system?*

The eyewitness experts with whom I consulted identified challenges to objectivity that vary along a continuum. At one end of the continuum are those situations in which it is easy to identify pressures to be nonobjective. One expert provided this example:

> The worst situation I ever had involved an attorney who wanted me to say something I couldn't say. The facts involved something like this: A witness who first thought the perpetrator was Caucasian but then identified a light-skinned Black individual. The lawyer wanted me to say that that was not humanly possible, calling on research on cross-racial identification. I tried to explain that the cross-racial identification research did not say what he thought. He didn't want to hear that and refused to pay me for my time involved in travel, testimony, etc.

More typical, however, are the more subtle situations at the other end of the continuum; these occur throughout the process, from pretrial consulting to testifying. What can be the challenges to an eyewitness expert's objectivity during pretrial consultation? One expert offered this view:

> I think of myself as an unbiased expert, but regularly face pressure to be an advocate for the [defense] attorney. Examples include being asked for advice about jury selection and how to cross-examine witnesses. These are questions that should be for the defense team, but not the expert witness. Are physicians who testify as experts asked to give advice about jury selection? I doubt it.

However, the opinions of the experts varied widely in terms of the acceptable scope of the pretrial consultation. Another expert said,

> I think the most basic ethical issue faced in this type of work is clearly separating the collaborative "strategy" work done with the attorney at the consultation-preparation stage from the objective testimony to be provided at trial. This is, of course, an issue in all cases. From the moment an attorney calls to the moment before I take the stand, I am their consultant. As their hired consultant, I do my very best to assist them in understanding the research in a manner that will help them build their case as effectively as possible as *they* zealously advocate for *their* client. However, once I take the stand, I must be an objective source of information, answering the questions raised by both sides in the most balanced and fair manner possible.

Whereas the former view emphasizes the need for objectivity on the part of the expert over advocacy for the defendant, the latter view considers the pretrial consultation as an opportunity to establish the foundation for the expert's testimony to strengthen its impact. Both experts agree, however, that objectivity is essential in their testimony. Nonetheless, based on the social psychology research on the impact of roles on behavior (Zimbardo, 1972), it is not clear that the type of role-switching suggested in the view of the latter expert is likely or even possible.

Prior to testifying, all witnesses take the oath that they will tell, "the truth, the whole truth, and nothing but the truth." But, what is "the whole truth?" The principal challenges to an expert's objectivity during trial testimony concern what is presented and how it is presented. In other words, to what extent does an eyewitness expert discuss factors that decrease versus increase the reliability of the eyewitness evidence, and is the research on both sides presented similarly? One expert emphasized the need to "accurately characterize research findings, avoiding overstating (or understating) the size of effects or generalizations of the findings, particularly as it pertains to the factors on both sides—those that would support and undermine an accurate identification." However, another expert framed the situation this way:

> During direct examination, the defense attorney usually shapes the expert testimony by only asking questions about the aspects of the eyewitness evidence that should decrease its likely accuracy, and not mentioning aspects that should increase its likely accuracy. I don't deliberately suppress factors that I notice that speak in favor of the eyewitness, but the adversarial nature of the situation imposes some biases on what my direct testimony will feature. I am retained by the defense, and the defense attorney asks the questions—usually questions that I have suggested. This is not usually a problem because I only agree to testify in cases in which the eyewitness evidence looks pretty bad overall in terms of system and estimator

variables, but there are times when it turns out that the evidence is not all that bad.

This is where extensive pretrial consultation—the type discussed in the middle section of this chapter—can be useful in identifying the factors that both foster and undermine the accuracy of the eyewitness evidence. Once the factors on both sides have been identified, the defense attorney can decide, first, whether to have the eyewitness expert testify at all, and if so, what the best strategy is for introducing the relevant material. However, it is important for the defense attorney to know, prior to trial, what the expert will say on any point, so that the expert's testimony is not shaped by the needs of the defense. This is one good strategy for maintaining the objectivity of the expert testimony.

It is easy for an eyewitness expert for the defense to be objective if he or she suspects that the defendant is innocent, but what about when this is not the case? The true test of an eyewitness expert's objectivity occurs when, during the process, the expert develops the view that the defendant is likely to be guilty even if the eyewitness evidence is dubious. This can occur while reviewing the case file in the pretrial stage, or it can occur as late in the process as during testimony. It has occasionally happened to me that, during cross-examination, the prosecutor asks, "How does it affect your opinion regarding the reliability of the eyewitness evidence that the defendant's fingerprints were found at the scene of the crime, and on the night of the murder, he told his sister that he shot the cashier by accident?" It is unlikely that facts such as these would only come to my attention at the trial, but is has occurred. When asked a question like this, I respond that I cannot evaluate the veracity of these other lines of evidence, and that I think it is important that each line of evidence be evaluated independently. This is true, and I think that it is an important point for jurors to understand that five lines of evidence against a defendant are not necessarily more compelling that two. When this occurs, I also use it as an opportunity to ask the prosecutor boldly if he is inviting me to comment on the culpability of the defendant. Nonetheless, it presents a challenge to my personal ethics if I feel that my testimony may be helping a guilty person.

This situation has arisen for other experts as well. One of the experts I surveyed said,

> Occasionally, I have a very strong suspicion that the defendant is guilty. The eyewitness evidence is bad because of improper, biased, suggestive testing by the police, so I am compelled to testify that the science raises questions about the validity of the identification. I am ethically bound to critique the eyewitness evidence for the jury, but I am ethically challenged by the belief that—maybe because of me—a guilty person may go free while victims suffer more.

Nonetheless, in these situations, it is important that the expert's testimony proceeds just as it would if he or she believed that the defendant was innocent. This is because, first, the expert witness does not actually know whether the defendant is innocent or guilty; this is not the role of the expert, and the expert rarely has sufficient information to make this determination. Further, we know from the research on interpersonal expectations that was previously discussed that an individual's covert expectations of a person affect how others perceive that person (Rosenthal, 2002). Thus, if the expert witness perceives that the defendant is guilty, this increases the probability that the jury will do so as well, and this far exceeds the appropriate influence of the expert witness.

Another expert witness has taken the very strong view that not only should eyewitness experts only consider the strength of the eyewitness evidence, ignoring other lines of evidence when they are preparing for testimony, but that it is equally important in deciding which cases to accept that an eyewitness expert not consider other factors that might suggest whether the defendant is guilty or innocent. In this expert's opinion, these actions would prejudge the case.

What criteria do eyewitness experts use to decide whether to accept a case? One expert witness offered this view:

> How selective should I be in accepting or rejecting cases? Some cases are better suited for expert testimony than others. But should this be a basis for accepting cases? I have heard good arguments for being selective, and I have heard good arguments for taking cases on a first-come-first-served basis. I have to make this decision virtually every time I receive a call from an attorney.

For all eyewitness experts, various practical considerations affect which cases they accept. These primarily include timing and scheduling issues. There are other issues as well. For example, I am more likely to want to work in the future with an attorney whom I perceive to be well organized and well prepared for trial than with one whose style is to shoot from the hip in the courtroom. Thus, even if I am very busy, I am more likely to say yes to some attorneys than to others; that is, my criterion increases with my availability. Although this does not affect my objectivity, I often wonder if this is fair to the client. Another expert expressed a similar decision rule in considering the severity of a case. That is, "if it involves the death penalty, I am more inclined to do it even if I am too busy." This makes sense if the expert's decision criterion is aimed at minimizing the consequence of a misidentification. However, this disadvantages innocent people accused of less serious crimes. I recently questioned a defense attorney why her client did not accept a 6-month deal rather than going to trial facing 15 years to life. She convinced me that, for this man, 6 months in jail would essentially ruin his life; he would lose his job, his house, and likely his family. Six months in jail for this man would be comparable to a much longer sentence for an individual with more resources. Thus, the "severity of the case" is a relative judgment, and one that the expert is not likely to be able to evaluate fully.

Sometimes the decision as to whether to accept an appointment or not is based on whether the expert's fee can be paid. Expert witnesses (along with everyone else working in the courtroom) are paid for their expertise. Ordinarily, each eyewitness expert has a court-approved rate, and they are appointed (for indigent clients) or paid a retainer (for private clients) based on this rate. However, periodically a lesser fee is offered. I consider it inappropriate to work on different cases, sometimes in the same county, at different rates. This would also open the door for dickering about the fee for every case, a practice I would not find pleasant. Therefore, sometimes I turn down cases because my fee cannot be paid. However, another expert admitted that "my requirement to be paid for my expert services arouses a large ethical concern about unequal access to resources to defend oneself. Requiring payment for testimony contributes to the bad reality that there is highly unequal access to justice in our legal system."

Let me return to the issue of what it means to be objective in the context of an adversarial system. Let's be honest. Even the calmest, best-intended expert witness can enter the courtroom committed to being an impartial educator and leave the courtroom in a rage, hoping that the defendant is acquitted just to spite the government's attorney. This situation was described by Schofield (1956) more than a half century ago when he recognized that something in the adversarial system "arouses the adrenals" (p. 2). The job of the government's attorney is to provide his best case against the defendant, and this often involves taking every possible step to discredit defense witnesses. The government's attorney will often (a) purposefully misstate the testimony of the expert to make him or her look foolish, (b) comb through transcripts of previous trials in which the expert has testified to attempt to perjure the witness, (c) try to identify weaknesses in the expert's academic record and provoke the expert by revealing his or her sensitivity about this, and (d) question the expert in detail about his or her fee and total income per year for the past several years. Schofield believed that, under such pressure, only a superhuman person could avoid taking sides and becoming invested in the outcome of the trial. Nonetheless, this should be avoided because it undermines the objectivity of the expert. How can this be avoided? Just anticipating this behavior during cross-examination helps minimize the sting when it occurs. But it is clear to anyone who has testified as an eyewitness expert that this line of work, although valuable to the courts, is not for the meek.

References

Adams, 137 Cal. App. 3d 346 (1982).

American Psychology-Law Society. http://www.ap-ls.org/links/SGFP%20 January%202006.pdf, Retrieved January 3, 2008.

California peace officers legal sourcebook (2001). Revision No. 104. Sacramento, CA: California Department of Justice.

Costanzo, M., Krauss, D., & Pezdek, K. (Eds.). (2007). *Expert psychological testimony for the courts* (pp. 99–117). Mahwah, NJ: Erlbaum.

Deffenbacher, K. A., Bornstein, B. H., Penrod, S. D., & McCorty, E. K. (2004). A meta-analytic review of the effects of high stress on eyewitness memory. *Law and Human Behavior, 28*, 687–706.

Dysart, J. E., Lindsay, R. C. I., MacDonald, T. K., & Wicke, C. (2002). The intoxicated witness: Effects of alcohol on identification accuracy from showups. *Journal of Applied Psychology, 87*, 170–175.

ForJustice. http://forJustice.org/wc/wrongful_conviction_websites.htm, Retrieved January 3, 2008.

Frye v. United States, 293 F. 1013 (D.C. Cir. 1923).

Innocence Project. http://www.innocenceproject.org/, Retrieved January 3, 2008.

Kassin, S. M., Tubb, V. A., Hosch, H. M., & Memon, A. (2001). On the "general acceptance" of eyewitness testimony research. *American Psychologist, 56*, 405–416.

Meissner, C., & Brigham, J.C. (2001). Twenty years of investigating the own-race bias in memory for faces: A meta-analytic review. *Psychology, Public Policy, and Law, 7*, 3–35.

Memon, A., Hope, L., & Bull, R. (2003). Exposure duration: Effects on eyewitness accuracy and confidence. *British Journal of Psychology, 94*, 339–354.

Morgan, C. A., Hazlett, G., Doran, A., Garrett, S., Hoyt, G., Thomas, P., Baronoski, M., & Southwick, S. M. (2004). Accuracy of eyewitness memory for persons encountered during exposure to highly intense stress. *International Journal of Law and Psychiatry, 27*, 264–279.

Munsterberg, H. (1908). *On the witness stand: Essays on psychology and crime.* Garden City, NY: Doubleday.

Nettles, B., Nettles, Z.S., & Wells, G.L. (November, 1996). Eyewitness identification: 'I noticed you paused on number three.' *The Champion Magazine.*

Nickerson, R. S., & Adams, M. J. (1979). Long-term memory for a common object. *Cognitive Psychology, 11*, 287–307.

Parker, J. F., & Ryan, V. (1993). An attempt to reduce guessing behavior in children's and adults' eyewitness identifications. *Law and Human Behavior, 17*, 11–26.

People v. McDonald, 37 Ca1.3d 351, 690 P.2d 709, 716, 208 Cal.Rptr. 236, 245 (1984).

Pezdek, K., & Blandon-Gitlin, I. (2005). When is an intervening lineup most likely to affect eyewitness identification accuracy? *Legal and Criminological Psychology, 10*, 247–263.

Pezdek, K., Blandon-Gitlin, I., & Moore, C. (2003). Children's face recognition memory: More evidence for the cross-race effect. *Journal of Applied Psychology, 88*, 760–763.

Rosenthal, R. (2002). Covert communication in classrooms, clinics, courtrooms, and cubicles. *American Psychologist, 57*, 839–849.

Santos, F. (2007, November 25). Vindicated by DNA, but lost man on the outside. *New York Times.* Retrieved from http://nytimes.com.

Scheck, B., Neufeld, P., & Dwyer, J. (2000). *Actual innocence.* New York: Random House.

Schofield, W. (1956). Psychology, law and the expert witness. *American Psychologist, 11*, 1–7.

Shapiro, P. N., & Penrod, S. (1986). Meta-analysis of facial identification studies. *Psychological Bulletin, 100,* 139–156.

Shaw, J. S., III (1996). Increases in eyewitness confidence resulting from postevent questioning. *Journal of Experimental Psychology: Applied, 2,* 126–146.

Sporer, S. L., Penrod, S. D., Read, J. D., & Cutler, B. L. (1995). Choosing, confidence, and accuracy: A meta-analysis of the confidence-accuracy relation in eyewitness identification studies. *Psychological Bulletin, 118,* 315–327.

Technical Working Group for Eyewitness Evidence. (1999). *Eyewitness evidence: A guide for law enforcement* [Booklet]. Washington, DC: United States Department of Justice, Office of Justice Programs.

Wells, G. L., & Bradfield, A. L. (1999). Distortions in eyewitnesses' recollections: Can the postidentification-feedback effect be moderated? *Psychological Science, 10,* 138–144.

Wells, G. L., Small, M., Penrod, S.D., Malpass, R. S., Fulero, S. M., & Brimacombe, C. A. E. (1998). Eyewitness identification procedures: Recommendations for lineups and photospreads. *Law and Human Behavior, 22,* 603–647.

Wells, G.L., & Olsen, E.A. (2003). Eyewitness testimony. *Annual Review of Psychology, 54,* 277–295.

Wells, G.L., Memon, A., & Penrod, S.D. (2006). Eyewitness evidence: Improving its probative value. *Psychological Science in the Public Interest, 7,* 45–75.

Wells, G.L., Olsen, E.A., & Charman, S.D. (2002). The confidence of eyewitnesses in their identifications from lineups. *Current Directions in Psychological Science, 11,* 151–154.

West's Ann. Cal. Evid. Code Sections 730 and 952.

Zimbardo, P. G. (1972). Pathology of imprisonment. *Society, 9,* 4–8.

Notes

1. A target-present showup is one that includes a picture of the suspect and assesses the hit rate to and the miss rate for the suspect. A target-absent showup is one that does not include a picture of the suspect and assesses the false alarm rate to filler faces.

2. During a trial, an eyewitness expert witness cannot be asked about or comment on whether he or she thinks that the defendant is the real perpetrator; that is, he or she cannot "speak to the ultimate issue." Nonetheless, this information can be offered by the eyewitness expert in a written report or work product that is not intended to be presented to the jury.

3. The classic study by Nickerson and Adams (1979) illustrates how poorly people can perform this simple memory task.

4. Here, I will not discuss the complexity of the legal definition of "confidential," but eyewitness experts should be aware when they put anything in writing that a difference exists between what is considered "work product," which is usually not discoverable by the opposing attorney, and a "report," which is usually discoverable.

3

Effectiveness of Traditional Safeguards Against Erroneous Conviction Arising From Mistaken Eyewitness Identification

Jennifer L. Devenport, Christopher D. Kimbrough, and Brian L. Cutler

For several decades now, scholars and social scientists have studied miscarriages of justice occurring in the American legal system and have drawn the same conclusion: Mistaken eyewitness identifications is the leading cause of wrongful convictions (Borchard, 1932; Connors, Lundregan, Miller, & McEwen, 1996; Huff, 1987; Huff, Rattner, & Sagarin, 1996; Scheck, Neufeld, & Dwyer, 2000). These conclusions continue to be validated by DNA evidence and the investigations of various nonprofit organizations working to free the innocent. For example, in 86 cases involving the death penalty, the Center on Wrongful Convictions found that, in 54% of these cases, testimony from an eyewitness helped to secure a conviction (Warden, 2001). Moreover, research by the Innocence Project has revealed that of the 208 wrongful convictions that have been exculpated by DNA testing, approximately 75% were predicated on mistaken eyewitness identification (see innocenceproject.org).

The legal system, however, acknowledges the potential for error and has built into itself a number of procedural safeguards designed to protect defendants from wrongful convictions resulting from mistaken eyewitness identifications. These safeguards include such procedures as presence of counsel at live, post-indictment lineups; motions to suppress identifications; voir dire; cross-examination of witnesses; and judicial instructions on the evaluation of eyewitness identification evidence. These safeguards are based on a number of assumptions regarding attorneys,' judges,' and jurors' knowledge about factors that influence eyewitness identification performance. The statistics from nonprofit organizations and the numerous cases of wrongful convictions flooding the media, however, suggest that these safeguards may not prevent judges and juries from being convinced beyond a reasonable doubt by a mistaken eyewitness. Thus, this chapter focuses on the assumptions underlying each safeguard and reviews the social science research examining the effectiveness of these safeguards. The effectiveness of expert psychological testimony, a relatively new safeguard, is reviewed in Chapter 8 by Leippe and Eisenstadt.

Presence-of-Counsel Safeguard

The presence-of-counsel safeguard is designed to protect defendants from wrongful convictions resulting from mistaken eyewitness identifications by allowing an attorney to attend her client's live, post-indictment lineups for the purpose of advising the client of his legal rights and obligations, observing and recording any suggestive procedures used during the identification test, and opposing the use of suggestive lineup procedures. This safeguard is predicated on two assumptions with regard to attorney knowledge and behavior. First, the presence-of-counsel safeguard assumes that attorneys are knowledgeable about factors influencing lineup suggestiveness and are able to recognize these factors when present in an identification test. Second, this safeguard assumes that attorneys attend their clients' lineups and document suggestive factors present in the lineup to support a pretrial motion to suppress the identification evidence or to challenge the identification through cross-examination at trial.

How Effective Is the Presence-of-Counsel Safeguard?

Although several studies have examined attorney knowledge of factors influencing identification accuracy, to date, only one study has examined the effectiveness of the presence-of-counsel safeguard by testing whether attorneys are sensitive to factors known to influence lineup suggestiveness and subsequent eyewitness identifications.

To test the effectiveness of the presence-of-counsel safeguard, Stinson, Devenport, Cutler, and Kravitz (1996) presented attorneys with a written description of a convenience story robbery and of the perpetrator. The attorneys were instructed to assume that the suspect in the case was their client, and after being provided with his photograph, they were asked to view a videotape of their client's lineup wherein the suggestiveness of the foils (biased vs. unbiased), instructions (biased vs. unbiased), and presentation (simultaneous vs. sequential) were manipulated between subjects. Simultaneous presentation is considered biased because it has been shown to increase the likelihood of false identifications relative to sequential presentation (Steblay, Dysart, Fulero, & Lindsay, 2001). After viewing the lineup, attorneys evaluated the overall suggestiveness and fairness of the lineup procedure as well as the suggestiveness of the foils, instructions, and presentation of the lineup.

The results revealed that attorneys were sensitive to foil bias, somewhat sensitive to instruction bias, and not at all sensitive to presentation bias. Thus, attorneys who viewed foil-biased lineups rated the overall lineup and the foils as more suggestive and less fair, and were more likely to indicate they would file a motion to have the identification suppressed than were attorneys viewing foil-unbiased lineups. Likewise, attorneys viewing instruction-biased lineups rated the overall lineup and the instructions as more suggestive than did attorneys viewing instruction-unbiased lineups. Attorneys' ratings of lineup fairness and their predictions as to whether they would file a motion to suppress the identification, however, were not affected by instruction bias. Last, attorneys were clearly unaware of the effects of presentation bias. Attorneys viewing the simultaneously presented (biased) lineup rated the lineup as less suggestive and more fair than attorneys viewing the sequentially presented (unbiased) lineup.

Although research suggests that attorneys are somewhat sensitive to factors influencing lineup suggestiveness, the presence-of-counsel safeguard is only effective if attorneys are actually present at their client's post-indictment lineups. Stinson, Devenport, Cutler, and Kravitz (1996) found that attorneys in their sample attended only approximately 5% of their clients' lineups. This finding is consistent with other research as well. Brigham and Wolfskeil's (1983) survey of attorneys indicates that, compared to prosecuting attorneys, defense attorneys were significantly less likely to believe that attorneys would be present at live lineups or photo arrays held either before or after the defendant's first court appearance. Moreover, a survey of police officers conducted by Wogalter, Malpass, and McQuiston (2004) provides further evidence that attorney presence at identification tests may not be standard procedure. Of the police officers who responded to their survey, 49% ($N = 199$) indicated that defense attorneys are routinely not present for the construction or presentation of identification tests. Officers reported, however, that attorneys were more likely to be present when a live lineup is constructed (36%) and presented to witnesses (61%) than when photo lineups (4% and 8%, respectively) are used. Officers also reported that the majority of identification tests they conduct are photo lineups (73%) as opposed to live lineups (27%).

In summary, the research investigating the effectiveness of the presence-of-counsel safeguard suggests that the effectiveness of this safeguard is severely limited by the lack of attorney presence at client post-indictment lineups. When present at the client's lineup, however, attorneys are effectively safeguarding their clients from foil-biased lineup procedures but may not be fully protecting their clients from mistaken identifications resulting from instruction-biased lineup procedures. Although attorneys appear to be sensitive to the deleterious effects of instruction bias and to recognize biased instructions when present in a lineup procedure, the biased instructions do not affect their evaluations of the fairness of the lineup or their intention to file a motion to suppress the identification. This is unfortunate, given research that has shown that judges are more likely to grant a motion to suppress an identification when the lineup instructions are biased as opposed to unbiased (Stinson, Devenport, Cutler, & Kravitz, 1997). Last, attorneys' lack of knowledge regarding the beneficial effects of sequentially presented lineups prevents them from effectively safeguarding their clients from presentation-biased lineup procedures.

Motion-to-Suppress Safeguard

The motion-to-suppress safeguard allows defense attorneys who believe their client's identification procedure was overly suggestive and thereby subject to unreliable identification to file a pretrial motion to suppress the identification. Once the pretrial motion has been filed with the court, the trial judge assesses the validity of the motion and either grants the motion, excluding the identification evidence at trial, or denies the motion, allowing the prosecution to present the eyewitness identification at trial. Two assumptions underlie the validity of the motion-to-suppress safeguard. First, as mentioned previously, attorneys must be sensitive to suggestive lineup procedures, so that they can distinguish between biased and unbiased procedures and persuade the judge of the legitimacy of their motions. Second, the judge must also be able to discriminate between suggestive and nonsuggestive procedures, so that her judgments reflect this knowledge.

How Effective Is the Motion-to-Suppress Safeguard?

Earlier in this chapter, we examined attorneys' abilities to recognize suggestive procedures, but what about the ability of judges? As yet, only one study has approached this question empirically. Stinson and associates (1997) surveyed 99 Florida judges, asking them to rule on simulated motion-to-suppress identification evidence. Judges received written descriptions of the events surrounding a crime and the perpetrator, color photocopies of the lineup members, a description of the identification procedure, a motion-to-suppress, and a questionnaire that assessed judges' ratings of lineup suggestiveness and judgment on the motion (grant or deny). Similar to the attorney study (Stinson et al., 1996), lineup suggestiveness was manipulated between subjects by presenting judges with information regarding either biased or unbiased foils, instructions, and presentations (simultaneous vs. sequential) of the lineup.

Results from the judges were somewhat more promising than the attorneys in that judges demonstrated sensitivity to both foil and instruction bias. Specifically, judges rated foil- and instruction-biased lineups as more suggestive and less fair than foil- and instruction-unbiased lineups. Furthermore, judges were more likely to grant a motion to suppress the eyewitness identification evidence when presented with evidence of biased foils (43% vs. 17% unbiased foils) and biased instructions (46% vs. 16% unbiased instructions).

Similar to attorneys, judges were not sensitive to presentation bias. In fact, judges rated sequentially (unbiased) presented lineup as significantly more suggestive and less fair than simultaneously (biased) presented lineups and, although nonsignificant, showed a tendency to grant the motion more often following a sequential lineup presentation (40%) than a simultaneous lineup presentation (23%).

This research would suggest that judges are aware of the harmful effects of foil and instruction bias, and more importantly, they are willing to safeguard defendants from erroneous convictions that may occur as a result of this type of bias by suppressing the identification evidence. Unfortunately, judges appear to be unaware of current psychological research indicating that sequential lineups produce fewer mistaken identifications than simultaneous lineups. In fact, the judges' data show a clear preference for simultaneously presented lineups. This preference, however, may be due, in part, to unfamiliarity with the sequential procedure. That is, sequential lineups are used less commonly than simultaneous lineups (Wogalter, Malpass, & Burger, 1993; Wogalter et al., 2004). As the beneficial effect of the sequential lineup becomes more widely known and the use of sequential lineups becomes a more customary practice in police departments, it is likely that judges' preference for simultaneous lineups may diminish.

Wells and Quinlivan (2009) have questioned the effectiveness of the motion-to-suppress safeguard for still other reasons. They argue compellingly that the two-stage inquiry typically used to evaluate the suppression is structurally flawed and destined to fail to suppress suggestive identification procedures. The first stage of the inquiry involves testing whether the procedures were unnecessarily suggestive. If the procedures were found to be unnecessarily suggestive (and they sometimes are), the judge proceeds to the second stage, and that is the determination of whether the identification was reliable despite the use of suggestive procedures. The problem laid out by Wells and Quinlivan is that the reliability test relies on self-reports of the witness (e.g., witness confidence, opportunity to view the perpetrator), and these self-reports are also influenced by suggestive procedures. Thus, suggestive procedures not only increase the likelihood of false identification but also cause witnesses to provide self-reports that give them high grades on the reliability test. Based on their analyses, Wells and Quinlivan call for alternative approaches to make the motion-to-suppress safeguard more effective.

Voir Dire Safeguard

When a criminal case moves forward to trial, the first stage of the trial is *voir dire*, or the jury selection process. In voir dire, prospective jurors are questioned about their relevant experiences in an effort to ascertain their suitability for jury service on a specific case. Prospective jurors who admit that they cannot be fair and impartial or are thought to be unable to be fair and impartial by the judge are excused from service on the specific case. Prospective jurors can be excused via *challenge for cause* when they have an obvious and demonstrable bias in the case (e.g., a relation to the defendant). Causal challenges are subject to approval by the judge, and there is no limit to the number of such challenges available. Prospective jurors can also be excused via *peremptory challenges*. Each attorney has a limited number of peremptory challenges available to her, and she can exercise a peremptory challenge without explanation (provided that she is not engaging in discrimination). Thus, through causal and peremptory challenges, the court—in theory—has the opportunity to excuse from service prospective jurors who are unwilling or unable to give careful scrutiny to the conditions under which a crime was witnessed and an eyewitness identification obtained.

How Effective Is the Voir Dire Safeguard?

For voir dire to serve as an effective safeguard in eyewitness cases, two conditions must be met. First, there must be an opportunity to query potential jurors about their attitudes toward eyewitnesses, and second, the information revealed from such queries must be predictive of juror bias in eyewitness cases. With respect to the first condition, voir dire practices vary considerably between federal and state courts, from one state to the next, and even from court to court within a state. In federal court, and in some state courts, the voir dire procedure is perfunctory. The questions are asked by the judge, and there is very limited opportunity for attorneys to query jurors about case-specific attitudes. On the other extreme, in some states attorneys have a very substantial role in voir dire and are given time and flexibility to query jurors. Thus, lack of opportunity to query jurors constrains the use of this safeguard in many courts.

The second condition requires that information revealed during voir dire (i.e., when opportunity to question prospective jurors about their attitudes toward eyewitnesses exists) is predictive of juror bias in identification cases. Narby and Cutler (1994) conducted a series of studies to empirically examine this condition. First, they developed a self-report instrument to assess prospective jurors' attitudes toward eyewitnesses. The Attitudes Toward Eyewitness Scale (ATES) contains nine items to which respondents rate their levels of agreement. Examples of items are "Eyewitnesses frequently misidentify innocent people just because they seem familiar," and "Eyewitness testimony is more like fact than opinion." Their first study established the reliability and psychometric properties of the scale in data from 651 students and jury-eligible community members. The reliability and psychometric properties were then replicated in a separate sample of 108 students and residents of the community. In that study, Narby and Cutler examined the relation between ATES scores, verdicts, and evaluations of trial evidence in a simulated trial. Although the ATES scores were reliable in the sample, the scores failed to significantly predict verdicts in a robbery case hinging on eyewitness identification. In a third study involving 57 students and community members, the ATES once again proved reliable but failed to predict juror judgments in a simulated robbery trial. In a subsequent study using trial simulation methodology with 497 students and jury-eligible community members (Devenport & Cutler, 2004), however, ATES scores did correlate significantly and in the expected directions with juror decisions.

In summary, the effectiveness of voir dire as a safeguard in eyewitness cases is limited in part by the lack of opportunity to question prospective jurors about their attitudes toward eyewitnesses in some courtrooms. When attorneys have the opportunity to question prospective jurors during voir dire, it is not clear whether the information revealed is predictive of juror judgments. The research on this issue produces mixed results.

Cross-examination Safeguard

At a trial, attorneys present witnesses who will testify as to the facts of the case. This testimony is obtained through direct examination of an attorney's witness, as well as through cross-examination of opposing counsel's witnesses. In cases involving eyewitness identifications, the prosecuting attorney may present testimony from the eyewitness as well as the officer in charge of administering the lineup. The defense attorney is then given an opportunity to scrutinize the validity of eyewitness memory and identification during cross-examination of these witnesses. Thus, cross-examination is the most commonly implemented safeguard in cases involving eyewitness identifications (Walters, 1985). This safeguard, however, is based on three psychological assumptions that must hold true in order for the safeguard to be effective. First, attorneys must be aware of conditions that can affect eyewitness identification performance and ask questions during examination and cross-examination that highlight for jurors the factors negatively associated with eyewitness identification accuracy. Naturally, this can only be done if the attorneys know which conditions negatively affect eyewitness memory for the event and the perpetrator. Second, jurors must also be knowledgeable about the factors influencing eyewitness identification performance and sensitive to the information highlighted by attorneys. Third, jurors must be able to incorporate this information into their decision-making process, evaluating appropriately the accuracy of the eyewitness identification.

How Effective Is the Cross-examination Safeguard?

Only a few studies have assessed attorney knowledge of the factors known to affect eyewitness memory and identification accuracy. For example, Rahaim and Brodsky (1982), using a multiple-choice format, assessed attorney ($N = 43$) knowledge of such factors as race, violence/stress, and eyewitness confidence on eyewitness identification accuracy. The results revealed that the attorneys were more likely to respond correctly to items testing for knowledge regarding the effects of violence/stress and eyewitness confidence than if the item tested for knowledge of the cross-race effect.

Brigham and Wolfskeil (1983) also assessed attorney knowledge to factors influencing eyewitness identification accuracy. In their survey, 235 defense and prosecuting attorneys were asked, via an open-ended question, to describe the factors most likely to influence eyewitness identification performance. Overall, the results were somewhat mixed. Although attorneys correctly indicated that factors such as physical attributes of the suspect, lighting at the scene of the crime, and length of exposure to the suspect were likely to affect accuracy of identification, they incorrectly included additional characteristics of the witness such as disposition, intelligence, and quality of memory. Additionally, attorneys failed to acknowledge factors such as the presence of a weapon, disguises, interval of retention, and biased identification procedures, implying that attorneys may be insensitive to other factors that affect eyewitness identification performance.

A more recent survey (Wise, Pawlenko, Safer, & Meyer, 2007) compared prosecutors' (N=73) and defense attorneys' (N=1184) knowledge of factors influencing eyewitness identification testimony. Attorneys were presented with 14 items and were asked to indicate their agreement with the statements on a 5-point Likert scale. Eight of the 14 questions were drawn from Kassin, Tubb, Hosch, and Memon's (2001) survey of expert psychologists. Overall, Wise and colleagues found that defense attorneys, although not completely accurate, were more knowledgeable than prosecutors regarding factors that can affect eyewitness testimony. Eighty percent of defense attorneys responded accurately to questions concerning witness attitude/expectations, lineup administrator bias, post-event information, eyewitness confidence, confidence malleability, the presence of a weapon, mugshots, stress, and jurors' ability to distinguish between accurate and inaccurate eyewitnesses. Furthermore, over 50% of defense attorneys demonstrated knowledge of the effects of a disguise, minor details, and lineup presentation. In contrast, a majority of prosecuting attorneys correctly identified five factors (i.e., witness attitude/expectations, post-event information, confidence malleability, mugshots, and stress). Only 22% of prosecuting attorneys, however, correctly indicated that eyewitness confidence was not a good predictor of identification accuracy, suggesting that they may not be fully aware of the role of witness confidence in eyewitness cases. For additional discussion of research on attorney knowledge, see Chapter 7, by Hosch and colleagues.

Although surveys of attorney knowledge are somewhat informative, Stinson and associates' (1996) study of attorney sensitivity to lineup suggestiveness would suggest that attorneys may not always use the various factors they know to influence eyewitness performance. As mentioned previously, Stinson and associates found that, when presented with lineups containing biased versus unbiased foils, instructions, and presentations, attorneys were sensitive to foil bias, moderately sensitive to instruction bias, but insensitive to presentation bias. Thus, attorneys may be somewhat knowledgeable about suggestive lineup procedures even though they failed to mention these factors in the Brigham and Wolfskeil (1983) study. This would suggest that additional studies manipulating the presence/absence of various eyewitness factors need to be conducted to test attorney sensitivity to these factors.

Research assessing the second assumption underlying the effectiveness of cross-examination has taken several methodological approaches. Specifically, juror sensitivity to factors affecting eyewitness memory and identification accuracy has been investigated via surveys of juror knowledge, assessments of jurors' ability to post-dict the outcome of eyewitness identification experiments, and the use of trial simulations to examine the influence of eyewitness evidence on jury decision-making.

Some survey research has assessed juror knowledge by administering the Knowledge of Eyewitness Behavior Questionnaire (KEBQ; Deffenbacher & Loftus, 1982; McConkey & Roche, 1989; Noon & Hollin, 1987). The KEBQ, developed by Deffenbacher and Loftus (1982), contains 14 multiple-choice items containing several eyewitness identification scenarios, and it assesses juror knowledge of the factors presented in each scenario. Results across a number of different populations of respondents (i.e., undergraduates, law students, and laypersons from the United States, United Kingdom, and Australia) were remarkably similar. In general, respondents appeared to be somewhat sensitive to the influence of both cross-race recognition and prior photo array identifications on identification accuracy but less sensitive to the negative effects of eyewitness age and retention interval on identification accuracy. Also, respondents wrongly believed that training would improve witness identification accuracy.

More recently, Schmechel, O'Toole, Easterly, and Loftus (2006) conducted a large-scale ($N = 1296$) phone survey of potential jurors in Washington, D.C. to determine whether factors that can affect eyewitness memory and subsequent identifications are indeed common knowledge. Results were somewhat mixed. A clear majority of respondents demonstrated an awareness of unconscious transference (73%) and the malleability of eyewitness confidence (85%) and eyewitness memory (80%), as well as the potential for error when an eyewitness has identified the same culprit in multiple lineups (89%). Respondents, however, were unaware of the negative effect that weapons and lineup instructions can have on the accuracy of eyewitness testimony and provided inconsistent answers when responding to multiple questions assessing knowledge of eyewitness confidence and violence/stress, suggesting that they do not fully understand the relationship between these factors and identification accuracy.

Most disconcerting were results indicating that respondents believed that eyewitness identification evidence was somewhat or very reliable (83%), that memories are like video recordings (48%), and that their own memories were excellent (77%). Schmechel and colleagues (2006) posit that jurors may transfer their unwarranted confidence in their own memories onto the eyewitness, thereby producing an overestimation of the eyewitness' accuracy.

To test whether the level of juror knowledge obtained in previous survey research is simply an artifact of confusion to unclear and complicated questions, Read and Desmarais (2009 created a variation of Kassin, Tubb, Hosch, and Memon's (2001) expert survey instrument, using concrete examples instead of abstract terms. The results of this survey revealed higher levels of lay knowledge than typically is demonstrated in the research. For example, over 60% of respondents demonstrated a correct understanding of factors such the wording of questions, confidence malleability, lineup instructions, alcohol intoxication, showups, unconscious transference, exposure time, and child suggestibility. The results obtained by Read and Desmarais suggest that laypersons may agree with experts on factors that affect eyewitness accuracy more than previous research has suggested. The research by Read and Desmarais and related research is reviewed in more detail in their chapter (Chapter 6).

In sum, survey research indicates that information about the factors influencing eyewitness identification performance may not be a matter of common sense. Specifically, jurors appear to be aware of some factors influencing eyewitness identifications but unaware of others.

Researchers have also conducted post-diction studies of eyewitness identification performance. In studies such as these, participants (often students or laypersons) read summaries of already completed experiments on eyewitness identification and then predicted the accuracy rates of the original participants in the experiment. By comparing the predicted accuracy rates with the results of the original experiment, the researchers are able to evaluate the sensitivity of potential jurors to factors known to reduce eyewitness identification accuracy.

Overall, researchers have found that laypersons tend to predict higher accuracy rates than those exhibited by participants in the original studies (Brigham & Bothwell, 1983; Kassin, 1979; Wells, 1984). Moreover, laypersons appear to be insensitive to the influence of crime seriousness (Kassin, 1979), instruction bias (Wells, 1984), and cross-racial identifications on eyewitness identification accuracy (Brigham & Bothwell, 1983). Furthermore, postdiction studies reveal that laypersons appear to place too much emphasis on eyewitness confidence and accuracy (Brigham & Bothwell, 1983; Wells, 1984).

A third set of studies used to assess juror knowledge of factors that can affect eyewitness identification accuracy involves the use of trial simulations and experimental designs. Thus, participants take part in some form of a mock trial (i.e., read a written summary, listen to an audio simulation, or view a video simulation), wherein portions of the testimony and evidence are manipulated (e.g., Bell & Loftus, 1988; Cutler, Penrod, & Dexter, 1990; Devenport, Stinson, Cutler, & Kravitz, 2002). In these studies, juror sensitivity is indicated by significant effects of factors known to influence identification accuracy and nonsignificant effects of factors known to not predict identification accuracy (Cutler et al., 1990).

Research examining juror sensitivity to eyewitness factors has taken two distinct approaches. One approach has examined jurors' abilities to discriminate between accurate and inaccurate eyewitnesses, whereas the other has examined juror sensitivity to those factors that influence eyewitness identification performance. Overall, these studies have reached similar and unsatisfying conclusions with regards to juror knowledge. Specifically, the experimental research indicates that jurors have difficulty distinguishing between accurate and inaccurate eyewitnesses (Lindsay, Wells, & O'Connor, 1989; Wells et al., 1979) and are insensitive to the effect of eyewitness factors such as length of exposure to the perpetrator, viewing conditions (Lindsay, Lim, Marando, & Cully, 1986), level of violence, use of a disguise, presence of a weapon (Cutler, Penrod, & Stuve, 1988), crime seriousness (Kassin, 1979), cross-race identifications (Abshire & Bornstein, 2003), and eyewitness confidence (Cutler et al., 1988; Lindsay, Wells, & Rumpel, 1981; Wells, Lindsay, & Ferguson, 1979) on identification accuracy. Jurors do, however, show some sensitivity to inconsistent eyewitness testimony (Berman & Cutler, 1996; Berman, Narby, & Cutler, 1995), foil, and instruction bias (Devenport et al., 2002). The research demonstrating juror sensitivity, however, reveals that, even when jurors are sensitive to the deleterious effects of factors such as foil and instruction bias (assessed via a direct measure of the specific lineup bias), this sensitivity does not appear to carry over to the decision-making portion of the trial, as indexed by their verdict decisions (Devenport et al., 2002).

Judicial Instructions Safeguard

Judicial instructions also serve to safeguard defendants from mistaken eyewitness identifications. In cases involving eyewitness testimony, defense attorneys may file a motion with the court requesting that the judge provide the jury with cautionary instructions about the eyewitness identification, along with the standard jury instructions. These special instructions are meant to assist jurors in the evaluation of eyewitness evidence, particularly in cases where proffered expert psychological testimony has been excluded (*United States v. Hicks*, 1996, *United States v. Rincon*, 1994).

How Effective Is the Judicial Instructions Safeguard?

The Telfaire instructions (*United States v. Telfaire*, 1972), the most well-known and commonly used form of cautionary instructions, are designed to inform jurors of the inherent dangers of eyewitness identification, the necessity of evaluating such evidence with caution, and the burden of proof that requires that they be convinced beyond a reasonable doubt that the defendant is the perpetrator. The instructions identify specific factors that jurors should consider when evaluating the testimony of an eyewitness. These factors include the witness's ability and opportunity to view the defendant, the strength of the identification (typically determined by prior misidentifications or failures by the eyewitness to make an identification), the viewing conditions that may have influenced the identification, and the witness's credibility.

Although the Telfaire instructions are designed to safeguard defendants from erroneous convictions resulting from mistaken identifications, the instructions are somewhat problematic. Specifically, the instructions fail to explain to jurors how the factors highlighted by the court actually influence eyewitness memory or how this information should be applied to the identi-fication evidence in a specific case. Furthermore, the Telfaire instructions are derived from legal precedent (i.e., *Neil v. Biggers*, 1972) rather than social scientific research. Thus, the instructions identify only a limited number of factors known to influence eyewitnesses and incorrectly mention one factor (i.e., eyewitness confidence) that research has shown to be only a modest predictor of eyewitness accuracy under the best of circumstances (Wells, Olson, & Charman, 2002).

Although a number of studies have examined the influence of judge's instructions on mock juror decisions, few studies have examined whether Telfaire instructions are an effective safeguard in cases involving eyewitness identifications. In a study conducted by Cutler, Dexter, and Penrod (1990), the effectiveness of the Telfaire instructions was examined by manipulating the eyewitnessing and identification conditions (good vs. poor) and the judge's instructions presented to jurors (Telfaire instructions vs. no instruc-tion). Mock jurors watched one version of a videotaped trial and then rendered verdicts and rated the defendant's culpability, the accuracy of the identification, and the strength of the prosecution's and defense's case. The Telfaire instructions did not appear to influence participants' verdicts or evaluations of the witness and evidence.

In a series of studies, Greene (1988) examined the effect of the Telfaire instruction on mock juror decisions and whether the instructions could be revised in such a way as to increase juror comprehension of factors influenc-ing eyewitness memory. In Experiment 1, participants watched a simulated videotaped trial involving a defendant who was identified as being the person responsible for throwing a glass bottle that left the victim partially blind, and they heard either strong or weak eyewitness testimony. Prior to group delib-eration, participants were presented with jury instructions that included either the Telfaire instructions or no cautionary instructions. Post-deliberation ver-dicts revealed no difference in jury verdicts for the two instruction conditions when the eyewitness testimony was weak. When the eyewitness testimony was strong, however, juries who did not hear the Telfaire instructions were more likely to convict the defendant (42%) compared to juries that heard the Telfaire instructions (6.5%). Furthermore, after hearing the Telfaire instruc-tions, jurors were no more accurate in completing a multiple-choice test assessing their understanding of the factors influencing eyewitness memory than were jurors who had not heard the cautionary instructions.

In Experiment 2, participants viewed the same videotaped trial, were once again exposed to weak versus strong eyewitness identification evidence, and received one of three versions of jury instructions (Telfaire instructions, revised cautionary instructions, or no cautionary instructions). The revised instructions included the use of simpler language and less convoluted sentences than those presented in the Telfaire instructions. In addition, the revised instructions explained how various factors influence eyewitness memory and included factors not mentioned in the Telfaire instructions, such as witness stress and lineup fairness, and correctly informed the juries of the weak relationship between witness confidence and accuracy. Post-deliberation decisions revealed that the juries who heard the Telfaire instructions and those who heard no cautionary instructions were similar in their conviction and acquittal rates, whereas juries that were presented with the revised instructions produced the highest acquittal rate. Likewise, jurors who heard the revised instructions had a better understanding of the factors influencing eyewitness memory than did jurors in the Telfaire or no cautionary instructions conditions. Thus, although the revised instructions primarily led to jury skepticism, there was some indication of jury sensitization as well.

In another series of studies, Ramirez, Zemba, and Geiselman (1996) also examined the effect of the Telfaire instructions on juror sensitivity to eyewitness identification evidence. In study 1, mock jurors viewed one version of a videotaped trial within which the eyewitnessing conditions (good vs. poor), and the timing of the instructions (before and after the trial evidence, before-only, after-only, or not at all) were manipulated. The results of this study revealed that the Telfaire instructions did not enhance juror sensitivity to factors influencing eyewitness identification accuracy but rather produced juror skepticism (depending on the timing of the instructions). Regardless of the quality of the identification evidence, Telfaire instructions given after the evidence was presented produced significantly fewer not-guilty verdicts.

In their second study, Ramirez and colleagues examined whether revising the Telfaire instruction could enhance jury sensitization. Thus, mock jurors viewed the same videotaped trial containing trial testimony and evidence suggesting either good versus poor eyewitnessing conditions. In addition, mock jurors were presented with either the standard Telfaire instruction or a set of instructions that were created by the researchers and based on information typically presented by experts testifying in eyewitness cases. When the eyewitness viewing conditions were good, participants who received the Telfaire instructions rendered fewer guilty verdicts than did those who heard the revised instructions or no cautionary instructions. When the viewing conditions were poor, however, there was no effect of cautionary instructions. Although there was no effect of the revised instruction (and this was probably due to a floor effect), these data are consistent with their first study and suggest that the Telfaire instructions produce juror skepticism rather than juror sensitization to factors influencing eyewitness identification accuracy.

In sum, judicial cautionary instructions, in their present state, may be an ineffective safeguard against erroneous convictions resulting from mistaken eyewitness identifications, and at best, their effectiveness is questionable. In fact, psychological research suggests that the cautionary instructions currently relied on by the courts (i.e., Telfaire instructions) either have no effect or enhance juror skepticism rather than juror sensitization to eyewitnessing and identification conditions. Thus, the courts may benefit from a set of cautionary instructions that more closely resemble expert psychological testimony, such as those set forth by the California Supreme Court in *People v. Wright* (1987). The Wright instructions differ from the Telfaire instructions in that the instructions can be customized so that they highlight the important factors in any given case, and they explain to jurors the influence of these factors on eyewitness identification accuracy rather than simply identifying the factors and then leaving it to jurors to determine the role of these factors on eyewitness memory. In addition, the Wright instructions address the issue of witness credibility by bringing into question the reliability of eyewitness identification accuracy and acknowledging that eyewitnesses may make mistakes and that errors have been know to occur. Certainly psychological research is needed to test whether these instructions are effective at sensitizing jurors, but the Wright instruction appears to be a step in the right direction. Indeed, Drouet and Kent (Chapter 11) suggest that defense attorneys make more use of jury instruction options in their attempts to discourage jurors from believing mistaken identifications.

Conclusion

In this chapter, we reviewed the effectiveness of traditional safeguards designed to protect defendants from erroneous conviction resulting from mistaken eyewitness identification. These safeguards included presence of counsel at live, post-indictment lineups, motions to suppress identifications, voir dire, cross-examination, and judicial instructions. The empirical research on these safeguards reveals that each has important limitations. That traditional safeguards have limitations should not come as a surprise, for if they were perfect, we would not have hundreds of clearly documented erroneous conviction cases based in part on mistaken identification. Beyond identifying limitations, the research on safeguards points to several avenues for improvement.

The first area of improvement is to reduce the likelihood of false identification in the first place by employing best practices in identification procedures, as identified in the research on eyewitness identification (Wells, Memon, & Penrod, 2006). Having fewer false identifications should reduce the number of erroneous convictions based on false identification.

The second area of improvement involves improving the effectiveness of individual safeguards. As indicated earlier, a common factor underlying the effectiveness of the traditional safeguards are attorney, judge, and juror knowledge of the factors known from the research to influence identification accuracy and the factors known to not be predictive of identification accuracy.

The knowledge produced from the research is not rocket science and should not require an advanced degree to acquire. Attorneys and judges, like most professionals, engage in continuing professional education through conferences, workshops, trade publications, and other media. Eyewitness research should be included in these curricula and publications. This requires psychologists to share their knowledge by giving continuing professional education workshops and writing for practice-oriented publications. Better-educated attorneys and judges will be better prepared for voir dire and cross-examination, and should be in a position to compose more informative and technically accurate judges' instructions.

The third area of improvement is to develop new and effective safeguards. Even with use of best practices in identification tests, witnesses will make mistakes, so it is imperative that additional safeguards exist to protect mistaken identifications from becoming erroneous convictions. Expert testimony is one such new safeguard, but its effectiveness is questionable for a variety of reasons (see Flowe, Finklea, & Ebbesen, Chapter 9; Bailey & Mecklenburg, Chapter 10), and effectiveness of the testimony itself has been questioned (Leippe & Eisenstadt, Chapter 8). Are there less expensive and more efficient means of educating jurors? It is possible that well-crafted judges' instructions can serve this purpose. Although initial research on judges' instructions is not promising, there is only one published study of judges' instructions that were developed based on research (Greene, 1988). Given the reach of judges' instructions, this topic should receive further investigation. Similarly, courts could consider other mechanisms for educating jurors, such as written materials or videotaped lessons.

In sum, there is much work to be done in improving the effectiveness of safeguards against erroneous convictions in eyewitness identification cases. This work involves reducing mistaken identification in the first place; educating attorneys, judges, and jurors about eyewitness memory; and improving the effectiveness of traditional safeguards. Psychological research can be used both to improve the safeguards and assess their effectiveness.

References

Abshire, J., & Bernstein, B. H. (2003). Juror sensitivity to the cross-race effect. *Law and Human Behavior, 27*, 471–480.

Berman, G. L., & Cutler, B. L. (1996). Effects of inconsistencies in eyewitness testimony on mock-juror decision making. *Journal of Applied Psychology, 81*, 170–177.

Berman, G. L., Narby, D. J., & Cutler, B. L. (1995). Effects of inconsistent eyewitness statements on mock-juror's evaluations of the eyewitness, perceptions of defendant culpability and verdicts. *Law and Human Behavior, 19*, 79–88.

Bell, B. E., & Loftus, E. F. (1988). Degree of detail of eyewitness testimony and mock-juror judgment. *Journal of Applied Social Psychology, 18*, 1171–1192.

Borchard, E. M. (1932). *Convicting the innocent*. Garden City, NY: Garden City Publishing Company, Inc.

Brigham, J. C., & Bothwell, R. K. (1983). The ability of prospective jurors to estimate the accuracy of eyewitness identifications. *Law and Human Behavior, 7*, 19–30.

Brigham, J. D., & Wolskeil, M. P. (1983). Opinions of attorneys and law enforcement personnel on the accuracy of eyewitness identification. *Law and Human Behavior, 7*, 337–349.

Connors, E., Lundregan, T., Miller, N., & McEwen, T. (1996). Convicted by juries, exonerated by science: Case studies in the use of DNA evidence to establish innocence after trial. U.S. Department of Justice Office of Justice Programs.

Cutler, B. L., Dexter, H. R., & Penrod, S. D. (1990). Nonadversarial methods for improving juror sensitivity to eyewitness evidence. *Journal of Applied Social Psychology, 20*, 1197–1207.

Cutler, B. L., Penrod, S. D., & Dexter, H. R. (1990). Jury sensitivity to eyewitness identification evidence. *Law and Human Behavior, 14*, 185–191.

Cutler, B. L., Penrod, S. D., & Stuve, T. E. (1988). Jury decision making in eyewitness identification cases. *Law and Human Behavior, 12*, 41–56.

Deffenbacher, K. A., & Loftus, E. F. (1982). Do jurors share a common understanding concerning eyewitness behavior? *Law and Human Behavior, 6*, 15–30.

Devenport, J. L., & Cutler, B. L. (2004). Impact of defense-only and opposing eyewitness experts on juror judgments. *Law and Human Behavior, 28*, 569–576.

Devenport, J. L., Stinson, V., Cutler, B. L., & Kravitz, D. (2002). How effective are the cross-examination and expert testimony safeguards? Jurors' perceptions of the suggestiveness and fairness of biased lineup procedures. *Journal of Applied Psychology, 87*, 1042–1054.

Greene, E. (1988). Judge's instruction on eyewitness testimony: Evaluation and revision. *Journal of Applied Social Psychology, 18*, 252–276.

Huff, C. R. (1987). Wrongful conviction: Societal tolerance of injustice. *Research in Social Problems and Public Policy, 4*, 99–115.

Huff, C. R., Arye Rattner, R., & Sagarin, E. (1996). *Convicted but innocent: Wrongful conviction and public policy*. Thousand Oaks, CA: Sage.

Kassin, S. (1979). Personal communication cited by Wells, G. L. (1984). How adequate is human intuition for judging eyewitness testimony. In G. L. Wells, & E. F. Loftus (Eds.), *Eyewitness testimony: Psychological perspectives* (pp. 256–272). New York: Cambridge University Press.

Kassin, S. M., Tubb, V. A., Hosch, H. M., & Memon, A. (2001). On the "general acceptance of eyewitness testimony research. *American Psychologist, 56*, 405–416.

Lindsay, R. C. L., Lim, R., Marando, L., & Cully, D. (1986). Mock-juror evaluations of eyewitness testimony: A test of metamemory hypotheses. *Journal of Applied Social Psychology, 16*, 447-459.

Lindsay, R. C. L., Wells, G. L., & O'Conner, F. J. (1989). Mock-juror belief of accurate and inaccurate eyewitnesses: A replication and extension. *Law and Human Behavior, 13*, 333–339.

Lindsay, R. C. L., Wells, G. L., & Rumpel, C. M. (1981). Can people detect eyewitness-identification accuracy within and across situations? *Journal of Applied Psychology, 66*, 79–89.

McConkey, K. M., & Roche, S. M. (1989). Knowledge of eyewitness memory. *Australian Psychologist, 24*, 377–384.

Narby, D. J., & Cutler, B. L. (1994). Effectiveness of voir dire as a safeguard in eyewitness cases. *Journal of Applied Psychology, 79*, 724–729.

Noon, E., & Hollin, C. R. (1987). Lay knowledge of eyewitness behaviour: A British survey. *Applied Cognitive Psychology, 1*, 143–153.

People v. Wright, 43 Cal.3d 399 (1987).

Rahaim, G. L., & Brodsky, S. L. (1982). Empirical evidence versus common sense: Juror and lawyer knowledge of eyewitness accuracy. *Law & Psychology Review, 7*, 1–15.

Ramirez, G., Zemba, D., & Geiselman, R. E. (1996). Judges' cautionary instructions on eyewitness testimony. *American Journal of Forensic Psychology, 14*, 31–66.

Read, J. D., & Desmarais, S. L. (2009). Lay knowledge of eyewitness issues: A Canadian evaluation. *Applied Cognitive Psychology, 23*, 301–326.

Scheck, B., Neufeld, P., & Dwyer, J. (2000). *Actual innocence: Five days to execution and other dispatches from the wrongly convicted*. New York, NY: Doubleday.

Schmechel, R.P., O'Toole, T. P., Easterly, C., & Loftus, E. F. (2006). "Beyond the ken?" Testing jurors' understanding of eyewitness reliability evidence. *Jurimetrics, 46*, 177, 214.

Steblay, N., Dysart, J., Fulero, S., & Lindsay, R. C. L. (2001). Eyewitness accuracy in sequential and simultaneous lineup presentations: A meta-analytic comparison. *Law and Human Behavior, 25*, 459–473.

Stinson, V., Devenport, J. L., Cutler, B. L., & Kravitz, D. A. (1996). How effective is the presence-of-counsel safeguard? Attorney perceptions of suggestiveness, fairness, and correctability of biased lineup procedures. *Journal of Applied Psychology, 81*, 64–75.

Stinson, V., Devenport, J. L., Cutler, B. L., & Kravitz, D. A. (1997). How effective is the motion-to-suppress safeguard? Judges' perceptions of the suggestiveness and fairness of biased lineup procedures. *Journal of Applied Psychology, 82*, 211–220.

Neil v. Biggers, 409 U.S. 188 (1972).

United States v. Hicks, 103 F.3d 837 (9th Cir. 1996).

United States v. Rincon, 36 F.3d 859 (9th Cir. 1994).

United States v. Telfaire, 469 F.2d 552, 558–59 (D.C.Cir. 1972).

Walters, C. M. (1985). Admission of expert testimony on eyewitness identification. *California Law Review, 73*, 1402–1430.

Warden, R. (2001). How mistaken and perjured eyewitness identification testimony put 46 innocent Americans on death row: An analysis of wrongful convictions since restoration of the death penalty following *Furman v. Georgia*. Northwestern University School of Law, Center on Wrongful Convictions. Retrieved March 12, 2009 from http://www.deathpenaltyinfo.org/studycwc2001.pdf.

Wells, G. L. (1984). How adequate is human intuition for judging eyewitness testimony. In G. L. Wells, & E. F. Loftus (Eds.), *Eyewitness testimony: Psychological perspectives* (pp 256–272). New York: Cambridge University Press.

Wells, G. L., Lindsay, R. C. L, & Ferguson, T. J. (1979). Accuracy, confidence, and juror perceptions in eyewitness identification. *Journal of Applied Psychology, 64*, 440–448.

Wells, G. L., & Quinlivan, D. S. (2009). Suggestive eyewitness identification procedures and the Supreme Court's reliability test in light of eyewitness science: 30 years later. *Law and Human Behavior, 33,* 1-24.

Wells, G. L., Memon, A., & Penrod, S. D. (2006). Eyewitness evidence: Improving its probative value. *Psychological Science in the Public Interest, 7,* 45–75.

Wells, G. L., Olson, E. A., & Charman, S. D. (2002). The confidence of eyewitnesses in their identifications from lineups. *Current Directions in Psychological Science, 11,* 151–154.

Wise, R. A., Pawlenko, N. B., Safer, M. A., & Meyer, D. (2007). What prosecutors and defense attorneys know and believe about eyewitness testimony. Manuscript submitted for publication.

Wogalter, M. S., Malpass, R. S., & Burger, M. A., (1993). How police officers construct lineups: A national survey. In *Proceedings of the Human Factors and Ergonomics Society* (pp. 640–644). Santa Monica, CA: Human Factors and Ergonomics Society.

Wogalter, M. S., Malpass, R. S., & McQuiston, D. E. (2004). A national survey of U.S. police on preparation and conduct of identification lineups. *Psychology, Crime & Law, 10,* 69–82.

4

Expert Testimony: Legal Standards for Admissibility

Jules Epstein

The course of the judicial response to motions seeking the admission of expert testimony in eyewitness cases may be viewed in two lights: historically/chronologically, and in terms of the application of seemingly principled evidentiary rules. Neither approach results in a consistent treatment of this issue. Rather, what can best be said is that, while the majority of courts have found the scientific underpinnings of this proposed testimony sufficient to meet the varying admissibility standards, in any specific case little or no guarantee exists that such proof will be admitted. This latter outcome is a result of two disparate but symbiotic factors—the great discretion vested in trial judges when deciding whether to permit expert testimony, and the perception of many judges that expert testimony in identification cases is needed only when little or no corroborating proof exists.

Historic Overview

Historically, prior to the 1980s, courts were adverse to expert testimony regarding eyewitness. A 1931 decision described the defense attempt to call such an expert and the court's multifaceted rationale for exclusion:

> E. E. Brooks was called as an expert by appellant, and a hypothetical question was submitted . . . [which] would have called for the opinion of the witness as to the powers of observation and recollection of Allen and Jones in the matter of their identification of appellant as one of the robbers, they never having seen him prior

to the robbery. The court properly excluded this testimony. There
was no contention that these witnesses were of unsound mind.
It was, of course, proper to inquire how badly the witnesses themselves were frightened by the robbery, and this information might
have been elicited by the examination of the witnesses themselves
on that subject. It would not have been improper to have asked
other witnesses present what opportunity Allen and Jones had to
observe the robbers, also what their conduct was during the
robbery. But the question whether these witnesses were mistaken in
their identification, whether from fright or other cause, was one
which the jury, and not an expert witness, should answer. This was
a question upon which one man as well as another might form an
opinion, and the function of passing upon the credibility and
weight of testimony could not be taken from the jury.
(*Criglow v. State*, 1931)

This decision pre-dated the emergence of a solid if not conclusive body of
research (see Chapter 2, by Pezdek) establishing (a) the weaknesses that can
plague eyewitness observation (encoding), retention, and recall, and (b) that
jurors' views of eyewitness accuracy are often counterintuitive or at odds with
established science.[1] Nonetheless, its reasoning (except for the emphasis on
whether the witness had a mental illness) is echoed by many judges today
when confronted with a request for the admission of eyewitness expert testimony. Thus, even in 2006, a federal court of appeals reasoned that, on most
issues, jurors can reasonably assess eyewitness reliability without an expert,
relying instead on cross-examination and jury instruction.[2]

Notwithstanding the persistence of these attitudes, state supreme courts[3]
began to approve the admissibility of eyewitness expert testimony in the
1980s, with Arizona in 1983 (*State v. Chapple*) and California in 1984 (*People
v. McDonald*) leading the way. Since then, the manifest trend in both state and
federal courts is to permit judges, on a case-by-case basis, to admit expert
testimony in eyewitness cases. The majority of federal[4] and state courts[5] now
accept the science as meeting the necessary reliability threshold for scientific
evidence, and allow trial judges to admit such proof *if* it is relevant (often
described as whether the expert testimony "fits" the facts of the particular
prosecution) *and* will be useful to the jurors (Wise, Dauphinais, & Safer,
2007).[6] (The different threshold tests for reliability, under the *Frye* and *Daubert*
standards, are discussed later in this chapter.)

Although some jurisdictions still categorically exclude such proof,[7] their
numbers are dwindling. Indeed, the two most recent challenges to the per se
exclusion of expert testimony in identification cases resulted in determinations that such proof is scientifically valid and appropriate for admission
(again, on a case-by-case basis). This conclusion was reached in both Tennessee
and New York in 2007.

Tennessee was confronted with its own recent (2000) precedent categorically barring expert testimony regarding eyewitness identification because

"eyewitness testimony has no scientific or technical underpinnings which would be outside the common understanding of the jury" (*State v. Coley*, 2000). Within 7 years, the Tennessee Court reversed itself, concluding that several points warranted the admission of such testimony:

- "There have been advances in the field of eyewitness identification . . . It is the educational training of the experts and empirical science behind the reliability of eyewitness testimony that persuades us to depart from the Coley rule."
- "[T]he research also indicates that neither cross-examination nor jury instructions on the issue are sufficient to educate the jury on the problems with eyewitness identification . . ."

New York precedent was equivocal regarding the admission of expert testimony in identification cases, but the focus of earlier decisional law was the absence of a compelling need for such proof in cases in which appeals were brought because corroborating evidence existed to support the eyewitness' claim. Once it was confronted with the no-corroborating-evidence case, the New York court quickly found the science to be "generally accepted," at least as to several propositions the defense hoped to prove:

- "As to three of these factors—correlation between confidence and accuracy of identification, the effect of post-event information on accuracy of identification and confidence malleability—the defense expert's testimony contained sufficient evidence to confirm that the principles upon which the expert based his conclusions are generally accepted by social scientists and psychologists working in the field" (*People v. LeGrand*, 2007).[8]

These two decisions confirm the trend toward a step-one (scientific reliability) acceptance of expert testimony regarding eyewitness identification. They are not contradicted by those courts that categorically bar expert testimony in identification cases,[9] as the rationale for exclusion may turn on other factors, such as impermissible usurpation of the jury's fact-finding function (*Commonwealth v. Simmons*, 1995).[10]

Yet, notwithstanding this continuing trend, expert proof regarding eyewitness capacity is often excluded at trial. The disconnect between general acceptance and exclusion in a particular case cannot be understood without a full grasp of the principles governing the admission of expert testimony generally, and the great amount of discretion vested in trial judges. It is to these topics that this chapter now turns.

Governing Law

More than three-quarters of a century ago, a federal court developed a test for the expert testimony that conditioned its admission on the science or theory being "generally accept[ed]" (*Frye v. United States*, 1923). The test focused on whether "the thing from which the deduction is made must be sufficiently established to have gained general acceptance in the particular field in which it belongs." In articulating the "general acceptance" standard, the *Frye* court addressed only the admissibility of novel scientific evidence. Subsequently, this test was expanded to all types of scientific proof. It did not, however, extend to nonscientific expert testimony (Crump, 2003).[11]

Under the *Frye* test, a preliminary showing would have to be made that the scientific validity of the theory or principle had achieved a level of acceptance. Although developed in the 1920s, it was not extensively applied until after World War II (Golan, 2008).[12] "By the 1970s, *Frye*'s general acceptance standard had become 'not only the majority view . . . but the almost universal view' in those criminal courts that considered the admissibility of new scientific evidence" (Golan, 2008, p. 931).

What is "general acceptance?" First, it does not mean "universal" acceptance (*United States v. Yee*, 1990, p. 196); rather, the acceptance must be "general," as when it is supported by "the testimony of experts in the particular field, the acceptance of the proponent's writings in professional journals, and the absence of rebuttal testimony . . . " (*United States v. Yee*, 1990, p. 1999; *United States v. Downing*, 1985).[13] At least some courts conflated "general acceptance" with "reliability." As the Sixth Circuit explained, "general acceptance . . . [is] nearly synonymous with reliability. If a scientific process is reliable, or sufficiently accurate, courts may also deem it 'generally accepted'" (*United States v. Distler*, 1981).

In addition to the problem of what acceptance is "general," there is the related concern of acceptance *by whom?* For example, the Florida Supreme Court defined this to mean "acceptance by a clear majority of the members of the relevant scientific community, with consideration by the trial court of both the quality and quantity of those opinions" (*Marsh v. Valyou*, 2005). Yet defining the "relevant" community itself may be subjective—is it all engineers (or all psychologists), or just those who have experience in a particular subspecialty? As one court explained,

> A court must not define the relevant field of experts so narrowly
> that the expert's opinion inevitably will be considered generally
> accepted. If the community is defined to include only those experts
> who subscribe to the same beliefs as the testifying expert, the
> opinion always will be admissible. The community of experts must
> include a sufficiently broad sample of experts so that the possibility
> of disagreement exists. (*Bernardoni v. Industrial Community*, 2005)

Albeit somewhat narrowing, this definition still provides little objective guidance.

In the context of eyewitness/identification expert testimony, one court has identified the relevant community as "the experts in this particular field [i.e., psychologists who study perception, memory and recall]" (*People v. LeGrand*, 2007). The court found general acceptance even though the prosecution offered an expert who disputed much of the science (*People v. LeGrand*, 2007). The debate over whether consensus exists among experts regarding issues pertinent to eyewitness identification is also detailed in Chapter 7 of this text.

The *Frye* test, despite its vague terminology and inconsistent application,[14] remains one of this country's two principal tests for determining the reliability of scientific testimony, the necessary but not sufficient condition for admissibility. (The additional criteria for admissibility are discussed in the later section, Grounds for Admission or Exclusion in Identification Cases.) Its principal counterpart is the *Daubert* test, which was mandated as applicable in all federal courts and selected by several states.[15] *Daubert* is a direct outgrowth of the adoption of a written evidence code, the Federal Rules of Evidence.

The history of this development is easily told. Some 50 years after the *Frye* court articulated its "general acceptance" threshold, Congress promulgated a rule of evidence that made no mention of this standard. Rule 702, entitled "Testimony by Experts," provided

If scientific, technical, or other specialized knowledge will assist the trier of fact to understand the evidence or to determine a fact in issue, a witness qualified as an expert by knowledge, skill, experience, training, or education, may testify thereto in the form of an opinion or otherwise.[16]

Confronted with this language, the United States Supreme Court had to decide whether the *Frye* test was still applicable. In the *Daubert* decision (*Daubert v. Merrell Dow Pharmaceuticals*, 1993), it answered the question with a resounding "no." In *Daubert*, the Court explained that the language of Rule 702 did not reflect a decision to adopt the *Frye* standard[17] (*Daubert v. Merrell Dow*, 1993, pp. 579, 588). Rather, the rule required that the evidence be "relevant" and "reliable," with the latter term defined by the words "scientific knowledge" (pp. 589–590). As the Court explained, "The adjective 'scientific' implies a grounding in the methods and procedures of science. Similarly, the word 'knowledge' connotes more than subjective belief or unsupported speculation" (p. 590).

The *Daubert* court required a two-step inquiry: whether the evidence is valid scientific knowledge, and *then* a determination of whether admission of such proof will "assist the trier of fact to understand or determine a fact in issue" (*Daubert v. Merrell Dow*, 1993, pp. 592–593). This chapter addresses the second prong later; here, the focus remains on whether the testimony reflects "good science." To the Court, this question "entails a preliminary assessment of whether the reasoning or methodology underlying the testimony is scientifically valid and of whether that reasoning or methodology properly can be applied to the facts in issue" (pp. 592–593).

Although not exclusive, the Court then identified a list of factors to be considered in assessing the validity of the proffered scientific theory and evidence:

- "A key question to be answered in determining whether a theory or technique is scientific knowledge . . . will be whether it can be (and has been) tested."
- "Whether the theory or technique has been subjected to peer review and publication."
- "The court ordinarily should consider the known or potential rate of error[.]"
- "Finally, 'general acceptance' can yet have a bearing on the inquiry." (*Daubert v. Merrell Dow*, 1993, pp. 593–594)

There was still more to the *Daubert* Court's framework. After emphasizing the flexibility of the inquiry, the Court made clear that the primary focus is methodology, not conclusions. "The focus, of course, must be solely on principles and methodology, not on the conclusions that they generate" (*Daubert v. Merrell Dow*, 1993, p. 595). This emphasis permits competing conclusions to be placed before the jury, and is consistent with the foundational approach of the Federal Rules of Evidence; to wit, that evidence with any relevance should be admitted and then weighed by the factfinder (p. 587).[18]

The Court's final statement in *Daubert* spoke to the role of the trial judge, one that has had great significance in assessing, case by case, the admissibility of eyewitness expert testimony. The trial judge was assigned the responsibility of "gatekeeper":

We recognize that, in practice, a gatekeeping role for the judge, no matter how flexible, inevitably on occasion will prevent the jury from learning of authentic insights and innovations. That, nevertheless, is the balance that is struck by Rules of Evidence designed not for the exhaustive search for cosmic understanding but for the particularized resolution of legal disputes. (*Daubert v. Merrell Dow*, 1993, p. 597)

Applying these standards to the science of eyewitness identification, courts have consistently found the principles to meet this reliability (scientific validity) threshold. (Whether a prosecutor should persist in challenging this threshold reliability determination is an issue raised and addressed in Chapter 10.) As the Sixth Circuit stated in 2007, "expert testimony on eyewitness identifications, once thought to be unreliable and overly prejudicial to the prosecution, is now universally recognized as scientifically valid . . ." (*Ferensic v. Birkett*, 2007). The Third Circuit has emphasized the "proliferation" of studies and accepts the proposition that "the science of eyewitness perception has achieved the level of exactness, methodology, and reliability of any psychological research" (*United States v. Brownlee*, 2006).

This recognition has come even in cases in which the expert's testimony is ultimately excluded; the exclusion derives not from it being "bad" science but from other considerations (as discussed later). As the Tenth Circuit explained,

> The rejection by these courts, as well as our own, of a per se approach to expert testimony on eyewitness identification reflects *Daubert*'s liberal definition of what constitutes reliable, scientific knowledge. Conversely, confinement of such testimony to limited circumstances reflects *Daubert*'s admonition that expert testimony assist the jury—indeed, an expert's testimony describing how certain factors, falling outside a typical juror's experience, may affect a eyewitness's identification is the very type of scientific knowledge to which *Daubert*'s relevance prong is addressed. (*United States v. Rodriguez-Felix*, 2006)

Daubert did not end the Supreme Court's foray into analyzing the standards under Rule 702. Two subsequent cases added significant components to expert witness jurisprudence. In *Kumho Tire* (*Kumho Tire Co. v. Carmichael*, 1999) the Court "conclude[d] that *Daubert*'s general holding . . . applies not only to testimony based on 'scientific' knowledge, but also to testimony based on 'technical' and 'other specialized' knowledge" (*Kumho Tire Co. v. Carmichael*, 1999). More significant to this chapter was the Court's third decision regarding expert testimony, rendered in *General Electric v. Joiner*, in 1997. There, the Court held that a reviewing (appellate) court could overturn a trial judge's decision to exclude expert witness testimony only if the decision was shown to be an "abuse of discretion" (*General Electric v. Joiner*, 1997). This standard of review is extremely deferential to the trial judge, and is found to be met only when the judge has made an error of law, relied on fact-findings that are clearly erroneous, or committed a clear error of judgment (*Kenny A. v. Perdue*, 2008).[19]

The effect of *Daubert* and its companion cases was far-reaching. It led to the amending of Rule 702 in 2000; that rule now provides:

> If scientific, technical, or other specialized knowledge will assist the trier of fact to understand the evidence or to determine a fact in issue, a witness qualified as an expert by knowledge, skill, experience, training, or education, may testify thereto in the form of an opinion or otherwise, if (1) the testimony is based upon sufficient facts or data, (2) the testimony is the product of reliable principles and methods, and (3) the witness has applied the principles and methods reliably to the facts of the case.

There have been further consequences of *Daubert*, in particular with the assignment of the role of gatekeeper to the judge. Although much of the language in *Daubert* seemed to invite the use of expert testimony,[20] the clear trend is for judges to *restrict* the use of expert proof. One study of civil cases showed that judges limited or excluded some of the testimony proffered by experts in 41% in 1998 (post-*Daubert*) cases, as opposed to imposing such limitations or bars in only 25% of case in 1991 (Krafka et al., 2002).[21] In the criminal context, a disparity exists between admitting prosecution expert testimony and proffered defense expert evidence. One study of federal appellate criminal cases found an admissibility rate of more than 95% for prosecution experts, whereas fewer than 8% of defense experts were allowed to testify (Groscup et al., 2002).

Another effect of *Daubert* was in the development of a relevance standard for expert testimony, beyond that of scientific reliability; even if reliable methodology was used, the conclusion of the expert had to "fit" the case. As one court recently explained, the admissibility of expert testimony involves an examination of three criteria—the expert's qualifications, the reliability of the methodology, and "fit," the last being explained as follows:

> We must also consider whether expert testimony proffered in the case is sufficiently tied to the facts of the case that it will aid the jury in resolving a factual dispute. Rule 702's "helpfulness" standard requires a valid scientific connection to the pertinent inquiry as a precondition to admissibility. This helpfulness requirement—which our Court of Appeals calls "fit"—is, in the end, the ultimate touchstone of admissibility. (*Perry v. Novartis Pharmaceutical Corp.*, 2008)

It is in the arena of "fit" that most of the litigation concerning expert testimony concerning eyewitness identification is fought.

Before turning to the specific bases for admissibility or exclusion relied upon by courts, it is worth examining the overall differences between the *Frye* and *Daubert* tests. Neither is overall more restrictive than the other; rather, the viability of expert testimony under either test is a function of the nature of the science or technology. The *Frye* test may be the more rigorous one when the type of knowledge is particularly novel; when there has been longstanding acceptance of a discipline but new research calls into question its validity, it is the *Daubert* standard that may raise the barrier to admission (Faigman, Porter, & Saks, 1994).[22]

Grounds for Admission or Exclusion in Identification Cases

At its most basic level, what can be said with certainty is that although courts have found the science behind eyewitness expert testimony to be reliable and/or "generally accept(ed)," the exclusion of such evidence is recurring, and is often affirmed by reviewing appellate courts.[23] This apparent disconnect arises from a number of factors.

The Presence of Corroborative Evidence

First is the perception of many courts that such testimony is not needed (and may be a distractor) in cases in which the prosecution has evidence corroborative of the eyewitness testimony. As one court summarized,

> In *Moore*, this court examined, and affirmed the exclusion of, expert testimony regarding eyewitness identification . . . Although expert eyewitness identification testimony may be critical when eyewitness testimony makes the entire difference between a finding of guilt or innocence, it obviously becomes considerably less critical when physical evidence of guilt substantiates such testimony. . . .
>
> In determining whether an expert witness' exclusion was an abuse of discretion (typically in the context of offering testimony regarding eyewitnesses), other circuits appear to examine both whether other evidence beyond the lay-witness testimony ties the defendant to the crime, and whether defense counsel was given an opportunity to thoroughly cross-examine those witnesses. (*United States v. McGinnis*, 2006)[24]

The prevalence of this view does not confirm its validity. Corroboration does not establish eyewitness accuracy. In the National Criminal Justice Reference Service (NCJRS) landmark study "Convicted by Juries, Exonerated by Science," a review of the first 28 DNA exonerations showed that all 28 involved eyewitnesses, while two-thirds also had conventional forensic corroboration, such as hair analysis.[25] A second flaw in this reasoning is the assumption that the availability of corroborating evidence equates with juror *acceptance* of that proof. There is no way of predetermining prior to a trial's conclusion whether the jurors will believe the corroborating evidence; and if they do not, the need for an expert is the same as in a case with no corroborative proof. The admissibility of defense evidence is supposed to be conditioned on relevance, not on the amount of prosecution proof, as was exemplified in *Holmes v. South Carolina*, in 2006.[26] Whether *Holmes* secures a defendant a due process right to present an expert on eyewitness identification has not been resolved.[27] *Holmes* certainly does raise questions about exclusions of experts when the sole ground is the presence of *some* corroborative evidence. Finally, such exclusion ignores the inefficacy of traditional litigation tools such as cross-examination and jury instructions in eyewitness cases.[28]

Whatever its deficiencies, this view remains widely held; but its inverse applies to support (if not mandate) the admission of expert testimony. Thus, in cases in which eyewitness testimony is the sole or primary proof of guilt, exclusion of expert testimony has been found to be an abuse of discretion.[29] This is true even when there are numerous eyewitnesses corroborating one another, but no other type of corroboration exists.[30]

Inadequate Qualifications

Courts have also excluded expert testimony based on a perceived lack of qualification of the expert. In particular, courts have distinguished between those with degrees in psychology and those with degrees and particularized credentials in eyewitness research. Illustrative is one recent Texas case, which upheld the exclusion of expert testimony because the witness lacked sufficient experience:

> Evidence adduced at the hearing shows that [the proffered expert] has some specific knowledge of eyewitness identification issues gleaned from reading some articles and attending conferences. However, . . . [e]yewitness identification is a small part of [his] wide-ranging practice, and he has not performed any research or published on the topic in a peer-reviewed publication. He has read only approximately .0025% of all published articles on eyewitness identification, and in his 16-year career has received only 10 days of seminar education on the topic. (*Garcia v. State*, 2007)

In another case, the court merged the issue of qualifications and reliability (which do have some analytical overlap) in affirming the exclusion of the expert. There, the court focused on the absence of testimony making clear whether the expert was relying on his own studies or those of other researchers, the lack of peer review for the research this witness had conducted, and the failure of the expert's pre-trial report to "sufficiently reference specific and recognized scientific research, which underlies [his] conclusions, such that the court could determine if this foundational research had been subjected to peer review, and, if so, whether it had been accepted in the community" (*United States v. Rodriguez-Felix*, 2006).

Expert Testimony Is Too Generic

Even when the science is solid and the witness' qualifications cannot be questioned, courts may uphold the exclusion of eyewitness expert testimony when it is either too generic or otherwise lacks "fit" to the facts of the particular case. As one court explained in upholding the exclusion of expert testimony, the defense did not "demonstrate that Dr. Rubenzer's opinions related to any of the specific facts of this case . . . nor did the appellant identify factors that could assist the jury in this case, other than in the most general sense" (*Baldree v. State*, 2007). The court criticized the expert because he "did not exhibit knowledge of the specific facts of this case or tie the scientific principles on which he sought to testify to the facts of this case" (*Baldree v. State*, 2007). Ultimately, the proffer was held inadequate as offering only "educational material for the jury, which is insufficient to demonstrate that the scientific principles will assist the trier of fact in this case . . ." (*Baldree v. State*, 2007).

This judicial response is not unique.[31] Conversely, in cases in which a clear link is made to the facts of the specific matter, admission of the expert's testimony is more likely. Admission has been required when the expert was shown to have reviewed the eyewitness statement and then linked the circumstances of the crime and the identification process to specific psychological research (*Stephenson v. State*, 2007).[32] Thus, the importance of a tailored, fact-specific proffer, and a well-written expert report, cannot be minimized.

No Juror Need for Expertise

The final, oft-relied-upon proposition for excluding expert testimony is that jurors have the capacity to evaluate the questioned identification testimony without assistance, either because it involves common-sense perceptions, or cross-examination is equally efficacious.[33] Courts have found that an expert is not needed to testify about differences among the photos in an identification array that might cause the accused to stand out, as jurors can see this for themselves[34] or to factors such as the impact of delay on memory and the problems with cross-racial identifications (*Commonwealth v. Bly*, 2007).[35] Such judicial perceptions cannot be effectively countered without including juror studies in the expert's report; and without proffering data to show that the concepts at issue are beyond the ken of the average juror and/or cannot be effectively demonstrated via cross-examination or jury instruction, the exclusion will be upheld on appeal.

The Scope of Expert Testimony

In those cases in which an expert is permitted to testify, the scope or breadth of the testimony will be determined by several considerations. (For an overview addressing the content, form, and ethics of expert testimony in eyewitness cases, see Chapter 2.)

First, as emphasized earlier, the testimony will be designed to have "fit"— relevance to the case at hand. A discussion of weapons focus will be irrelevant and inadmissible in a case in which no weapon was utilized. Second, the expert will be permitted to testify in the form of opinions and respond to hypothetical questions.[36]

Much more likely than opinion testimony and responses to hypothetical questions will be statements of an educational nature, ones in which the expert will describe the science of perception, memory, and recall and explain the types of factors that can enhance or diminish accuracy at each stage. Such educational or informational testimony is what is contemplated by the language in evidence codes permitting an expertise to testify in the form of an opinion "or otherwise." The hypothetical or opinion may come into play when the expert is asked to explain whether the combination of factors in a particular case—for example, bad lighting, the brevity of the crime, the different races of the victim and the perpetrator, and the high level of stress admitted by the witness—create an increased risk of a mistaken identification.

The sources an expert may rely on in forming an opinion are myriad, and they are proper as long as they are "of a type reasonably relied upon by experts in the particular field in forming opinions or inferences upon the subject . . ."[37] This means that the witness may rely on her own research or research of others, consultation with other experts, visits to the crime scene, police and investigative reports, witness statements and testimony, the actual lineups or photo displays utilized in the investigation, government studies,[38] and/or other sources of information that are of the type normally used by experts in the field. The items need not themselves be admissible at trial; the only requirement is that they be regularly relied upon by experts in the discipline.

The law generally permits experts to give opinions on the "ultimate issue" in a case.[39] In a criminal trial, the "ultimate issue" is the defendant's guilt or non-guilt, and that subsumes the issue of whether the eyewitness is accurate. Notwithstanding the absence of a prohibition to this type of proof, an eyewitness expert typically will not tread near this issue. Unless the witness herself has been tested by the expert, the expert cannot conclude that the particular individual is correct or incorrect; rather, the expert can only opine about risk factors.

This distinction was noted by a federal court discussing the propriety of expert testimony in eyewitness cases. After concluding that the testimony should have been allowed, the appellate court responded to government concerns about one portion of the proffer from the expert, the contention that "had Mr. Smithers been the robber, the eyewitnesses would have observed and been able to recall the large scar on Mr. Smithers's neck" (*United States v. Smithers*, 2000). The court concluded that such a statement was impermissible, as "no expert may testify as to what a witness did or did not see" (*United States v. Smithers*, 2000). Nonetheless, this was not a ground to exclude the expert's testimony, but only to narrow it:

> The proper solution would have been to excise the inappropriate portion of the proffer rather than to exclude all of the testimony, the remainder of which dealt only with the psychological factors which may have impacted the perception and memory of the witnesses in this case. This evidence would have been both relevant and helpful to the jury. (*United States v. Smithers*, 2000)

The Need for Counsel to Consult with an Expert

Given the vast body of science that informs the issue of eyewitness accuracy, the legal question arises of whether defense counsel in a criminal case could be constitutionally ineffective if he fails to consult with an eyewitness expert prior to trial. Such claims have been raised on appeal by defendants convicted at trial.

The standard for whether counsel is ineffective to the level of depriving an accused of the Sixth Amendment guarantee of the assistance of counsel is found in *Strickland v. Washington* (1984). There, the Court determined that counsel is ineffective only when it is proved both that counsel's performance was "deficient" and that this deficient performance "prejudiced the defense." The latter occurs when the defendant is deprived of "a fair trial, a trial whose result is reliable" (*Strickland v. Washington*, 1984).

In the context of an identification case, an ineffectiveness claim may arise in either of two regards—the failure to present an expert at trial, and/or the failure to consult with an expert to assist in trial strategy and preparation. In general terms, it has been recognized that counsel must become informed about eyewitness issues: "an identification expert might assist an attorney in developing a cross-examination methodology or might provide helpful expert testimony in a particular case (*Ex parte Huerta*, 2007). At the same time, the recurring theme in decisions assessing ineffectiveness claims is that "it is not the law that every defense counsel must—upon pain of being found constitutionally incompetent—hire such an expert in a one-witness identification case" (*Ex parte Huerta*, 2007). Indeed, courts pay great deference, in the post hoc evaluation of ineffectiveness claims, to counsel's tactical judgment.[40]

Counsel will not be held ineffective when he is shown to have made a sound tactical judgment that an expert was not necessary on the facts of the particular case (*Currie v. Burt*, 2008).[41] Counsel may not be ineffective for failing to petition the trial court to admit expert testimony when that court has barred such proof in other cases (*Easter v. Fleming*, 2005; *Kennedy v. Warden*, 2008). Similarly, counsel may not be ineffective when cross-examination and other proof can show the defects in eyewitness testimony sufficiently to demonstrate what the expert testimony would have shown (*Switzer v. Hannigan*, 1999). At the same time, one court has found counsel ineffective for failing to retain and present an expert in eyewitness identification, when the case revolved around eyewitness credibility and there was minimal corroborative evidence (*People v. Kindle*, 2002).

That courts generally defer to counsel's decision when conducting a post-conviction review should not be seen as an approval of the failure of trial counsel to at least consult with an eyewitness expert or otherwise extensively study the science of perception, memory, and recall. Often, the post-trial record is inadequate to show ineffectiveness because new counsel has not secured an expert report to demonstrate how an expert would have materially improved the chances for acquittal.[42] Separately, much of the justification for court approval of an attorney's decision has focused on trial counsel's use of cross-examination (or cross coupled with jury instructions) as being equally efficacious in explaining the vagaries of eyewitness testimony.[43] If research and study show such tools to be inadequate, there may be no valid tactical grounding to counsel's omission.[44] And it is likely that only after consultation with an expert or ample self-education in the science can a well-designed cross, and well-crafted jury instructions, be prepared.

Conclusion

The admissibility of expert testimony in eyewitness identification cases remains problematic. The absolute bar on its use, restricted to a handful of jurisdictions, is ripe for challenge, particularly given the trend nationally toward discretionary admissibility. The question of whether discretion is abused when such evidence is excluded in a particular case may also be subject to continued testing, particularly as studies assess juror knowledge (or misperceptions) regarding eyewitness accuracy and as DNA exonerations show that the presence of corroborating evidence is no guarantee that an eyewitness is accurate.[45] (The current state of research surveying layperson knowledge of eyewitness science issues is detailed in Chapter 6.)

At the same time, a clear impracticality exists to having an expert testify in every case in which eyewitness testimony is presented; issues of cost and efficiency preclude this. As well, in some of those cases, no expert will be needed, given the particular facts. What courts, litigators, and policy makers must struggle with is a two-fold concern—finding a fairer guiding principle for determining those cases in which expert testimony is appropriate; and assessing whether means other than expert testimony, such as taking judicial notice of the science of perception, memory, and recall, or well-crafted jury instructions, can properly educate factfinders and ensure more reliability in eyewitness-based prosecutions.

References

Baldree v. State, 248 S.W.3d 224, 230 (Tex. App. Houston 1st Dist. 2007).

Benton, T. R., McDonnell, S. A., Thomas, J. N., et al. (Spring, 2006). On the admissibility of expert testimony on eyewitness identification: A legal and scientific evaluation. *Tennessee Journal of Law and Policy*, 2, 392.

Bernardoni v. Industrial Commission (Huntsman Chem. Co.), 840 N.E.2d 300, 311 (Ill. App. Ct. 3d Dist. 2005).

Commonwealth v. Bly, 862 N.E.2d 341, 360 (Mass. 2007).

Commonwealth v. Christie, 98 S.W.3d 485 (Ky. 2002).

Commonwealth v. Santoli, 424 Mass. 837, 680 N.E.2d 1116 (1997).

Commonwealth v. Simmons, 541 Pa. 211, 662 A.2d 621 (Pa. 1995), cert. denied, 516 U.S. 1128, 133 L. Ed. 2d 870, 116 S. Ct. 945 (1996).

Commonwealth v. Simmons, 662 A.2d 621, 631 (Pa. 1995).

Criglow v. State, 183 Ark. 407, 409 (1931).

Crump, D. (Winter, 2003). The trouble with DaubertKumho: Reconsidering the Supreme Court's philosophy of science. *Missouri Law Review*, 68, 1, 3.

Currie v. Burt, U.S. Dist. LEXIS 63308, 55–56 (N.D. Iowa Aug. 13, 2008).

Daubert v. Merrell Dow Pharmaceuticals, 509 U.S. 579 (1993).

Doyle, J. (2004). *True witness.* New York: Palgrave Macmillan.

Easter v. Fleming, 132 Fed. Appx. 706, 708 (9th Cir. Wash. 2005).

Engberg v. Meyer, 820 P.2d 70 (Wyo. 1991).

Epstein, J. (Spring, 2007). The great engine that couldn't: Science, mistaken identifications, and the limits of cross-examination. *Stetson Law Review, 36,* 727.

Ex parte Huerta, Tex. Crim. App. Unpub. LEXIS 660 **7–8 (2007).

Ex parte Williams, 594 So. 2d 1225 (Ala. 1992).

Faigman, D. L. (2008). Admissibility regimes: The "opinion rule" and other oddities and exceptions to scientific evidence, the scientific revolution, and common sense. *Southwestern University Law Review, 36,* 699, 717.

Faigman, D. L., Porter, E., & Saks, M. J. (April 1994). Check your crystal ball at the courthouse door, please: Exploring the past, understanding the present, and worrying about the future of scientific evidence. *Cardozo Law Review, 15,* 1799.

Ferensic v. Birkett, 501 F.3d 469, 482 (6th Cir. Mich. 2007).

Frye v. United States, 54 App. D.C. 46, 293 F. 1013, 1014 (D.C. Cir. 1923).

Garcia v. State, Tex. App. LEXIS 10059 *17 (Tex. App. Houston 14th Dist. Dec. 6, 2007).

Garrett, B. L. (January, 2008). Judging innocence. *Columbia Law Review, 108,* 55, 82. Eyewitness testimony was also occasionally bolstered by a false confession.

General Electric v. Joiner, 52 U.S. 136, 142 (1997).

Giannelli, P. C. (1980). The admissibility of novel scientific evidence: Frye v. United States, a half-century later. *Columbia Law Review 80,* 1197.

Gibson v. State, 661 S.E.2d 850, 855 (Ga. Ct. App. 2008).

Golan, T. (Spring, 2008). A crossdisciplinary look at scientific truth: What's the law to do? Revisiting the history of scientific expert testimony. *Brooklyn Law Review, 73,* 879, 930.

Groscup, J. L., et al. (2002). The effects of Daubert on the admissibility of expert testimony in state and federal criminal cases. *Psychology, Public Policy & Law, 8,* 339, 344.

Holmes v. South Carolina, 547 U.S. 319, 330 (2006).

Jones v. State, 314 Ark. 289, 862 S.W.2d 242 (Ark. 1993).

Kennedy v. Warden, Conn. Super. LEXIS 997 (Conn. Super. Ct. Apr. 29, 2008).

Kenny A. v. Perdue, 532 F.3d 1209, 1219 (11th Cir. Ga. 2008).

Krafka, C., Dunn, M. A., Johnson, M. T., Cecil, J. S., Miletich, D., & Federal Judicial Center. (2002). *Judge and attorney experiences, practices, and concerns regarding expert testimony in federal civil trials.* Washington, D.C.: Federal Judicial Center.

Kumho Tire Co. v. Carmichael, 526 U.S. 137, 141 (1999).

Marsh v. Valyou, 917 So. 2d 313, 320 (Fla. Dist. Ct. App. 5th Dist. 2005).

McMullen v. State, 714 So. 2d 368, 370 (Fla. 1998).

National Criminal Justice Reference Service (NCJRS). Convicted by juries, exonerated by science: Case Studies in the use of DNA evidence to establish innocence after O'Toole, T. P., et al. (Apr. 2005). District of Columbia Public Defender Eyewitness Reliability Survey. *Champion, 28,* 28–32.

People v. Bryant, 2008 Cal. App. Unpub. LEXIS 3154 (Cal. App. 1st Dist. 2008).

People v. Campbell, 847 P.2d 228 (Colo. Ct. App. 1992).

People v. Enis, 139 Ill. 2d 264, 564 N.E.2d 1155, 151 Ill. Dec. 493 (Ill. 1990).
People v. Farrow, 2007 Mich. App. LEXIS 2614 (Mich. Ct. App. Nov. 20, 2007).
People v. Goodwillie, 147 Cal. App. 4th 695, 726 (Cal. App. 4th Dist. 2007).
People v. Kindle, Cal. App. Unpub. LEXIS 6453 (Cal. App. 2d Dist. 2002).
People v. LeGrand, 867 N.E.2d 374, 380 (N.Y. 2007).
People v. McDonald, 690 P.2d 709 (Cal. 1984).
People v. Mooney, 76 N.Y.2d 827, 559 N.E.2d 1274, 560 N.Y.S.2d 115 (N.Y. 1990).
People v. Varnado, 2007 Cal. App. Unpub. LEXIS 8389 (Cal. App. 2d Dist. 2007).
Perry v. Novartis Pharmaceutical Corp., U.S. Dist. LEXIS 52407 *14 (E.D. Pa. July 9, 2008) (citations and quotations omitted).
Silva v. State, 2006 Tex. App. LEXIS 9599, 3–5 (Tex. App. Houston 14th Dist. Oct. 24, 2006).
State v. Chapple, 135 Ariz. 281, 660 P.2d 1208 (Ariz. 1983).
State v. Chapple, 660 P.2d 290 (Ariz. 1983).
State v. Coley, 32 S.W.3d 831, 833 (Tenn. 2000).
State v. Gaines, 260 Kan. 753, 926 P.2d 641 (Kan. 1996).
State v. Gardiner, 636 A.2d 710 (R.I. 1994).
State v. Goldsby, 59 Ore. App. 66, 650 P.2d 952 (Ore. Ct. App. 1982).
State v. Kemp, 199 Conn. 473, 507 A.2d 1387 (Conn. 1986).
State v. Moon, 45 Wash. App. 692, 726 P.2d 1263 (Wash. Ct. App. 1986).
State v. Percy, 156 Vt. 468, 595 A.2d 248 (Vt. 1990).
State v. Riofta, 2003 Wash. App. LEXIS 1880 (Wash. Ct. App. Sept. 2, 2003).
State v. Whaley, 305 S.C. 138, 406 S.E.2d 369 (S.C. 1991).
State v. Wooden, 658 S.W.2d 553 (Tenn. Ct. Crim. App. 1983).
Stephenson v. State, 226 S.W.3d 622, 627–629 (Tex. App. Amarillo 2007).
Strickland v. Washington, 466 U.S. 668, 687 (1984).
Switzer v. Hannigan, 45 F. Supp. 2d 873, 879 (D. Kan. 1999).
Torres v. State, 962 P.2d 3, 20 (Okla. Crim. App. 1998).
United States v. Brien, 59 F.3d 274 (1st Cir. 1995).
United States v. Brown, 540 F.2d 1048 (10th Cir. 1976).
United States v. Brownlee, 454 F.3d 131, 142 (3d Cir. Pa. 2006).
United States v. Carter, 410 F.3d 942, 950 (7th Cir. Ill. 2005).
United States v. Curry, 977 F.2d 1042 (7th Cir. 1992).
United States v. Daniels, 64 F.3d 311 (7th Cir. 1995), cert. denied, 516 U.S. 1063, 116 S. Ct. 745, 133 L. Ed. 2d 693 (1996).
United States v. Distler, 671 F.2d 954, 961 (6th Cir. Ky. 1981).
United States v. Downing, 753 F.2d 1224, 1236 (3d Cir. Pa. 1985).
United States v. George, 975 F.2d 1431 (9th Cir. 1992).
United States v. Harris, 995 F.2d 532 (4th Cir. 1993).
United States v. Holloway, 971 F.2d 675 (11th Cir. 1992).
United States v. Kime, 99 F.3d 870 (8th Cir. 1996), cert. denied, 519 U.S. 1141, 136 L. Ed. 2d 892, 117 S. Ct. 1015 (1997).
United States v. Langan, 263 F.3d 613, 624 (6th Cir. 2001).
United States v. Mathis, 264 F.3d 321, 336 (3d Cir. N.J. 2001).
United States v. McGinnis, 201 Fed. Appx. 246, 251–252 (5th Cir. La. 2006).
United States v. Moore, 786 F.2d 1308 (5th Cir. 1986).
United States v. Rincon, 28 F.3d 921 (9th Cir. 1994).
United States v. Rodriguez-Felix, 450 F.3d 1117, 1125–1126 (10th Cir. N.M. 2006).
United States v. Smithers, 212 F.3d 306, 317 (6th Cir. Mich. 2000).

United States v. Villiard, 186 F.3d 893, 895 (8th Cir. 1999).
United States v. Yee, 134 F.R.D. 161, 196, 199 (N.D. Ohio 1990).
White v. State, 112 Nev. 1261, 926 P.2d 291 (Nev. 1996).
Wise, R. A., Dauphinais, K. A., & Safer, M. A. (2007). A tripartite solution to
    eyewitness error. *Journal of Criminal Law and Criminology, 97*, 807–872.

Notes

1. See, for example, Timothy P. O'Toole (2005) who found, in a survey of approximately 1000 potential jurors, that they overestimate the reliability of eyewitness identification testimony in many circumstances in which science calls it into question. Chapter 6 of this text reviews the studies on juror understanding of eyewitness identification research and findings.
2. In *United States v. RodriguezFelix*, 450 F.3d 1117, 1125 (10th Cir. N.M. 2006): "Jurors, assisted by skillful cross-examination, are quite capable of using their commonsense and faculties of observation to make this reliability determination."
3. Trial courts permitted such proof in individual cases, starting in the early 1970s. A compelling retelling of the battles over admissibility is found in Doyle (2004). The significance of state supreme court decisions is found in the setting of a state-wide policy with some normative controls.
4. Federal decisions include: *United States v. Smithers*, 212 F.3d 306 (6th Cir. 2000); *United States v. Kime*, 99 F.3d 870 (8th Cir. 1996), cert. denied, 519 U.S. 1141, 136 L. Ed. 2d 892, 117 S. Ct. 1015 (1997); *United States v. Daniels*, 64 F.3d 311 (7th Cir. 1995), cert. denied, 516 U.S. 1063, 116 S. Ct. 745, 133 L. Ed. 2d 693 (1996); *United States v. Brien*, 59 F.3d 274 (1st Cir. 1995); *United States v. Rincon*, 28 F.3d 921 (9th Cir. 1994); *United States v. Harris*, 995 F.2d 532 (4th Cir. 1993); *United States v. Curry*, 977 F.2d 1042 (7th Cir. 1992); *United States v. George*, 975 F.2d 1431 (9th Cir. 1992); *United States v. Moore*, 786 F.2d 1308 (5th Cir. 1986); and *United States v. Brown*, 540 F.2d 1048 (10th Cir. 1976).
5. Examples of state decisions admitting such evidence include *Ex parte Williams*, 594 So. 2d 1225 (Ala. 1992); *State v. Chapple*, 135 Ariz. 281, 660 P.2d 1208 (Ariz. 1983); *Jones v. State*, 314 Ark. 289, 862 S.W.2d 242 (Ark. 1993); *People v. Campbell*, 847 P.2d 228 (Colo. Ct. App. 1992); *State v. Kemp*, 199 Conn. 473, 507 A.2d 1387 (Conn. 1986); *McMullen v. State*, 714 So. 2d 368, 370 (Fla. 1998); *State v. Gaines*, 260 Kan. 753, 926 P.2d 641 (Kan. 1996); *Commonwealth v. Christie*, 98 S.W.3d 485 (Ky. 2002); *People v. Enis*, 139 Ill. 2d 264, 564 N.E.2d 1155, 151 Ill. Dec. 493 (Ill. 1990); *Commonwealth v. Santoli*, 424 Mass. 837, 680 N.E.2d 1116 (Mass. 1997); *White v. State*, 112 Nev. 1261, 926 P.2d 291 (Nev. 1996); *People v. Mooney*, 76 N.Y.2d 827, 559 N.E.2d 1274, 560 N.Y.S.2d 115 (N.Y. 1990); *State v. Gardiner*, 636 A.2d 710 (R.I. 1994); *State v. Whaley*, 305 S.C. 138, 406 S.E.2d 369 (S.C. 1991); *State v. Percy*, 156 Vt. 468, 595 A.2d 248 (Vt. 1990); *State v. Moon*, 45 Wash. App. 692, 726 P.2d 1263 (Wash. Ct. App. 1986); and *Engberg v. Meyer*, 820 P.2d 70 (Wyo. 1991).
6. This decision-making pyramid has been described in an alternative formulation as "Courts must generally make three determinations in ruling on the admissibility of eyewitness expert testimony. First, is the expert testimony reliable in both the sense that the methodology and reasoning employed by the eyewitness expert have scientific validity, and that the expert's conclusion is supported by the facts of the

case? Second, is the eyewitness expert's testimony relevant to the case? . . . Third, is the probative value of the eyewitness expert's testimony substantially outweighed by its prejudicial value?" See Wise, Dauphinais, & Safer (2007).

7. See, for example, *United States v. Holloway*, 971 F.2d 675 (11th Cir. 1992); *State v. Goldsby*, 59 Ore. App. 66, 650 P.2d 952 (Ore. Ct. App. 1982); *Commonwealth v. Simmons*, 541 Pa. 211, 662 A.2d 621 (Pa. 1995), cert. denied, 516 U.S. 1128, 133 L. Ed. 2d 870, 116 S. Ct. 945 (1996).

8. *People v. LeGrand*, 867 N.E.2d 374, 380 (N.Y. 2007). The New York court found regarding the evidentiary proffer as to the fourth category, weapons focus, that "there was insufficient evidence to confirm that the principles expounded by defendant's expert witness are generally accepted by the relevant scientific community."

9. A limited number of jurisdictions exclude such testimony categorically. See, for example, *United States v. Holloway*, 971 F.2d 675 (11th Cir. 1992); *State v. Goldsby*, 59 Ore. App. 66, 650 P.2d 952 (Ore. Ct. App. 1982); *Commonwealth v. Simmons*, 541 Pa. 211, 662 A.2d 621 (Pa. 1995), cert. denied, 516 U.S. 1128, 133 L. Ed. 2d 870, 116 S. Ct. 945 (1996); *State v. Wooden*, 658 S.W.2d 553 (Tenn. Ct. Crim. App. 1983).

10. This is the rationale of the Pennsylvania Supreme Court, which has twice upheld the across-the-board exclusion of eyewitness expert testimony. From *Commonwealth v. Simmons*, 662 A.2d 621, 632 (Pa. 1995): "Such testimony would have given an unwarranted appearance of authority as to the subject of credibility, a subject which an ordinary juror can assess."

11. Crump notes that the *Frye* standard did not apply to "financial witnesses, economists, and even physicians. . . ."

12. For another history of the development of evidentiary rules governing the admission of expert testimony, see Faigman, Porter, and Saks (April 1994).

13. From *United States v. Yee*, 134 F.R.D. 161, 196, 199 (N.D. Ohio 1990): "a court need not find that there is unanimity, or consensus within the scientific community concerning such acceptability". See also, *Bernardoni v. Industrial Commission* (Huntsman Chemical Co.), 840 N.E.2d 300, 311 (Ill. App. Ct. 3d Dist. 2005) (citation omitted): "'General acceptance' does not mean universal acceptance, and it does not require that the methodology in question be accepted by unanimity, consensus, or even a majority of experts. Instead, it is sufficient that the underlying method used to generate an expert's opinion is reasonably relied upon by experts in the relevant field."

The Third Circuit surveyed decisional law and found disparate definitions of this standard. From *United States v. Downing*, 753 F.2d 1224, 1236 (3d Cir. Pa. 1985): "One court has described 'general acceptance' as 'widespread; prevalent; extensive though not universal,' while another has suggested that the test requires agreement by a 'substantial section of the scientific community.'"

14. A well-regarded critique of *Frye* is found in Giannelli (1980). States that continue
to apply the *Frye* decision or a variant include Arizona, California, District of Columbia, Florida, Illinois, Kansas, Maryland, Michigan, Minnesota, Mississippi, Missouri, Nebraska, New York, North Dakota, Pennsylvania, and Washington. Georgia, Utah, Virginia, and Wisconsin have developed their own tests (neither *Frye* nor *Daubert*).

15. Because the *Daubert* decision interprets a federal evidence rule, it is not binding on states, which may select their own rules or guidelines. Nonetheless,

many states now follow *Daubert* principles, in total or in large part. These include Alaska, Arkansas, Colorado, Connecticut, Delaware, Idaho, Indiana, Iowa, Kentucky, Louisiana, Maine, Montana, Nebraska, New Mexico, North Carolina, Ohio, Oklahoma, Oregon, Rhode Island, South Carolina, South Dakota, Tennessee, Texas, Vermont, West Virginia,
and Wyoming. Several states apply *Daubert*-like criteria: Alabama, Hawaii, Massachusetts, Nevada, New Hampshire, and New Jersey.

16.   Federal Rules of Evidence, Pub. L. No. 93595, 88 Stat. 1926, 1937 (1975). Rule 702 has been modified since the *Daubert* decision to further reflect the language used by the Court. See text following footnote 19, quoting amended Rule 702.

17.   In *Daubert v. Merrell Dow*, U.S. (1993) p. 588: "Nothing in the text of this Rule establishes 'general acceptance' as an absolute prerequisite to admissibility. Nor does respondent present any clear indication that Rule 702 or the Rules as a whole were intended to incorporate a 'general acceptance' standard."

18.   In *Daubert v. Merrell Dow*, 509 U.S. (1993) p. 587: "The Rules' basic standard of relevance thus is a liberal one."

19.   *Kenny A. v. Perdue*, 532 F.3d 1209, 1219 (11th Cir. Ga. 2008) showed that it is this broad authority vested in trial judges that sometimes leads to the exclusion of expert testimony, even when the science is deemed valid. The reasons for such exclusions are discussed, in this case.

20.   From *Daubert v. Merrell Dow*, 509 U.S. 579, 596 (U.S. 1993): "Vigorous cross-examination, presentation of contrary evidence, and careful instruction on the burden of proof are the traditional and appropriate means of attacking shaky but admissible evidence."

21.   See also Faigman (2008).

22.   From Faigman, Porter, and Saks (pp. 1799, 1810): "The conventional view that *Frye* sets a higher threshold for admissibility is an erroneous one. Whether *Frye* or the Federal Rules constitute the more rigorous test of admissibility depends on certain features of the proffered knowledge."

23.   For a survey of decisions showing this pattern, see Benton, McDonnell, Thomas, et al. (Spring, 2006).

24.   See also *United States v. Carter*, 410 F.3d 942, 950 (7th Cir. Ill. 2005): "the government had significant additional evidence (e.g., getaway car, shoe print, crack pipe DNA) to corroborate Hernandez's identification." *United States v. Langan*, 263 F.3d 613, 624 (6th Cir. 2001), noting the "substantial amount of other evidence"; *United States v. Villiard*, 186 F.3d 893, 895 (8th Cir. 1999), explaining "we are especially hesitant to find an abuse of discretion. . . unless the government's case against the defendant rested exclusively on uncorroborated eyewitness testimony."

25.   See National Criminal Justice Reference Service. Convicted by juries, exonerated by science. Retrieved January 23, 2009 from http://www.ncjrs.gov/txtfiles/dnaevid.txt. Commentary by Edward J. Imwinkelried.

26.   In *Holmes*, the Court considered a rule of evidence that excluded defense evidence of a third-party suspect's guilt if the prosecution proof appeared strong. The Court rejected such a rule as unconstitutional: "The rule applied in this case appears to be based on the following logic: Where (1) it is clear that only one person was involved in the commission of a particular crime and (2) there is strong evidence that the defendant was the perpetrator, it follows that evidence of third-party guilt must be weak. But this logic depends on an accurate evaluation of

the prosecution's proof, and the true strength of the prosecution's proof cannot be assessed without considering challenges to the reliability of the prosecution's evidence. Just because the prosecution's evidence, if credited, would provide strong support for a guilty verdict, it does not follow that evidence of third-party guilt has only a weak logical connection to the central issues in the case. And where the credibility of the prosecution's witnesses or the reliability of its evidence is not conceded, the strength of the prosecution's case cannot be assessed without making the sort of factual findings that have traditionally been reserved for the trier of fact. . . ."

27.   See, for example, *People v. Goodwillie*, 147 Cal. App. 4th 695, 726 (Cal. App. 4th Dist. 2007), rejecting a due process claim on facts of particular case; *People v. Bryant*, 2008 Cal. App. Unpub. LEXIS 3154 (Cal. App. 1st Dist. 2008), the same; and contrary opinions in *Stephenson v. State*, 226 S.W.3d 622, 628–629 (Tex. App. Amarillo 2007): "the trial court's decision to exclude the testimony of Dr. Wills significantly impaired Appellant's ability to present his defense and was, therefore, of constitutional proportions."

28.   See, for example, Chapter 3 of this book; see also, Epstein (Spring, 2007).

29.   See, for example, *United States v. Brownlee*, 454 F.3d 131, 142 (3d Cir. Pa. 2006); *United States v. Mathis*, 264 F.3d 321, 336 (3d Cir. N.J. 2001); *United States v. Smithers*, 212 F.3d 306, 317 (6th Cir. Mich. 2000) "expert testimony should be admitted in the precise situation presented to the trial court in this case—that is, when there is no other inculpatory evidence presented against the Defendant with the exception of a small number of eyewitness identifications"; *United States v. Moore*, 786 F.2d 1308, 1313 (5th Cir. 1986), finding that "in a case in which the sole testimony is casual eyewitness identification, expert testimony regarding the accuracy of that identification is admissible and properly may be encouraged. . ."

30.   See, for example, *United States v. Downing*, 753 F.2d 1224 (3d Cir. 1985), excluding expert testimony an abuse of discretion in case with 12 eyewitnesses but no other type of corroboration.

31.   See, for example, *People v. Varnado*, 2007 Cal. App. Unpub. LEXIS 8389 (Cal. App. 2d Dist. 2007), "Mere generic factors affecting the reliability of eyewitness observations do not usually warrant expert testimony"; *Silva v. State*, 2006 Tex. App. LEXIS 9599, 3–5 (Tex. App. Houston 14th Dist. Oct. 24, 2006), "[the expert] did not relate most of the abstract principles of which he spoke to the facts of the case or specify how any of the eyewitness identification factors could have affected the eyewitness identification in this case."

32.   In *Stephenson v. State*, 226 S.W.3d 622, 627 (Tex. App. Amarillo 2007): "Dr. Wills reviewed the statement given to the police by Maria Moreno. He also reviewed the probable cause affidavit and the photographic lineup in question. He applied the concept of 'relative judgment' to simultaneous photographic lineups and opined the benefits of sequential photographic lineups versus simultaneous photographic lineups. Furthermore, he applied the concepts of 'cueing and unintentional behavior' to the process of preparing and presenting non-suggestive photographic lineups."

33.   Studies regarding whether the science has penetrated the lay community and thus is known to prospective jurors are detailed in Chapter 6 of this text.

34.   See, for example, *Silva v. State*, 2006 Tex. App. LEXIS 9599, 3–5 (Tex. App. Houston 14th Dist. Oct. 24, 2006): "Regarding the use of photo spreads, most of Dr. Rubenzer's testimony focused on matters not involving scientific, technical, or other specialized knowledge. For instance, he expressed concerns over the

differences between appellant's photo and those of the other subjects. He stated that the differences in the backgrounds of the photos and appellant's hair style compared to the other subjects could have caused appellant's photo to stand out on the photo spreads."

35.   In *Commonwealth v. Bly*, 862 N.E.2d 341, 360 (Mass. 2007): "The nature of Woodsum's identification, including the circumstances of her original sighting, the time delay, the television broadcast, and the cross-racial aspect were such that the jury's evaluation could be accomplished through its common understanding without need of expert testimony."

36.   See, for example, Federal Rule of Evidence 702, which permits the expert witness to testify "in the form of an opinion or otherwise. . ."

37.   See Federal Rule of Evidence 703.

38.   The National Institute of Justice, for example, has published materials on guidelines for law enforcement in eyewitness cases: Eyewitness evidence: A guide for law enforcement (October, 1999). http://www.ncjrs.gov/pdffiles1/nij/178240.pdf.

39.   See, for example, Federal Rule of Evidence 704, which provides that "testimony in the form of an opinion or inference otherwise admissible is not objectionable because it embraces an ultimate issue to be decided by the trier of fact."

40.   See, for example, *State v. Riofta*, Wash. App. LEXIS 1880 (Wash. Ct. App. Sept. 2, 2003): "Even the best attorney does not retain such an expert in every case; rather, he or she makes a judgment whether the expert is likely to help. In this case, [counsel's] judgment was that the expert might not have helped, and even might have hurt. This was a tactical decision within his province, and thus not deficient performance."

41.   From *Currie v. Burt*, U.S. Dist. LEXIS 63308, 5556 (N.D. Iowa Aug. 13, 2008): "The record indicates that trial counsel was familiar with transracial identification problems and eyewitness identification experts, but he decided an expert was not required in this case. Since the robber wore a mask, trial counsel did not believe an eyewitness identification expert was needed to explain the potential problem with identifying someone wearing a mask, regardless of race."

42.   See, for example, *Torres v. State*, 962 P.2d 3, 20 (Okla. Crim. App. 1998): "Torres has not presented any evidence to show what that expert testimony would have revealed and he has failed to show how the failure to present such expert evidence prejudiced him."

43.   See, for example, *Gibson v. State*, 661 S.E.2d 850, 855 (Ga. Ct. App. 2008): "The record shows that defense counsel thoroughly cross-examined Vernard Anderson at trial about his tentative identifications, and that the trial court instructed the jury on identification. It is clear that trial counsel made a strategic choice not to attempt to suppress the identification evidence, but instead to attack the identification testimony on cross-examination."

44.   See also *People v. Farrow*, Mich. App. LEXIS 2614 (Mich. Ct. App. Nov. 20, 2007).

45.   In a study of the first 200 DNA exonerations, many identification cases had corroborating evidence. For example, "in forty-six of the exonerees' cases (23%), there was an eyewitness identification added to the serological evidence." See B.L. Garrett (January, 2008).

5

Appellate Review and Eyewitness Experts

Jennifer Groscup and Steven Penrod

Expert testimony has posed special problems for the justice system for over a century. As an example, Learned Hand (1901) commented: "How can the jury judge between two statements each founded upon an experience confessedly foreign in kind to their own? It is just because they are incompetent for such a task that the expert is necessary at all" (p. 54). Hand correctly identified the purpose of expert testimony in the legal system. Sometimes the issues that must be resolved by the factfinder in legal disputes include concepts that are outside of the knowledge and experience of the factfinder. Expert testimony is provided to aid the factfinder in appropriately resolving these issues.

Since that time, many problems have been identified with expert testimony. One problem that recently has been the focus of the debate over expert testimony is its reliability, largely due to a troika of Supreme Court cases that attempted to clarify the standards for the expert testimony admissibility. Judges are given the authority to admit or exclude expert evidence. Expert testimony can cover a broad range of topics, from beekeeping to epidemiology. In rendering admissibility decisions, judges are expected to have a rudimentary understanding of all of these topics in order to assess the reliability of the evidence. This assessment can be particularly difficult when courts are faced with complex scientific testimony.

Admissibility Standards

Prior to 1993, the legal standards that were applied to the admissibility of expert testimony were the *Frye* general acceptance test and the requirements of the Federal Rules of Evidence (FRE). In *Frye v.United States*, the D.C. Circuit Court considered the admissibility of an early form of polygraph evidence. In short, *Frye* stated that, in order for expert testimony to be admissible "the thing from which the deduction is made must be sufficiently established to have gained general acceptance in the particular field it belongs" (*Frye v. United States*, 1923, p. 1014). This standard became known as the "general acceptance" test, and it was used as the basis for determining expert admissibility in many courts.

Another common source of admissibility standards are the Federal Rules of Evidence. The Federal Rules are controlling in all federal jurisdictions, but many states have enacted substantially similar language in their state evidence codes. Federal Rule of Evidence 702 governs the admission of expert testimony. It states that "if scientific, technical, or other specialized knowledge will assist the trier of fact to understand the evidence or to determine a fact in issue, a witness qualified as an expert by knowledge, skill, experience, training, or education, may testify thereto in the form of an opinion or otherwise" (Mueller & Kirkpatrick, 1999). When the Federal Rules of Evidence governing expert testimony were codified, no general acceptance requirement for admissibility was present in the language of those Rules. The adoption of these Rules did not specifically preclude the use of the *Frye* standard to evaluate expert testimony, nor did it endorse it. In the wake of the adoption of the Rules, it was unclear whether evaluating the general acceptance of scientific knowledge remained a valid approach to determining the admissibility of expert testimony.

In a series of landmark cases, the Supreme Court attempted to clarify the standards for the admissibility of expert testimony. First, the Court had to resolve the question of which admissibility standard should be used for expert testimony. In *Daubert v. Merrell Dow Pharmaceuticals, Inc.* (1993), the Court had to consider the admissibility of novel scientific expert evidence about epidemiology. The Court held that the Federal Rules superseded *Frye* as the appropriate admissibility standard for expert evidence. Additionally, the Court stated that the reliability of scientific evidence should be evaluated by the trial court judge as part of the admission decision under the Rules. The opinion re-emphasized the trial judge's "gatekeeping" duty to evaluate the quality of the evidence being presented, including the underlying quality of the science presented via expert testimony. When evaluating scientific knowledge, the reliability of the scientific methods must be assessed. Four factors were suggested to aid judges in this reliability analysis: falsifiability, peer review, error rate, and general acceptance.

One of the many questions raised by the *Daubert* decision concerned the distinction between scientific and nonscientific testimony. *Daubert* was silent on the applicability of its criteria to nonscientific testimony, and the proper standard to be applied to the admissibility of nonscientific testimony was unclear. In *Kumho Tire Co. v. Carmichael* (1999), the Supreme Court resolved this issue and determined that the reliability analysis suggested in *Daubert* should be applied to both scientific and nonscientific testimony. The trial judges' gatekeeping role was extended to include a reliability assessment of nonscientific evidence, as well as scientific evidence. However, no guidelines were provided by the Court in the *Kumho* opinion to assist judges in this task. The Court suggested that the nonexclusive factors for evaluating scientific evidence listed in the *Daubert* opinion could provide some assistance in screening nonscientific evidence, but the use of these factors was not required. Trial judges were granted discretion to determine the standard for the admissibility of nonscientific evidence on a case-by-case basis (*Kumho*, 1999).

Psychological Expert Testimony

Daubert and *Kumho* required the trial judge to assume the role of a "gatekeeper" of all expert evidence. After these cases were decided, much legal and psycho-legal commentary appeared on how these newly clarified rules would affect the admissibility of behavioral science expert evidence (Goodman-Delahunty, 1997; Sparks, 1995). One potential problem in determining the appropriate application of *Daubert* to psychological testimony was the distinction between scientific and nonscientific testimony. Whether psychology is a specialized field or a scientific field was a subject of debate, and it was unclear how the courts were supposed to treat specialized and scientific testimony under *Daubert* (Faigman, 1995a, b). Even though the post-*Daubert* commentary and the *Kumho* decision itself attempted to clarify the standard to be applied to nonscientific testimony, speculation abounded concerning whether psychological testimony should be considered scientific or nonscientific. Some domains of psychological testimony were identified by commentators as being nonscientific (Faigman, 1995a, b; Renaker, 1996; Savage, 1999). These types of psychology are problematic under *Daubert* because many of their concepts are inherently untestable (Richardson, Ginsburg, Gatowski, & Dobbin, 1995). For example, some have drawn a distinction between clinically based psychological expert testimony and empirically based psychological expert testimony, arguing that some clinical testimony lacks scientific validity (Shuman & Sales, 1999). Syndrome evidence generally (Duncan, 1996; Faigman, 1995; Renaker, 1996; Slobogin, 1998), battered woman syndrome specifically (Faigman & Wright, 1997; Morse, 1998), the existence of repressed memories (Spadoro, 1998; Steele, 1999), and the presence of child sexual abuse in a particular child (Richardson et al., 1995) have been identified as topics falling into the category of psychology that may be less scientifically reliable or for which scientific reliability would be more difficult to prove. It was predicted that courts would have a difficult time evaluating the reliability of testimony on these topics as required by *Daubert*.

On the other hand, some types of psychological testimony are arguably scientific (Faigman, 1995a, b). The reliability of eyewitness identifications is among the topics of psychological expert testimony that has been identified as scientific (Fradella, 2006). The research underlying the testimony of eyewitness experts has been described by legal commentators as reliable and valid (Fradella, 2006). In theory, this type of testimony should fare very well under an admission standard focused on the reliability of its research methodology. However, research on eyewitness experts demonstrates that admission decisions about them are not as favorable as we might expect.

Research on Courts' Treatment of Eyewitness Experts

Commentators have identified expert testimony on eyewitness reliability as particularly problematic for the courts (Sparks, 1995). The court in *United States v. Downing* (1985) summarized the negative attitude judges have toward this type of expert testimony in its discussion of why courts may decide it is proper to exclude all expert testimony on this topic. In this case, the decision to affirm the exclusion of an eyewitness expert who was not permitted to testify at trial as being per se inadmissible at the trial court level was reversed on appeal. The appellate court stated that "judicial resistance to the introduction of this kind of expert testimony is understandable given its innovativeness and the fear of trial delay spawned by the specter of the creation of a cottage industry of forensic psychologists" (p. 1232). Although the appellate court ruled that eyewitness experts may be admissible under some circumstances, the opinion clearly summarizes the negative general feeling courts may have toward this type of testimony.

One question regarding the admissibility of eyewitness experts is whether eyewitness experts are treated differently from other psychological experts. Our previous research demonstrates that different types of psychological testimony are treated differently in terms of the admissibility of expert testimony (Groscup & Penrod, 2003). We compared the treatment of police officers, clinical psychologists, and experimental psychologists (consisting mostly of eyewitness experts) in criminal appellate cases. The mostly eyewitness experimental experts were excluded more often than clinical psychologists. Experimental psychologists were more likely to be found prejudicial, not relevant, and not providing assistance to the trier of fact than police and clinical psychologists. In addition, experimental psychologists mostly testified for the defense, and expert testimony for the defense, as stated earlier, was more likely to remain excluded at the appellate level (Groscup & Penrod, 2003). Fradella, Fogarty, and O'Neill (2003) also compared eyewitness experts to other psychological experts. They looked for themes in cases including different types of psychological testimony. They examined a total of 73 federal cases, including some appellate court cases, 11 of which were cases with eyewitness experts. They concluded that courts treat eyewitness experts inconsistently relative to other types of psychological testimony (Fradella et al., 2003).

Research examining the admissibility of eyewitness experts relative to other psychologists highlights that eyewitness experts may have more problems being admitted than other psychologists. Within cases involving eyewitness experts, variation occurs in courts' general approaches to admitting their testimony, as indicated by the different approaches taken by the trial and the appellate courts in *Downing*. Benton and colleagues (2006) argue that two basic approaches are taken to eyewitness expert admission decisions post--*Daubert*. They term one "discretionary," in which the court making the admission decision can exercise its discretion in determining admissibility. The second approach is "prohibitory," in which eyewitness experts are always excluded, and that decision is not within the discretion of the trial court. Benton and colleagues argue that discretionary is the most commonly articulated approach, but that courts' actual treatment of eyewitness experts more closely resembles prohibitory (Benton et al., 2006). How are these two approaches observed in courts' overall treatment of eyewitness experts?[1]

Consistent with Benton and colleagues' argument that many courts effectively prohibit expert testimony about eyewitness reliability regardless of case circumstances, most researchers argue that eyewitness experts are admitted less frequently than they should be (Benton et al., 2006; Fradella, 2006; Fradella et al., 2003). Some commentators argue that decision making about eyewitness experts is inconsistent across jurisdictions (Benton et al., 2006). Some argue that admission of eyewitness expert testimony is on the rise, but provide little evidence of this increase (Woller, 2003). Many others observe that it is mostly excluded (Benton et al., 2006; Fradella, 2006; Groscup & Penrod, 2003). Overall, research confirms that a generally negative stance toward eyewitness experts is taken by the courts.

For example, Benton and colleagues (2006) reviewed state and federal appellate court admission decisions for eyewitness experts. They selected the most recent cases from each state and federal circuit. They characterized the largest group of cases falling into a category they referred to as "may be admissible: discretion not abused in excluding." In this category, the appellate courts deferred to the trial courts on their reasoning for exclusion, even if the court could have reached a different decision and admitted the evidence. Reasons for exclusion in these cases varied but included the presence of corroborating evidence for the eyewitness identification, the certainty to which the expert could state the opinion, and whether the expert had personal experience with the case. The authors conclude that the reasons appear to be little more than excuses to support exclusion and that these cases indicate that courts have the potential to admit an eyewitness expert but admission is unlikely (Benton et al., 2006).

In Benton and colleagues' review of federal cases, they observed that none of the eyewitness experts were admitted. However, in the courts' opinions, there was nothing to indicate that the federal circuits had taken a prohibitory approach to admitting eyewitness experts. Like the state courts in their analysis, they found the federal courts arguing that eyewitness experts may be admissible in some cases, even though they did not find them to be admissible in any of the cases they reviewed. The authors concluded that the variability in admission decision making stems from a lack of clear admission standards, the deference given to the trial court judge, and the personal views of those trial court judges. The large degree of deference given to trial judges prevents the system from changing its approach to eyewitness experts (Benton et al., 2006).

Reasons for Exclusion [of Eyewitness Experts]

Assisting the Trier of Fact

Several reasons for the frequent exclusion of eyewitness experts from testifying in court have been proffered. The most common observation is that courts find eyewitness experts do not assist the trier of fact and are therefore inadmissible under Rule 702. The barrier to eyewitness experts assisting the trier of fact is the argument that jurors already understand what makes an eyewitness reliable. An expert must provide information outside the common knowledge of the average juror and, under this argument, they would not (Fradella, 2006; Sparks, 1995; Woller, 2003). Related reasons for exclusion are that eyewitness experts would usurp the function of the jury or mislead the jury (Fradella, 2006).

As part of judges' inquiry into whether the testimony provides assistance to the trier of fact, they should ideally determine if jurors' knowledge in relevant areas is lacking. It is argued, and research demonstrates, that expert testimony on memory and perception as they relate to eyewitnesses provides information that is outside the common knowledge of the average juror (Kassin & Barndollar, 1992; Fradella, 2006). Because the expert could explain some of the underlying processes that could make some eyewitnesses less accurate, their testimony would assist jurors in evaluating eyewitness identifications, particularly identifications made under less than ideal circumstances (Fradella, 2006). Research comparing laypersons' knowledge of eyewitness reliability and the knowledge of eyewitness experts indicates that there are many topics upon which laypersons' understanding could be improved with expert testimony (Kassin & Barndollar, 1992). Specifically, they found that, although topics such as weapon focus were well understood by potential jurors, topics such as the confidence–accuracy relationship were outside of laypersons' common knowledge (Kassin & Barndollar, 1992). A detailed discussion of jurors' common knowledge about the reliability of eyewitnesses can be found in Read and Desmarais, Chapter 6. As these factors may be crucial to evaluating the reliability of an eyewitness, it stands to reason that expert testimony on these topics should be judged as assisting the trier of fact and therefore admissible.

The research conducted thus far on legal decision making indicates that courts do not follow this logic. For example, Fradella and associates (2003) examined a total of 73 federal cases, including some appellate court cases, 11 of which were cases with eyewitness experts. The courts in this research excluded 81.8% of eyewitness expert testimony because it would not assist the trier of fact or because it had the potential to mislead the jury. Judges admitting eyewitness experts recognized that factors affecting eyewitness reliability may not be in the common understanding of the average juror. Benton and colleagues (2006) observed that a common rationale of courts when excluding eyewitness experts was that the information in their testimony was not outside the ken of the average jurors and therefore would not assist the trier of fact. Very few state appellate courts in the recent cases reviewed overturned decisions to exclude eyewitness experts. Those that did reasoned that jurors do not understand the psychological factors underlying eyewitness identifications or that they have a misunderstanding of these factors. Another factor in their decision that exclusion was an abuse of discretion was whether the eyewitness identification was the main piece of evidence presented by the prosecution. Overall, there is some hope that judges can appropriately identify areas for which an eyewitness expert would assist the trier of fact, but there is far more evidence that they do not.

General Acceptance

General acceptance has also been identified as a problematic requirement for the admission of eyewitness experts (Sparks, 1995; Woller, 2003). A large body of empirical research has been conducted on the factors affecting eyewitness reliability. Within this body of research, many phenomena have been examined, and many explanations for these phenomena have been tested. Although experts tend to agree on many of the findings in this area of research, disagreement exists in other areas. For example, the vast majority of eyewitness researchers agree that an eyewitness's reliability can be affected by the wording of questions posed to them, lineup instructions, and post-event information, among others (Kassin, Ellsworth, & Smith, 1989; Kassin, Tubb, Hosch, & Memon, 2001). However, there is less agreement that other phenomena are likely to occur in an eyewitness situation, such as the long-term repression of memory and the effects of witnessing event violence and stress on an eyewitness (Kassin et al., 2001). This disagreement is in part due to contradictory research findings. These contradictory findings and disagreement can result in a trial court judge finding that the research underlying an eyewitness expert's testimony is not generally accepted and therefore not admissible (Woller, 2003), even though there is a large amount of general acceptance in the field (Kassin et al., 2001). For a complete review of research on the perceptions of general acceptance of the factors affecting eyewitness reliability within the eyewitness expert community, see Hosch, Jolly, Schmersal, and Smith, in Chapter 7.

   To investigate how general acceptance and other potential decision-making criteria were treated by courts, Fradella (2003) conducted a qualitative analysis on post-*Daubert* cases involving all types of social science evidence.

A subset of those social science expert witnesses testified about eyewitness reliability. Complementing his other research findings, Fradella observed that generally accepted eyewitness reliability findings were excluded in this study. Even when courts find eyewitness reliability experts to be testifying about topics on which we know consistent research findings exist (i.e., cross-race identification), they are not admitted. The courts' reasoning in these situations was that eyewitness experts in this context are of little consequence to the case. The courts reasoned that when research findings are so well established, then the jury should be capable of evaluating the reliability of an eyewitness for themselves, without the assistance of an expert (Fradella, 2003). Therefore, research topics for which we have the most convergent validity, and which would have the most impact, are still likely to be kept away from the jury. Although there has been some discussion by courts about how general acceptance will be determined for eyewitness experts, there has been little investigation into how the other three *Daubert* factors have been applied to eyewitness experts.

Reliability of Scientific Methodology

Distinctions have been drawn between different topics of psychological expert testimony based on the underlying science (Faigman, 1995a, b; Renaker, 1996; Richardson et al., 1995; Savage, 1999). Fradella and associates (2003) argued that psychological testimony could have problems in court post-*Daubert* because a lot of it is based on anecdote and has not been tested empirically, such as testimony about the effects of child sexual abuse. Contrary to testimony based on case studies and anecdote, eyewitness reliability research is arguably based on hard science (Fradella, 2006). In his earlier research (Fradella et al., 2003), he looked for judicial reasoning about eyewitness experts in court opinions that would indicate they were being negatively evaluated on their scientific reliability. Unlike the prediction that psychological testimony would be excluded more after *Daubert* because it is a "soft" science, they found no cases in which a psychological expert was excluded because he used faulty methodology. Overall, they observed that many types of psychological testimony were readily admitted. However, this trend was not observed for psychologists testifying about eyewitness reliability. We also found little indication that eyewitness experts were excluded for methodological reasons in our previous findings (Groscup & Penrod, 2003).

Party Proffering the Expert

As discussed earlier, commentators offered a variety of hypotheses regarding which parties would benefit most from *Daubert* and *Joiner*. Given that most eyewitness experts are proffered by the defense, any trend favoring or biased against defense-proffered experts could affect the admission of eyewitness experts. Groscup and colleagues (2002) found that defendants in criminal cases were not as successful in their expert admissibility appeals as the prosecution. Risinger (2000) and Groscup and Penrod (2003) also found a related effect that eyewitness experts were less likely to be admitted than prosecution experts such as police officers. In our previous research, we found that psychologists testifying on the same topics were more likely to be deemed admissible at the appellate level if they testified for the prosecution than when they testified for the defense (Groscup & Penrod, 2003).

Negative Attitudes About Social Science Evidence

Finally, the difficulty that eyewitness experts experience in admissibility hearings may be rooted in judges' negative attitudes about social science evidence generally. In survey research, judges express fairly negative attitudes toward the social sciences and find little relevance for social science research in their courtrooms (Manuto & O'Rourke, 1991). From their research findings, Benton and colleagues (2006) also conclude that an overall hostility exists toward social science evidence. They argue that the source of this hostility is a distrust of statistics and their potential to usurp the decision making of the jury with their aura of infallibility. This may be especially true when the statistics indicate phenomena that run counter to laypersons' commonsense impressions (Benton et al., 2006). This could explain a general hostility toward eyewitness reliability experts, given that they typically testify about research findings including statistics, and those findings typically run counter to the commonsense impressions jurors have of eyewitnesses.

Summary of Research on Courts' Treatment of Eyewitness Experts

Overall, trial courts have not been terribly receptive to psychologists testifying as experts on eyewitness reliability issues. Courts often exclude this type of expert testimony, and some courts prohibit eyewitness experts from testifying altogether. The most frequent reason for exclusion is that the factors affecting the reliability of an eyewitness are already in the common knowledge of the average juror. However, research demonstrates that many of these concepts are not, and commentators argue that eyewitness experts would assist the trier of fact in properly evaluating the reliability of an eyewitness. Because appellate courts are able to provide guidance to the trial courts about how rules should be applied, such as those provided by *Daubert* and *Kumho*, it is important to understand how appellate courts are making decisions about eyewitness experts and how their decisions might affect the trial courts.

Appellate Court Decision Making About Expert Testimony

Standard of Review

To understand appellate decision making about eyewitness experts, it is important to understand the relationship between the trial and appellate courts in this context. The decision to admit or exclude expert testimony in a case is made by the trial court judge. The trial court is privy to all of the evidence presented or offered for presentation to the factfinder first-hand. The *Daubert* and *Kumho* decisions were directed at trial court judges and were intended to give them guidance in their decisions. When a case is appealed, the appellate court reviews the trial court's actions. Because the trial court judge is exposed to all of the evidence during the trial, higher courts are often deferential to the trial court judge's opinions and rulings. The degree of deference afforded to the trial court reasoning and decision by the appellate court is called the *standard of review*. Some standards of review require the appellate court to review the evidence presented to the trial court with a very critical eye. One such standard is *de novo*, in which the appellate court must review all of the evidence anew. Others do not allow the appellate court to conduct any independent review of the evidence.

After *Daubert*, there was no agreement among the appellate courts about which standard of review should be used to review trial courts' admission decisions about expert testimony. During this time, it was argued that different levels of review should be applied to the decision to admit expert testimony depending on the impact of the decision (Faigman, 1995b, 1997). For example, aspects of expert testimony that have broad ramifications for subsequent cases, including theory and procedures, should be reviewed under a *de novo* standard. Other aspects relating to the specific case in question should be reviewed under some deferential standard, such as abuse of discretion (Faigman, 1995b, 1997). In *General Electric Co. v. Joiner* (1997), the Supreme Court answered the question of the appropriate level of appellate review to be utilized. In *Joiner*, the plaintiffs' medical expert, who was attempting to prove that exposure to polychlorinated biphenyls (PCBs) caused Joiner's lung cancer, was excluded as lacking scientific support. The issue on appeal was the appropriate standard of appellate review to be applied to the consideration of the trial courts' admission decisions regarding expert testimony. The Court determined that an abuse of discretion standard should be applied to all aspects of trial court determinations of admissibility of expert testimony. The decision in this case is binding on federal courts, but many state courts also use the same appellate standard for expert testimony admissibility.

Abuse of discretion is a fairly deferential standard of review. Under an abuse of discretion standard, the trial court judge's admission decision should only be overturned if that decision was impermissible under the current law or if it was unreasonable (Jonakait, 1999). Abuse of discretion does not necessitate that the appellate court review the evidence presented to the trial, nor does it necessarily mean that a trial court decision will be overturned when the appellate court disagrees with it. The appellate court's job is to determine if the trial court properly used the guidelines it was given. Although this is the function of the appellate court under an abuse of discretion review, many continue to argue that a less deferential standard of review should be applied to scientific evidence admission decisions and that a less deferential version of abuse of discretion would be permissible and desirable under *Joiner* (Gibbons, 2003; Jonakait, 1999).

After *Joiner*, there was much discussion about how this standard of review would affect both trial and appellate court decision making about expert testimony and about the proper role of the appellate courts in applying the standards set forth in *Daubert* and *Kumho*. Although the *Joiner* Court attempted to further clarify the way courts should treat expert testimony, several issues were raised about the abuse of discretion standard that indicate it may have created more potential for confusion than clarity. First, the uniform standard raised questions about how involved the appellate courts could and should be in implementing and clarifying the Supreme Court's mandate to assess the reliability of expert evidence (Jonakait, 1999). One function of appellate courts is to provide guidance to the trial courts in their jurisdictions. Appellate courts can determine rules that will apply generally to all cases of a similar type in the trial courts over which they preside (Jonakait, 1999). Under a deferential standard of review like the abuse of discretion, it was unclear if appellate courts would be able to serve this function and provide much guidance to the trial courts.

Effects of the Abuse of Discretion Standard on Appellate Courts

One supervisory function the appellate courts could perform is to clarify the application of a reliability analysis to expert testimony beyond what was specified by *Daubert. Daubert* provided generally applicable guidelines, but the appellate courts could provide more specific direction for the trial courts in their jurisdiction. Many scholars argued that the abuse of discretion standard would prohibit the appellate courts from standardizing the trial court responses to expert testimony because the standard is too deferential (see, e.g., Frampton, 2007; Harvard Journal of Law and Public Policy, 2006; Gottesman, 1998). For example, it is not likely that a trial court judge's decision to exclude an eyewitness expert will be overturned on appeal using abuse of discretion as the standard of review (Frampton, 2007). It has been argued that the abuse of discretion standard of review may be preventing courts from refining the standards of admission (Harvard Journal of Law and Public Policy, 2006). With flexibility in the standard to be applied, it is difficult for appellate courts to determine if discretion was abused. A clearer standard for admission would be preferable, because the abuse of discretion allows inconsistent and erroneous trial court admission rulings to stand (Harvard Journal of Law and Public Policy, 2006). Fear was expressed that the use of an abuse of discretion appellate review standard will result in an "anything goes" standard, giving too much deference to trial judges and increasing the admissibility of unreliable testimony (Gottesman, 1998, p. 775).

If the appellate courts are prevented from overseeing trial court decision making about expert testimony admissibility under this standard, one possible result is that decisions in cases with similar circumstances will be inconsistent across trial courts (Jonakait, 1999). Because the appellate court is not determining whether the trial court judge made the "right" decision to admit or exclude expert testimony under an abuse of discretion standard, it is possible that testimony admitted by one court could be excluded by another court even under similar circumstances (Jonakait, 1999). This type of deferential standard of review may prevent consistent rules regarding admissibility from being created. Gibbons argues that the standards, as clarified by the Supreme Court in *Daubert* and *Kumho*, still contain much ambiguity in their proper implementation (Gibbons, 2003). Because the application of *Daubert* and *Kumho* is ambiguous, it would be possible for judges to set the bar for expert testimony admission at an unreasonably high level (Gibbons, 2003). Ambiguity in the rules judges should use to determine admissibility that cannot be resolved by the appellate courts could in turn increase the burden on the court system and make the trial process more complex (Jonakait, 1999). Difficulty in planning litigation may be one possible way that this burden may be observed in the trial courts. With no overarching guidelines, uncertainty will exist in the decisions that will be made in any given case. It will be difficult for lawyers to determine the quality of a case or the appropriate time and terms for settlement (Jonakait, 1999).

Clarifying admission guidelines for expert testimony may not be an easy task for the appellate courts, even if clarification was a task permissible under an abuse of discretion standard. A wide variety of cases and case facts arise, and rules that are generally applicable across that variation could be difficult to establish (Jonakait, 1999). However, Jonakait argues that it may be easier to create broad rules for scientific evidence. Although individual non–expert witnesses and case facts will vary widely across trials, the science underlying expert testimony will be somewhat consistent across trials (Jonakait, 1999). The reasoning behind admission decisions about science will therefore cut across trial court cases, allowing for the higher courts to establish some precedent for the admission of scientific evidence (Jonakait, 1999). One caveat is that scientific developments are constantly emerging, thus making it difficult for courts to set longstanding precedents about the *content* of scientific evidence (Jonakait, 1999). Jonakait argues that a precedent about the content of scientific evidence should only be set when there is confidence in the permanence of that knowledge, such that a good rule will result (Jonakait, 1999). However, precedent could be set for the consideration of the methodology underlying scientific evidence. Since methodology was the focus of the *Daubert* opinion, this may be an appropriate task for appellate courts.

Although the Supreme Court did not extensively articulate its reasoning for choosing an abuse of discretion standard in *Joiner*, one reason for such deference to the trial court is to save appellate judicial resources (Jonakait,

1999). Jonakait argues that this argument is not persuasive regarding expert testimony decisions. First, although deference may save the appellate court time, the savings in time will likely be complemented by an increase in trial court time, as each judge has to make admission decisions about every type of science anew, with no guidance from higher courts (Jonakait, 1999). Second, the appellate courts would not have to review the entire trial in order to review the admission decisions. The appellate courts would only have to review the *Daubert* hearing information. For these reasons, decisions about the admissibility of science may be appropriate for a less deferential standard of review (Jonakait, 1999).

Arguments for a Less Deferential Standard of Review

A standard of review that permits the appellate court to more thoroughly review the trial court admission decision would allow the appellate courts to take a more active role in setting an appropriate standard (Harvard Journal of Law and Public Policy, 2006). Gibbons, an appellate court judge, argues that *Joiner* should not be read as preventing the appellate courts from reviewing lower courts admission decisions with a careful eye (Gibbons, 2003). Overall, Gibbons argues that *Joiner* could and should be read broadly, so that an abuse of discretion includes many levels of review (Gibbons, 2003). Gibbons provides several reasons supporting his argument for a less strict approach to abuse of discretion. First, he argues that when the bar is set too high or the standards appear ambiguous, a less deferential version of the abuse of discretion should be used (Gibbons, 2003). This may be true when a type of testimony is per se excluded or is excluded more frequently than is appropriate, or when there is great variability in the admissions standards applied to a particular type of testimony.

Gibbons also argues that the abuse of discretion standard should be less deferential if there is a reasonable fear that judges are misinterpreting the rules by which they are making their decisions (Gibbons, 2003). One of the major concerns raised by the *Daubert* opinion was the ability of judges to evaluate reliability in the absence of training in scientific methodology. The effectiveness of legal education in providing judges with these skills provides a starting place for this inquiry. Research suggests that law school does not by itself prepare lawyers and future judges to recognize flaws in empirical research (Lehman, Lempert, & Nisbett, 1988). A next step in determining if there should be concern about judges misinterpreting the decision rules they are to follow is investigating the abilities of actual judges related to the assessment of expert testimony. Surveys conducted on actual judges to assess their abilities indicate that judges may lack knowledge about social science methods and therefore lack the ability to evaluate scientific reliability (Manuto & O'Rourke, 1991). Kovera and McAuliff (2000) conducted a study that manipulated the quality of the science being presented to the court, including some of the *Daubert* factors. Although judges with some prior scientific training were somewhat sensitive to experimental validity, judges without scientific training were insensitive to variations in the quality of science presented before the courts (Kovera & McAuliff, 2000). Gatowski and colleagues (2001) conducted a national survey of state trial court judges to assess their understanding of *Daubert*'s scientific factors, their willingness to apply the *Daubert* factors, and their ability to apply the *Daubert* factors. Results indicated that judges' demonstrated level of understanding of the factors was quite low. The majority of judges demonstrated understanding of peer review and general acceptance, but only a small percentage of judges who thought falsifiability and error rate were useful factors clearly understood the meaning of those terms (Gatowski et al., 2001). In sum, research conducted on judges' abilities to apply the *Daubert* factors and to judge scientific reliability in general indicates that misinterpretation of the rules by judges might be a valid concern.

Another argument for a more flexible and less deferential form of the abuse of discretion review focuses on the nature of scientific investigation. Jonakait (1999) argues that a less deferential standard of review is appropriate for the admissibility of science when new empirical information is collected between trial and appeal. If novel scientific discovery must be ignored under the abuse of discretion standard, even when it would change the ultimate decision of the trial court, this might result in negative perceptions of the fairness of the legal system overall (Jonakait, 1999). The idea that the trial court can make the best decisions about the evidence because it has the opportunity to view firsthand all of the evidence underlies a deferential standard of appellate review (Jonakait, 1999). Jonakait argues that this is not persuasive for admission decisions about scientific experts. "Personal credibility is seldom at the core of a decision regarding the admissibility of scientific evidence. *Daubert* commands the trial court to assess the science, and science is based not on the word of a scientist but data which is available to all" (Jonakait, 1999, p. 317). Therefore, the appellate court should be in an equally good position to judge the quality of scientific evidence as the trial court, with the added benefit of having a broad perspective on multiple trial court decisions in similar cases (Jonakait, 1999). It is also argued that appellate courts are better positioned to make good decisions about scientific evidence by virtue of their composition (Jonakait, 1999). Several appellate court judges may make better complex decisions about the quality of science than a single trial court judge by virtue of their ability to bring multiple perspectives to the process (Jonakait, 1999).

A final set of arguments in favor of a less deferential standard of review is the degree to which the decision to exclude an expert can affect the viability of a case. It has been argued that the admissibility of expert testimony is a unique issue that requires the opportunity for careful appellate review because of its power to make or break a case (Gibbons, 2003). The appellate court should be given the opportunity for more careful review of the trial court when the court's admission decision is more influential to the outcome of the case such as one that immediately leads to summary judgment for one of the parties (Gibbons, 2003). Exclusion of an expert, especially in a civil case, can be tantamount to a summary judgment ruling when it prevents a party from adequately making a claim or a valid case. This potential to affect the ultimate outcome of the trial makes the admission decision one that is unlike decisions to admit or exclude other types of evidence. Gibbons argues that since the legal system would not create policy that would create such a deferential level of appellate review for an ultimate decision like summary judgment, then the legal system should not be so deferential to expert admission decisions (Gibbons, 2003).

Given that the decision about expert admissibility can effectively stop a case from proceeding, there was also some discussion of which parties would receive the most benefit from abuse of discretion appellate review. It was unclear whether plaintiffs or defendants will be the recipients of any benefits from this deference (Marlin, 1998). Some have argued that plaintiffs in civil cases will be the beneficiaries. However, many have argued that it will impede even worthy plaintiffs from mounting civil cases. The admissibility of expert testimony can be dealt with at pre-trial, resulting in more summary judgments against plaintiffs if their experts are excluded, and the abuse of discretion standard prevents the appellate court from overturning many trial court decisions (Gibbons, 2003). Consistent with Gibbons argument, Risinger (2000) found that civil defendants opposing plaintiff experts on appeal were successful in more than the majority of appeals in his research. However, the effect of abuse of discretion in criminal cases, in which eyewitness experts are more likely to testify, is unclear.

Summary of Factors Affecting Appellate Court Decision Making

Overall, the abuse of discretion standard when applied to expert testimony admission decisions may have created more problems than it solves. Appellate courts may not take as active a role in guiding the trial courts in their new gatekeeping duties as they would have under a less deferential standard of review. This may result in ambiguity about the standards for admission and inconsistent decision making across similar cases. Several arguments have been raised that a less deferential standard of review would be appropriate under *Joiner*, including judicial misunderstanding of science or the development of new science. Both of these arguments could apply to eyewitness experts. Therefore, it is possible that appellate courts reviewing the admission or exclusion of an eyewitness expert may exercise some of their supervisory power in their opinions.

Our Research on the Appellate Admissibility of Eyewitness Experts

Our research has investigated how *Daubert*, *Joiner*, and *Kumho* affected the appellate admissibility of all types of expert testimony (see Groscup, 2002,

2004; Groscup et al. 2002; Groscup & Penrod, 2003). Experts testifying about eyewitness reliability were included in that investigation. The findings reported here add to the research on eyewitness experts already described here by focusing solely on appellate court opinions and by expanding the scope of the investigation. To determine how *Daubert, Joiner,* and *Kumho* affected judicial decision making about eyewitness reliability expert testimony, appellate court opinions were read and coded for content. Appellate court opinions were chosen because of their potential to demonstrate trends in judicial decision making about expert testimony, their potential to set jurisdictional precedent, and their provision of additional information about trial court decision making. Decisions involving admissibility decisions about psychological expert testimony were located using Westlaw. The cases identified were an exhaustive sample of all federal cases decided between 5½ years before *Daubert* and 2 years after *Kumho,* and all state cases decided between 5½ years before *Daubert* and 5½ years after *Daubert.*

Opinions with discussion of these experts were coded for content. A complete list of the variables in the coding scheme appears in Groscup (2002). The categories of variables used in these analyses included: information about the case in general, the expert, the admission decision, and courts' use of *Frye, Daubert, Joiner,* and *Kumho,* and selected Federal Rules.[2] All of the coders were graduate students in both psychology and law, who had taken at least 1 year of classes in law school, including evidence law. Cases were randomly assigned to raters and were coded in a random order. If a case contained substantive admissibility discussion of more than one expert, then each expert was coded separately. More information about the methodology for this and the overall research can be found in our previously published research (e.g., Groscup, 2002, 2004; Groscup et al. 2002; Groscup & Penrod, 2003). A total of 798 appellate court decisions concerning the admissibility of a psychological expert were coded. Of those cases, 76 involved experts testifying about eyewitness reliability. Fifty-six (73.7%) of these cases were tried in state courts, and 20 (26.3%) in federal courts. Only one of the cases was tried in civil court; the rest were criminal cases.

Appellate Nature of the Admission Decision

Among the primary questions raised about appellate review of eyewitness expert admissibility were what standard of review is applied to these decisions and whether that standard of review changed after *Joiner.* Even though *Joiner* signaled that there might be a change in the appellate standard of review used for eyewitness expert admission decisions, no statistically significant change occurred in the standard of review for eyewitness experts after *Joiner.* Eighty-five percent of the cases were decided before *Joiner,* and 15% were decided after *Joiner.*[3] All of the expert admission decisions except one were reviewed under an abuse of discretion standard. The one remaining decision was reviewed under a manifest error standard. Therefore, it would appear that trial court decisions about eyewitness experts were being reviewed under an abuse of discretion standard prior to *Joiner*, leaving little change in the appellate court consideration of this type of expert after *Joiner*.

Another question raised about abuse of discretion was whether it would prevent appellate court oversight of the trial courts. Although many legal commentators have argued that an abuse of discretion standard of review would allow for no policing of the trial courts by the appellate courts, some evidence suggests that the appellate courts did not defer totally to the trial courts. The majority of trial court decisions regarding admissibility, 80.3% ($n = 61$), were affirmed by the appellate courts. However, that means that almost 20% ($n = 15$) of the decisions made about eyewitness expert admissibility were reversed or remanded back to the trial court. In fact, a significant amount of change occurred between the trial and appellate court admission decisions, $X^2 (1, N = 69) = 6.77, p = .009, V = .313$. Only one eyewitness expert in our sample of cases that were appealed was admitted at the trial court level, and 98.6% of the experts were excluded at the trial court level. At the appellate court level, seven additional experts (10.7% increase) were found admissible.

The rate of admission of eyewitness experts at the appellate court level was very low. Overall, only 13% of eyewitness experts whose admission decision was appealed were deemed admissible at the appellate level. This low number can be contextualized by contrasting it with the significantly higher admission rate of almost 56% we observed for clinical psychologists (Groscup & Penrod, 2003). However, there was a significant increase over time in the likelihood that an eyewitness expert would be found admissible at the appellate level, $X^2 (2, N = 68) = 10.65, p = .005, V = .396$. Most of this increase occurred after *Kumho*, when the rate of admission went from 22.2% to 66.7%. This may indicate that appellate courts are beginning to view eyewitness experts more favorably than they have in the past.

As addressed earlier, previous research indicated that admission rates may be driven by the party for whom the expert testifies (Groscup et al., 2002; Groscup & Penrod, 2003; Risinger, 2000). One of the explanations for the rates of admission at the appellate level is that testimony may be admitted at different rates depending upon which party in the case offered the testimony. In fact, eyewitness expert testimony was not significantly more likely to be admitted when it was proffered by the prosecution than when it was proffered by the defense, $X^2(1, N = 69) = .632, p = .514, V = .06$. For the prosecution-proffered testimony, this was true both before and after *Daubert* and after *Kumho*. The pattern of admission rates did not change significantly for prosecution-proffered eyewitness experts across time, $X^2(1, N = 5) = .361, p = .361, V = .41$. However, the pattern of admission rates changed significantly for defense-proffered psychological experts, $X^2(1, N = 72) = 10.08, p = .006, V = .40$. Defense-proffered eyewitness experts were more likely to be excluded across all time periods until after *Kumho*. After *Kumho*, they were more likely to be admitted. However, it is likely that this is the change reflected in the overall change in admission rates, because 87.5% of the experts were proffered by the defense. Therefore, it is difficult to conclude, based on this data, that the party offering the eyewitness expert is a likely explanation for the admission decisions, as the vast majority of eyewitness experts are called by the defense.

Factors Influencing Admission Decisions

When investigating judicial decision making about eyewitness experts, it is important to examine what decision criteria they use and the relationship of those criteria to their admission decisions. To determine the effects of the FRE requirements and the *Daubert* factors on decision making, coders rated the importance of these criteria to the opinion on a 9-point scale, with 9 indicating the most importance. This importance rating gives us some information about the rationale judges are using in their decisions. We also recorded whether the appellate courts explicitly stated that the eyewitness expert either met or did not meet each of the selected admission criteria. This gives us a more objective measure of judges' opinions about eyewitness expert testimony. Then, we related these judgments to the admission decision to see what factors are related to this ultimate decision.

Assisting the Trier of Fact

One criterion for admission that has been repeatedly identified as problematic for eyewitness experts is the Rule 702 requirement that the testimony assist the trier of fact. Our research indicates that this criterion and the arguments associated with it are the biggest impediment to the admission of eyewitness experts. As a criterion, it had the highest importance rating of any of the other requirements of the FREs or any of the *Daubert* factors (*Mean* = 6.92, *SD* = 2.85). This rating of importance did not change significantly over time, and it was not related to the admission decision. Assisting the trier of fact was also the criterion most frequently mentioned by judges as having been met or not met by the eyewitness experts (almost three times more often than the next most frequently mentioned criterion). Eyewitness experts were judged as assisting the trier of fact in 15.9% ($n = 11$) of the cases. The testimony was significantly more likely to be admitted when it was judged as assisting the trier of fact, $X^2(1, N = 69) = 29.53, p <.001, V = .65$. Of the experts who assisted the trier of fact, 77.8% ($n = 7$) were admitted. On the other hand, eyewitness experts were judged as not assisting the trier of fact in 76.8% ($n = 53$) of the cases. These experts were significantly more likely to be excluded, $X^2(1, N = 69) = 17.32, p <.001, V = .50$. Eyewitness experts were excluded in 96.2% ($n = 51$) of the cases in which they did not assist the trier of fact. As past research and commentary indicated, assisting the trier of fact may be at the heart of the exclusion of eyewitness experts.

If assisting the trier of fact is so influential, how do judges evaluate it? Assisting the trier of fact is often discussed as resting on whether the testimony is outside the common knowledge of the jurors. We coded whether judges' stated that the testimony was within or outside the jurors' common knowledge (or was not mentioned). Eyewitness experts were judged to be outside the jurors' common knowledge in 16.9% ($n = 13$) of the cases and within their common knowledge in 41.6% ($n = 32$) of the cases. Determinations that an eyewitness expert provided information within the common knowledge of the jurors were significantly associated with explicit judicial statements that the testimony did not assist the trier of fact, $X^2(2, N = 76) = 16.06$, $p < .001$, $V = .46$. Judges stated that the testimony was within the common knowledge of the jurors in 56.6% ($n = 30$) of the cases in which they also determined that the testimony did not assist the trier of fact. Eyewitness experts providing information outside the jurors' common knowledge were also more likely to be found to assist the trier of fact, $X^2(2, N = 76) = 15.29$, $p < .001$, $V = .45$. Judges stated that the testimony was outside the common knowledge of the jurors in 53.8% ($n = 7$) of the cases in which they also determined that the testimony assisted the trier of fact. As with assisting the trier of fact, decisions about common knowledge were significantly related to judges' admission decisions, $X^2(2, N = 69) = 15.11$, $p = .001$, $V = .47$. The testimony was excluded in 100% ($n = 32$) of the cases when it was judged to be within the jurors' common knowledge and admitted in 55.6% ($n = 5$) of the cases when it was judged to be outside the jurors' common knowledge. Overall, what we learn from these results is that appellate courts frequently find that expert testimony about eyewitness reliability is within the jurors' common knowledge, and that finding is highly associated with a finding that the testimony does not assist the trier of fact, ultimately resulting in the exclusion of the testimony.

General Acceptance

Contrary to the findings of other research, we did not observe any significant effects of general acceptance on the admission decision for eyewitness experts. General acceptance was rated as significantly less important than assisting the trier of fact over all cases (*Mean* = 1.04, *SD* = 2.15, $t(75) = 14.07$, $p < .001$). The rating of importance for general acceptance did not change significantly over time, although we may have expected it to decrease, and it was not related to the admission decision. Judges were not more likely to explicitly state that general acceptance was met when the testimony was admitted or not met when the testimony was excluded. Explicit statements about general acceptance were also not related to the timing of the case. The lack of significant findings for general acceptance influencing admission decisions were also observed for the other three *Daubert* factors. Therefore, although other researchers concluded that general acceptance determinations could prevent the admission of eyewitness experts, we find no evidence of this in our research.

Reliability of Scientific Methods

The main focus of the *Daubert* and *Kumho* opinions was for judges to assess the reliability of the methods used to derive expert knowledge. Jonakait (1999) suggested that research methods could be evaluated under a less deferential standard of review, allowing for clearer guidelines to be available to the trial courts. Fradella (2003) found no indication of eyewitness experts being excluded because their methodology was unreliable. That research suggests that reliability might be particularly important for eyewitness experts and that they may be positively evaluated based on this criterion. Although reliability was not rated as important overall (*Mean* = 1.19, *SD* = 2.91) as assisting the trier of fact, $t(75) = 10.49$, $p < .001$, it was rated as more important than general acceptance $t(75) = 3.03$, $p = .003$. Unlike assisting the trier of fact and general acceptance, the rated importance of reliability did increase after *Daubert*, $F(2, 73) = 3.66$, $p = .031$, and was more important to court opinions in which the expert was admitted, $F(1, 69) = 13.30$, $p = .001$. Judges' explicit statements about reliability indicate that eyewitness experts were being judged favorably on this criterion. Although they were not more likely to explicitly mention that reliability was met or not met after *Daubert* or *Kumho*, judicial findings that the eyewitness expert was reliable were significantly related to admission decisions. Eyewitness experts who were found to be reliable were also more likely to be admitted, $X^2(1, N = 69) = 28.62$, $p < .001$, $V = .64$. Consistent with Fradella (2003), judges only specifically said the eyewitness expert testimony was not reliable in 5.8% of cases, and that determination was not significantly related to exclusion. Our research confirms the arguments and findings of others regarding reliability in that eyewitness experts are not likely excluded on these grounds and may fare better in the admission process when evaluated based on their reliability.

Conclusion

For eyewitness experts, commentators and researchers have observed that admission decision making is fairly consistent and generally negative. Courts tend to exclude this type of psychological expert more often than any other that has been the focus of empirical research. Past research demonstrated that when eyewitness experts are excluded by the trial court, it is often because the court believes they do not assist the trier of fact, their testimony is not generally accepted in their field, and they were not relevant to the case. These criteria may be applied inconsistently across eyewitness experts testifying in similar cases. Because the appellate standard of review that is applied to these decisions is very deferential to the trial court, it was argued that little opportunity existed for the appellate court to provide consistent guidelines to the trial courts for the consideration of eyewitness experts.

Overall, we observed the same fairly negative treatment of eyewitness experts that was observed in previous research. In cases that were appealed, the trial courts almost uniformly excluded the eyewitness experts. Even though the standard of review applicable to these decisions is very deferential, we found some evidence that the appellate courts performed some oversight regarding the trial courts. Some exclusions of eyewitness experts were reversed and/or remanded by the appellate courts. The evidence is hardly overwhelming, because the numbers of cases in which this occurred are small. However, some appellate courts are finding means to question trial court decisions under an abuse of discretion standard.

If this slight tendency for admission decisions to be overturned on appeal is co-occurring with a message to trial courts about how to make these decisions in the future, then the reasoning in the appellate opinions is important. What signals are the appellate courts potentially sending to the trial courts? First, they are signaling that the topics of eyewitness expert testimony are already understood by the average juror and that expert testimony on these topics is therefore unnecessary. This may be occurring even though research indicates that many topics about eyewitness reliability are poorly understood by laypersons. They may also be sending the message that the bases for eyewitness expert testimony are not generally accepted within their scientific community, if previous research is correct. This may be occurring even though research indicates that there is significant agreement among experts in the field on most of the topics covered by eyewitness expert testimony. Under the abuse of discretion standard of review, it is argued that it is not likely that appellate courts will be able to exert much influence over the admission decisions about eyewitness experts. Without a catalyst for change from a higher court, the ambiguity in standards and the reasoning observed in the admission decisions are likely to continue to be the picture of decision making about eyewitness experts at the trial court level.

Overall, many researchers and legal scholars argue that appellate courts should be allowed to provide guidance to the trial courts in these decisions. Among others, Jonakait (1999) concludes that we should examine whether the appellate courts could establish broadly applicable precedent regarding the admission of scientific evidence that would help the trial courts and that would increase consistency in admission decisions across cases. If this is possible, then it may be appropriate for a less deferential standard of review to be applied to admission decisions about scientific evidence (Jonakait, 1999). Jonakait alternatively suggests that a deferential standard of review could be applied to the trial courts' reasoning about an individual expert, but that the overall decision to admit or exclude the evidence be reviewed more carefully. Giving the appellate courts more latitude in their review of trial court decisions could help standardize the decision making about eyewitness experts and perhaps inform it with empirical research.

References

Benton, T., McDonnell, S., Thomas, N., Ross, D., & Honerkamp, N. (2006). On the admissibility of expert testimony on eyewitness identification: A legal and scientific evaluation. *Tennessee Journal of Law & Policy, 2,* 392–448.

Daubert v. Merrell Dow Pharmaceuticals, 509 U.S. 579, 113 S.Ct. 2795 (1993).

Duncan, K. L. (1996). "Lies, damned lies, and statistics"? Psychological syndrome evidence in the courtroom after *Daubert. Indiana Law Journal, 71,* 753–771.

Faigman, D. L. (1995a). The evidentiary status of social science under *Daubert:* Is it "scientific," "technical," or "other" knowledge? *Psychology, Public Policy, & Law, 1,* 960–979.

Faigman, D. L. (1995b). Mapping the labyrinth of scientific evidence. *Hastings Law Journal, 46,* 555–579.

Faigman, D. L. (1997). Appellate review of scientific evidence under *Daubert* and *Joiner. Hastings Law Journal, 48,* 969–979.

Faigman, D. L., Kaye, D.H., Saks, M. J., & Sanders, J. (1997). *Modern scientific evidence: The law and science of expert testimony* (Vol. *1, section* 1–3.4, 29–37, 1999 pocket part).

Faigman, D. L. & Wright, A. J. (1997). The battered woman syndrome in the age of science. *Arizona Law Review, 39,* 67–115.

Federal Rule of Evidence, 2000 Federal Rule of Evidence 702 & Advisory Committee Notes. (2000).

Fradella, H. (2003). A content analysis of federal judicial views of the social science "researcher's black arts." *Rutgers Law Journal, 35,* 103–169.

Fradella, H. (2006). Why judges should admit expert testimony on the unreliability of eyewitness testimony. *Federal Courts Law Review, 2006,* 3–29.

Fradella, H., Fogarty, A., & O'Neill, L. (2003). The impact of *Daubert* on the admissibility of behavioral science testimony. *Pepperdine Law Review, 30,* 403–444.

Frampton, J. (2007). Can a jury believe my eyes, and should courts let experts tell them why not: The admissibility of expert testimony on cross-racial identification in New York after *People v. Young. Pace Law Review, 27,* 433–465.

Frye v. United States, 293 F. 1013 (1923).

Gatowski, S. I., Dobbin, S. A., Richardson, J. T., Ginsburg, G. P., Merlino, M. L., & Dahir, V. (2001). Asking the gatekeepers: A national survey of judges on judging expert evidence in a post-*Daubert* world. *Law & Human Behavior, 25,* 433–458.

General Electric Co. v. Joiner, 522 U.S. 136, 118 S.Ct. 512 (1997).

Gibbons, J. (Hon.) (2003). Tenth anniversary of the Supreme Court's decision in Daubert v. *Merrell Dow Pharmaceuticals, Inc.: The respective roles of trial and appellate courts in Daubert-Kumho rulings. Seton Hall Law Review, 34,* 127–140.

Goodman-Delahunty, J. (1997). Forensic psychological expertise in the wake of *Daubert. Law & Human Behavior, 21,* 121-140.

Gottesman, M. H. (1998). From *Barefoot* to *Daubert* to *Joiner:* Triple play or double error? *Arizona Law Review, 40,* 753–780.

Groscup, J. (2002). *Legalized gambling, beekeeping, or science? Judicial decision making about expert testimony in the aftermath of Daubert and Kumho.* Unpublished dissertation.

Groscup, J. (2004). Judicial decision making in the aftermath of *Daubert* and *Kumho. Journal of Forensic Psychology Practice, 4,* 57–66.

Groscup, J., & Penrod, S. (2003). Experts in criminal cases: Police versus psychologists. *Seton Hall Law Review, 33,* 1141–1165.

Groscup, J, Penrod, S., Huss, M., Studebaker, C., & O'Neil, K. (2002). The effects of Daubert v. Merrell Dow Pharmaceuticals on the admissibility of expert testimony in state and federal criminal cases. *Psychology, Public Policy, & Law, 8,* 339–372.

Hand, L. (1901). Historical and practical considerations regarding expert testimony. *Harvard Law Review, 15,* 40.

Harvard Journal of Law and Public Policy (Note). (2006). Flexible standards, deferential review: *Daubert's* legacy of confusion. *Harvard Journal of Law and Public Policy, 29,* 1085–1105.

Jonakait, R. (1999). The standard of appellate review for scientific evidence: Beyond *Joiner* and *Scheffer. U.C. Davis Law Review, 32,* 289–340.

Kassin, S. M., & Barndollar, K. A. (1992). The psychology of eyewitness testimony: A comparison of experts and prospective jurors. *Journal of Applied Social Psychology, 22,* 1241–1249.

Kassin, S., Ellsworth, P., & Smith, V. (1989). The 'general acceptance' of psychological research on eyewitness testimony: A survey of the experts. *American Psychologist, 44.* Page numbers

Kassin, S., Tubb, V., Hosch, H., & Memon, A. (2001). On the 'general acceptance' of eyewitness testimony research. *American Psychologist, 56,* 405–416.

Kumho Tire Co. v. Carmichael, 119 S.Ct. 1167 (1999).

Kovera, M. B., & McAuliff, B. D. (2000). The effects of peer review and evidence quality on judge evaluations of psychological science: Are judges effective gatekeepers? *Journal of Applied Psychology, 85,* 574–586.

Lehman, D. R., Lempert, R. O., & Nisbett, R. E. (1988). The effects of graduate training on reasoning: Formal discipline and thinking about everyday-life events. *American Psychologist, 43,* 431–42.

Manuto, R., & O'Rourke, S. P. (1991). Federal judges' perceptions of social research in judicial decision making. *Communications Reports, 4,* 103–106.

Marlin, R.D. (1998). Scientific evidence: Standard of review raises questions of fit. *General Electric Co.* v. *Joiner,* 118 S.Ct. 512 (1997). UALR Law Review, *21,* 133-149.

Morse, A. (1998). Social science in the courtroom: Expert testimony and battered women. *Hamline Law Journal, 21,* 287-321.

Mueller, C.B., & Kirkpatrick, L.C. (1999). *Federal Rules of Evidence, with Advisory Committee Notes, Legislative History, and Cases* (1999 ed.). Gaithersburg, NY: Aspen Law & Business.

Renaker, T. S. (1996). Evidentiary legerdemain: Deciding when *Daubert* should apply to social science evidence. *California Law Review, 84,* 1657–1693.

Richardson, J., Ginsburg, G., Gatowski, S., & Dobbin, S. (1995). The problems of applying *Daubert* to psychological syndrome evidence. *Judicature, 79,* 10–16.

Risinger, D. M. (2000). Navigating expert reliability: Are criminal standards of certainty being left on the dock? *Albany Law Review, 64,* 99–152.

Savage, D.G. (May, 1999). Putting the brakes on junk analysis; A tire case pumps up judicial power over opinion testimony. *ABA Journal, 85,* 38-39.

Shuman, D.W., & Sales, B.D. (1999). The impact of *Daubert* and its progeny on the admissibility of behavioral and social science evidence. *Psychology, Public Policy, & Law, 5,* 3-15.

Slobogin, C. (1998). Psychiatric evidence in criminal trials: To junk or not to junk? *William & Mary Law Review, 40,* 1-56.

Sparks, J. (1995). Admissibility of expert psychological evidence in federal courts. *Arizona State Law Journal, 27,* 1315–1333.

United States v. Downing, 753 F.2d 1224 (3rd Cir., 1985).

Woller, S. (2003). Rethinking the role of expert testimony regarding the reliability of eyewitness identification in New York. *New York Law School Law Review, 48,* 323–352.

Notes

1. This section describes research conducted on courts' decision making about eyewitness experts. A thorough analysis of the courts' legal treatment of eyewitness experts on a case-by-case basis is presented by Epstein in Chapter 4.

2. Because federal courts are bound by the *Daubert* decision, the actual date of the Court's decision was used to divide the federal cases in the sample into cases decided "before" or "after" *Daubert.* State courts were not required to adopt the *Daubert* decision as their standard for the admissibility of expert testimony. Some state courts chose to adopt *Daubert,* while others kept *Frye* as their standard or developed their own standard (see Epstein, Chapter 4, for a list of states using each standard). Those states that did adopt *Daubert* did so at different times (Faigman, Kaye, Saks, & Sanders, 1997). To distinguish between cases decided before and after *Daubert* among the state cases in the sample, the date that each state adopted *Daubert* was used. If a state did not adopt *Daubert,* all cases from that state were considered to be "before" *Daubert.*

3. We used a chi-square (X^2) to conduct tests of whether there were statistically significant patterns of relationship between variables that were recorded as frequencies or as categories. When these relationships are significant, the chi-square (X^2) is reported in the text. The error rate (p) is also reported, which must be below the traditional cutoff of .05 to be considered significant. Cramer's Phi (V) is also reported, which indicates the strength of the relationship between the variables in the analysis (the relationship is considered stronger as these values get further away from zero and closer to 1). For these analyses, description of the pattern of relationship is given in terms of percentages and frequencies (n). We used t-tests (t) to compare two means, and ANOVA (F) to compare means across multiple categories. These tests are reported when the means were significantly different from each other, and the p-values are reported. For analyses of mean differences, means and standard deviations (SD) are provided.

6

Expert Psychology Testimony on Eyewitness Identification: A Matter of Common Sense?

J. Don Read and Sarah L. Desmarais

When attorneys proffer expert opinion on the topic of eyewitness testimony at trial, the judge decides on the basis of several legal criteria whether the expert will be heard. One of these criteria is the judge's assessment of lay or juror knowledge about eyewitness testimony. If the eyewitness factors to be discussed by an expert (for either side) are deemed to be relevant to the case and are also deemed to be outside the jurors' ken, experience, or common sense, expert testimony intended to inform the trier of fact may be judged admissible. In the United States, for example, Federal Rule of Evidence 702 assigns to judges the task of determining whether an expert's testimony will assist the trier of fact to understand or determine a fact in issue. In Canada, the *Mohan* decision (*R. v. Mohan*, 1994) provides the criteria by which a judge may render a decision on the same issue. As a result, based upon her own knowledge and evaluation of the specific testimony offered by an expert, the judge decides whether members of the jury are, as a group, sufficiently informed and, if they are not, that the quality and reliability of their deliberations will benefit from presentation of information about the relevant eyewitness factors.

Although the focus here is on the judges' perceptions of juror knowledge, it follows that in judge-alone trials, judges must evaluate their own knowledge of the domain for which expert testimony is offered and determine whether their own fact finding would be informed by its admission. Given the adversarial nature of common law procedures, it is possible that opposing counsel may also wish to proffer another expert who may have a different interpretation of the relevant eyewitness factors. Benton, McDonnell, Ross, Thomas, and Bradshaw (2007), Schmechel, O'Toole, Easterly, and Loftus (2006), Epstein (2007, Chapter 4), and Groscup and Penrod (Chapter 5) have thoroughly reviewed the legal issues raised by expert testimony on the topic of eyewitness memory.

Judges regularly rule that many components of proffered expert opinion on eyewitness testimony are common sense and known to jurors (see Benton et al., 2007; Epstein, 2007, Chapter 4 of this volume; Hosch, Jolly, Schmersal, & Smith, Chapter 7; Leippe, 1995; Leippe & Eisenstadt, Chapter 8; Schmechel et al., 2006; Stuesser, 2005; Yarmey, 2001). However, regardless of the decisions made by judges in these situations, no data can tell us whether their assessments of jurors' knowledge about eyewitness factors have, in fact, been correct. Their decisions would have a stronger foundation if based upon an empirical description of juror knowledge rather than upon their own idiosyncratic estimates of such knowledge (cf. Kassin & Barndollar, 1992; Schmechel et al., 2006). Many scientific investigations of lay knowledge or public beliefs about eyewitness factors have been completed and, on occasion, judges' assessments are perhaps informed by these lines of research, although there is little empirical evidence in support of this speculation (cf. Schmechel et al., 2006; Wise, Pawlenko, Meyer, & Safer, 2007; Lane, Groft, Roussel, & Alonzo, 2007; Lane, Groft, & Alonzo, 2008). Further, although a topic of research interest in its own right, limited data assess whether judges themselves have correct knowledge of eyewitness issues (but see Benton, Ross, Bradshaw, Thomas, & Bradshaw, 2006; Benton et al., 2007; Hosch et al., Chapter 7; Lane et al., 2007, 2008; Schmechel et al., 2006; Wise & Safer, 2004; Wise et al., 2007). In this chapter, we do not describe this research nor that on knowledge of eyewitness issues held by other players in the criminal justice system, such as attorneys and police (but for Canada, the United States, and Sweden see Benton et al., 2006; Devenport, Cutler, & Penrod, 1997; Devenport, Kimbrough, & Cutler, Chapter 3; Granhag, Strömwall, & Hartwig, 2005; Hosch et al., Chapter 7; Lane et al., 2008; R. C. L. Lindsay, MacDonald & McGarry, 1990; Schmechel et al., 2006; Wise et al., 2007; Wise & Safer, 2004).

This chapter reviews the methods and outcomes of survey research strategies that have been used to provide information about lay knowledge to the judiciary. Briefly, the field of eyewitness memory research examines the myriad factors that *may* influence witnesses' recollections of an event, the people present, their behaviors, and the context in which the event occurred (for recent and extensive reviews of these factors, see Toglia, Read, Ross, &. Lindsay, 2007; R. C. L. Lindsay, Ross, Read, & Toglia, 2007). The lion's share of the research described in these reviews involves research participants who served as witnesses to mock (staged or videotape), rather than spontaneous or naturally occurring events; however, considerable data has also been gathered from field studies as well as archival analyses of real-world criminal cases.

A number of schemes have been proposed for categorizing the various eyewitness factors (Turtle, Read, Lindsay, & Brimacombe, 2008; Wells &

Loftus, 2003). Most frequently, the distinction made is that offered by Wells (1978) between those factors that are under the control of the criminal justice system (i.e., *system variables*) and, as a result, may be manipulated to improve the reliability of eyewitness evidence (such as the suspect identification procedures used and instructions given to the eyewitness) and those for which their impact on the reliability of testimony may only be estimated (i.e., *estimator variables*) and that are not under the control of the justice system. This second group is large and includes variables that have often been shown to be related to eyewitness memory performance in laboratory and real-world contexts, such as the age of the witness, lighting at the crime scene, levels of anxiety or confidence held by eyewitnesses, presence of a weapon, and witness suggestibility. Research has demonstrated that although these factors can have effects on memory in general they are variable and unpredictable in regard to specific individuals (Flowe, Ebbesen, & Finklea, Chapter 9; Malpass, Meissner, Ross, & Marcon, Chapter 1).

A recent groundswell of interest has occurred in assessing what jurors understand about eyewitness topics (e.g., Alonzo & Lane, 2006; Benton et al., 2006; Desmarais & Read, 2008; Devenport & Cutler, 2008; Hope, Memon, Houston, & Read, 2008; Lane et al., 2007, 2008; Martire & Kemp, 2007; McAuliff & Kovera, 2007; Mitchell & Haw, 2008; J. D. Read & Desmarais, 2009; Schmechel et al., 2006; Simon, Strenstom, & Read, 2008). Most surveys concerning eyewitness issues have reported that student and community samples in North America, the United Kingdom, and Australia demonstrate infrequent agreement with the opinions of experts and the outcomes of empirical research (e.g., Benton et al., 2006; Deffenbacher & Loftus, 1982; Kassin & Barndollar, 1992; Schmechel et al., 2006; Yarmey & Jones, 1983) and therefore suggest that juror knowledge on many eyewitness issues is an inadequate basis for understanding the facts of a case. Accordingly, many researchers and legal scholars (e.g., Benton et al., 2006; Benton et al., 2007; Cutler & Penrod, 1995; Epstein, Chapter 4; Leippe, 1995; Leippe & Eisenstadt, Chapter 8; Schmechel et al., 2006) have argued that expert testimony on eyewitness factors should not be ruled inadmissible as a matter of course. We first discuss the history and variety of the research procedures.

Expert Knowledge and Belief of Eyewitness Phenomena

To assess the accuracy and depth of understanding of lay knowledge, an appropriate or "gold" standard must exist against which it can be compared. What is needed for trial counsel and the judiciary is a distillation of eyewitness research that provides the "correct" answers about the effects of eyewitness factors thought to be relevant to a specific case. These answers have been determined in two ways. In one, researchers surveyed the "eyewitness experts" to determine what they believe are the purported effects of variables upon eyewitness reliability. On the basis of these data, courts may then determine what is an acceptable level of agreement or "general acceptance" among experts allowing for admissible opinion evidence, according to appropriate legal standards (that may place differential emphasis upon the demonstration of such general acceptance; see Epstein, Chapter 4; Hosch et al., Chapter 7) such as *Frye* (*Frye v. United States*, 1923) or *Daubert* (*Daubert v. Merrell Dow Pharmaceuticals, Inc.*, 1993) in the United States and *Mohan* in Canada. Two surveys of experts have provided the criteria for these decisions.

First, Kassin, Ellsworth, and Smith (1989) constructed statements that described the direction of the relationship between 21 eyewitness variables and memory performance. Five assessments of each proposition or "phenomenon" were provided by 63 eyewitness experts, but we restrict our discussions here to the first two: (a) the extent to which the proposition was supported by research evidence on a 7-point Likert scale and (b) whether the proposition met (Yes/No) the expert's standard of reliability for its presentation in court. For nine items, Kassin and associates (1989) suggested that a criterion for the experts' "general acceptance" of a proposition was met if at least 70% of experts in the sample agreed that the phenomenon was sufficiently reliable to be presented in court. More recently, to update the survey and reflect the explosion over the intervening decade of research investigations into the original and new eyewitness factors, Kassin, Tubb, Hosch, and Memon (2001) reported a second investigation with data from another sample of 64 experts. This survey included 17 of the earlier and 13 new items and followed the same format. However, the criterion offered as a measure of general acceptance among experts was increased from 70% to 80%. This level of consensus was achieved on 16 of 30 propositions that were judged to be sufficiently reliable for court presentation. For example, whereas 90% agreed that there is a detrimental effect of cross-race perpetrators on the identification reliability of eyewitnesses, only 60% agreed that stress has a detrimental effect on memory. To date, no eyewitness factor has received complete unanimity from the experts as to its impact on eyewitness testimony. Indeed, among experts there often can be considerable disagreement as to a variable's effect upon testimony (cf. Hosch et al., Chapter 7; Bailey & Mecklenburg, Chapter 10).

In the second method of conveying to the judiciary what is "correct," survey researchers have explicitly provided their own interpretations of what the scientific literature has revealed about eyewitness factors (e.g., Deffenbacher & Loftus, 1982; McAuliff & Kovera, 2007; Schmechel et al., 2006; Seltzer, Lopes, & Venuti, 1990; Yarmey & Jones, 1983). The goals of these studies were twofold because they also examined correspondences between their beliefs and those of laypersons. In these surveys, the number of eyewitness factors examined has been smaller than in the two Kassin-led expert surveys described earlier, but they have sometimes achieved greater depth of analysis. These investigations reveal researchers' differing views of the effects of eyewitness variables, and they sometimes reflect positions contrary to the consensual views of experts described in the Kassin surveys. For example, whereas Schmechel and colleagues (2006) summarized the research literature as providing strong support for the proposition that event violence reduces recall by eyewitnesses, only 37% of experts in the Kassin and associates' (2001) survey agreed with this proposition, a percentage not far removed from the 30% of the laypersons in Schmechel and colleagues' survey who agreed with the statement. Of course, continuing research often alters our understanding, and the Schmechel study characterization of event violence may have reflected the publication of research not available to the experts surveyed by Kassin and associates in 2001.

It is striking that, compared to the 23 surveys of laypersons to be described later, really only two surveys of experts are available to us, both by Kassin and associates, both now somewhat dated (1989 and 2001), and both based upon fairly small sample sizes ($N = 63$ and 64, respectively). Presentation of the results from these samples begs the question as to whether they provide accurate reflections of the views of the larger population of researchers and practitioners, some of whom no doubt will have strikingly different, albeit perhaps minority positions on eyewitness factors. Thus, the question of exactly whose expert opinion should be heard is one with which courts regularly grapple and highlights the importance of making current summaries of expert opinion available to the triers of fact. Chapters by Flowe and colleagues and Hosch and colleagues both address these issues in detail elsewhere in this volume.

Research Approaches to Assessing Lay Beliefs

To assess public beliefs on the other hand, researchers have used both *direct* and *indirect* methods. Direct methods emphasize a survey approach in which respondents answer questions about the general effects of eyewitness variables, whereas indirect methods examine the ways in which lay participants make use of their knowledge about eyewitness factors in order to estimate, for example, the probability that an eyewitness would make an accurate memory report or identification decision. To demonstrate, one factor considered relevant to the reliability of eyewitness identification is the correspondence between the race of the witness and that of the suspect. When both are members of the same racial group, identification reliability has often been found to be higher than when the two people belong to different racial groups, an outcome often called the *cross-race effect*. Using a direct approach to the assessment of lay knowledge, respondents might be presented with a statement such as "People are better at recognizing members of their own racial group than those of a different race" and then asked whether they believe the statement is true or false. Alternatively, they may be asked to choose one of several answers to the question "When people are asked to identify someone of a racial group different from their own, they are (a) *just as likely*, (b) *more likely*, (c) *less likely*, (d) *don't know* to be correct as when the person is of their own racial group."

On the other hand, if an indirect approach is used, respondents may receive a brief written vignette in which the races of the witness and perpetrator are either not mentioned at all (a control condition), are described as being the same, or as different. Their use of this information is assessed by the nature and frequency of their judgments about the case; for example, predictions of the effects of specific variables on person identification, the credibility of the eyewitness evidence, and/or the ability to render a verdict. Differences in these assessments from participants who received the different vignettes are taken to reflect the public's beliefs about or sensitivity to the direction and magnitude of the relationship between race and eyewitness memory (see also Devenport et al. and Leippe & Eisenstadt, Chapter 8). The examination of mock jurors' usage of expert testimony evidence (offered by prosecution, defense, or court-appointed experts) concerning the general or specific factors relevant to a written or videotaped trial is an even less direct approach to the assessment of juror knowledge. Depending upon the mock jurors' subsequent decisions regarding the verdict and the credibility of witnesses, inferences may be drawn about both the jurors' pre-trial beliefs about relevant eyewitness factors and the effectiveness of expert testimony on the topic. However, because Leippe and Eisenstadt have thoroughly reviewed and examined these studies in this volume, they will not be discussed in detail here.

Research Review

Benton and colleagues (2007) and Schmechel and colleagues (2006) have provided thorough reviews of the research on lay beliefs about the effects of eyewitness factors prior to 2000; accordingly, our summary will primarily focus upon research completed since that time. Nonetheless, we provide here a tabular summary of the extent to which all samples ($N = 23$) of research participants gathered from 1982 to the present agreed with the experts about a number of system and estimator variables for which a sample of experts had, among themselves, achieved substantial agreement (see Tables 6.1 and 6.2, respectively). Beginning with the earliest survey studies in the 1980s, generally comparable results have been obtained and similar conclusions drawn. For example, using a direct method, Deffenbacher and Loftus (1982) administered to university students the Knowledge of Eyewitness Behavior Questionnaire (KEBQ), a 14-item, four-alternative, multiple-choice questionnaire. Most participants did *not* give the correct answer (as determined by the authors) to many of the items (e.g., often within the range of chance responding), including the effects of violence on recall accuracy, of training or experience on identification performance, the relationship between witness accuracy and confidence, and the cross-race effect. The KEBQ was also administered to students and community respondents in the United Kingdom (Noon & Hollin, 1987) and Australia (McConkey & Roche, 1989) with similar results. In 1983, Yarmey and Jones surveyed primarily Canadian legal

Table 6.1 Summary of Percent Correct Agreement for System Variables Across Surveys of Lay Knowledge

Surveys of Lay Knowledge	Sample Type	n	Survey Format	Confidence Malleability	Lineup Instructions	Mugshot-Induced Bias	Presentation Format	Question Wording
Australia								
McConkey & Roche (1987) Sample 1	U	124	MC	–	–	49; 68	–	90
McConkey & Roche (1987) Sample 2	U	47	MC	–	–	70; 70	–	96
Canada								
Desmarais & Read (2009) Sample 1	U	270	MC	89'	95	71	–	94'
Desmarais & Read (2009) Sample 2	C	449	MC	77'	72	50	–	91'
Read & Desmarais (2009) Survey 1	C	201	AG	79	76	85	56	90
Read & Desmarais (2009) Survey 2	C	200	AG	87	84	94	55	93
Read & Desmarais (2009) Survey 3	C	598	AG	83	84	–	–	94
Yarmey & Jones (1983)	U	60	MC	–	–	43	–	80
Yarmey & Jones (1983)	C	60	MC	–	–	45	–	55
United Kingdom								
Hope et al. (in prep)	C	197	MC	–	–	63	–	66
Noon & Hollin (1989) Sample 1	U	28	MC	–	–	61; 68	–	92
Noon & Hollin (1989) Sample 2	C	24	MC	–	–	42; 67	–	71

(*Continued*)

Table 6.1 (Cont'd)

Surveys of Lay Knowledge	Sample Type	n	Survey Format	Confidence Malleability	Lineup Instructions	Mugshot-Induced Bias	Presentation Format	Question Wording
United States								
Benton et al. (2006)	C	111	AG	50	41	59	31	85
Deffenbacher & Loftus (1982) Sample 1	U	76	MC	–	–	**60; 71**	–	89
Deffenbacher & Loftus (1982) Sample 2	U	100	MC	–	–	52; 54	–	83
Deffenbacher & Loftus (1982) Sample 3	C	46	MC	–	–	54	–	–
Devenport & Cutler (2008)	U	222	MC	51	77	**74**	–	95
Kassin & Barndollar (1992)	C; U	79	AG	–	**68**	–	–	**90**
Lane et al. (2008)	U	52	MC	50	31	63	40	72
Loftus (1979)	U	500	MC	–	–	–	–	**90**
Rahaim & Brodsky (1982)	C	28	AG; MC	–	–	–	–	–
Schmechel et al. (2006)	C	1007	AG	**85; 86**	–	–	–	–
Seltzer et al. (1990)	C	190	MC	–	–	–	–	–
Unweighted Means				*74*	*70*	*62*	*46*	*85*
Weighted Means				*81*	*75*	*65*	*49*	*87*

C, community; U, university students; MC, multiple-choice; AG, Agree–Disagree (or some similar variation). Percentages in bold reflect consensus of 60% agreement or greater. The authors considered two options to be consistent with the Kassin et al. (2001) item—item not included in survey. Law student samples were excluded.

professionals, potential jurors, and eyewitness experts with a similar 16-item multiple-choice questionnaire. These authors also found that more than half of lay and legal professional participants did not identify the known relationships between eyewitness accuracy and variables including confidence, event violence, event duration estimates, trained observers, older witnesses, verbal descriptions, and child suggestibility. With only five KEBQ questions, on the other hand, Seltzer and colleagues (1990) surveyed actual jurors from Washington, D.C. Overall, they found that less than half of participants agreed with the correct responses.

In the early 1990s, following the first survey of experts just mentioned (Kassin et al. 1989), some researchers presented the experts' items to laypersons for evaluation as to their truth. In no study using the expert items have survey participants been presented with response options identical to those provided to experts. Instead, studies have used primarily dichotomous options as to the truth or falsity of a statement or the extent to which participants agreed with it. Thus, Kassin and Barndollar (1992) found that almost one-half of their small college and community respondent sample ($N = 79$) disagreed with statements judged to be accurate by experts when asked whether each statement was "generally true" or "generally false." If one accepts Kassin and Barndollar's premise (see later discussion) that these juror judgments may be likened to the experts' "Yes/No" judgments of whether the statement's proposition has sufficient reliability to be presented in court, then lay responses were similar to those of experts on six of the items, but differed significantly on 13. Specifically, they agreed with experts in regard to the eyewitness factors of attitudes and expectations, wording of questions, weapon focus, event violence, and estimates of the duration of events but differed with experts on, for example, lineup construction techniques, exposure time, confidence, cross-race effect, trained observers, and hypnotic suggestibility. Throughout this chapter, we make use of the shorthand descriptions provided by Kassin and associates (2001) to refer to 30 specific eyewitness factors.

More recently, Benton and colleagues (2006) provided 111 potential jurors in Tennessee with the 30 statements evaluated by Kassin and associates' second sample of experts. As in Kassin and Barndollar, respondents were asked whether each statement was "generally true" or "generally false." All statements, save one, were presented in their original format from the survey of Kassin and associates (2001). The single altered item was that of "presentation format," an item that assesses whether respondents understand the conceptual distinctions between relative and absolute judgment and between simultaneous and sequential lineup presentations. In any case, Benton and colleagues' potential jurors responded significantly differently on 26 of 30 items, with magnitudes of disagreements ranging from 11% to 67%. There were no significant differences on items pertaining to child suggestibility, alcoholic intoxication, wording of questions, and attitudes and expectations. Kassin and Barndollar had found a similar lack of difference on the latter two items in 1992. Surprisingly, however, Benton and colleagues' participants

Table 6.2 Summary of Percent Correct Agreement for Estimator Variables Across Surveys of Lay Knowledge

Surveys of Lay Knowledge	Sample Type	n	Survey Format	Accuracy & Confidence	Alcohol Intoxication	Attitudes & Expectations	Child Suggestibility	Cross-Race Bias	Exposure Time	Forgetting Curve	Hypnotic Suggestibility	Post Event Info	Unconscious Transference	Weapon Focus
Australia														
McConkey & Roche (1987) Sample 1	U	124	MC	15	–	–	–	56; 38	–	–	–	–	–	32
McConkey & Roche (1987) Sample 2	U	47	MC	68	–	–	–	79; 62	–	–	–	–	–	68
Canada														
Desmarais & Read (2009) Sample 1	U	270	MC	78	96	98'	75	81	55	68'	59	84	44'	71
Desmarais & Read (2009) Sample 2	C	449	MC	49	93	83'	63	58	64	65'	45	59	61'	44
Read & Desmarais (2009) Survey 1	C	201	AG	67	84	88	82	69	68	55	59	81	74	63
Read & Desmarais (2009) Survey 2	C	200	AG	51	91	84	81	75	71	71	58	86	69	62
Read & Desmarais (2009) Survey 3	C	598	AG	87	91	90	89	69	80	46	55	88	90	74
Yarmey & Jones (1983)	U	60	MC	37	–	–	–	48	–	–	–	–	–	52
Yarmey & Jones (1983)	C	60	MC	33	–	–	–	43	–	–	–	–	–	63

		N		1	2	3	4	5	6	7	8	9	10	11
United Kingdom														
Hope et al. (in prep)	C	197	MC	32	**92**	–	**64**	59	**68**	–	–	**60**	**77**	47
Noon & Hollin (1989) Sample 1	U	28	MC	18	–	–	–	**79**; 21	–	–	–	–	–	39
Noon & Hollin (1989) Sample 2	C	24	MC	17	–	–	–	**67**; 21	–	–	–	–	–	**63**
United States														
Benton et al. (2006)	C	111	AG	38	**96**	**81**	**82**	47	47	33	24	**60**	30	39
Deffenbacher & Loftus (1982) Sample 1	U	76	MC	33	–	–	–	54; 22	–	–	–	–	–	51
Deffenbacher & Loftus (1982) Sample 2	U	100	MC	24	–	–	–	57; 19	–	–	–	–	–	45
Deffenbacher & Loftus (1982) Sample 3	C	46	MC	–	–	–	–	20	–	–	–	–	–	–
Devenport & Cutler (2008)	U	222	MC	**69**	**97**	**95**	**70**	**66**	**75**	**85**	**60**	**73**	**71**	**65**
Kassin & Barndollar (1992)	C; U	79	AG	49	–	**89**	–	58; 22	37	41	46	**75**	**65**	**60**
Lane et al. (2008)	U	52	MC	29	**75**	59	**76**	43	45	–	–	57	43	33
Loftus (1979)	U	500	MC	–	–	–	–	55	–	–	–	–	–	39
Rahaim & Brodsky (1982)	C	28	AG; MC	24	–	–	–	24	–	–	–	–	–	–
Schmechel et al. (2006)	C	1007	AG	55	–	–	–	**66**	–	–	–	–	**73**	–
Seltzer et al. (1990)	C	190	MC	36	–	–	–	33	–	–	–	–	–	–
Unweighted Means				43	**91**	**85**	**76**	50	**61**	**58**	**51**	**72**	**63**	53
Weighted Means				51	**92**	**88**	**75**	57	**65**	**61**	**53**	**74**	**69**	52

C, community; U, university students; MC, multiple-choice; AG, Agree–Disagree (or some similar variation). Percentages in bold reflect consensus of 60% agreement or greater. The authors considered two options to be consistent with the Kassin et al. (2001) item—item not included in survey. Law student samples were excluded.

responded at substantially lower levels of accuracy than did Kassin and Barndollar's respondents some 14 years earlier. Because discussions of many memory-related concepts such as wrongful convictions and lineup misidentifications, long-term repression, trauma, sexual abuse, and childhood memories have inundated the media over the last decade (cf. Desmarais, Price, & Read, 2008), we might have anticipated improved performance over time (cf. Flowe et al., Chapter 9).

Schmechel and colleagues (2006) contacted 1007 potential jurors in Washington, D.C. and used varied and contextualized approaches to examine "10 specific reliability factors" derived from Kassin and associates' and other studies. For three of the 10 topics surveyed, statement format and content overlapped fairly closely with those of the Kassin study, but seven did not. In addition to the specific reliability factors examined, Schmechel and colleagues also assessed lay understanding of memory in general by asking for judgments about a number of statements concerning general memory processes and eyewitness reliability. For example, one item asked whether remembering a traumatic event reflects a videorecorder type of operation in which details are recalled as if they had been burned into one's brain. Because over half (52%) either thought this statement true or could not judge its truth, the authors argued that the respondents' answers reflected a general deficiency in their understanding of basic memory processes.[1] Their ambivalence on this and other general memory items, however, contrasts with their generally good performance on six other true–false items related to confidence malleability, unreliability of person identification, and the effects of post-event information. On several specific items related to identification procedures or system variables (e.g., lineup instructions, blind testing, presentation format), the respondents fared much less well and, like Benton's participants, performed poorly compared to the author-determined correct answers (cf. Devenport et al., Chapter 3). Like Benton and colleagues, the authors argued that their results support the view that potential jurors often differ significantly from experts in their opinions about and understanding of the issues, very frequently on those topics for which experts have demonstrated consensus.

Recently, we (J. D. Read & Desmarais, 2009) reported assessments of 29 of the 30 Kassin and associates (2001) expert statements by members of three large Canadian jury-eligible community samples ($N = 999$). In the first survey, and in a manner identical to that of Benton and colleagues (2006), 201 participants received the Kassin items on 29 topics. Lay performance was substantially higher than previously reported and, when scored for accuracy as per Benton (i.e., focusing only on expert consensus items), they received an average score of 67% (whereas the Benton study participants scored an average of 51% on the same items). Two subsequent surveys administered in the same geographical area incorporated wording changes and background contextual information intended to improve the potential jurors' comprehension of the statements themselves (i.e., through the reduction of jargon and specific terms used by experts). Taken together, the participants' responses to items across surveys formats demonstrated considerable consistency and, as a result of the wording changes made in Surveys 2 and 3, accuracy significantly improved from 67% to 71%. Thus, in contrast to earlier work, the respondents often answered survey items in ways that approximated the responses of experts and suggested substantial understanding of these topics, particularly those on which experts themselves had reached consensus. On the other hand, and as has been demonstrated in all prior surveys, substantial differences in knowledge and familiarity between experts and laypersons were readily apparent for 50% of the eyewitness topics.

Summary of Direct Method Research Studies

Tables 6.1 and 6.2 present the percentages of lay respondents in surveys from 1982 forward who "agreed" with the truth of propositions that were similar or identical to the Kassin and associates' expert survey statements. Bold print designates sample responses that met or exceeded a 60% level of agreement with the Kassin experts on the courtroom reliability question. In several studies, variations in the wordings of the statements concerning cross-race identification reliability were received by different respondents; for these samples, both values are presented. Because most samples neither received the exact Kassin study statements nor the specific response options provided by experts, we have taken some license to reflect in a general way whether lay respondents agreed with a statement or proposition concerning one of the Kassin study topics. For example, whereas seven samples received some variant of true–false, agree–disagree questions, the remaining 16 used a multiple-choice format providing options concerning the direction of a relationship and that occasionally allowed for more than one "correct" response.[2] Questionnaires varied in length and format from one researcher to another. The tables summarize the results for *only* the 16 propositions on which the Kassin (2001) experts had agreed among themselves at the level of an 80% consensus as to their having adequate reliability to be presented in court. We restrict this table to these factors because without an 80% level of agreement between experts, courts may (although unknown, to be sure, and related to the court's use of a *Frye* or *Daubert* standard; see Groscup & Penrod, Chapter 5) be unlikely to admit expert testimony on the topics and, if not admitted, the survey results gathered from lay respondents would not likely be heard either. Tables 6.1 and 6.2 provide a picture of the central tendencies, variability, and ranges of lay response distributions to the 16 eyewitness factors presented in different formats across populations, jurisdictions, and time. Average performances on items were calculated with respect to both samples (unweighted means) and respondents (weighted means).

As may be seen, researchers generally assessed only a handful of the eyewitness factors. In fact, only one topic (cross-race bias) was assessed in all 23 surveys. Three other topics were assessed in 75% of the samples (i.e., mugshot-induced bias, question wording, and accuracy–confidence). The modal value of the number of assessments made of any topic was nine.

Although it was rare for the same format to be used across studies, Tables 6.1 and 6.2 do include four recently completed but as-yet-unpublished studies (in Canada, the United States, and the United Kingdom) that employed the identical multiple-choice response items from Desmarais and J. D. Read (2008; Samples 1 and 2). Of the four studies, three assessed lay knowledge of 14 of the 16 consensus factors, whereas the fourth (Hope et al., 2008) examined only eight factors but also did so in depth from the perspective of response format (i.e., compared multiple-choice and response generation). Overall, from Desmarais and J. D. Read's Sample 1 of university students ($n = 270$), and Sample 2 of community volunteers ($n = 449$), Devenport and Cutler's sample of university students ($N = 222$), and Hope and associates' sample of community respondents ($N = 197$), mean accuracy scores ranged from 65% to 87% on the four system and from 55% to 95% on the ten estimator variables examined. Generally, as may be seen, consistency characterized the results across these items and diverse samples, but for a few items, substantial variability was evident. Specifically, for the confidence malleability item, sample proportions correct ranged from 51% to 87% ($M = 72\%$), and for accuracy–confidence ($M = 57\%$), from 32% to 78%. Because the item wordings remained constant across these samples, the observed variability appears to reflect the specific populations sampled, but certainly not in an obvious way. For example, we might anticipate that university students would better understand the nature of many eyewitness factors than would members of community samples. Generally, this was true, but not in every case (cf. confidence malleability).

Across all item types and samples, Tables 6.1 and 6.2 often demonstrate consistencies in responding and, in our opinion, the data often reflect good agreement with the experts. For example, on "attitudes and expectations," the nine relevant samples averaged 92% agreement with the experts. However, it is also very clear that inconsistent levels of agreement between samples can and do occur when similar (university or community) samples are assessed with identical survey formats at approximately the same points in time; for example, strikingly different outcomes on estimator variables were achieved by Benton and colleagues (2006) and J. D. Read and Desmarais (2009). In our opinion, recognition of the variability across surveys is useful because it is likely to stimulate further research to determine whether these differences arise from variations in question wordings, questionnaire formats (e.g., written vs. telephone), jurisdictions and sample demographics, or some combination of the above.

Summary of Direct Method Data

Determining the necessity of expert testimony on these eyewitness factors at court would first require a determination of the level of accuracy that denotes adequate familiarity with a topic; that is, whether it is within the ken of jurors' understanding. As noted earlier, no information has been collected as to a numerical judicial standard employed in decisions of admissibility of expert opinion evidence (cf. Kassin et al., 1989; Kassin & Barndollar, 1992; Schmechel et al., 2006). For experts, however, the criterion for "general acceptance" or consensus among experts has varied from 70% to 80% (Kassin et al., 1989; Kassin et al., 2001, respectively) and arguments for the admission of expert testimony based on these levels of agreement appear to have been successful on some occasions (e.g., cases described by Epstein, Chapter 4, or Groscup & Penrod, Chapter 5). Clearly, it is an empirical question as to whether courts using either the *Frye* or *Daubert* standard would agree that such levels of agreement are required.

Perhaps more important for the present discussion is whether courts would consider similar or lesser pluralities among laypersons to be similarly sufficient criteria by which to rule expert evidence admissible or inadmissible. This is also an empirical question. Benton and colleagues (2006) reported that a difference as small as 11% in agreement rates (e.g., 92% vs. 81% for experts and laypersons on the topic of attitudes and expectations) signaled significant disagreement between experts and jurors. In our opinion, a statistically significant difference alone seems an insensitive or inappropriate criterion and likely would not be convincing to judges faced with a decision on admissibility. On the other hand, if courts heard that a plurality or majority of jurors hold the deemed correct opinion, would such opinion be considered an adequate safeguard against overbelief of eyewitness evidence?

Benton and colleagues (2007), Groscup and Penrod (Chapter 5), and Hosch and colleagues (Chapter 7) summarized reasons given by a number of U.S. courts for denying admissibility of expert testimony on eyewitness factors. One interpretation of their synopses and the rationales provided by the judges themselves (e.g., Benton et al., 2007, pp. 476–477) is that judges have applied the proffered expert testimony to jurors whose life experiences are "common" or "ordinary" and whose knowledge and understanding is "average." In other words, it would be surprising if judges required experiences beyond "ordinary" and "common" to render expert evidence inadmissible. Life experiences that are common or ordinary are those that are prevalent and shared by many. But what levels of knowledge and understanding are held by the "average juror"? On one hand, it may be that jurors, taken together, could demonstrate average knowledge and understanding (relative to the experts); or, on the other hand, "average" could refer to a level of knowledge that is anticipated of every juror. As noted, no data specify which criterion would satisfy the meaning of these terms, but it seems reasonable that a judge would rule an eyewitness factor to be within the jurors' understanding if some plurality of the relevant jury pool was demonstrated to be familiar with its correct interpretation. This kind of information may be accessible in those cases in which a voir dire was used to assess the jurors' knowledge about eyewitness factors prior to a determination of the necessity of expert evidence. Unfortunately, this appears to have been done infrequently (e.g., Benton et al.,

2007; *State v. Nordlund*, 2002; Devenport et al., Chapter 3). In Tables 6.1 and 6.2, we arbitrarily set the criterion of plurality at 60% simply to highlight the frequency of samples that achieved at least this level of agreement with the experts.

Determining "Average" Knowledge: What Data Provide for Appropriate Comparisons of Experts and Laypersons?

Kassin and associates' experts answered two questions about the reliability of each statement: First, whether research evidence supported or did not support the assertion made in each statement, and second, whether each "phenomenon" (the empirical claim made in each statement) was sufficiently reliable to be presented in court. Because survey researchers have judged evaluations of scientific reliability to be inappropriate requests of the lay participants, they were asked different questions. Specifically, Kassin and Barndollar (1992) and Benton and colleagues (2006) asked participants whether they thought each statement was "generally true" or "generally false." Schmechel and colleagues asked simply whether a statement was "true or false." It is not at all clear what a frequency judgment denoted by "generally" adds to lay participants' interpretations of statements about events that they likely have never personally experienced (e.g., showups, mugshot-induced bias, unconscious transference, and lineup instructions; cf. see Memorandum of Opinion in *United States v. Lewis Libby*, 2006). Despite their belief that the sufficient (for courtroom presentation) reliability question should not be answered by lay participants, Kassin and Barndollar (1992) and Benton and colleagues (2006) nonetheless directly contrasted their respondents' true–false responses with the experts' reliability question (see also Hosch et al., Chapter 7). In our view, these comparisons have been inappropriate.

Closer inspection of the experts' responses to the different questions asked of them reveals additional grounds for concern. First, when Kassin and associates' experts provided an assessment of the cumulative research evidence in favor of or against a proposition, they sometimes indicated that research evidence in support of the proposition was weak or even absent. It is striking that, having done so they went on to indicate that the phenomenon was nonetheless sufficiently reliable to be presented in court. For example, whereas 45% of the experts thought that the statement regarding the effect of hypnosis on accuracy was sufficiently reliable to be presented in court, not a single expert in the 64-person sample had previously responded that the research evidence in any way either "tends to favor," is "generally reliable," or "very reliable" in support of the statement "Hypnosis increases the accuracy of an eyewitness's reported memory." In other words, data presented for the second (courtroom) reliability question appear to reflect considerable expert opinion *against* rather than for the proposition. Benton and colleagues, on the other hand, had explicitly characterized the experts' responses to the second question as reflecting 45% agreement with or endorsement of the proposition to which the laypersons' 19% endorsement of "generally true" could be compared. However, a more appropriate comparison would have been with the 0% of experts who agreed with the proposition by endorsing any level of research support in its favor. Similarly, with respect to the statement on lineup fairness, only 54% of experts had positively evaluated (at any level) the research evidence in favor of the proposition, but 70% indicated there was sufficient reliability for its presentation in court. It was, of course, the 70% figure that was compared to the 32% lay judgments of "generally true," not the 54% who had indicated that any research at all supported the proposition. These discrepancies are even larger if a higher standard of the research evidence by experts ("generally" or "very reliable") is used.

Second, for some items, many experts who stated they were insufficiently familiar with the relevant research and therefore provided no assessment of research support (by choosing "I don't know") nonetheless went on to judge the statement to be of sufficient reliability to be presented in court. In one remarkable example, fully 68% of respondents said they did not know about research evidence regarding the color perception statement, yet 63% of the complete sample went on to indicate that the specific statement was of sufficient reliability to be presented in court. Similarly, for the statement on description-matched foils, 31% of the experts chose "I don't know" regarding its scientific reliability and another 16% said scientific evidence was contrary to the proposition, leaving a maximum of 54% of the sample in agreement that research supported the proposition. Despite the logical implausibility of doing so, 71% of the sample thought the statement sufficiently reliable for courtroom presentation. Of the jurors sampled by Benton and colleagues, 35% thought the statement to be generally true. Yet, it is the 71% of experts, not the 54%, figure that was compared to the jurors' 35% by Benton and colleagues and others (e.g., Leippe & Eisenstadt, Chapter 8; Schmechel et al., 2007; Epstein, 2007). Similar arguments may be made for the items of showups and presentation format.

Kassin and associates explicitly commented upon some of these apparent dissociations, and conflated the specific and general meanings of their propositions by suggesting instead that the data reflect opinions on "topics" (see also Epstein, 2007, p. 740). However, what is important here is the fact that laypersons had not been asked to assess and did not likely assess the truth or falsity of *topics*. Further, given the kinds of confusions between causal and associative relationships inherent in the Kassin statements described by Wright (2006), it is possible that the statements were interpreted differently by experts from the first to the second question. Specifically, some statements may have connoted a "causal" relationship on their first appearance and "associative" on their second. Possibly, the latter interpretation has seeming greater generality and, as a topic, could safely be heard in court, hence their higher percentages. Despite these ambiguities, commentators of what it is that laypersons understand about eyewitness factors appear to have concluded that direct comparisons between the experts' and laypersons' responses are indeed justified (e.g., Benton et al., 2007; Hosch et al., Chapter 7; Leippe & Eisenstadt, Chapter 8; Schmechel, 2006). We believe otherwise.

It seems clear that reliance upon the courtroom reliability question alone can exaggerate both the level of consensus among experts (as to the meaning of a specific proposition) and the magnitudes of some differences between jurors and experts. These discrepancies between experts on the first two questions are, however, smallest on those items that received their highest levels of agreement to the second question. Nonetheless, it would be valuable to examine which comparisons of these expert and layperson data have been cited in courtroom hearings on the admissibility of expert evidence. If expert testimony has not gone beyond a presumptive judgment that the experts' reliability responses reflect agreement with each proposition, then courts may have received misleading information about some of these issues.

To provide a more appropriate standard of comparison, J. D. Read and Desmarais (2009) calculated from Kassin and associates' data presentation the percentage of experts who "agreed" with each proposition through their choices of either "tends to favor, generally reliable, or very reliable" in their initial evaluation of reliability. As noted, the differences in the calculations do not substantially alter the magnitudes of differences on the 80% consensus items between experts and jurors reported by Benton and colleagues, but they frequently do alter the differences on items for which the overall levels of agreement (on either question) were lower. Doing so also highlights the fact that on three additional items, 80% of experts achieved a high level of consensus by their indication that there was no empirical support for the specific propositions.

Review of Indirect Approaches

In contrast to the direct survey methods just described, a number of researchers have employed alternative or *indirect* methods to assess juror understanding of eyewitness factors. A variety of these methods exist, ranging from the estimation of probabilities of person identification to the assessment of juror sensitivity to eyewitness factors in case studies (written or videotaped scenarios) either with or without the receipt of expert opinion. Chapters by Malpass and colleagues, Devenport and colleagues, and Leippe and Eisenstadt in this volume also provide discussion of these approaches. As a result, we focus on a limited sample of studies.

First, research participants have often been asked to estimate the likelihood of accurate person identification in situations that varied along levels of several eyewitness factors, manipulated one at a time, such as witness confidence, crime seriousness, and lineup bias. For example, McAuliff and Kovera (2007) recently asked jurors and jury-eligible undergraduates to estimate the direction and magnitude of effects of the single specific factor of misleading information on witness accuracy and compared their estimates to the assessments provided by experts. The researchers' goal was to gain an in-depth understanding from experts, jurors, and potential jurors of the moderating effects of the scientifically examined variables of witness age, warnings, delay, source prestige, event detail centrality, and witness involvement upon witness suggestibility. The study was remarkably thorough and provides an impressive demonstration of the benefits of exploring a single eyewitness factor in great depth and going well beyond the question of whether someone simply agreed or disagreed with the truth of a statement. Doing justice to the full range of their findings is not possible in this chapter. Suffice it to say that, despite their reported unfamiliarity with witness suggestibility research, lay participants were generally aware that information following an event can be incorporated into memory for the event, and they demonstrated awareness of the risks of misleading post-event information and anticipated, apparently as well as experts, the impact of witness age, delay, and pre-misinformation warnings on the magnitude of these risks.

There were, however, significant differences between experts and laypersons on questions concerning the effects on witness suggestibility of detail centrality, witness participation, and source prestige. Although laypersons thought that expert witness testimony would be helpful to jurors, the researchers recommended a more limited approach. In particular, they recommended that such testimony may be warranted with respect to those variables for which laypersons demonstrated inferior understanding, but they explicitly suggested that expert testimony on the points of agreement between experts and laypersons would not be helpful (i.e., effects of age-related trends in suggestibility, positive effects of warnings, and the negative effects of delay).

Similarly, Schmechel and colleagues (2006) asked their participants to estimate identification outcomes and compared their responses to the effects of manipulations of these same variables in laboratory research. This was also the primary approach taken by Mitchell and Haw (2008), who asked members of the public (and a small sample [$N = 22$] of eyewitness experts) to estimate the probabilities of successful person identification in the context of specific scenarios (e.g., multiple witnesses, stress). In general, participants' estimates did not match the research findings in these situations because they either substantially under- or overestimated the effects of variables known to influence eyewitness memory performance. Finally, a study by Simon, Strenstom, and S. J. Read (2008) obtained from a large sample of Internet users estimated probabilities of correct identification in a number of person identification vignettes (i.e., quick or slow ID, botched or induced ID, and showups). As in the previous studies, respondents often appeared to be surprisingly insensitive to factors expected to undermine any possibility of a reliable ID.

A second indirect approach compares research participants' estimates of the effects of specific variables on person identification with data collected from research participants who acted as mock jurors and who were provided with case descriptions in which the variables of interest were actually manipulated. For example, R. C. L. Lindsay (1994) asked participants to rate the likelihood that an eyewitness would make an accurate identification under a series of varied circumstances, which included two manipulations on each of 19 variables or factors. Lindsay found that the factors rated by lay respondents as important determinants of eyewitness accuracy generally had not been shown to influence mock jurors' verdicts or credibility evaluations. These results suggest that the factors that potential jurors think are relevant to the reliability of eyewitness testimony often prove to be unimportant when case evidence is actually presented to them.

Finally, other researchers have asked participants to provide what they believe are the important factors determining the reliability of eyewitness testimony. For example, Shaw, Garcia, and McClure (1999) asked 276 jury-eligible university students to list those things that would affect the reliability of witness recall (along with the recall of other players in the system). Relatively few research participants (university students) listed system variables such as the type of lineup and investigator bias. Instead, they focused on estimator variables related to the context in which a hypothetical crime occurred (e.g., the lighting), the characteristics of the crime (e.g., violent), and the personal features of the witness (e.g., age, gender). Unfortunately, they were not asked for the direction of the effects they believed the factors would have on eyewitness reliability so that, even for the factors they generated, it is difficult to assess the accuracy of their inclusion. More recently, in a similar vein, Hope and associates (2008) required laypersons in the United Kingdom to provide descriptions of the relationships between a number of system and estimator variables following their reading of a statement similar to a "stem" used in corresponding multiple-choice items assigned to a comparable sample (and discussed earlier). When scored for accuracy and compared to the second sample's performance, those who generated their own responses performed at much lower levels on most of the items. In short, these laypersons were unsuccessful at generating the correct answers for the various eyewitness factors. Overall, the use of indirect methods does not provide an optimistic view of the sensitivity of laypersons to relevant eyewitness factors.

Consistency in Responses Across Surveys

Few investigations have examined the consistency of lay beliefs across surveys. J. D. Read and Desmarais (2009) reported that their lay participants demonstrated high consistency across three surveys in which attempts were made to improve understanding of the eyewitness statements. However, as seen in Tables 6.1 and 6.2, consistency has usually been lacking when studies using different formats are compared. For example, to questions in a true–false format Schmechel and colleagues' participants responded in a manner that very closely agreed with experts and current research on the malleability of eyewitness confidence (e.g., investigator feedback effects), post-event information, unconscious transference, and cross-race identification) and demonstrated appropriate caution about the predictive value of confidence statements and multiple witnesses (cf. Devenport, Kimbrough, & Cutler, Chapter 3; Bailey & Mecklenburg, Chapter 10). However, when given the opportunity to assess the effects of a variable like lineup instructions using multiple-choice options, their caution is less evident, suggesting that they hold a much more optimistic view of eyewitness reliability. These inconsistencies raise the question as to whether, when jurors have knowledge about eyewitness factors, such knowledge is, in fact, incorporated into their decision-making.

This question emphasizes the distinction between *having* knowledge and *making use* of it. To date, most studies speak to the former issue and not the latter. Further, it is one thing to be able to identify correctly an explicitly stated, general relationship between a factor and memory, but quite another to have the requisite depth of knowledge to appreciate conceptual distinctions made at trial by experts and to apply subtle relationships between relevant factors and eyewitness memory to the facts in specific cases. To examine these questions, researchers may ask whether existing knowledge held by jurors (without benefit of expert testimony) is used when they are presented with case descriptions that include the relevant eyewitness factors (e.g., cross-race effect). That is, do the respondents apply their knowledge to the case at hand? In one of the early studies directed to this question, Cutler, Penrod, and Dexter (1989) found that even when jurors had knowledge of the limitations of eyewitness identification, the information was not well integrated into their decision-making. A review by Devenport and colleagues in 1997 reached a similar conclusion across a variety of research methodologies. Similarly, Alonzo and Lane (2006) assessed knowledge of eyewitness factors among their research participants and hypothesized that those with greatest knowledge would reach different decisions than those with least knowledge of eyewitness factors. However, that did not prove to be the case, and the researchers concluded that there was little evidence that the existing knowledge held by mock jurors was incorporated into their decisions regarding a written vignette. A similar outcome was recently obtained by Devenport and Cutler (2008), who examined individual differences in knowledge about eyewitness factors among 222 research participants and asked whether those with greater knowledge would respond differently to case facts (that included manipulated levels of witness intoxication, lineup instructions, and witness confidence) than would those who held much lower levels of knowledge. Consistent with the earlier mentioned studies, their answer was "no."

As noted earlier, Leippe and Eisenstadt (Chapter 8) have reviewed research on this question, often when information about eyewitness factors was provided through expert testimony, and have concluded that it is—like most psychological questions—complicated because circumstances exist in which it is clear that mock jurors did indeed apply either pre-existing knowledge or expert-provided information and other circumstances when they did not. Leippe and Eisenstadt's point is that a trial itself is complex and there are few situations in which eyewitness testimony is the sole or necessarily even the most salient evidence heard by triers of fact. In addition, even when eyewitness factors are relevant and perhaps salient, jurors may nonetheless prefer to rely upon those factors that we know are most weakly related to eyewitness accuracy (e.g., eyewitness confidence, testimonial inconsistency). As a result, knowledge of eyewitness factors may account for very little of the variance in trial outcomes. In short, these studies suggest that the presentation of relevant testimony does not remediate impoverished juror knowledge or, if it does, the jurors' newly acquired information does not always appear to be incorporated into their decision-making. Thus, if knowledge of eyewitness factors held or gained through expert testimony is recommended as a safe-guard against weak juror understanding, it has not been demonstrated to be particularly effective in reflecting differential sensitivity to eyewitness factors as seen in credibility and verdict outcomes (cf. Devenport, Kimbrough, & Cutler, Chapter 3).

Evaluations of Juror Knowledge: Additional Concerns

We have four final points we wish to make. First, we expect that any evaluation of lay knowledge has a limited shelf life. Citation of research studies from 30 years ago can provide historical backdrop to current investigations and their results, but that is all. Over time, we anticipate that public beliefs and knowledge will change because psychological research, as well as our under-standing of forensic psychological issues, will change (cf. Egeth, 1995; Kassin et al., 2001, 2002; Schmechel et al., 2006). In many cases, the changes will result from improved scientific understanding of factors by experts and its dissemi-nation to the general public (Desmarais et al., 2008; Kassin et al., 2001).

Second, the various assessment procedures of lay knowledge need to be monitored continually to assess whether research participants and mock jurors have been evaluated in a manner that accurately reflects what they believe or know. If, for example, the Kassin and associates' items (constructed to be answered by experts) are offered without alteration to lay survey partici-pants, on what basis can we be assured that they comprehend the questions? The inconsistencies seen across question formats and methodologies in our review strongly suggest that participants may often not understand the ques-tions nor, perhaps, their chosen answers. As Hope and associates (2008) have suggested, the provision of a limited set of available responses or choices (that includes the correct answer) to participants in these studies may result in an overestimation of their levels of knowledge. The translation of the expert items into meaningful statements for lay respondents is difficult and demon-strates that real understanding of these issues by jurors (and by judges and experts alike) will likely only be gained with more in-depth interviews and the use of techniques that can assess response consistency within individuals (not samples), both across question formats and time (Alonzo & Lane, 2006; McAuliff & Kovera, 2007; Schmechel et al., 2006).

Third, as reviewed earlier, whereas the outcomes of direct method studies provide some optimism that laypersons are often aware of many unreliable aspects of eyewitness testimony, the outcomes from indirect methodologies, however, do not paint an equally optimistic picture of their knowledge and ability to apply such awareness to a case at hand. Which type of information will be welcomed and heard by courts and jurors? It is our opinion that courts are likely more ready to receive and digest information derived from the direct question-and-answer surveys than they are from the set of considerably more complex studies that often (but not always) demonstrate juror insensitivity to the very factors assessed by the survey methodologies (see Leippe & Eisenstadt, Chapter 8). Reliance upon the survey approaches alone, of course, will provide an unbalanced view of the state of juror knowledge.

Finally, difficulties with sample selection are evident in juror knowledge research. Many studies have relied upon undergraduate students who, arguably, are neither demographically representative of actual jurors (although they are jury-eligible in most cases), nor do they frequently serve on actual juries (Bornstein, 1999). Even those studies in which community samples were included may suffer from representativeness concerns because there may be important demographic and attitudinal differences between community members who do or do not volunteer to participate in research studies and who are or are not available to the researchers. A more ecologically valid approach would be to collect data from actual jurors who have participated in trials (e.g., Seltzer et al., 1990), or to survey community members who have been called and appear for jury duty, but have yet to be assigned to a particular case (e.g., Benton et al., 2006). Among the latter group, however, issues of generalizability may still apply; for example, differences likely exist among those who do or do not appear at court at the appointed time. Further, if surveys are distributed on-site among those appearing for jury duty, one may question whether all are highly motivated to demonstrate their knowledge of legally related topics. Indeed, many may prefer to appear unaware of these topics as the basis for being excluded from jury duty. Some insight into this possibility may be gained by examining their response distributions of correct and incorrect answers, and the "I don't know" option. Some data, however, suggest that these fears may be unwarranted because results across mock jury, community, and actual jury samples have been reasonably consistent in other research domains (cf. Bornstein, 1999).

In summary, with respect to eyewitness factors that have received consensus agreement by experts, the conclusion is murkier than one might like. On the one hand, using direct methods of assessment, laypersons have demonstrated reasonable agreement with the experts (see Tables 6.1 and 6.2) and have done so in a fairly consistent fashion. On the other hand, using more indirect methods, jurors often appear to have an erroneous or limited understanding of many of these same eyewitness issues and research findings. As a consequence, many researchers (Benton, et al., 2006, 2007; Cutler & Penrod, 1995; Devenport et al., 1997; Leippe, 1995; Leippe & Eisenstadt, 2007,

Chapter 8; Schmechel et al., 2007) have argued that juror decisions may benefit from expert testimony. Our review has focused upon those eyewitness topics for which the vast majority of researchers believe they know the correct answer. Using the experts' consensus on these topics, however, leaves the disposition unknown of an equal number of other factors studied (and included in the Kassin et al., 2001 survey) for which such agreement was not achieved. Further, a great many other factors have also been researched, and there exists as well an unknown number of other factors to be examined in the future that could be presented to experts for assessment of their effects on eyewitness reliability (cf. Turtle et al., 2008).

References

Alonzo, J., & Lane, S. M. (2006, March). Saying versus judging: Assessing juror knowledge of eyewitness memory. *Paper presentation at the Meetings of the American Psychology-Law Society,* St. Petersburg, FL.

Behrman, B. W. & Richards, R. E. (2005). Suspect/foil identification in actual crimes and in the laboratory: A reality monitoring analysis. *Law and Human Behavior, 29,* 279–301.

Benton, T. P., McDonnell, S., Ross, D., Thomas, W. N., & Bradshaw, E. (2007). Has eyewitness testimony research penetrated the American legal system? A synthesis of case history, juror knowledge, and expert testimony. In D. W. Ross, R. C. L. Lindsay, M. P. Toglia, & J. D. Read (Eds.), *Handbook of eyewitness psychology: Vol. 2: Memory for people* (pp. 453–500). Mahwah, NJ: Erlbaum.

Benton, T. R., Ross, D. F., Bradshaw, E., Thomas, W. N., & Bradshaw, G. S. (2006). Eyewitness memory is still not common sense: Comparing jurors, judges, and law enforcement to eyewitness experts. *Applied Cognitive Psychology, 20,* 115–130.

Bornstein, B. H. (1999). The ecological validity of jury simulations: Is the jury still out? *Law and Human Behavior, 23,* 75–92.

Brewer, N., & Wells, G. L. (2006). The confidence–accuracy relationship in eyewitness identification: Effects of lineup instructions, foil similarity and target-absent rates. *Journal of Experimental Psychology: Applied, 12,* 11–30.

Cutler, B. L., & Penrod, S. D. (1995). *Mistaken identification: The eyewitness, psychology, and the law.* New York: Cambridge University Press.

Cutler, B. L., Penrod, S. D., & Dexter, H. R. (1989). The eyewitness, the expert psychologist, and the jury. *Law and Human Behavior, 13,* 311–332.

Daubert v. Merrill Dow Pharmaceuticals, Inc., 509 U.S. 579, 125 L.Ed.2d. 469, 113 S.Ct. 2786 (1993).

Deffenbacher, K. A., & Loftus, E. F. (1982). Do jurors share a common understanding concerning eyewitness behaviour? *Law and Human Behavior, 6,* 15–30.

Desmarais, S. L., Price, H. L., & Read, J. D. (2008). "Objection Your Honor, television is not the relevant authority!" Crime drama portrayals of eyewitness issues. *Psychology, Crime, & Law, 14,* 225–243.

Desmarais, S. L., & Read, J. D. (2009). *Re-examining juror knowledge of eyewitness issues*. Manuscript in preparation.

Devenport, J., & Cutler, B. L. (2008). *Juror knowledge and sensitivity to eyewitness identification testimony in a simulated trial*. Manuscript in preparation.

Devenport, J. L., Cutler, B. L., & Penrod, S. D. (1997). Eyewitness identification evidence: Evaluating commonsense evaluations. *Psychology, Public Policy, and Law, 3*, 338–361.

Egeth, H. (1995). Eyewitness testimony: An update. In W. Kessel (Ed.), *Psychology, science and human affairs: Essays in honor of William Bevan* (pp. 151–166). Boulder, CO: Westview.

Epstein, J. (2007). The great engine that couldn't: Science, mistaken identifications, and the limits of cross-examination. *Stetson Law Review, 36*, 727–787.

Frye v. United States, 293 F. 1013 (D.C. Cir. 1923).

Granhag, P. A., Strömwall, L. A., & Hartwig, M. (2005). Eyewitness testimony: Tracing the beliefs of Swedish legal professionals. *Behavioral Sciences & the Law, 23*, 709–27.

Hope, L., Memon, A., Houston, K. A., & Read, J. D. (2008). *Do we need eyewitness expert testimony? A preliminary examination of the methodological considerations in evaluating juror 'commonsense.'* Manuscript in preparation.

Kassin, S. M., & Barndollar, K. A. (1992). The psychology of eyewitness testimony: A comparison of experts and prospective jurors. *Journal of Applied Social Psychology, 22*, 1241–1249.

Kassin, S. M., Ellsworth, P. C., & Smith, V. L. (1989). The "general acceptance" of psychological research on eyewitness testimony: A survey of the experts. *American Psychologist, 44*, 1089–1098.

Kassin, S. M., Tubb, V. A., Hosch, H., & Memon, A. (2001). On the "general acceptance" of eyewitness testimony research. *American Psychologist, 56*, 405–416.

Kassin, S. M., Tubb, V. A., Hosch, H., & Memon, A. (2002). 'Eyewitness researchers as experts in court: responsive to change in a dynamic and rational process': Comment. *American Psychologist, 57*, 378–379.

Lane, S. M., Groft, S., & Alonzo, J. (2008, March). *What judges know about what jurors know: Consistency of beliefs about eyewitness memory*. Paper presented at the annual meeting of the American Psychology-Law Society, Jacksonville, FL.

Lane, S. M., Groft, S., Roussel, C., & Alonzo, J. (2007, March). *Beliefs about eyewitness memory: Differences among judges, jurors, and jury-eligible college students*. Poster presentation at the "Off the Witness Stand Conference", John Jay College of Criminal Justice, New York, NY.

Leippe, M. R. (1995). The case for expert testimony about eyewitness memory. *Psychology, Public Policy, and Law, 1*, 909–959.

Leippe, M. R., & Eisenstadt, D. (2007). Eyewitness confidence and the confidence-accuracy relationship in memory for people. In D. W. Ross, R. C. L. Lindsay, M. P. Toglia, & J. D. Read (Eds.), *The handbook of eyewitness psychology: Vol. 2: Memory for people* (pp. 377–426). New Jersey: Erlbaum.

Lindsay, D. S., Read, J. D., & Sharma, K. (1998). Accuracy and confidence in person identification: The relationship is strong when witnessing conditions vary widely. *Psychological Science, 9*, 215–218.

Lindsay, R. C. L. (1994). Expectations of eyewitness performance: Jurors' verdicts do not follow from their beliefs. In D. F. Ross, D. J. Read, & M. P. Toglia

(Eds.), *Adult eyewitness testimony: Current trends and developments*. New York: Cambridge University Press, 362–384.

Lindsay, R. C. L., Ross, D. F., Read, J. D., & Toglia, M. P. (Eds.) (2007). *Handbook of eyewitness psychology: Vol. 2: Memory for people*. Mahwah, N.J.: Lawrence Erlbaum Associates.

Lindsay, R. C. L., MacDonald, P., & McGarry, S. (1990). Perspectives on the role of the eyewitness expert. *Behavioral Sciences and the Law, 8*, 457–464.

Martire, K., & Kemp, R. (2007, July). *Quantifying the expertise of an eyewitness expert. Paper presentation at the meetings of the Society for Applied Research in Memory and Cognition (SARMAC)*, Lewiston, ME.

McAuliff, B. D. & Kovera, M. B. (2007). Estimating the effects of misleading information on witness accuracy: Can experts tell jurors something they don't already know? *Applied Cognitive Psychology, 21*, 849–870.

McConkey, K. M., & Roche, S. M. (1989). Knowledge of eyewitness memory. *Australian Psychologist, 24*, 377–384.

Mitchell, T. L., & Haw, R. M. (2008). *What we know: A survey comparison of community and expert opinion*. Manuscript in preparation.

Noon, E., & Hollin, C. R. (1987). Lay knowledge of eyewitness behaviour: A British survey. *Applied Cognitive Psychology, 1*, 143–153.

Porter, S., & Peace, K. A. (2007). The scars of memory: A prospective, longitudinal investigation of the consistency of traumatic and positive emotional memories in adulthood. *Psychological Science, 18*, 435–441.

R. v. Mohan, 2 S.C.R. 9 (1994).

Rahaim, G. L., & Brodsky, S. L. (1982). Empirical evidence versus common sense: Juror and lawyer knowledge of eyewitness accuracy. *Law & Psychology Review, 7*, 1–15.

Read, J. D., & Desmarais, S. L. (2009). Lay knowledge of eyewitness issues: A Canadian survey. *Applied Cognitive Psychology, 23*, 301-326.

Schmechel, R. S., O'Toole, T. P., Easterly, C., & Loftus, E. F. (2006). Beyond the ken? Testing jurors' understanding of eyewitness reliability evidence. *Jurimetrics, 46*, 177–214.

Seltzer, R., Lopes, G. M., & Venuti, M. (1990). Juror ability to recognize the limitations of eyewitness identifications. *Forensic Reports, 3*, 121–137.

Shaw, J. S. III, Garcia, L. A., & McClure, K. A. (1999). A lay perspective on the accuracy of eyewitness testimony. *Journal of Applied Social Psychology, 29*, 52–71.

Simon, D., Strenstom, D., & Read, S. J. (2008). *Jurors' background knowledge and beliefs. Paper presentation at American Psychology-Law Association Meetings*, Jacksonville, FL.

State v. Nordlund, 2002 Wash, App (Wash.2002).

Stuesser, L. (2005). Experts on eyewitness identification: I just don't see it. *International Commentary on Evidence, 3*(1), Article 2.

Toglia, M. P., Read, J. D., Ross, D. W., & Lindsay, R. C. L. (Eds.) (2007). *Handbook of eyewitness psychology: Vol. 1: Memory for events*. Mahwah, N.J.: Lawrence Erlbaum.

Turtle, J., Read, J. D., Lindsay, S. D., & Brimacombe, E. (2008). Toward a more informative psychological science of eyewitness evidence. *Applied Cognitive Psychology, 22*, 769–778.

United States v. Lewis Libby, Cr. No. 05-394 (2006).

Wells, G. L. (1978). Applied eyewitness testimony research: System variables versus estimator variables. *Journal of Personality and Social Psychology, 36,* 1546–1557.

Wells, G. L., & Loftus, E. F. (2003). Eyewitness memory for people and events. In A. M. Goldstein (Ed.), *Handbook of psychology: Forensic psychology, Vol. 11* (pp. 149–160). New York: Wiley.

Wise, R. A., Pawlenko, N. B., Meyer, D., & Safer, M. A. (2007). A survey of defense attorneys' knowledge and beliefs about eyewitness testimony. *The Champion, 31*(9), 18–27, 33.

Wise, R. A., & Safer, M. A. (2004). What US judges know and believe about eyewitness testimony. *Applied Cognitive Psychology, 18,* 427–443.

Wright, D. B. (2006). Causal and associative hypotheses in psychology: Examples from eyewitness testimony research. *Psychology, Public Policy, and Law, 12,* 190–213.

Yarmey, A. D. (2001). Expert testimony: Does eyewitness memory research have probative value for the courts? *Canadian Psychology, 42,* 92–100.

Yarmey, A. D., & Jones, H. P. T. (1983). Is the psychology of eyewitness identification a matter of common sense? In S. M. A. Lloyd-Bostock & B. R. Clifford (Eds.), *Evaluating witness evidence* (pp. 13–40). Toronto, Canada: Wiley.

Notes

1. It is interesting that a recent paper published in *Psychological Science* offers support for the "memory burning" or memory scarring kind of metaphor endorsed by the Schmechel participants (Porter & Peace, 2007).

2. For example, one question asks respondents to decide who is the more reliable witness: someone who is absolutely certain versus another witness who has less confidence in his identification. According to the authors, the answer of "slightly more reliable" as opposed to "much more reliable" or "equally reliable" is the correct option. However, in recent years several studies have demonstrated that when eyewitnesses express maximum confidence at the time of identification, they are, in fact, much more likely to be accurate than someone with lower confidence (D. S. Lindsay, Read, & Sharma, 1998; Behrman & Richards, 2005; Brewer & Wells, 2006).

7

Expert Psychology Testimony on Eyewitness Identification: Consensus Among Experts?

Harmon M. Hosch, Kevin W. Jolly, Larissa A. Schmersal, and Brooke A. Smith

Manhattan cab driver Joaquin Liriano was stabbed to death early on June 15, 1991. The assailant escaped the scene before the police arrived; however, four witnesses to the attack were able to create a composite sketch of the assailant. Two years later, when Nico LeGrand was arrested for an unrelated burglary charge, officers determined that he resembled the 1991 composite sketch. In April 1998, LeGrand, arrested for a second burglary, again was determined to resemble the 1991 composite sketch, and the four witnesses were brought in to view a lineup. One witness positively identified LeGrand in a photo lineup; two witnesses believed LeGrand to be similar to the perpetrator, but not an exact match. Additional witnesses shown the photo array were unable to identify LeGrand as the assailant. No physical evidence connected LeGrand to the stabbing; the only evidence was the resemblance to the composite sketch and the inconsistent eyewitness identifications made 7 years after the stabbing occurred.

When the case went to trial in 2001, an expert witness on eyewitness identification was ruled in a *Daubert* hearing to be qualified, and the proposed testimony was declared beyond the ken of a typical juror. Still, the court refused to admit the expert, stating that the testimony was based upon scientific principles that were not generally accepted by the relevant scientific community.

In deciding the *Daubert v. Merrell Dow Pharmaceuticals* (1993) case, the U.S. Supreme Court articulated four questions that may help trial courts decide on the admissibility of expert testimony. These were: (a) whether the theories and methods used by the expert to come to an opinion can be tested,

(b) whether they have been subjected to peer review, (c) if there is a measurable error rate, and (d) whether the theories or methods are generally accepted within the expert's scientific community.

Prior to the *Daubert* decision, the standard judges were to use to decide if expert testimony should be admitted into evidence was the *Frye* rule (*Frye v. United States*, 1923). When the *Frye* standard became law, trial courts were to use the criterion of "general acceptance" within the scientific community to consider a scientific technique and the results of research using that technique to be admissible. Indeed, the U.S. Court of Appeals for the District of Columbia created this standard when it asserted that "the thing from which the deduction is made must be sufficiently established to have gained general acceptance in the particular field in which it belongs" (p. 1).

In this chapter, we briefly review the legal standards by which trial courts are to decide whether experts may testify. The reader should note that a more comprehensive review of the legal history and the standards for the admissibility of expert testimony from the perspective of legal precedent is available in Chapter 4. We then focus on the legal and empirical research that establishes the criteria and the evidence that attests to the general acceptance of research data focusing on the factors that influence the accuracy of eyewitness identifications. Studies that compare the understanding of experts in the field and that of other trial participants, such as judges, attorneys, and the lay public who may serve as jurors, will then be addressed. Finally, we look at additional sources such as textbooks that can be construed as evidence of community consensus with regard to factors that influence identifications.

Legal Standards for Acceptance of Expert Testimony

For nearly 70 years, the "general acceptance" standard, derived from *Frye v. United States* (1923), served as the authoritative guideline for the evaluation of expert testimony in the federal court and was adopted by many state courts (see Epstein, Chapter 4). The Frye test requires that both the theory and methods used by the expert to testify in court be "generally accepted" within the relevant scientific community. Although the *Frye* standard has been criticized for being obscure on the exact definition of "general acceptance," overall, research scientists and legal scholars agree that scientists from each particular field are the most appropriate judges of the reliability of a technique (Fisher, 1994). Thus, if a theory or technique has gained sufficient support from researchers in that area, expert testimony about that topic may be appropriate in a court of law.

The Federal Rules of Evidence (FRE) were adopted in 1976, but it was not until the *Daubert v. Merrell Dow Pharmaceuticals, Inc.* ruling in 1993 that the Court firmly established the Federal Rules as the predominant standard on which the admissibility of scientific expert testimony should be based in all federal cases, thus making the *Frye* test obsolete in federal cases (Fisher, 1994;

Groscup, Penrod, Studebaker, Huss, & O'Neil, 2002). Under the Federal Rules of Evidence, Article VII directs the admissibility of expert testimony in federal courts. Specifically, Rule 702 indicates that an expert witness is qualified to provide testimony only if "(1) the testimony is based upon sufficient facts or data, (2) the testimony is the product of reliable principles and methods, and (3) the witness has applied the principles and methods reliably to the facts of the case" (FRE 702, amended in 2000).

Thus, for all federal cases, the *Daubert* ruling of 1993 placed the trial judge in the role of gatekeeper, responsible for ensuring that any expert admitted into court provided testimony that was both firmly grounded on a reliable foundation and relevant to the particular case. This differed drastically from the *Frye* standard, which held the scientific community to which the expert belonged accountable for establishing the credibility of an expert's testimony (Fisher, 1994). The federal court no longer required general acceptance, but focused on the relevance and reliability of the information provided by the testimony.

Under the Frye standard, the scientific community was responsible for determining the reliability of a technique (Fisher, 1994); however, under *Daubert*, it is the judge's responsibility to ensure that the expert's testimony is both reliable and relevant to the issue at hand. The Court's ruling provided general guidelines for determining the reliability and relevance of the proposed testimony. Although no longer required to secure admissibility, the "general acceptance" standard remained singled out as an important factor for determining admissibility; however, the Court remained vague on how much emphasis should be placed on this factor (Fisher, 1994).

The *Daubert* ruling takes its definition of relevant evidence from FRE 401. Specifically, relevant evidence is any "that which has any tendency to make the existence of any fact that is of consequence to the determination of the action more probable or less probable than it would be without the evidence" (FRE 401). When determining the relevance aspect of an expert's testimony, a judge must assess whether the reasoning underlying the testimony fits properly with the facts of the case in question and whether the testimony could be applied to these facts in a manner that would aid the trier of fact (*United States v. Smithers*, 2000).

In addition to rising to the *Daubert* guidelines for reliability, the testimony to be proffered also must be relevant to the case at bar. *Daubert* and subsequent ruling concerning expert testimony, such as *General Electric v. Joiner* (1997) and *Kumho Tire Co. v. Carmichael* (1999) apply solely to federal cases; however, most state courts have followed the federal lead, at least in part. The majority of states have adopted portions of the rulings, or use the rulings in *Daubert*, *Joiner*, and *Kumho* as a guideline in evaluating expert testimony (Bernstein & Jackson, 2004). Still, a sizable minority of states continue to apply the *Frye* standard (Bernstein, 2001), and many *Daubert* jurisdictions continue to emphasize the "general acceptance" factor, thus making the consensus of experts an important topic for continued exploration, both under

Frye and *Daubert* (refer to Chapter 4 for details on which states use *Frye* and which use *Daubert* principles to decide an expert testimony admission).

Expert Surveys

Researchers in psychology have surveyed experts within their own field to gauge the level of consensus on a number of topics. For example, surveys of expert opinion on legally relevant topics such as the accuracy of the polygraph (Iacono & Lykken, 1997), the use of standardized intelligence tests (Murphy, Cronin, & Tam, 2003), or the use of forensic tests (Lally, 2003), and the ability of sexual abuse victims to serve as credible witnesses (Kovera, Borgida, Gresham, Swim, & Gray, 1993) now exist. In addition, some scholars had put forth their opinions on the issue of expert testimony about eyewitness identification accuracy (e.g., Elliott, 1993; Goodman & Loftus, 1988; Loftus, 1986; McCloskey, Egeth, & McKenna, 1986; McKenna, Treadway, & McClosky, 1992) for a couple of decades. Despite the volume of work exploring the factors that influence eyewitness identifications, no general assessment of how eyewitness researchers perceived the totality of results of these numerous studies existed until recently. For a summary of surveys on eyewitness factors, consult Table 7.1.

Table 7.1 Consensus[1] Among Experts on Eyewitness Factors as Reported in Published Literature[2]

Eyewitness Factor	Psychological Experts		Judges	Law Enforcement	Jurors	
	Kassin et al. (1989)	Kassin et al. (2001)	Safer & Wise. (2004)	Benton et al. (2006)	Benton et al. (2006)	Seltzer et al. (1990)
Question Wording	97%	98%	-	88%	83%	-
Lineup Instructions	95%	98%	84%	74%	64%	-
Post-event Information	87%	94%	-	81%	75%	-
Accuracy-Confidence Relationship	87%	87%	32%	64%	50%	36%
Role of Expectations and Attitudes	87%	92%	94%	86%	87%	-
Exposure Time	85%	81%	-	71%	54%	-
Unconscious Transference	85%	81%	-	48%	46%	-
Showups	83%	74%	-	83%	64%	-
Forgetting Curve	83%	83%	31%	41%	50%	33%
Cross-Race Identification	-[3]	90%	-	81%	79%	-

Table 7.1 (Cont'd)

Eyewitness Factor	Psychological Experts		Judges	Law Enforcement	Jurors	
	Kassin et al. (1989)	Kassin et al. (2001)	Safer & Wise. (2004)	Benton et al. (2006)	Benton et al. (2006)	Seltzer et al. (1990)
Lineup Fairness	77%	70%	-	65%	48%	-
Time Estimation	75%	-	-	-	-	-
Stress	71%	60%	-	81%	73%	-
Color Perception	66%	63%	-	26%	50%	55%
Trained Observers	59%	61%	-	29%	50%	42%
Weapon Focus	57%	87%	69%	67%	69%	-
Hypnotic Suggestibility	69%	91%	-	17%	29%	-
Event Violence	36%	37%	-	26%	25%	13%
Sex Differences	11%	-	-	-	-	-
Confidence Malleability	-	95%	89%	81%	75%	-
Mug-Shot Induced Bias	-	95%	74%	76%	79%	-
Child Suggestibility	-	94%	-	88%	81%	-
Alcoholic Intoxication	-	90%	-	100%	90%	-
Presentation Format	-	81%	19%	29%	37%	-
Description Matched Foils	-	71%	-	43%	60%	-
Child Accuracy	-	70%	-	45%	23%	-
False Childhood Memories	-	68%	-	56%	50%	-
Older Witnesses	-	50%	-	12%	48%	-
Hypnotic Retrieval	52%	-	-	-	-	-
Hypnotic Accuracy	-	45%	-	5%	39%	-
Identification Speed	-	40%	-	36%	65%	-
Discriminability	-	32%	-	21%	31%	-
Long-term Repression	-	22%	-	50%	65%	-
Effects of Hat	-	-	44%	-	-	-
Minor Details	-	-	23%	-	-	-
Conducting Lineups	-	-	62%	-	-	-
Attorneys' Knowledge	-	-	41%	-	-	-
Jurors' Knowledge	-	-	64%	-	-	-
Jurors Distinguish Eyewitnesses	-	-	39%	-	-	-
Voice Identification	-	-	-	-	-	-

Yarmey and Jones (1983) were among the first to gauge measures of knowledge of eyewitness research among populations of participants in the legal system. Judges, psychologists, law students, and jurors who had been sampled from the community and the academy were mailed a 16-item multiple-choice questionnaire. A brief question, statement, or vignette was presented for each item, and participants indicated which of four provided statements was correct. The correct answers were those the authors had identified as being the best response to the question from their understanding of the literature. Yarmey and Jones (1983) acknowledged that they may have not truly measured consensus among the respondents on the topics queried. The intent of the research was to identify to what extent those surveyed had "correct" knowledge on each topic; responses may have reflected the best answer to each scenario and not the experts' general knowledge of the extant literature or their degree of agreement with it. It was not surprising that the subsample of psychologists, who were all published experts in the field of eyewitness identification research, answered more questions correctly than did any of the other groups of respondents. Even these expert psychologists did not endorse the correct answer unanimously on some questions (e.g., the accuracy of eyewitness voice recognition), however.

In 1989, Kassin, Ellsworth, and Smith published an article describing the results of a study designed to gauge the level of general acceptance of factors influencing eyewitness identifications among a sample of experts in the field. In addition, they assessed the extent of the research experts' experiences testifying as expert witnesses. Experts responded by indicating their judgments about a set of assertions concerning 21 phenomena that had been empirically investigated. The respondents indicated whether a proposition was supported by the research results, whether the empirical findings were inconclusive, or merely tended to favor the proposition, and whether the results were generally reliable or were very reliable. The experts were asked to indicate if, from their understanding of the research literature, the evidence suggested the opposite of the proposition was true or if he did not know enough to assert a position on the particular issue. Experts also indicated if they believed that lay jurors would be aware of the eyewitness phenomenon because it was simply a matter of common sense. Finally, for each eyewitness phenomenon, experts indicated whether they thought that the results were sufficiently reliable to justify expert witness testimony in court and if he, as an expert, would be willing to testify about it and whether or not he had already testified on that matter.

Kassin and his associates consulted the published literature and the membership lists of the American Psychology-Law Society to identify a panel of experts in the field of eyewitness research. Of the 119 individuals identified, 63 returned the questionnaire. Questions about the individual's professional background revealed that three-quarters of the respondents had authored or co-authored at least one scientific paper or book chapter on eyewitness identification topics and that over half (54%) had testified in court as an expert witness.

A generally accepted eyewitness phenomenon was one identified by 70% of the experts as having reliable empirical results (Kassin et al., 1989). Nine phenomena met or exceeded that criterion. Experts agreed that an eyewitness who has only a small amount of time in which to view a crime can only remember a limited amount of information about the event. They also agreed that memory for an incident precipitously declines soon after an event, and the remaining memory remains stable from that point on. Experts thus support the police practice of interviewing witnesses soon after a crime occurs rather than weeks or months afterward. Consensus emerged on topics highlighting the malleability of memory, with over 80% of respondents endorsing that question wording (e.g., "Did you see *a* gun?" vs. "Did you see *the* gun?") can influence reported memories. They also agree that post-event information (e.g., "Other witnesses reported that the suspect was wearing glasses"), and attitudes and expectations (e.g., the belief that certain violent crimes are predominantly committed by individuals of a particular racial or socio-economic background) color memory for an event. The biasing nature of showups, in which suspects are presented to a witness in isolation or in the sole custody of the police, and lineup instructions (e.g., whether or not a witness is told that the perpetrator may or may not be in a lineup) were identified as being sufficiently reliable phenomenon to introduce to the courts. Reliable phenomena also included the absence of a strong accuracy–confidence correlation and the existence of unconscious transference.

Experts agreed that the empirical research shows that the correlation between witnesses' confidence in their identification and their actual accuracy is very modest in magnitude or nonexistent. Confidence would then not be a suitable predictor of accuracy, in that the most confident or the least confidence eyewitness may make a correct or an incorrect identification. Unconscious transference refers to the tendency of a person to consider people encountered in one situation to be incorrectly recalled as having been seen at the scene of a crime (e.g., image of a homeless man sitting outside of the bank is incorrectly recalled as that of the perpetrator).

Finally, there is a phenomenon known as the *cross-race effect*. The cross-race effect refers to the reduced accuracy in identification of individuals of a race or ethnic group different from one's own in comparison to the accuracy of identifying someone of one's own race or ethnicity. The experts agreed that the cross-race effect hampered the ability of European American eyewitnesses to identify accurately African Americans at a level very close to the threshold for consideration as a reliable phenomenon, being endorsed as reliable by 79.4% of the sample. Only 48.3% of the expert respondents believed that the cross-race effect was reliable for African Americans, suggesting that researchers were divided on the generalizability of the phenomenon. The only eyewitness factor that reached consensus among the polled experts as being commonsense to jurors was the notion that exposure time could affect memory.

When the eyewitness phenomenon was believed to be very reliable, 91.9% of respondents indicated that they would offer expert testimony to that fact;

however, when the evidence was inconclusive, only 17.3% would testify in court. A notable proportion of respondents (31.7%) would testify when there was no support for a phenomenon, although this sizable proportion may be willing to testify simply to refute any incorrect interpretations of the literature (Kassin et al., 1989).

Important legal decisions, notably *Daubert* (1993) and *Kuhmo* (1999), and government publications such as the Technical Working Group for Eyewitness Evidence (1999) that appeared after the first expert survey (Kassin et al., 1989) provided the impetus for a reevaluation of expert opinion on eyewitness factors. Thirteen new items were included to survey expert opinions on eyewitness topics not previously known at the time of the 1989 assessment; two items were dropped while the pair of statements regarding the cross-race effect were combined into a general measure of the phenomenon (Kassin, Tubb, Hosch, & Memon, 2001). As with the first expert survey (Kassin et al., 1989), the 64 individuals who comprised the sample in the second survey (Kassin et al., 2001) were exceptionally well qualified as experts in the field, averaging nearly 13 peer-reviewed journal articles apiece.

Results suggested that experts continued to share consensus on eyewitness issues previously identified as being reliable (e.g., longer exposure time facilitates reliable recall, the relationship between eyewitness confidence and the eyewitness' accuracy is low to nonexistent, such that confidence cannot be used to judge accuracy); topics on which experts did not previously meet or exceed 80% consensus remained at levels of agreement reported by Kassin and associates (1989). The passage of 10 years had not changed expert consensus on whether individuals seen under a single type of light are unreliable. Additionally, there was no change in consensus observed on an item that measured whether or not those who have received training in identifying individuals (e.g., law enforcement personnel) are more accurate at identifications than are average individuals (they are not). However, in the decade that passed since the results of the first expert survey were published, significant increases were observed in the proportions of experts who were persuaded that two factors were sufficiently reliable to introduce in court. The proportions of experts who reported that the research on the weapon focus effect and hypnotic suggestibility was sufficiently reliable to testify about increased from 57% to 87% and from 69% to 91%, respectively. Expert consensus on when testimony is appropriate given the state of the literature mirrored that of the Kassin and associates (1989) survey (Kassin et al., 2001).

A critique of the Kassin and associates (1989) survey of experts indicated that the current state of the science of eyewitness identification is unreliable and too complex to provide adequate expert testimony (Elliot, 1993). Elliot (1993) explained that the extrapolation of information that is not validated by sound research poses dangerous consequences to the reputation of the science. In the 1989 survey, 83% of experts replied that evidence existed to support the idea that showups increase the risk of misidentification of a suspect and that this finding was reliable enough on which to provide testimony.

Elliot (1993) points out that there was no research at the time to validate that assumption. In addition, the main effects for topics that experts showed high confidence in have weakened and even reversed with the collection of more data. Examples of this include the effect that stress or the presentation of a weapon have on eyewitness identification.

In the rebuttal to Elliot (1993), Kassin, Tubb, Hosch, and Memon (2002) explain that the topics focused on in the critique (showups, stress, weapon focus, forgetting curve, and unconscious transference) were relatively low ranked on reliability by experts, coming in, respectively, 8th, 13th, 17th, 9th, and 7th. Those topics that were judged as highly reliable by experts in the survey—the effects of post-event information and the relationship between accuracy and confidence—have a body of literature supporting the experts' opinions. Kassin and associates (2002) argue that the critique completely discounts the 70% of experts who have never testified on the topics that have inconsistent findings and explains that experts may have testified on a topic to say it is *not* a reliable phenomenon. Kassin and his colleagues also assert that the critique overgeneralizes the lack of reliability in the research and underqualifies the state of the science for expert testimony.

A lengthy critique of the probative versus the prejudicial value of eyewitness memory research was authored by Ebbesen and Konečni (1996) and has at its heart the assertion that there is no generally accepted *theory* of eyewitness identification. They argue in addition that the external validity of the research that has been conducted is low, thus limiting its applicability to real cases in which eyewitness identifications are a critical component of the prosecution's evidence against a defendant. Therefore, they argue that experts should not be testifying as to the research evidence and its implications for particular cases. Brian Clifford (1997) authored a concurring opinion in which he agrees with Ebbesen and Konečni's conclusion that expert evidence on factors that influence eyewitness identifications should not be admitted in courts of law, but argues that they overstate the case and that their reasoning is faulty. He concludes his paper by suggesting four ways for researchers to inform and bring about change in the criminal justice system, only one of which is to present expert evidence in courts. The other three include working with the criminal justice system to improve its work at stages earlier in the processing of cases, to publish what is known in outlets that are more accessible to the general public than are professional journals, and to work with greater vigor in the development of a general theory of eyewitness identification. Clifford's view, at least as presented in the late 1990s, was that the least defensible of the four is the expert testimony, and he urged the research community to pursue the other methods of disseminating their results.

Another critique, prompted by Kassin and associates (2001), highlighted some concerns regarding the purpose of the article and perceived methodological flaws (McCullough, 2002). McCullough felt that Kassin and associates (2001) overstated the importance and impact of expert eyewitness testimony on jurors' understanding of eyewitness factors when compared to the 1989 work. By primarily focusing on the experts' expectations of jurors' or laypersons' knowledge and the discrepant findings between the two Kassin and associates' studies (1989, 2001), the critique sought to unveil a hidden endorsement of eyewitness expert testimony by the authors. Kassin, Tubb, Hosch, and Memon (2002) responded that the article merely served to update the prior survey, not support or rebuff expert testimony. It was explained that the experts' opinions of juror knowledge was not employed as an actual measure of juror knowledge. In addition, they argued that changes in expert opinion were to be expected for an active area of scientific research. The authors argued that variability is not evidence of expert incompetence, but that scientific information and knowledge change over time.

Daftary and Penrod (2008) recently replicated and extended the Kassin and associates (2001) survey. Their study was conducted with two major goals in mind. The first was to assess again the changes that may be occurring over time in the consensus among experts in eyewitness identification. In addition, since the Kassin and associates (2001) study had been published, several meta-analyses and major research papers had appeared in the literature. The second purpose of the Daftary and Penrod study was to assess the changes that may have occurred in the experts' views of the state of the science given these new data. Seventy-one respondents completed the entire survey and were more productive in their research and publication than even the highly accomplished sample on which the 2001 Kassin study data are based.

The first finding of note from Daftary and Penrod's research is that, if anything, the level of general acceptance in the field is higher than it was in 2001.They also noted a very high level of stability in responses to the items used in the two surveys. For example, in the Daftary and Penrod study, the agreement among experts was 94% for mugshot-induced bias, which was virtually identical to the 95% agreement for the same item found by Kassin and associates. Similarly, the cross-race effect reached 94% agreement in the recent survey, in comparison to the 90% agreement in 2001.

The expert surveys conducted by Kassin and associates in both 1989 and 2001 are, as McCullough (2002) and Elliot (1993) indicated, not without limitation. Response rates were low in both surveys; Kassin and associates reported a 56% response rate on the first expert survey (1989), while the second expert survey reported a 34% response rate (Kassin et al., 2001). The low response rates are concerning because the experts who returned the survey may have been systematically different on any number of variables from those who did not return the survey. As an example, those who did not take the time to return the survey may have felt that their time could have been more productively spent engaging in activities that would enhance their credentials as experts (e.g., writing manuscripts, reading eyewitness literature, testifying in court). Or, those who did not reply to the survey may not have felt sufficiently qualified as an expert to respond to the survey. Indeed, six respondents excused themselves from participation in the first expert survey because they did not consider themselves experts (Kassin et al., 1989). In their 2001 study, however, Kassin and associates attempted to ensure that all potential respondents were equally qualified to participate in the survey by first compiling a list of experts from the rosters of major national and international conferences and then by referring to PsycINFO and consulting with the PSYCHLAW listserve subscribers; these electronic databases were not available at the time of the earlier survey. Despite these efforts, some experts may have been excluded because they had not published in the decade before the survey, other qualified experts may have been simply overlooked, or individuals may have become qualified as experts over the duration of the survey by publishing a scientific manuscript on eyewitness research. Finally, the authors selected the eyewitness factors that were included in the surveys and the statements that were used to describe them. Important eyewitness phenomena may not have been included in the surveys. Even the responses to the listed eyewitness phenomena may not adequately measure consensus; an expert may not have endorsed an eyewitness phenomenon due solely to how it was described in the survey.

Surveying eyewitness experts may provide a brief snapshot into the consensus that exists among researchers at a given time. It fails, however, to provide empirical evidence as to how that agreement was developed. The changes in consensus could have been explained as a result of renewed vigor in the exploration of the factors that influence identifications or a result of influential publications (Kassin et al., 2001). For example, researchers may turn to meta-analyses to form a basis for their testimony in court. We note as well that the experts in the Daftary and Penrod survey were very active in the courts, as they had collectively been asked to testify more than 2700 times. They had agreed to testify 66% of the times ($n = 1818$) they had been asked. They actually did so 88% of the times ($n = 1609$) in which they had agreed to serve as expert witnesses. This group of experts was more willing to testify than were the respondents to the previous surveys. At least some of this increase may be due to the publication of new research and meta-analyses to which we now turn.

Meta-analyses

Meta-analyses are reviews of a body of research that allows the analyst to describe the combined results of a multitude of studies in quantitative terms. For example, reviewers who perform more traditional qualitative reviews may assert that seven studies support the existence of an outcome whereas four do not. A meta-analyst can go beyond this assertion to report the overall combined result across the sets of studies and specify the magnitude of the effect.

Steblay (1997) noted the practical benefits to expert witnesses of being familiar with studies that have adopted this methodological approach:

Researchers who provide information to the criminal justice system need more than familiarity with isolated studies or a simple tally of results for and against a hypothesis. The probability and effect size indicators generated through meta-analysis provide a substantial step toward a thorough assessment of the literature, particularly allowing for recognition of a pattern of effect across studies, thus helping to overcome the limitations of small sample size. (p. 285)

Meta-analyses may help expert witnesses to synthesize disparate research findings to provide a general assessment of the literature to the court. Moderators that attenuate findings can also be identified in meta-analyses; these moderators may include specific methodological tools or samples reported in the paper. Meta-analyses are not uncommon in the eyewitness literature. Topics that have been subjected to meta-analytic review include the effects of biased instruction on eyewitnesses (Steblay, 1997), the relationship between accuracy and confidence (Bothwell, Deffenbacher, & Brigham, 1987; Cutler & Penrod, 1989; Sporer, Penrod, Read, & Cutler, 1995), the cross-race effect (Anthony, Copper, & Mullen, 1992; Bothwell, Brigham, & Malpass, 1989; Meissner & Brigham, 2001), the effects of post-identification feedback (Douglass & Steblay, 2006), lineup format and presentation (McQuiston-Surrett, Malpass, & Tredoux, 2006; Steblay, Dysart, Fulero, & Lindsay, 2001; Steblay, Dysart, Fulero, & Lindsay, 2003), stress (Deffenbacher, Bornstein, Penrod, & McGorty, 2004), the weapon focus effect (Steblay, 1992), facial recognition and identification (Shapiro & Penrod, 1986), and eyewitness repudiation (Whitley, 1987).

Consensus on Eyewitness Expert Testimony Among Key Actors in the Courts

In 2004, the American Bar Association (ABA) adopted a resolution with the aim of using scientific evidence to better inform the legal community on the topic of eyewitness identifications. The resolution's ultimate goal was to ensure justice (i.e., protect the innocent from the specter of false imprisonment; prosecute and imprison guilty parties). Specifically, the resolution stated that "courts should have the discretion, where appropriate in an individual case, to allow a properly qualified expert to testify both pre-trial and at trial on factors affecting eyewitness accuracy" (p. 2).

Because judges decide whether to admit expert testimony or not, it is important to understand whether these judges are accurate in their perceptions of the impact of the factors that influence identifications. We are also interested the accuracy of other individuals who may be involved in the adjudication of cases that rely on eyewitness identification testimony. The benchmark against which trial participants are compared is the perception of generally accepted research findings by scientific experts. What do the empirical data reveal in this regard?

Judicial Rulings

Historically, the courts have been hesitant to embrace expert testimony concerning eyewitness reliability. Most courts have not allowed defendants to use experts on eyewitness testimony, and even courts that have allowed them to testify have only done so on a limited basis (Handberg, 1995). Prior to *Daubert*, courts opting to exclude such testimony often did so without even mentioning *Frye* or the "general acceptance" standard (Woller, 2004). Although acceptance of expert testimony is becoming more common (see Epstein, Chapter 4), in recent years, courts operating under the *Daubert* criteria also remain reluctant to admit eyewitness experts (Fradella, 2006). A review of federal cases ruled under Daubert from its inception to the end of 2000 found that, out of 11 cases concerning an eyewitness expert, nine cases excluded the expert from testifying (Fradella, Fogarty, & O'Neill, 2003).

The reasons for exclusion have not always followed directly from *Frye* or *Daubert*. In fact, numerous rulings have held that the *Frye* standard did not apply to expert testimony on eyewitness reliability (*Bloodsworth v. Maryland*, 1986; *People v. McDonald*, 1984; *People v. Mooney*, 1990, *People v. Smith*, 2002). In one of the earliest cases to address expert testimony on eyewitnesses, the Court ruled in *Criglow v. State* (1931) that an eyewitness expert would invade the province of the jury. Since then, in rulings under both *Frye* and *Daubert*, the courts consistently reject such testimony on the grounds that it would not add anything beyond jurors' common knowledge (*United States v. Fosher*, 1979; *United States v. Rincon*, 1993); would not assist the trier of fact (*Green v. United States*, 1998; *People v. Slack*, 1987; *People v. Valentine*, 1976; *State v. Cromedy*, 1999; *State v. Hubbard*, 2004; *United States v. Hall*, 1999); would replace the jury in determining the credibility of a witness (*United States v. Lumpkin*, 1999); would mislead the jury (*United States v. Walton*, 2000); would serve no purpose beyond that of cross-examination (*Parker v. State*, 1998; *United States v. Crotteau*, 2000); would serve no purpose beyond that of jury instructions (*State v. Maestas*, 2002; *State v. Miles*, 1998); would unduly influence the jury (*United States v. Benson*, 1991); or would not be applicable to the case at hand (*State v. McClendon*, 1999). Still, a handful of jurisdictions have permitted expert testimony on eyewitness reliability (*Campbell v. Colorado*, 1991; *People v. Brooks*, 1985; *State v. Buell*, 1986; *State v. Chapple*, 1983), and a growing number of appeals have succeeded in getting experts into the courts (*People v. LeGrand*, 2007; *United States v. Downing*, 1985; *People v. McDonald*, 1984).

The ruling of the *People v. LeGrand* (2002) noted the inconsistencies in previous rulings and indicated that an "energized debate" existed on whether the consensus had been reached on issues concerning eyewitness reliability. It is interesting that, over a decade earlier in *People v. Mooney* (1990), the Court recognized that "psychological research data is (sic) by now abundant, and the findings based upon it concerning cognitive factors that may affect identification are quite uniform and well documented" (retrieved from Westlaw).

Still, despite this precedent, the Court in *LeGrand* (2002) originally ruled that expert testimony should be excluded on the basis that general acceptance had not yet been achieved.

Judges

Judges play an important role in the trial process, as they are the gatekeepers who decide whether an expert witness will be allowed to testify in court. Judges are solely responsible for determining if an expert witness meets the *Daubert* (or *Frye*) criteria, thus deciding if their scientific testimony will be admitted into court proceedings. Judges, like jurors, law enforcement, and attorneys are capable of falling prey to false beliefs and knowledge about aspects of eyewitness identification. The reliance on common sense is a general problem-solving strategy, yet in the case of eyewitness testimony, it can often lead to misinterpretation and false "knowledge" of factors affecting eyewitness identification accuracy.

Wise and Safer (2004) surveyed 160 U.S. judges and found that, when questioned about their beliefs and knowledge of factors affecting eyewitness identification, judges were correct, on average, in 55% of their responses. Compared to eyewitness experts, judges were less knowledgeable than the experts and more likely to have false beliefs about the ability of jurors to know the facts as derived from empirical research. That being said, 64% of judges disagreed with a statement that said that jurors are aware of *most eyewitness factors that affect identification accuracy*, showing that although judges fare worse than experts in regards to juror ability to interpret eyewitness testimony, over half are aware of juror misconceptions on the subject (Wise & Safer, 2004).

One might presume that judges who have served on the bench for many years would have a higher correct response rate, well above the average 55%, and would fall more in line with the eyewitness experts, but data from Wise and Safer show otherwise. Judicial experience and position were not correlated with knowledge of eyewitness factors. A relationship was observed between correct knowledge and certain judicial beliefs, however. For example, judges were aware of the fact that eyewitness misidentifications are one of the leading factors associated with wrongful convictions, and they believed that rarely, if ever, a defendant should be convicted exclusively on the basis of eyewitness testimony.

In a survey designed to compare the knowledge of eyewitness factors of judges and other participants in the criminal justice system to that of eyewitness experts, consensus was observed between judges and experts on 40% of the test items (Benton, Ross, Bradshaw, Thomas, & Bradshaw, 2006). Judges were less knowledgeable than experts about the possible misidentifications due to the presentation format used (simultaneous vs. sequential), less knowledgeable about mugshot-induced bias, and less knowledgeable about how the wording of questions may affect an eyewitness's testimony about an event, among other factors. Correspondence between judges and experts emerged on items concerning eyewitness confidence and the effects of lineup fairness. Ninety-five percent of experts and 88% of judges believe that confidence is malleable, and 70% of experts and 65% of judges believe that as the number of similar lineup foils increases, the higher the likelihood that the identification is correct.

A comparison of a survey of judges' practices regarding expert testimony on eyewitness factors in 1991 and again in 1998, showed that the *Daubert* (1993) ruling had an important impact on judges' legal decision making (Krafka, Dunn, Johnson, Cecil, & Miletich, 2002). Following the *Daubert* decision, judges were more stringent with the evidence they allowed experts to present at trial. Judges permitted 75% of cases to proceed with no evidence limitations in the initial survey, compared to 59% in the 1998 survey. Those judges who excluded expert testimony in both surveys cited reasons such as having unqualified witnesses and testimonial content that was irrelevant to the case.

Law Enforcement and Attorneys

Although law enforcement officers do not usually play a direct role in the interpretation of eyewitness testimony in the courtroom, it is important to understand the general acceptance of eyewitness factors among officers in the field. Law enforcement personnel are often responsible for investigating individuals who match descriptions given by eyewitnesses. It is imperative for officers to have an in-depth understanding of the influence of factors surrounding eyewitnesses' descriptions. Officers also play a vital role in lineup procedures, by creating the lineup and conducting the identification of the accused from the lineup. Law enforcement officers should be aware of the possible biasing effect of lineup procedures to make the identification of a suspect as impartial and accurate as possible. Law officers play an important role in assessing eyewitnesses, deciding which ones to believe, and then which ones to follow up on and which witness' statements to pursue. They also play an important role in helping the prosecutors decide which cases to pursue.

Law enforcement officers' responses to the survey on knowledge of eyewitness factors showed some similarity to the responses from judges (Benton et al., 2006). Police and judges only differed significantly on eight out of the 30 items, or 27% of the items. This was minimal in comparison to the differential responses between police and jurors' (43%) and between jurors' and judges' (53%). Analogous to the data collected from judges, law enforcement personnel showed consensus with experts on 40% of the items. Items that showed the greatest difference between experts and law enforcement officers included lineup instructions, presentation format, and child witness accuracy. Law enforcement had less knowledge about the effect that instructions can have on an eyewitness's willingness to make an identification, less knowledge about the influence of presentation format (simultaneous vs. sequential) on identification accuracy, and less knowledge about the lower accuracy rate of children's identifications compared to adults. Items of correspondence included but are not limited to knowledge that intoxication lowers the ability to recall persons and events, showups may increase false identification, and accuracy is not increased for identifications made under hypnosis.

Research on attorney knowledge and beliefs regarding eyewitness factors is a bit aged in comparison to the just mentioned studies, but it follows a similar pattern in that attorneys, too, are limited in their understanding of factors associated with eyewitness identification. At the time of Brigham and WolfsKeil (1983), there was no literature on eyewitness experts, so a direct comparison between attorneys and experts could not be made. With that being said, Brigham and WolfsKeil surveyed 235 public defenders, prosecutors, and private attorneys on items resembling those that would later appear in the survey by Benton and colleagues (2006). When questioned about factors that would have the most influence on identification accuracy, attorneys often mentioned exposure time and physical attributes of the suspect, frequently overlooking factors associated with system variables such as lineup procedures and wording of questions. It is unclear whether the absence of these items in the attorney's responses can be attributed to a lack of knowledge or a limitation of the survey.

Attorneys reported in a 1999 survey about beliefs and practices of expert eyewitness testimony that *Daubert* rulings have altered their behavior concerning eyewitness factors (Krafka et al., 2002). This was attributed to the fact that *Daubert* has drawn attention to important aspects of eyewitness testimony, making it more likely for lawyers to examine their own experts to determine if they are qualified to testify. They also reported that, post-*Daubert*, they are more likely to file motions of exclusion for opposing expert eyewitness testimony and are more involved in the preparation of their own experts. Attorneys also reported that in their experience after *Daubert*, judges have been more likely to scrutinize experts' credibility, which increased the amounts of excluded testimony. Taking into account the expected limitations of self-report surveys, this research lends support for a stronger and more vigilant legal system in respect to expert testimony in a post-*Daubert* era.

Jurors

It is true that the majority of cases are settled through plea agreements. Yet, the seemingly small numbers of jury trials are still a significant part of the American legal system. For cases that are tried by a jury of peers, jurors are key players in the verdict and, in some jurisdictions, the sentencing phase of a trial. In a jury trial that involves eyewitness testimony, jurors are not only responsible for interpreting the validity of the testimony, but also for deciding to what extent the testimony will play a role in the deliberation, and ultimately the verdict. Eyewitness experts can supply jurors with testimony on reliable evidence to assist them in their decision-making with the intent of alleviating any concerns regarding eyewitness factors. As mentioned earlier, 96% of experts said they *would not* testify if they felt the research was "inconclusive" on a topic, compared to approximately 91% who said they *would* testify on research evidence that was "very reliable" (Kassin et al., 2001). These numbers should provide the legal system and jurors alike with a level of confidence in the testimony of expert witnesses. When asked about their role as expert witnesses, more than three-fourths of the experts said that their primary purpose was to educate the jury, and much of the remainder said their primary purpose was to educate other legal-minded bodies such as judges, law enforcement officers, and policy makers.

Jurors and experts differed on their answers to survey items 87% of the time, indicating the lack of correct knowledge held by jurors with respect to eyewitness phenomena (Benton et al., 2006). Items that showed the greatest discrepancy between the two groups were those dealing with lineup instructions and presentation format. The inaccuracy of jurors' knowledge was demonstrated in that more jurors tended to think that observers can accurately tell the difference between true and false memories and that a clear relationship exists between accuracy and identification speed.

We should mention here that the majority of these data come from jury-eligible individuals, college students, or members of the public, not community residents who served on a jury. That being said, studies have validated the use of mock jurors by demonstrating their empirical similarity to actual jurors (Bornstein, 1999; Cutler, Penrod, & Dexter, 1989; Devenport & Cutler, 2004; Diamond, 1997; cf. Flowe, Finklea, & Ebbesen, Chapter 9).

In a study that used an actual jury sample, Seltzer, Lopes, and Venuti (1990) found that on average jurors possessed insufficient knowledge of factors affecting eyewitness identifications. One-hundred and ninety jurors in the District of Columbia were interviewed within 90 days of the trial date. Of those jurors, 60 had sat on a case in which the eyewitness identification was contested, and 130 more sat on a case in which there was no dispute about the identification. The jurors were asked general questions pertaining to potential problems associated with eyewitness identifications, and data from five of the questions were analyzed.

No significant differences in juror understanding of potential problems associated with eyewitness identification were found between the 60 jurors who had the eyewitness testimony contested and the 130 who did not on four out of the five questions (Seltzer et al., 1990). This was an unexpected finding because it was assumed that the problems surrounding eyewitness identification would be more salient for those who heard the contested testimony, thus increasing their understanding of problems associated with eyewitness identification. This was not the case for the one question, on which the two groups differed significantly. Jurors who decided the case in which the eyewitness testimony was challenged were *less likely* than were the other jurors to correctly believe that the relationship between identification confidence and accuracy is zero. It also was found that jurors who were undecided in verdict when they first entered the deliberation phase were more likely to believe that no association existed between eyewitness identification accuracy and confidence in that identification. Seltzer and his colleagues provided one of the first studies that analyzed actual juror beliefs regarding factors surrounding accurate eyewitness identification. The psycho-legal field would further benefit from an updated study that utilizes real jurors' perceptions and knowledge of similar factors, since there have been dynamic changes in the legal system as well as increased publicity and public awareness of problems associated with correct identification.

In Chapter 6 of this volume, by Read and Desmarais, a compelling case is made that the available data testing public awareness of the factors that influence eyewitness accuracy and the direction in which these factors work are complex. They argue that the outcome of any particular empirical study depends upon the method used to assess potential jurors' knowledge. In brief, when public knowledge is assessed directly, the data do show that people understand the influence of some variables (e.g., question wording, the impact of alcohol intoxication), but are not aware of the impact of other factors (e.g., sequential or simultaneous lineups; the relation between identification accuracy and confidence). Possibly more importantly, Read and Desmarais conclude that when the jurors are asked to apply what they know, and their knowledge is assessed indirectly, they perform quite poorly. We urge you to read their insightful analysis.

Textbook Coverage of Eyewitness Issues

A final method to assess the general acceptance of expert testimony in the field is to examine the degree to which the literature has made it into college and university textbooks. A lag is to be expected between the time studies are published as they typically are in journal formats and when they begin to be cited in texts. Textbook authors and their publishers are motivated to have their books be up to date as possible, so that they remain as current with the state of research in the field as possible. Texts from four topical domains seem most pertinent here: legal psychology or psychology and law, social psychology, cognitive psychology, and those designed for introductory courses in psychology.

We conducted a review of available texts to explore these fields. We want to make it clear that our review can only be called a casual one. The texts we reviewed were made available to us by colleagues who typically teach these courses at but one university. They did have a large number of current textbooks, however, so we are pretty sure we have been able to capture the essence of the data we would have obtained had we taken the time and energy to do an exhaustive, systematic search.

The basic question we asked was: Are the factors that influence eyewitness identifications discussed under that rubric in the texts? If so, what are the most prominent sub-themes and studies?

First, we looked at texts written to be the primary resource of information for courses in introduction to psychology, cognitive psychology, social psychology, and psychology and law. It should be the case that textbook writers in these domains are closest to the issues surrounding testimony by eyewitness experts. It was expected that their texts would reflect that knowledge. The introductory psychology texts were chosen because they represent the broadest market and the first survey course taught at virtually all colleges and universities. The majority of researchers who are studying issues in eyewitness identification have been trained in cognitive or in social psychology, and the issues themselves typically would be classified as factors under the general rubrics of social or cognitive psychology. If an institution offers a major or a minor field of study in psychology, it is very likely that it will provide courses in cognitive and in social psychology in its curriculum. Finally, some institutions teach a specialty undergraduate course in psychology and law, as the field has become quite popular among faculty and undergraduate students alike.

Introductory Psychology

We focused on some 20 texts currently on the market and found that almost all of them addressed at least some issues of eyewitness identification and some of the factors that influence eyewitness testimony. These themes were almost always discussed in the section or chapter of the texts in which memory was the primary focus. The most important studies, based on their citation frequency, were those of Elizabeth Loftus and her colleagues, in which the influence of question wording on identifications was explored. Another frequent theme was the impact on child witnesses' testimony of suggestions made by adults.

Social Psychology

Seven textbooks in social psychology revealed an emphasis on three main themes: that eyewitnesses are imperfect, that certain factors can systematically influence eyewitness' performance, and that judges, lawyers, and juries are not adequately informed about the these factors. Specific topics discussed frequently look at factors that influence memory acquisition, storage, and retrieval. Some of these were: the fact that arousal impairs memory for less central details of witnessed events and contexts, how alcohol makes eyewitnesses less accurate, that identifications of individuals of different race or ethnic group than the witness are less likely to be accurate, that attention focuses on a weapon rather than the perpetrator if a weapon is present, that the wording of questions can influence the reconstruction of memories, that people recall events that did not actually take place, that reconstructing culprits' faces from an array of features rarely results in an image that actually looks like the culprit, that lineup formats may influence identification accuracy rates, and that retelling a story facilitates recollection even if the story and thus the memory is incorrect. Finally, social psychology texts emphasize the fact that jurors overestimate the correlation between eyewitness accuracy and confidence.

Cognitive Psychology

Seven recent texts in the subfield of cognitive psychology were reviewed and were found to have major sections of the content focused on issues in attention deployment, perception, language processing, memory processes, and the like. It should be obvious then that these texts would incorporate the research of psychologists whose work on basic cognitive processes plays out or can be applied in forensic settings. For example, major works by Elizabeth Loftus focusing on memory distortion and the impact of suggestion are again cited in these texts; Robert Sternberg (2006) cites 10 publications in which Loftus is first author. It is clear that the research of eyewitness experts is a major component of the content of cognitive psychology courses.

Psychology and Law

There are texts for courses introducing students to the domain of psychology and law, but there are fewer because the market is smaller than that for introductory, or social, or cognitive psychology. The five that were reviewed discussed factors that influence eyewitness identifications. Indeed, the texts reserve whole units or chapters to discussions of eyewitness identification factors. These sections add important qualifiers to broad eyewitness identification phenomena. In addition to the factors mentioned earlier, factors discussed included change blindness, that people cannot detect subtle changes in visual field (Grimes, 1996; Simons & Ambinder, 2005); the effect of age of the eyewitness on identification accuracy, that older people and young children make more mistakes; the potential impact of experimenter bias in research designs and the use of double blind methods reduce such bias; that hypnosis should not be used with eyewitness and that the data indicate that there is no increase in accuracy as a result of witness hypnosis (Newman & Thompson, 2001; Steblay & Bothwell, 1994; Webert, 2003); that recovered memories that have been repressed have not been scientifically validated as accurate memories (Gerrie, Garry, & Loftus, 2005; Holmes, 1995); and the distinction between system and estimator variables (Wells, 1978). *System variables* are those that may be modified by the justice system such as the manner in which a lineup is conducted. *Estimator variables*, on the other hand, cannot be modified by the justice system, and experts can only hope to quantify their influence. An estimator variable is exemplified in cross-race identification. The police must take witnesses and suspects as they are with respect to the race of the individuals involved. Race cannot be controlled by the system.

It is clear from these casual survey data that textbook writers who endeavor to reflect the status of the field of psychology in the content of their books (lest they not be adopted for use in college and university courses), have accepted the primary themes of the eyewitness experts as de rigueur for inclusion in their books. We suggest, therefore, that general acceptance of these factors is quite widespread.

In addition to textbooks that have devoted valuable space to this issue, we note as well that sessions of professional meetings are regularly devoted to the topic, that the U.S. Attorney General convened a group of eyewitness researchers and practitioners as early as 1999 to consider policy and best practices in the domain, and that millions of dollars have been invested to advance the research in this field. Finally, we note that the most prestigious of journals devote space to publishing the research in the area.

General Summary

What testimony by experts on the factors that have an impact on eyewitness identification is generally accepted by the relevant scientific community? From what legal precedents does the criterion of general acceptance emanate? To what degree are the factors that influence identification known and accepted beyond the scientific community? This chapter focused on these issues and presented historical and empirical evidence to identify and support the answers.

The results of the empirical research focusing on experts' judgments as to the results of the empirical work suggest considerable agreement. Issues of disagreement among eyewitness experts focus on the application of the empirical findings to specific cases at bar and the benefit that expert testimony will have for legal decision makers. Wells (1997) summarized the state of affairs quite nicely when he said:

> The fact that disagreement among eyewitness experts has revolved primarily around these two concerns is interesting for a number of reasons. First, these concerns by eyewitness experts are similar to concerns that have been raised by the courts in addressing the question of the admissibility of expert testimony. In *Daubert v. Merrill Dow Pharmaceuticals*, for instance, the Court stresses the importance of whether the expert knows something the jury does not, whether the knowledge applies to the facts of the case, and whether the expert would assist the jury. These areas of concern among eyewitness experts, however, are not borrowed from judicial rulings regarding the admissibility of expert testimony but instead were developed from within psychology as a natural outgrowth of the question of what can be done to address the problem of inaccuracy in eyewitness identification. Second, it is interesting to note that eyewitness experts may be the only scientific group that has

taken so seriously the question of whether they can assist the juror that they have actually conducted studies to try to answer the question. (p. 478)

We began this chapter with a discussion of the *LeGrand* case, in which an expert witness was not allowed to testify to factors that may have influenced an eyewitness identification. The picture has now changed. Indeed, the ruling in *LeGrand* took an interesting turn in 2007 when the New York Court of Appeals held that the defendant's expert should have been admitted, citing that the principles upon which the expert in question based his conclusions were generally accepted by scientists in the relevant field. Further, the court noted that in cases in which little or no corroborating evidence existed connecting the defendant to the crime, testimony on the reliability of eyewitness identification needed to be included. The court enumerated conditions that must be satisfied in order for an expert to testify in such cases, including that the testimony be "(a) relevant to the witness's identification of defendant, (b) based on principles that are generally accepted within the relevant scientific community, (c) proffered by a qualified expert and, (d) on a topic beyond the ken of the average juror" (*People v. LeGrand*, 2007). Thus, recent developments suggest that judicial perception of the value of expert testimony may be changing. We leave it to the reader to attach a value to that change.

References

American Bar Association. (2004). *Report to the House of Delegates Recommendation, American Bar Association, Criminal Justice Section.* Retrieved November 10, 2007, from www.abanet.org/leadership/2004/annual/111c.doc.

Anthony, T., Copper, C., & Mullen, B. (1992). Cross-racial facial identification: A social cognitive integration. *Personality and Social Psychology Bulletin, 18,* 296–301.

Benton, T.J., Ross, D.F., Bradshaw, E., Thomas, W.N., & Bradshaw, G.S. (2006). Eyewitness memory is still not common sense: Comparing jurors, judges and law enforcement to eyewitness experts. *Applied Cognitive Psychology, 20,* 115–129.

Bernstein, D.E. (2001) *Frye, Frye, Again: The Past, Present, and Future of the General Acceptance Test.* George Mason University School of Law, Law and Economics Research Papers Series, Paper No. 01-07-2001, Retrieved July 12, 2007 from http://papers.ssrn.com/paper.taf?abstract_id=262034.

Bernstein, D. E., & Jackson, J. D. (2004). The Daubert trilogy in the states. *Jurimetrics Journal, 44,* 351–366.

Bloodsworth v. State, 307 Md. 164, 167 (1986).

Bornstein, B.H. (1999). The ecological validity of jury simulations: Is the jury still out? *Law and Human Behavior, 23,* 75–91.

Bothwell, R. K., Brigham, J. C., & Malpass, R. S. (1989). Cross-racial identification. *Personality and Social Psychology Bulletin, 15,* 19–25.

Bothwell, R. K., Deffenbacher, K. A., & Brigham, J. C. (1987). Correlation of eyewitness accuracy and confidence: Optimality hypothesis revisited. *Journal of Applied Psychology*, *72*, 691–695.

Brigham, J.C., & WolfsKeil, M.P. (1983). Opinions of attorneys and law enforcement personnel on the accuracy of eyewitness identifications. *Law and Human Behavior*, *7*, 337–349.

Campbell v. *People*, 814 P.2d 1(Colo. 1991).

Clifford, B.R. (1997). A commentary on Ebbesen and Konečni's "Eyewitness memory research: Probative v. prejudicial value." *Expert Evidence*, *5*, 140–143.

Criglow v. State, T83 Ark. 407, 36 S.W.2d 400 (1931).

Cutler, B.L., & Penrod, S. D. (1989). Forensically relevant moderators of the relation between eyewitness accuracy and confidence. *Journal of Applied Psychology*, *74*, 650–652.

Cutler, B.L., Penrod, S.D., & Dexter, H.R. (1989). The eyewitness, the expert psychologist, and the jury. *Law and Human Behavior*, *13*, 311–332.

Daftary, T. & Penrod, S.D. (2008). General acceptance among experts of eyewitness search findings: A 2007 update. Unpublished manuscript, John Jay College of Criminal Justice, City University of New York.

Daubert v. Merrill Dow Pharmaceuticals, Inc., 509 U.S. 579 (1993).

Deffenbacher, K. A., Bornstein, B. H., Penrod, S. D., & McGorty, E. K. (2004). A meta-analytic review of the effects of high stress on eyewitness memory. *Law and Human Behavior*, *28*, 687–706.

Devenport, J. L & Cutler, B. L.(2004). Impact of defense-only and opposing eyewitness experts on juror judgments. *Law and Human Behavior*, *28*, 569–576.

Diamond, S. S. (1997). Illuminations and shadows from jury simulations. *Law and Human Behavior*, *21*, 561–571.

Douglass, A. B., & Steblay, N. M. (2006). Memory distortion in eyewitnesses: A meta-analysis of the post-identification feedback effect. *Applied Cognitive Psychology*, *20*, 859–869.

Ebbesen, E. B., & Konečni, V. J. (1996). Eyewitness memory research: Probative v. prejudicial value, *Expert Evidence, 5*, 2–28.

Elliott, R. (1993). Expert testimony about eyewitness identification: A critique. *Law and Human Behavior*, *17*, 423–437.

Federal Rules of Evidence Rule 702, 28 U.S.C.A.

Federal Rules of Evidence Rule 401, 28 U.S.C.A.

Fisher, D. E. (1994). *Daubert v. Merrell Dow Pharmaceuticals*: The Supreme Court gives federal judges the keys to the gate of admissibility of expert scientific testimony. *South Dakota Law Review*, 141. Retrieved July 12, 2007 from Westlaw Campus Research database.

Fradella, H. F. (2006). Why judges should admit expert testimony on the unreliability of eyewitness testimony. *Federal Courts Law Review*, 1. Retrieved July 12, 2007 from Westlaw Campus Research database.

Fradella, H. F., Fogarty, A., & O'Neill, L. (2003). The impact of Daubert on the admissibility of behavioral science testimony. *Pepperdine Law Review*, 403. Retrieved July 12, 2007 from Westlaw Campus Research database.

Frye v. United States, 293 F. 1013 (D.C. Cir. 1923).

General Electric v. Joiner, 522 U.S. 136 (1997).

Gerrie, M. P., Garry, M., & Loftus, E. F. (2005). False memories In N. Brewer (Ed.), *Psychology and law: An empirical perspective* (pp. 222–253). New York: Guilford Press.

Goodman, J., & Loftus, E. F. (1988). The relevance of expert testimony on eyewitness memory. *Journal of Interpersonal Violence, 3,* 115–121.

Green v. United States, 718 A.2d 1042 (1998).

Grimes, J. (1996). On the failure to detect changes in scenes across saccades. In K. Akins (Ed.), *Perception* (Vol. 2, pp. 89–110). New York: Oxford University Press.

Groscup, J. L., Penrod, S. D., Studebaker, C. A., Huss, M. T., & O'Neil, K. M. (2002). The effects of Daubert on the admissibility of expert testimony in state and federal cases. *Psychology, Public Policy, and Law, 8,* 339–372.

Handberg, R. B. (1995). Expert testimony on eyewitness identification: A new pair of glasses for the jury. *American Criminal Law Review, 32.* Retrieved July 12, 2007 from Westlaw Campus Research database.

Holmes, D. S. (1995). The evidence for repression: An examination of sixty years of research. In J. L. Singer (Ed.), *Repression and dissociation: Implications for personality theory, psychopathology and health* (pp. 85–102). Chicago: University of Chicago Press.

Iacono, W. G., & Lykken, D. T. (1997). The validity of the lie detector: Two surveys of scientific opinion. *Journal of Applied Psychology, 82,* 426–433.

Kassin, S. M., Ellsworth, P. C., & Smith, V. L. (1989). The "general acceptance" of psychological research on eyewitness testimony. *American Psychologist, 44,* 1089–1098.

Kassin, S. M., Tubb, V. A., Hosch, H. M., & Memon, A. (2001). On the "general acceptance" of eyewitness testimony research: A new survey of the experts. *American Psychologist, 56,* 405–416.

Kassin, S. M., Tubb, V. A., Hosch, H. M., & Memon, A. (2002). Eyewitness experts as experts in court: Responsive to change in a dynamic and rational process. *American Psychologist, 57,* 378–379.

Kovera, M. B., Borgida, E., Gresham, A. W., Swim, J., & Gray, E. (1993). Do child sexual abuse experts hold pro-child beliefs?: A survey of the International Society for Traumatic Stress Studies. *Journal of Traumatic Stress, 6,* 383–404.

Krafka, C., Dunn, M. A., Johnson, M. T., Cecil, J. S., & Miletich, D. (2002). Judge and attorney experiences, practices, and concerns regarding expert testimony in federal civil trials. *Psychology, Public Policy, and Law, 8,* 309–332.

Kumho Tire Co. v. *Carmichael,* 526 U.S. 137 (1999).

Lally, S. J. (2003). What tests are acceptable for use in forensic evaluations? A survey of experts. *Professional Psychology, Research, and Practice, 34,* 491–498.

Loftus, E. F. (1986). Ten years in the life of an expert witness. *Law and Human Behavior, 10,* 241–263.

McCloskey, M., Egeth, H., & McKenna, J. (1986) The experimental psychologist in court: The ethics of expert testimony. *Law and Human Behavior, 10,* 1–13.

McCullough, M. L. (2002). Do not discount lay opinion. *American Psychologist, 57,* 376–377.

McKenna, J., Treadway, M., & McClosky, M. E. (1992). Selling psychology before its time. In P. Suedfeld & P. E. Tetlock, (Eds.), *Psychology and social policy,* (pp. 283–294). New York: Hemisphere Books.

McQuiston-Surrett, D., Malpass, R. S., & Tredoux, C. G. (2006). Sequential vs. simultaneous lineups: A review of methods, data, and theory. *Psychology, Public Policy, and Law, 12,* 137–169.

Meissner, C. A., & Brigham, J. C. (2001). Thirty years of investigating the own-race bias in memory for faces: A meta-analytic review. *Psychology, Public Policy, and Law, 7,* 3–35.

Murphy, K. R., Cronin, B. E., & Tam, A. P. (2003). Controversy and consensus regarding the use of cognitive ability testing in organizations. *Journal of Applied Psychology,* 660–671.

Newman, A. W., & Thompson, J. W. (2001). The rise and fall of forensic hypnosis in criminal investigation. *Journal of the American Academy of Psychiatry and Law, 29,* 75–84.

Parker v. State, 333 Ark. 137, 968 S.W.2d 592 (1998).

People v. Brooks, 128 Misc 2d 608 (Westchester County Ct. 1985).

People v. LeGrand, 196 Misc.2d 179 at 202 (New York County 2001).

People v. LeGrand, 8 N.Y.3d 449, 835 N.Y.S.2d 523, 867 N.E.2d 374 (2007).

People v. McDonald, 37 Cal.3d 351 208 Cal. Rptr. 236 (California Supreme Court 1984).

People v. Mooney, 76 NY2d 827, 829–830 (1990).

People v. Slack, 516 N.Y.S.2d 309 (N.Y App. Div. 1987).

People v. Smith, 191 Misc.2d 765 (New York County 2002).

People v. Valentine, 53 App. Div. 2d 832, 385 N.Y.S.2d 545, 546 (1976).

Seltzer, R., Lopes, G. M., Venuti, M. (1990). Juror ability to recognize the limitations of eyewitness identifications. *Forensic Reports, 3,* 121–137.

Shapiro, P. N., & Penrod, S. (1986). Meta-analysis of facial identification studies. *Psychological Bulletin, 100,* 139–156.

Simons D. J., Ambinder M. S. (2005) Change blindness: theory and consequences. *Current Directions in Psychological Science, 14,* 4448.

Sporer, S. L., Penrod, S., Read, D., & Cutler, B. (1995). Choosing, confidence, and accuracy: A meta-analysis of the confidence-accuracy relation in eyewitness identification status. *Psychological Bulletin, 118,* 315–327.

State v. Buell, 22 Ohio St.3d 124 (1986).

State v. Chapple, 660 P.2d 1208 (Ariz. 1983).

State v. Cromedy, 727 A.2d 457, 467-68 (N.J. 1999).

State v. Hubbard, 267 Neb. 316, 673 N.W.2d 567 (2004).

State v. Maestas, 63 P.3d 621 (Utah 2002).

State v. McClendon, 248 Conn. 572 (Conn. 1999).

State v. Miles, 585 N.W.2d 368, 371-72 (Minn. 1998).

Steblay, N. M. (1992). A meta-analytic review of the weapon focus effect. *Law and Human Behavior, 16,* 413–424.

Steblay, N. M. (1997). Social influence in eyewitness recall: A meta-analytic review of lineup instruction effects. *Law and Human Behavior, 21,* 283–297.

Steblay, N. M., & Bothwell, R. K. (1994). Evidence for hypnotically refreshed testimony: The view from the laboratory. *Law and Human Behavior, 18,* 635–651.

Steblay, N. M., Dysart, J. E., Fulero, S., & Lindsay, R. C. L. (2001). Eyewitness accuracy rates in sequential and simultaneous lineup presentations: A meta-analytic comparison. *Law and Human Behavior, 25,* 459–473.

Steblay, N. M., Dysart, J. E., Fulero, S., & Lindsay, R. C. L. (2003). Eyewitness accuracy in police showup and lineup presentations: A meta-analytic comparison. *Law and Human Behavior, 27*, 523–540.

Sternberg, R. J. (2006). *Cognitive Psychology* (Fourth Ed.). Belmont, CA: Thompson Wadsworth.

Technical Working Group for Eyewitness Evidence. (1999). Eyewitness evidence: A guide for law enforcement. Washington, DC: National Institute of Justice.

United States v. Benson, 941 F.2d 598, 604-606 (7th Cir. 1991).

United States v. Crotteau, 218 F. 3d 826, 832 (7th Cir. 2000).

United States v. Downing, 609 F.Supp. 784 (D.C. Pa. 1985).

United States v. Fosher, 590 F.2d 381 (1st Cir. 1979).

United States v. Hall, 165 F. 3d 1095, 1107 (7th Cir. 1999).

United States v. Lumpkin, 192 F. 3d 280, 289 (2d Cir. 1999).

United States v. Rincon, 921 F.3d 28 (9th Cir. 1993).

United States v. Smithers, 212 F 3d 306, 316 (6th Cir. 2000).

United States *v.* Walton, 217 F.3d 443, 449 (7th Cir. 2000)

Webert, D. (2003). Are the courts in a trance? Approaches to the admissibility of hypnotically enhanced witness testimony in light of empirical evidence. *American Criminal Law Review, 40*, 1301–1327.

Wells, G. L. (1978). Applied eyewitness-testimony research: System variables and estimator variables. *Journal of Personality & Social Psychology, 36*, 1546–1557.

Wells, G. (1997). The scientific status of research on eyewitness identifications. In D.L. Faigman, D.H. Kaye, M.J. Saks, & J. Sanders (Eds.). *Modern scientific evidence: The law and science of expert testimony,* Vol. 1, 451–479. St. Paul, MN: West Publishing Co.

Whitley, Jr., B. E. (1987). The effects of discredited eyewitness testimony: A meta-analysis. *Journal of Social Psychology, 127*, 209–214.

Wise, R. A., & Safer, M. A. (2004). What U.S. judges know and believe about eyewitness testimony. *Applied Cognitive Psychology, 18*, 427–433.

Woller, S. (2004). Rethinking the role of expert testimony regarding the reliability of eyewitness identification in New York. *New York Law School Law Review,* 323. Retrieved July 12, 2007 from Westlaw Campus Research database.

Yarmey, A. D., & Jones, H. P. T. (1983). Is the psychology of eyewitness identification a matter of common sense? In S. Lloyd-Bostock & B. R. Clifford (Eds.), *Evaluating witness evidence: Recent psychological research and new perspectives* (pp. 13–40). New York: Wiley.

8

The Influence of Eyewitness Expert Testimony on Jurors' Beliefs and Judgments

Michael R. Leippe and Donna Eisenstadt

Jurors typically find confident eyewitness testimony quite convincing, even when the product of a witnessing experience is unfavorable to formation of a good memory (Leippe, 1995). Especially when placed against the mounting evidence that eyewitness testimony is prone to error and suggestion that is often produced—unwillfully and willfully—by the police to whom eyewitnesses report their memories, this ready belief in confident eyewitnesses is a worrisome matter. Mistaken identifications, if believed in the courtroom, result in miscarriages of justice.

The influential power of and associated problems with eyewitness testimony have been recognized by the courts for some time, albeit often in an understated and underappreciative fashion. Legal scholars point out that several remedies or safeguards are in place within the legal system that help protect the falsely identified and accused from the persuasive pointing finger of an eyewitness. These safeguards include, at the time of trial, cross-examination of eyewitnesses and judge's cautionary instructions to jurors that eyewitnesses can err. Before trial, when a suspicion exists that identification procedures were unduly suggestive, attorneys have opportunities to seek suppression of eyewitness identifications, thereby keeping them from any possibility of misleading a jury. Research into the efficacy of these safeguards, however, suggests they are often ineffective (Devenport, Kimbrough, & Cutler, Chapter 3; Leippe, 1995; Patterson, 2004). A major reason for this is that, as Devenport, Penrod, and Cutler (1997) noted, "these safeguards are based on assumptions regarding attorneys,' judges,' and jurors' commonsense knowledge about factors that influence eyewitness identifications" (p. 339), and, as we shall see later and as reviewed elsewhere in this volume (Devenport et al., in Chapter 3; Read & Desmarais, in Chapter 6), the requisite knowledge is often lacking. Accordingly, for more than 30 years now, a number of psycho-legal scholars (and some merely legal scholars) have championed the remedy of expert testimony that informs jurors about the nature of eyewitness memory and the factors scientifically known to affect it, and thereby, ideally, gives them the knowledge and understanding they need to better judge the accuracy of an incriminating identification (see, e.g., Leippe, 1995).

Eyewitness expert testimony may be defined as "the delivery to a jury by a qualified research psychologist of information about research and theory on eyewitness behavior" (Leippe, 1995, p. 910). As such, it is primarily an educational endeavor. But, it can also be seen as an information- or cognitively based persuasive appeal. Although the expert's goal usually (and prescriptively) is not to persuade jurors to trust or distrust the eyewitness, or to judge the defendant as more or less guilty, there is the intent to persuade jurors to believe that eyewitness memory has certain qualities. The qualities happen to be negative, accuracy-inhibiting ones for the most part (i.e., the expert notes that people may overestimate the likely accuracy of recognition of strangers, and describes witnessing and testing factors in terms of how they may decrease accuracy). As a result, new or heightened belief in these attributes of eyewitness memory—the desired increase in knowledge and understanding that is the intended proximal, direct effect of the expert testimony—can be expected to have the more distal, indirect effect of persuading jurors to believe the eyewitness less.

At least that is what many parties in the research and legal communities, including the defense attorneys who eagerly seek eyewitness experts, hope will happen. In this chapter, we review and summarize research on the impact of eyewitness expert testimony, concentrating on research reported in the years since the last comprehensive review of the literature in this area by Leippe (1995). We first examine just what level of juror knowledge—or ignorance—is likely to greet experts as they take the witness stand. Just how deficient is it? And, what is the usual impact of eyewitness evidence when, as in the vast majority of eyewitness-based cases, no eyewitness expert enters the courtroom picture? With this baseline of sorts established, we then look at the effects of expert testimony in research that has manipulated its presence or absence, mainly in trial simulations. Last, we discuss, largely theoretically, what the process of expert influence might entail.

Juror Beliefs and Knowledge in the Absence of Expert Advice: Evidence of a Need for Expert Testimony

Belief and Overbelief

Trial simulation studies, among other research endeavors, reveal that eyewitness testimony is highly incriminating. Loftus (1974) provided an early demonstration of this. Participants read a summary of a court case that either included or did not include the positive identification testimony of an eyewitness along with some other incriminating evidence. The percentage of participants voting guilty was 18% when no eyewitness was present, and 72% when there was. More recently, Sigler and Couch (2002) found that adding a single, vaguely described eyewitness to the circumstantial evidence described in a case summary increased guilty votes from 45% to 68%.

Consistent with this impression of belief gleaned mainly from college students' responses to simulated trial evidence, archival data from the real world reveals clear evidence that eyewitness evidence by itself is persuasive. Research undertaken by the Devlin Commission in England in the 1970s examined more than 300 trials in which the only evidence was a positive lineup identification. In 75% of these cases, the defendant was convicted (Devlin, 1976). More recently, in the United States, the number of exonerations of convicted prisoners through DNA testing reached 211 by 2008 (Scheck & Neufield, 2008). More than 75% of the cases involved a positive, but clearly false, identification, and often the identification was pretty much the only truly incriminating evidence.

Eyewitness testimony, then, is persuasive, and perhaps to a fault. Two lines of evidence, reviewed by Leippe (1995) and Boyce, Beaudry, and Lindsay (2007), suggest that eyewitnesses are *overbelieved*. In one line, participants read descriptions of an actual study in which witnesses attempted a lineup identification of the culprit in a staged event, and then estimated what percentage of such witnesses would make an accurate identification. Overestimation has been the rule in such research, and is best exemplified in a study by Brigham and Bothwell (1983). These researchers found that, on average, participants guessed that 71% of the witnesses wouldmake an accurate identification in a staged-crime condition in which only 12.5% of the witnesses actually were accurate. In the second line of research, using the so-called two-phase paradigm, "participant jurors" watch the videotaped testimony of "participant witnesses" who had made an accurate or inaccurate identification of the culprit in a staged crime. In these studies, not only are participant jurors generally incapable of discriminating between accurate and inaccurate eyewitnesses, they also believe an inaccurate participant witness was accurate anywhere from 40% to 80% of the time (e.g., Lindsay, Wells, & Rumpel, 1981; Wells, Lindsay, & Ferguson, 1979).

What appears to cinch factfinders' belief is the confidence of the eyewitness, asserted, apparent, or both. In the two-phase studies, it has been found that the perceived confidence of participant witnesses accounts for half of all the variance in participant jurors' estimates of whether their identifications were accurate, and that an experimental treatment (e.g., coaching) that raises the apparent confidence of inaccurate witnesses raises the belief of participant witnesses who watch their testimony (e.g. Wells, Ferguson, & Lindsay, 1981; Wells & Leippe, 1981). In trial simulations, moreover, both witness believability and guilty verdicts are increased when the prosecution's eyewitness openly asserts more confidence or emits nonverbal signs of confidence (Whitley & Greenberg, 1986).

In actual trials, of course, eyewitnesses are very likely to express strong confidence in the correctness of their identification. They have become publicly committed to their identification, are aware that the police agree that they "have the right guy," are aware of any additional evidence that the police and prosecution believe corroborate their testimony, and have probably been coached to be confident. Confidence has proven to be only a modest indicator of accuracy even in the absence of these forces that drive up confidence for accurate and inaccurate eyewitnesses alike (Bothwell, Deffenbacher, & Brigham, 1987; Leippe & Eisenstadt, 2007; Penrod & Cutler, 1995). One advocated role of expert testimony is to disabuse jurors of their belief that confident witnesses are accurate witnesses.

The Knowledge Gap

Factfinders may too-readily believe confident eyewitnesses because of their belief in a strong confidence–accuracy relationship, as well as for other reasons. The assumption that confidence bespeaks accuracy may be part of an overall stereotype about eyewitnesses comprised of meta-memorial beliefs or assumptions about how memory works (cf. Leippe, Eisenstadt, Rauch, & Stambush, 2006). Many of these beliefs may be wrong, however, to the extent that most individuals have little or no experience with eyewitness-like memory tasks (Wells, Lindsay, & Ferguson, 1979) and may misapply their greater experience in recognizing familiar faces to the unfamiliar or once-seen face recognition required of most eyewitnesses.

Indeed, the primary culprit in overbelief is that would-be jurors lack knowledge of how important and frequently present factors in the witnessing experience negatively impact on memory and the reporting of memory. Researchers have been assessing the knowledge of would-be jurors since the early 1980s and have consistently found it to be rather severely lacking (Benton, Ross, Bradshaw, Thomas, & Bradshaw, 2006; Deffenbacher & Loftus, 1982; Kassin & Barndollar, 1992; Schmechel, O'Toole, Easterly, & Loftus, 2006; Yarmey & Jones, 1983). This is well-illustrated in one of the more recent surveys. Replicating a methodology used by Kassin and Barndollar (1992), Benton and colleagues (2006) assessed the extent to which 111 Tennessee residents summoned to jury duty agreed with statements describing findings regarding eyewitness accuracy that eyewitness experts had judged in terms of accuracy when surveyed by Kassin, Tubb, Hosch, and Memon (2001). This survey of experts revealed 16 findings that 70% or more of 64 experts declared were reliable enough to present in courtroom expert testimony—findings that, by the criterion of expert agreement, could be considered generally accepted. Benton and colleagues (2006) found that, for 15 of these 16 items, the percentage of prospective jurors who judged the finding as "generally true" (vs. "generally false" or "don't know") was significantly lower than the percentage of eyewitness experts who judged the finding as "reliable enough to testify about in court." In some cases, and for some of the most important variables in eyewitness cases, the difference was dramatic. For example, only 41% of the jurors (vs. 98% of the experts) thought that police instructions can affect willingness to make a positive identification, 32% (vs. 70%) thought that identification accuracy is more likely the more the lineup members resemble the suspect, 59% (vs. 95%) agreed that seeing a mugshot of the suspect increased the likelihood of choosing the suspect later in a lineup, 50% (vs. 95%) agreed that confidence can be influenced by factors unrelated to identification accuracy, 39% (vs. 87%) agreed that the presence of a weapon impairs face identification accuracy, 38% (vs. 87%) agreed that eyewitness confidence was not a good predictor of accuracy, 47% (vs. 90%) believed in own-race recognition bias, 33% (vs. 83%) thought that memory loss is greatest right after the event and then levels off (forgetting curve), and 47% (vs. 81%) agreed that the less time to observe an event, the poorer the memory for it. Symmetrically consistent with these contrasts, the large majority (73%) of prospective jurors thought true the finding that the highest percentage (78%, or 22% endorsing) of experts agreed was *not* reliable ("Traumatic experiences can be repressed for many years and then recovered").

Another way of looking at Benton and colleagues' (2006) survey results is to treat the survey as a knowledge exam, with performance defined in terms of the percentage of items answered correctly, and "correctly" defined as responding "generally true" to statements endorsed by the large majority of experts. When this is done, most jurors "fail" the exam. The average score, on a test that included only items that at least three-quarters of the experts agreed on, was 50.7%. Clearly, prospective jurors have insufficient knowledge about and understanding of eyewitness memory and the factors that affect it. Importantly, Benton and colleagues (2006) also report some results with different samples that suggest that little corrective courtroom education could be provided by attorneys and judges. The survey was administered to 42 judges and 52 law enforcement personnel (e.g., police officers and detectives) in Tennessee. The two groups scored 65.9% and 63.8%, respectively.

As noted, there are plenty of other surveys of lay knowledge about eyewitness memory and behavior that have yielded a similarly dismal picture of highly insufficient knowledge and erroneous beliefs. A somewhat different take on the knowledge gap issue, however, is offered by Read and Desmarais in Chapter 6, and echoed by Bailey and Mecklenburg, in Chapter 10. These authors contend that the knowledge of potential jurors is actually better than we have construed it. Read and Desmarais provide averages of agreement with consensual expert items across most or all of the surveys of would-be jurors conducted to date, some of which indicate considerable agreement with the experts. Across surveys, to cite just three examples, a decided majority of laypersons agree with what experts know about the malleability of eyewitness confidence (74%), the effects of question wording on eyewitness reports (85%), and the influence of expectations and attitudes on memory (85%).

They also report that their own very recent surveys involving more than 1700 community and college-student respondents yielded notably higher agreement percentages than other, mostly older, surveys.

This is all good news; but Read and Desmarais's survey of surveys also shows that agreement with expert opinion on some of the most critical eyewitness factors is alarmingly low even when aggregated across 10 or more surveys totaling over 2000 participants. About half or more of the participants disagree with the experts about the confidence–accuracy relationship, own-race bias, weapon focus, and similarity of lineup foils. Nearly 40% disagree about mugshot-induced bias and effects of exposure time. Moreover, as Read and Desmarais also observe, and as we will see later in this chapter, indirect tests of prospective juror knowledge, as evidenced in mock jurors' sensitivity to information about the eyewitness evidence presented in trial simulations, suggests that, whether or not they have the knowledge, jurors may not spontaneously apply it even when prompted. Finally, even if prompted knowledge is better than the bulk of the evidence suggests, general overbelief, as described previously, may lead would-be jurors to underestimate the magnitude of the effects of factors for which they have accurate directional knowledge but an inaccurate sense of effect sizes.

Overall, the research rather compellingly suggests that when the trial features eyewitness evidence that is pivotal to the crux of the evidence, eyewitness expert testimony is a needed commodity.

Yet another dissenting take on this conclusion merits mention. Elsewhere in this volume, the argument is raised that many experts' knowledge about memory is either incorrect or irrelevant regarding real-life eyewitness situations and psychology (Flowe, Finklea, and Ebbeson, Chapter 9; Bailey & Mecklenburg, Chapter 10), rendering the extant "knowledge gap" moot and raising the possibility that experts are actually miseducating jurors. Some judges apparently also share this concern (Hosch, Jolly, Schmersal, & Smith, Chapter 7). We acknowledge that there is possibly some legitimacy to this claim regarding a *limited* number of variables an expert might be permitted to discuss at trial. However, numerous counterarguments (e.g. Leippe, 1995; Wells, 1993), considerable scientific research aimed precisely at this issue (see, e.g., Lindsay, Ross, Read, & Toglia, 2007, for reviews), and the opinions of a large majority of eyewitness experts, many of whom have knowledge of and experience in the "real world" of law and crime (Kassin et al., 2001), converge to rather convincingly dispel the general veracity of this startling idea that, somehow, most experts are wrong about most eyewitness matters. This chapter makes the assumptions that eyewitness experts are capable of providing relevant information about eyewitness evidence that many or most jurors lack at least in part, and that experts commonly include appropriate cautions about the applicability of strong scientific findings to specific cases (see, e.g., Pezdek, Chapter 2). Our main question, of course, is how such expert testimony might influence jurors and trial outcomes. And we now turn to this question.

The Need for Expert Testimony, Defined

Eyewitness expert testimony is needed in the service of two related proximal goals—both primarily educational—that seem appropriate. The first is to convince the jury that eyewitness identifications are less likely to be accurate than they intuitively believe; the second is to educate the jury about the nature of eyewitness memory and the factors that affect it. In effect, the first goal involves an adjustment of the initial belief orientation from a predisposition to believe the eyewitness to a predisposition to be analytical in evaluating the eyewitness evidence (cf. Pezdek, 2007) and skeptical of the certainty with which the claims of the eyewitness are sure to be offered by the prosecution. The second goal involves giving the jurors the ability to gauge, in the case at hand, just how skeptical they should be. These goals can be met, however, and yet make no difference in a case, if the downward adjustment in initial belief orientation and greater knowledge about eyewitness testimony do not, in turn, impact more distal juror responses. Jurors must apply, hopefully in a valid manner, their new knowledge about eyewitness testimony to the eyewitness(es) in the case at trial. And, at an even more distant level, any change in the evaluation of the eyewitness evidence attributable to the expert may or may not influence jurors' verdicts. Presumably, the extent to which this most indirect effect occurs will depend on how large a piece of the total evidence picture the eyewitness evidence comprises.

Most of the research on the impact of expert testimony has focused on the more distal outcome variables, believability of the case-specific eyewitness, and verdicts, with only a bit of attention given to the proximal educational goals and how, if they are achieved, they may translate into the distal outcomes. We will have more to say about this gap in the research later, after we have a look at what the extant research has found. From the baselines of verdict preferences and belief in the trial eyewitness associated with the status quo of juror overbelief and ignorance regarding eyewitness evidence, to where does eyewitness expert testimony move those perceptions?

Trial Simulation Studies of the Impact of Expert Testimony: Evidence About Whether It Helps

With a couple of early exceptions described in a subsequent section, all studies of this question of moving baseline trial judgments with eyewitness expert testimony have used some form of a trial simulation paradigm. These studies, of which there are fewer than two dozen all together, can be divided into an older set that were included in Leippe's (1995) review, and the newer set of studies conducted since that review. We first present essentially Leippe's (1995) summary of the older set, and then describe in more detail the studies conducted since then.

Eyewitness Expert Research Before 1995

Leippe (1995) identified a dozen mock-juror studies in which factfinders were asked to judge the believability of an eyewitness after receiving or not receiving expert information about the psychology of eyewitness evidence. These studies varied in methodology. In some studies, a brief written description of an eyewitness expert's testimony was either included or not included in a short narrative summary of a trial and its corresponding eyewitness testimony. In other studies, involving a visible witness and a minimal trial, written or videotaped expert testimony was either included or not included, and videotapes of an eyewitness giving testimony were presented to participant jurors along with a minimal written description of the case. In a final set of studies, an entire trial, albeit abbreviated relative to actual trials, was presented to participant jurors via video- or audiotape, and the trial was varied to include or not include an eyewitness expert. This last, "whole trial" procedure, which has the highest mundane realism and ecological validity, has characterized all of the studies that have been conducted subsequently (although some have presented the trial in a written transcript form). Regardless of procedure, however, the effect of the expert testimony on juror perceptions of the specific eyewitness and specific case tended to be same in the first wave of studies. In 10 of the 12 studies, participant jurors evinced less belief in the prosecution eyewitness, less propensity to render a guilty verdict, or both when expert testimony was offered, compared to when it was not offered. Such lessened belief in normally incriminating eyewitness evidence has been referred to as the *skepticism* effect, and would seem to reflect success at achieving the proximal and distal goals of expert testimony that we have identified.

Some of the studies reviewed by Leippe (1995) were designed to test for another, arguably more desirable, outcome of eyewitness expert testimony, namely a *sensitivity* effect. As we have noted, proponents of expert testimony view it as a means of educating jurors about the nature of eyewitness behavior and the factors that influence it, so that they can more knowledgeably gauge the likely veracity of the eyewitness(es) they encounter in the courtroom. If expert testimony succeeds at this goal, jurors who have had the benefit of expert testimony, compared to those who have not, should be more sensitive to the quality of eyewitness evidence defined in terms of what is known to be conducive or not conducive to accuracy. Thus, for example, eyewitnesses who experienced good witnessing or testing should be more believed, and eyewitnesses who experience poor conditions should be less believed by factfinders who received expert testimony than by factfinders who did not. Leippe's review of the eight studies that provided a test of some form of sensitivity revealed that only two did so. Sensitivity appeared to be more the exception than the rule.

Among the studies reviewed by Leippe (1995), one of the most comprehensive and ambitious at the time was that of Cutler, Penrod, and Dexter (1989). This study employed the whole-trial procedure that has become the norm since Leippe's review, and was especially well executed, testing a large sample of college students and experienced jurors and presenting them with a relatively realistic videotaped armed-robbery trial. Presaging later studies in terms of methodology and, to some extent, findings, Cutler and colleagues' main study fell into the minority camp regarding both skepticism (limited) and sensitivity (some). It is instructive to review their study because it set the stage—the paradigm and research questions—for most of the research that has followed.

Each participant viewed one of essentially eight versions of the trial, which varied regarding two aspects of the eyewitness evidence and whether or not an eyewitness expert testified for the defense. When the expert testified, the testimony was quite elaborate, covering memory processes, many influences on eyewitness memory, and, under cross-examination, some limitations of eyewitness research. The prosecution's eyewitness either enjoyed good conditions of witnessing and identification or endured poor conditions, in terms of weapon presence, robber disguise, time between witnessing and the identification opportunity, and the suggestiveness of lineup instructions. This eyewitness reported either high (100%) or lower (80%) confidence in her identification. Expert testimony was found to increase sensitivity to witnessing and identification conditions. When no expert testified, guilty verdicts and belief in the eyewitness were the same whether the eyewitness's conditions were good or poor. When the expert testified, in contrast, guilty verdicts and belief were significantly higher when conditions were good than when they were poor. Moreover, a skepticism effect of expert testimony was evident only in the appropriate condition—when witnessing and identification conditions were poor. When these conditions were good, hearing the expert, if anything, tended to raise belief in the eyewitness.

Two other outcomes are of interest. First, overall, expert testimony did not improve sensitivity regarding eyewitness confidence. In the absence of expert testimony, the eyewitness was believed more when she was 100% confident than when she admitted to being only 80% confident, and this common confident-is-persuasive effect was not eliminated by an expert who actually mentioned the weak confidence–accuracy relationship in his testimony. Second, Cutler and colleagues (1989) additionally included a questionnaire to assess jurors' knowledge of eyewitness psychology—a dependent measure focused on one of the educational outcomes that expert testimony should deliver. Scores were reliably higher in the expert testimony conditions compared to the no-testimony conditions.

So, expert testimony had some desired effects in the Cutler and colleagues (1989) study. As a consequence of listening to an expert's detailed description of eyewitness psychology, mock jurors became more knowledgeable about eyewitness memory and used their new knowledge to more appropriately evaluate at least some accuracy-relevant aspects of the eyewitness testimony at hand. When compared to the other extant studies at the time, this positive educational impact of expert testimony, evident in both beliefs and sensitivity to eyewitness conditions, was somewhat unique. Given the high level of mundane realism, it could be hoped that, while anomalous among other extant findings, it had better external validity and would be more typical of real world effects. What has research told us since then?

Eyewitness Expert Testimony Studies Since 1995

Two studies involving a whole-trial paradigm similar in realism to Cutler and colleagues' (1989) suggest that jurors' may have significant, but limited, sensitivity to some factors that correlate with eyewitness accuracy, and that expert testimony improves this sensitivity only slightly. Devenport, Stinson, Cutler, and Kravitz (2002) had 800 college students and jury-eligible citizens watch one of several videotaped versions of a simulated robbery-murder trial. The presence of eyewitness expert testimony was manipulated, along with three qualities of the lineup identification procedure administered to the lone eyewitness and described on the witness stand by a police officer. Mock jurors learned from the police officers that the lineup procedure included instructions that were either unbiased or biased (i.e., strongly implied the perpetrator was in the lineup without acknowledging a "none of them" option), included foils that either were well-matched or not well-matched (biased) to the description of the perpetrator, and used either a simultaneous (biased) or sequential lineup. The expert, as described by Devenport and colleagues (2002), "testified about the encoding, storage, and retrieval stages of memory" and, additionally, "about factors known to influence identification accuracy, specifically focusing on factors affecting lineup suggestiveness. Testimony regarding foil, instruction, and presentation bias was elicited by the prosecution when an unbiased identification procedure was used and by the defense when a biased identification procedure was used" (p. 1046).

Mock jurors who did not hear the expert testimony correctly rated the lineup procedure as more suggestive and unfair when foils were biased, but their ratings were not much affected by instruction bias or lineup presentation. So, unaided by the expert, there was sensitivity only to the suggestive and unfair influence of a lineup in which the defendant tended to stick out. This sensitivity to foil bias among unaided mock jurors showed up in ratings of defendant culpability but not on dichotomous individual verdicts.

What about the rather pointed expert testimony? Expert testimony created sensitivity to instruction bias, where there had been none without it. However, it did not foster sensitivity to the possible biasing effects of lineup presentation method, and did not heighten the existing sensitivity to foil bias. Overall, then, there was a sensitivity effect, but it was limited. Regarding skepticism, expert testimony had a monolithic effect of increasing the perceived suggestiveness of the identification procedures across all trial conditions—whether or not there was suggestiveness in the procedures. This would seem to qualify as a skepticism effect on proximal judgments. But because there was no such overall expert testimony main effect on the distal variables verdicts and ratings of defendant culpability, Devenport and colleagues (2002) concluded that no forensically meaningful skepticism effect occurred.

A trial simulation reported by Ramirez, Zemba, and Geiselman (1996) produced results that are similar to these in that they showed some evidence of juror sensitivity to eyewitness conditions that was not especially enhanced by expert advice. In this study, more than 200 college students watched a videotaped trial of a burglary case. In one version of the trial, the prosecution eyewitness testified about 10 factors in her witnessing and identifying situation that added up to rather poor conditions. In a second version, all the witnessing and identification conditions were better on all counts. The poor-versus-good conditions factor was crossed with whether or not, in closing instructions, the judge included an instruction about how and what to consider regarding eyewitness testimony. Although, this was not expert testimony per se, the instruction was based on what eyewitness experts would typically discuss, as inferred from an earlier survey of experts reported by Kassin, Ellsworth, and Smith (1989), which resembled the later survey by Kassin and associates (2001). In the authors' words, "thirteen eyewitness factors were incorporated into the instructions toward educating the subjects about eyewitness phenomena and to sensitize jurors to good versus poor eyewitnessing conditions" (p. 49).

Ramirez and colleagues (1996) found that, without expert-based instructions, mock jurors were sensitive to the rather extreme variation in eyewitness conditions, in that 29.0% voted for conviction when conditions were good, and only 4.3% did so when conditions were poor. This sensitivity seems a bit limited, given the very low conviction rate even when the eyewitness enjoyed relatively *good* conditions. In addition, no sensitivity was evident in mock jurors' ratings of the eyewitness's believability; regardless of conditions, the eyewitness was rated equivalently "somewhat believable." The expert-based judge's instructions did not alter these patterns. Among mock jurors who received these instructions, the conviction rates were 24.6% and 5.5% in the good and poor conditions, respectively. Sensitivity was sustained, but not improved, by expert-based instructions.

A post-trial questionnaire assessing knowledge of eyewitness factors was also administered by Ramirez and colleagues (1996). The statements about factors generally agreed on by the Kassin and associates (1989) experts were presented and mock jurors asked to indicate if they considered the statement true. These, of course, were precisely the statements that were presented in the expert-based instructions. Perhaps it is not too surprising, then, that, compared to mock jurors who did not receive instructions about eyewitness testimony (51%), those who received expert-based instructions answered a significantly higher percentage (70%) of statements correctly. This replicates conceptually Cutler and colleagues' (1989) findings regarding juror knowledge gains, and suggests that there can be some achievement of the proximal educational goal of increasing jurors' knowledge of eyewitness evidence through presentation of expert knowledge. On the other hand, given that the expert-based instructions essentially "taught to the test" administered less than an hour later, the 70% score is not terribly impressive. The knowledge gap was narrowed but not closed, despite rather pointed pressure to move one side of it.

Getting Specific in the Testimony

Both in research and courtroom reality, eyewitness expert testimony may vary on a general to specific continuum. At the general extreme, the expert presents only an overview of the scientific study and findings of eyewitness memory. Less extreme, but still fairly general, is expert testimony that explicitly lists and describes factors known to influence eyewitness accuracy, but does not specifically tailor the list to the eyewitness evidence at hand. More extreme on the specific end of the spectrum is expert testimony that is highly specific, in that the expert describes research findings regarding the accuracy-threatening influence of witnessing and testing factors that are explicitly present (and explicitly noted by the expert as present) in the eyewitness testimony for the case at trial. The three studies reviewed in detail so far have tended to cluster at the general-with-some-specificity range of the continuum, with the Devenport and colleagues (2002) study extending the most into the specific side. An important question is whether the impact of expert testimony varies with its content in terms of the general–specific dimension. An early study involving a minimal trial surrounding a videotaped rendition of the eyewitness and the expert testimony found that both very general and more specific expert testimony produced significant skepticism effects on verdicts and ratings of eyewitness believability, with the effects being a bit stronger when the testimony was specific (Fox & Walters, 1986).

More recently, Geiselman, Putman, Korte, Shahriary, Jachimowicz, and Irzhevsky (2002) conducted two videotaped trial simulations in which the general-versus-specific nature of the eyewitness expert testimony was manipulated. Although the description of the general expert testimony is somewhat vague in their report, both the general and specific testimony seem to have involved a listing of factors that are known to generally affect eyewitness accuracy, with the specific testimony additionally indicating the level or presence versus absence of each factor in the case at trial. Undergraduate psychology students served as mock jurors and read a summary of a robbery-homicide that included descriptions of the prosecution's allegations, prosecution and defense evidence, judge's instructions, and, in some conditions, the testimony of a court-appointed eyewitness expert. The prosecution's eyewitness evidence was varied in terms of 10 conditions of witnessing and testing that were mentioned in the description of what the sole eyewitness saw and experienced. The conditions were all favorable for eyewitnessing (e.g., bright illumination, close distance, no disguise, no police suggestiveness) in the good eyewitnessing conditions case, and all less favorable in the poor eyewitnessing conditions case. The results suggest that mock jurors were modestly sensitive to the quality of the eyewitness evidence without the benefit of expert testimony; 61% of the mock jurors delivered an individual guilty verdict when eyewitnessing conditions were good, whereas only 40% did so when eyewitnessing conditions were poor. The general expert testimony failed to improve juror sensitivity (56% vs. 37%), but the specific testimony did improve it (78% vs. 21%). Thus, coupling this with the earlier findings of Fox and Walters (1986), somewhat more specific expert testimony seems to be somewhat more effective, probably because, as discussed later, it clarifies better to jurors the relevance of the expert testimony to the case.

However, in a second experiment, Geiselman and co-workers (2002) added the adversarial closing arguments of the prosecutor and the defense attorney. Both attorneys addressed the eyewitness evidence in the manner one would expect, with the prosecutor touting its highly likely reliability and the defense attorney emphasizing how bad eyewitness memory can be. Importantly, the effect of the adversarial arguments was to nullify the heightened sensitivity that had been afforded by the specific testimony and to promote a skepticism effect. That is, mock jurors exposed to both the specific expert testimony and closing arguments discriminated—but no more than did mock jurors who were not exposed to an expert—and these jurors also were more likely to vote not guilty (relative to the no-expert control participants) whether eyewitnessing conditions were bad or good.

In a follow-up to this research that used the same trial scenario and tested more than 600 college-student participants, Geiselman and Mendez (2005) included a version of the trial summary in which the judge, just prior to the attorney's closing arguments, instructed jurors that closing arguments were opinions, not evidence and that jurors should be careful not to construe the attorney's statements as evidence. The effect of this admonition was to partially restore the heightened sensitivity afforded by specific expert testimony observed in the first study by Geiselman and co-workers (2002). That is, significant sensitivity to eyewitness conditions was again found when there was no expert (and no closing arguments) and the level of sensitivity when there was an expert was reliably greater still. The authors provide little conceptual accounting of this restorative effect of the judge's instruction. One plausible explanation, though, is that, in being directed about what they should and should not be considering, mock jurors became motivated to "correct" (Wegener & Petty, 1997) for any bias the judge implied would be inherent in the attorney's "advice," and therefore took pains to judge the eyewitness evidence for themselves; and, this could, of course, be aided by heeding the testimony of the impartial expert.

A close look at Geiselman and co-workers' (2002; Geiselman & Mendez, 2005) results, however, reveals an interesting and very revealing pattern concerning sensitivity and skepticism. In the absence of attorney's closing arguments, specific expert testimony increased guilty verdicts when eyewitnessing conditions were good, and decreased it when conditions were poor. The influence of attorneys' closing arguments, whether commented on by a judge or not, was limited to the good eyewitnessing conditions, in which it eliminated or reduced the heightened guilt rate. Closing arguments did not moderate the impact of specific expert testimony in any study or study condition in this group, when eyewitnessing conditions were poor. Specific expert testimony invariably reduced the guilt rate in the poor witnessing trials to between 21% and 24% (from 39% to 40%) when there was no expert. Thus, in the kind of case for which an eyewitness expert would be most likely to testify—when the eyewitness evidence is questionable—an expert who gives specifics appears to robustly make jurors sensitive to poor eyewitness evidence, which naturally emerges as skepticism.

Several other trial simulation studies have reported findings regarding sensitivity, skepticism, or both. One of these, by Devenport and Cutler (2004), failed to find evidence of even the limited sensitivity observed in most of the studies we have seen thus far. Devenport and Cutler presented the videotaped trial used by Devenport and colleagues (2002) to nearly 500 community members and college students. The eyewitness evidence in the trial involved either biased or unbiased lineup foils and either biased or unbiased lineup instructions. In addition, the trial included either no expert, an expert called by the defense who gave general testimony and a specific opinion about the bias(es) when present, or the defense expert plus an opposing expert called by the prosecution who criticized the methodology of eyewitness research and opined that the lineup procedures in the case were not unduly suggestive. Overall, mock jurors correctly rated the foil-biased (vs. unbiased) and instruction-biased (vs. unbiased) lineups as more suggestive, and rated the witness as less accurate when instructions were biased (vs. unbiased). Yet these ratings, as well as individual verdicts and ratings of defendant culpability, were completely unaffected by the expert testimony variable, either through main effects (i.e., skepticism) or interactions with the presence-or-absence-of-bias factors (i.e., sensitivity).

Leippe, Eisenstadt, Rauch, and Seib (2004) examined the influence of eyewitness expert testimony using a whole-trial scenario in written form. College students read a transcript of a robbery-murder trial in which a single eyewitness observed a hold-up at knifepoint that led to a fatal stabbing. The transcript included critical excerpts from the trial, including opening and closing arguments, direct and cross examination of the eyewitness and other witnesses, and judge's instructions. Included or not included in the transcript was general expert testimony by an experimental psychologist that consisted of a summary of theory and research on the factors that influence eyewitness accuracy. The expert, called as a friend of the court, testified either at the beginning of the trial or after all evidence had been heard. Leippe and associates (2004) were interested not only in this timing factor, but in whether eyewitness expert testimony would influence jurors even when the prosecution had a highly incriminating case without the eyewitness. To this end, the extra-eyewitness prosecution case strength was varied to be either relatively strong or quite weak.

The main thrusts of Leippe and associates' (2004) results are twofold. First, expert testimony was associated with reduced guilty verdicts and reduced belief in the accuracy of the eyewitness—a skepticism effect—but only when the expert testimony followed the evidence and the judge reminded jurors of what the expert said as part of final instructions. Second, as constrained as the skepticism effect was, it occurred under the same conditions to about the same degree whether the prosecution's noneyewitness case was weak, moderate, or, in a second study, moderately strong. Regarding the first finding, perhaps, as Leippe and associates (2004) suggested, expert testimony influences jurors' thinking primarily when it is both memorable as jurors reach a decision stage in their thinking and when the judge has "authorized" or prompted them to incorporate the still salient testimony by mentioning it in the instructions with which jurors are sent to the deliberation room. As for the second finding, it may imply that consideration of the expert testimony is not terribly thoughtful or integrative in terms of the entire body of trial evidence. Mock jurors were swayed by the salient and authorized expert testimony toward acquittal even in the face of considerable corroborative evidence that the defendant was guilty.

As we have seen in this review of recent studies, expert testimony effects can be a bit slippery and elusive. Effects found in one study by both the Geiselman and the Devenport/Cutler groups disappear or become qualified in the next published study. The same is true for Leippe and associates' limited skepticism effect. In a subsequent study (Leippe, Eisenstadt, & Kiddoo, 2005) that presented only their strongest case to mock jurors, and in which expert testimony followed the evidence and the judge reminded jurors of it, the skepticism effect disappeared, at least on verdicts. However, expert testimony did influence jurors on other relevant measures. When an expert testified (vs. did not), participants rated the eyewitness as less believable, judged the likelihood that the defendant committed the crime as marginally less likely ($p = .10$), and expressed marginally less certainty in their verdicts ($p < .09$). This would seem to suggest that at least a bit of skepticism was aroused by the expert testimony in the minds of the mock jurors, but not enough to overcome or negate the rather large amount of incriminating circumstantial evidence presented by the prosecution. From the perspective of the mock juror as a rational and careful information processor, the limited and selective impact of expert testimony in Leippe and associates' (2005) study is understandable.

Expert Testimony in Whole-Trial Simulations: Summary

At first glance, the findings of the trial simulation studies reviewed here appear to lack consistency and coherence. However, although an element of slipperiness is present, in that there are some inconsistencies in terms of whether or not a given effect is significant, few or no inconsistencies exist in terms of opposite or contradictory effects. Moreover, some generalities can be identified, especially when some of the earlier studies are looked at in addition to the post-1995 work. In the following paragraphs, we highlight several implications and conclusions that may be taken from the research.

Expert Testimony Yields Modest Gains in Juror Knowledge That Can Yield Sensitivity Effects—But They May Not Often Be Applied

Ramirez and colleagues (1996) essentially replicated Cutler and colleagues' (1989) early findings that mock jurors do learn from eyewitness expert testimony, endorsing more correct statements about influences on eyewitness reports after hearing or reading an expert's presentation of them. Devenport and colleagues' (2002) results also suggest a positive learning outcome in that mock jurors more readily recognized the suggestiveness of various lineup procedures when they had heard expert testimony than when they had not. It seems safe to assume from these findings that similar knowledge gains have occurred in the studies of expert testimony that did not directly test for them. Although observed increases in knowledge do not seem to be large, they nonetheless suggest that expert testimony is likely to achieve some degree of success in meeting the goal of increasing juror knowledge.

Yet, it is also obvious from the studies that the influence of expert testimony on eyewitness believability (and more distal variables associated with defendant culpability) is often not isomorphic with the influence, observed or inferred, on knowledge and beliefs. Participant jurors do not seem to apply readily their new knowledge to the case. One reason for this, of course, is that the relevance of the particular knowledge gained to the specific eyewitness(es) in the trial may not be recognized unless the expert makes very clear connections. But larger hurdles may exist here. It may be the case that jurors see the relevance to the case but reject its applicability to the actual eyewitness they encounter at trial. Lindsay (1994) found that, despite their asserted beliefs in the importance of biased lineups and lineup procedures, mock jurors' verdict preferences were not influenced in the direction these beliefs would imply by manipulations of lineup biases in a mock trial involving videotaped testimony of an eyewitness to a staged crime. This was so even when an eyewitness expert specifically discussed biased lineups and their effects on memory reports. One reason for these findings that Lindsay (1994) referred to as "startling," is that the eyewitness's testimonial behavior may be so salient that it dominates judgments about the eyewitness. The ignoring of what one knows about a present eyewitness factor may be analogous to the well-known fundamental attribution error in which observers see causes in the dispositions of an actor despite having evidence of a situational cause (Ross, 1977). In the classic and oft-replicated classic study of this, Jones and Harris (1967; Jones, 1990) found that an audience tended to attribute to a speech-maker an attitude that was consistent with the position espoused in the speech even though the position was decidedly counter-normative and the audience was informed in no uncertain terms that the speaker had been arbitrarily assigned the position to take and given help preparing it. The parallel to the believed eyewitness whose "speech" occurred in the presence of factors that should compromise its accuracy are noteworthy.

A recent study involving expert testimony using a visible-witness/minimal-trial procedure rather dramatically underscores the idea that belief in the witness can be unfazed even by very specific and relevant expert information that factfinders embrace. Martire and Kemp (2009) had Australian college students read a brief summary of a criminal event and then watch either no expert testimony or expert testimony conveying that confidence either was or was not a good predictor of accuracy. These participant jurors then watched the direct and cross-examination of an actual eyewitness to a videotaped bag-snatch crime who either was accurate and confident in her or his identification, or inaccurate and not confident. Participant jurors who were told by the expert that confidence predicted accuracy were more sensitive to witness confidence in that, when compared to participant jurors who were exposed to an expert who asserted a nil confidence–accuracy relationship, they rated witnesses who they believed to be accurate as more confident and witnesses who they believed to be inaccurate as less confident. Yet, despite this and the actual strong positive confidence–accuracy relationship among viewed witnesses in this study, participant jurors who were informed by an expert of a general positive confidence–accuracy relationship did no better than other participant jurors in discriminating between accurate and inaccurate witnesses in terms of whether they believed them. Again would-be jurors seem to learn the lesson but not apply it, perhaps, in this case, because they are moved mainly by the global act of affirmative eyewitness testimony and less by any specific confidence assertions that the expert mentioned as relevant.

It may be, then, that when beliefs instilled by an expert do not translate to ratings of the eyewitness, it is sometimes because the eyewitness's behavior has the lion's share of influence on judgments. Alternatively, it may be that, although jurors report knowledge that suggests informed beliefs about eyewitness memory, they do not really embrace those beliefs. A number of studies have examined jurors' reactions to psychological findings and theories presented by psychiatrists and other mental health professionals when testifying about matters such as insanity, competence, dangerousness, and self-defense (see Vidmar, 2005, for a review). These studies find that, when the expert's ideas and analysis of human psychology conflict with their own preconceived notions, jurors may ignore the expert and keep their prior beliefs or, more commonly, reinterpret the expert's statements in terms of their own preconceived notions. Eyewitness expert testimony, of course, also presents concepts and relationships involving psychological states, and some of them conflict with commonsense understandings. Thus, it is possible that jurors may learn the expert's beliefs about eyewitnesses and perhaps accept them superficially or in the abstract, yet not buy them as relevant or accurate in the concrete memory drama told in the courtroom. This possibility that the eyewitness expert's information may not be truly accepted under certain conditions deserves empirical investigation, as it would help explain the generally weak overall impact of eyewitness expert testimony, especially on the sensitivity outcome, which involves application of what is learned from the witness.

Skepticism Is Typical, but Conditional

For some of the studies we have reviewed, the researchers report an absence of skepticism, based on the failure to find a main effect of expert testimony characterized by lower defendant culpability and fewer guilty verdicts when expert testimony was (vs. was not) presented. There are two problems with this reasoning, however. First, the overall expert testimony main effect may not be the most appropriate test of skepticism, because it may include conditions in which the eyewitness evidence was quite strong. Expert testimony, realistically, is only likely to be tendered in cases that involve at least somewhat questionable eyewitness testimony. Moreover, if the strong eyewitness evidence is saliently characterized by qualities that the expert has noted are favorable to good memory, it would be truly surprising—and very difficult to explain by any psychological theory—if a reduced belief in that evidence occurred as a result of only expert testimony. So, the overall main effect test puts up a high hurdle for finding skepticism. The second problem is that defendant culpability and verdicts are not direct measures of skepticism. Skepticism is about the accuracy and hence perceived believability of the eyewitness, and a measure of this will therefore provide the most direct, sensitive, and valid test of skepticism.

What can be gleaned about skepticism from a look at the studies in light of these considerations? Pretty much that it usually happens when it should and sometimes when it should not.

SKEPTICISM PREVAILS WHEN THERE ARE BAD WITNESSES. Leippe and associates (2004; 2005) found that expert testimony was associated with fewer guilty verdicts, lessened eyewitness believability, or both, in some conditions of all three experiments they conducted involving eyewitness evidence that was somewhat fallible (e.g., brief, distant, somewhat dark viewing conditions). As noted previously, Geiselman and co-workers (2002; Geiselman & Mendez, 2005) found a significantly lower guilt rate in all three conditions involving abjectly poor witnessing conditions. In Devenport and colleagues' (2002) study, there is evidence of a skepticism effect in the trial condition that included an eyewitness identification that was flawed in a manner that the expert addressed (biased lineup instructions) and unflawed in a manner that mock jurors seemed to understand intuitively (unbiased foils). In the biased-instructions/ unbiased-foils condition, ratings of both the fairness of the lineup and the culpability of the defendant were lower when there was expert testimony compared to when there was not. The only post-1995 whole-trial study in which skepticism effects appear to have been utterly absent despite the weakness of the eyewitness evidence is that reported by Devenport and Cutler (2004).

SALIENCE OF THE EXPERT AND THE EYEWITNESS.   Recall that Leippe and associates (2004) observed a skepticism effect only when the expert testified at the end of the trial and the judge reminded jurors of the expert testimony in final instructions to the jury. Their interpretation of this includes the idea that the expert testimony must be salient to mock jurors as they consider the evidence, and is consistent with evidence that other kinds of experts are more influential in trials when they give repetitive testimony (Kovera, Gresham, Borgida, Gray, & Regan, 1997). Perhaps, more aptly, what needs to be salient is that the eyewitness evidence is an *issue*. If the eyewitness is but one piece of evidence embedded in a large body of trial evidence, arguments, and other information, the eyewitness is likely to have relatively little influence on the trial outcome. If the expert testimony about the eyewitness evidence is similarly embedded, it is apt to have only modest influence on judgments about the eyewitness and very negligible influence on the distal verdict-related variables—its effects on verdicts should be mainly through its effects on perceptions of the eyewitness evidence, which is having little effect itself in this elaborate trial scenario. This would help account for the absence of a skepticism effect in Devenport and Cutler's (2004) study, as well as for the relative weakness of skepticism effects, on average, in the whole-trial simulations we have reviewed here—all of which have involved relatively elaborate trial stimuli (cf. Devenport & Cutler, 2004).

The necessity-of-salience idea may also be related to some other variables that have been found to moderate the skepticism impact of expert testimony. As described previously, Geiselman and co-workers (2002) found that a skepticism effect in a case in which the eyewitnessing conditions were good occurred only when the prosecuting and defense attorneys addressed the eyewitness evidence very explicitly in their closing arguments. Such highlighting of the eyewitness evidence certainly increases the salience of the eyewitness evidence as an important issue in the trial, providing a bigger canvas, as it were, on which jurors could draw implications from the *defense* eyewitness expert's testimony.

Heightened salience of importance might also underlie another finding, this one from among the earlier studies of eyewitness expert testimony. Employing the whole-trial paradigm used by Cutler and colleagues (1989), Cutler, Dexter, and Penrod (1990) manipulated whether expert testimony was delivered by an expert testifying for the defense or by a court-appointed expert. Mock jurors evinced a larger skepticism effect in the latter, court-appointed condition. Unlike those who heard the defense expert, mock jurors who heard the court-appointed expert had lower guilt rates than those who heard no expert, even when the eyewitness experienced good witnessing conditions. Cutler and colleagues (1990) conjectured that mock jurors did not process the court-appointed expert's testimony as systematically and carefully as they did that of the defense expert. Instead, they processed the testimony heuristically, as described by contemporary theories of persuasion (Chaiken, Liberman, & Eagly, 1989; Petty & Cacioppo, 1986). That is, because it was court-appointed and thus likely to be impartial, the expert testimony was automatically deemed valid by mock jurors, and also assumed, more or less automatically, to be critical of the eyewitness. This may very well be what happened. But it is also possible that the fact that the court apparently saw the need to appoint an expert signaled that the eyewitness evidence was at issue— important and somewhat suspect. The eyewitness testimony was brought into figural focus by the expert testimony, out of the background of an elaborate trial.

THE OTHER EVIDENCE. One likely necessary condition for a skepticism effect of eyewitness expert testimony, at least on defendant culpability variables, is that the prosecution's case not be decisively incriminating even without the eye-witness evidence. Information integration approaches to juror decision making suggest that jurors attempt to integrate all of the evidence at hand into a judgment of likely guilt (e.g., Kaplan & Kemmerick, 1974; Moore & Gump, 1995). Thus, even if some skepticism about the eyewitness evidence is aroused by the expert's presentation, if the eyewitness evidence is only a small piece of the evidence, a downgrade in its incriminating value will do little to alter the equation. The limiting condition of a very strong prosecution case does not seem to have been present in any of the trial simulations we have reviewed. Judging by the guilt rates in no-expert control conditions, all involved trials in which the prosecution case—even including the eyewitness—was at best modest in strength. As we have seen, Leippe and associates (2004) actually manipulated the strength of the extra-eyewitness evidence and found that a skepticism effect on verdicts of about the same size occurred across three levels of prosecution case strength in which the no-expert control yielded guilt rates ranging from 42% to 74%. At first glance, this would suggest that a strong extra-eyewitness case is not a barrier to a skepticism effect on verdicts. However, it should be noted that, with a guilt rate of 74%, even the strongest prosecution case fell well short of infallible. And some evidence hints at a barrier. Within the strongest prosecution case condition, the skepticism effect fell short of significance on verdicts in Leippe and associates' (2004) research, and using the strongest case only, Leippe and associates (2005) later found no skepticism effect on verdicts, despite some evidence of skepticism about the eyewitness. A reasonable hypothesis is that the impact of an expert, at least on verdicts, should be stronger, the less the other evidence favors the prosecution—unless perhaps the other factors we have identified—a bad eyewitness and a highly salient expert—are present. This matter requires some future research attention.

All in all, then, eyewitness expert testimony can be expected to create skepticism in trials in which the (a) eyewitness evidence is both important to the case and questionable in its quality, (b) circumstantial or extra-eyewitness evidence is not convincingly incriminating by itself, and (c) eyewitness expert testimony is salient and memorable as jurors move toward deliberation.

The Proper and Realistic Goals of Expert Testimony

What should we make of this skepticism effect in terms of the goals of eyewitness expert testimony? Skepticism under the conditions just described would seem to satisfy the primary need we have identified for expert testimony—to correct jurors' tendencies to overbelieve eyewitness reports and to underadjust for factors in an eyewitness situation that are known to reduce the likely accuracy of the identification. To accomplish this, as we have seen, the expert presents research findings regarding the accuracy-inhibiting effects of variables relevant to the case, as well as the general finding that eyewitness errors are more frequent than people normally think. If jurors apply their new knowledge and beliefs, the consequence should indeed be reduced belief in weak eyewitness evidence—a skepticism effect—and that is what the trial simulation research has found. The ideal that the worse the conditions of witnessing and testing, the more jurors should be skeptical of the eyewitness evidence appears to be at least approximated in the research. And, importantly, if skepticism occurs primarily when the eyewitness evidence is fallible, such skepticism, in effect, is a sign of sensitivity. Moreover, this conditional nature of expert influence would seem to help allay fears (e.g., Flowe et al., Chapter 9) that experts' impact may be larger than the scientific findings merit. In short, the goals of creating accurate beliefs about eyewitness memory and having jurors apply those beliefs so as to become more skeptical of eyewitness evidence is not only prescriptively appropriate, it seems realistically attainable, to at least a modest degree in the courtroom through expert testimony.

Yet, a different goal of expert testimony may merit some discussion, namely that jurors should become better able to judge the *actual* accuracy of an eyewitness. In a probabilistic sense, this outcome is achieved by greater skepticism when the eyewitness evidence is bad, to the extent that jurors were inclined to believe an eyewitness who experienced conditions under which a majority of eyewitnesses would be inaccurate. But, should or could we expect expert testimony to help discriminate between accurate and inaccurate witnesses who experienced *identical* conditions? The answer would seem to be "no" on both should and could counts. Expert testimony should not help with discerning the accuracy of any one witness because the very message of the expert is that jurors should pay less attention to the characteristics of witnesses, such as their verbal and nonverbal expressions of confidence, and more attention to witnessing and identification conditions. This is sound advice in that, by the time they reach the courtroom, most eyewitnesses to crimes have become or been coached to become highly confident in their memory and to have gotten their "stories straight." In addition, variance in accuracy due to eyewitness conditions is likely to be far greater than variance in accuracy associated with witness characteristics that jurors can observe beyond the veneer of on-the-stand self-presentation. And for these very reasons that experts direct attention to eyewitness conditions and away from scrutinizing the eyewitness per se, expert testimony could not readily increase accuracy discernibility. Although there may be some relatively valid cues to memory accuracy (Leippe, 1994), they are not likely to be readily available in the testimonial behavior of individuals on the witness stand whose behavior is also being influenced by prior coaching and current stressors associated with adversarial questioning. In short, evaluating the efficacy of expert testimony based on its ability to teach jurors to better judge the accuracy of a single witness seem inappropriate. It is not clear that this is an achievable criterion.

Indeed, the little evidence that does exist about whether expert advice can assist jurors in discerning individual eyewitness accuracy suggests that discernment is not likely to be achieved even when accuracy-related cues are not masked by meddlesome coaching. Using the two-phase paradigm, two studies had participant jurors watch the question-and-answer memory report of accurate and inaccurate participant witnesses after hearing or not hearing "expert advice" about eyewitness memory. In both studies, without the expert advice, participant jurors evinced the same rate of belief in the identification accuracy of accurate and inaccurate witnesses. Expert testimony had absolutely no ameliorating influence on this in one study (Wells, Lindsay, & Tousignant, 1980) and only a small helpful influence in the other study (Wells & Wright, 1983, cited in Wells, 1986).

Of course, in an ideal world, jurors could be provided with more information about eyewitnesses' behavior than just their courtroom testimony. Their early reports to the police, lineup identifications, or both could be videotaped and presented to jurors. The speech, paralinguistic, and temporal (e.g., decision time) qualities evident in these slices of eyewitness behavior may indeed include diagnostic cues to accuracy (Leippe, 1994), although they are not likely to be very strong or reliable. It is possible that expert testimony that identifies known valid cues for jurors would result in better sensitivity to specific witness accuracy when additional, non-courtroom behaviors were scrutinized. But this intervention would involve more than merely expert testimony; so it is rather beyond the scope of our interest in this chapter, and untested in any event.

The Processes and Conditions of Eyewitness Expert Influence: Some Thoughts on the Psychology of Persuasion and Education

Having reviewed the research and drawn some conclusions, the final task of this chapter is to offer a theoretical framework for understanding how and why eyewitness expert testimony may influence jurors. A popular approach to this problem is to view delivery, receipt, and impact of expert testimony as a persuasion process (e.g., Cooper & Hall, 2000; Kovera et al., 1997). Persuasion is certainly a central process, but it is important to be clear about what actually is the "attitude object" toward which the expert's "persuasive communication" is directed. If expert testimony, general or specific, is practiced as we have defined it, then the direct objects of persuasion are jurors' beliefs about eyewitness memory in general and, to the extent that connections can be made by implication, beliefs about the quality of the eyewitness witnessing and identification conditions in the particular trial. From this view, the believability of the specific eyewitness(es) is not the attitude object, but rather an indirect outcome that requires jurors to apply and integrate the beliefs instilled by the expert to their impressions of the eyewitness as well as of other witnesses and evidence. Nevertheless, because beliefs about eyewitness memory—general and specific to the case—are an essential contributor to eyewitness believability judgments, the persuasive impact of the expert testimony is indirectly gauged by changes in those judgments.

From a persuasion perspective, the impact of expert testimony should depend on the cognitive responses (Petty, Ostrom, & Brock, 1981) of jurors to the expert and the expert's message, which may be affected by reception, source, and message factors.

Reception

Generally, it is assumed that jurors are motivated to carefully attend to and evaluate trial information, and to engage in systematic or central-route processing of the information, as opposed to more casual processing characterized by reliance on heuristic decision rules suggested by peripheral cues (Petty & Wegener, 1998). After all, theirs is a task with important consequences involving the liberty of an individual, as well as social justice and security. It is also likely that processing of the expert's message will be relatively open-minded, with jurors motivated to *construct* opinions about eyewitness evidence rather than defend existing ones (cf. Fazio, 1979; Leippe, 1991). Much of the expert's message will be novel to most jurors, involving domains and dimensions of memory and memory reporting that they have not often thought about. To the extent that this is true, the process is more one of education and belief formation than of persuasion. Jurors are likely to have some beliefs that conflict with message information, so a change or persuasion process may also be involved. But, under normal circumstances, people should not be highly committed to, identified with, or ego-involved in their beliefs about eyewitness memory and the factors that affect it.

If processing is thus likely to be relatively systematic and objective/unbiased, the degree to which the expert's message has impact on beliefs mainly should be a matter of how much information the expert gives and how clearly and articulately it is presented. Individuals are more persuaded by communications that present strong, information-based arguments (Leippe & Elkin,

1987; Petty & Cacioppo, 1984) and that are designed to foster comprehension (Eagly, 1974). Messages that are stripped of confusing "legalese" while retaining the same content also have greater persuasive impact (Chaiken & Eagly, 1976; Horowitz, Bordens, Victor, Bourgeois, & ForsterLee, 2001). Eyewitness expert testimony, involving scientific principles, complex relationships, and psychological jargon, of course, can be complex and challenging to understand. The situation is not helped by adversarial trappings of cross-examination and questioning intended to cause confusion. One consequence of this complexity would be poor understanding of the message and limited belief acquisition. This, then, may be one reason why, as we have seen, expert testimony in trial simulation studies has led to increases in knowledge of eyewitness psychology that, while often significant, have been of limited magnitude. Many mock jurors simply may have not fully comprehended the information-packed message or how it relates to the eyewitness evidence in the case.

Message complexity, however, may have other effects on reception of expert testimony. According to the elaboration likelihood model of persuasion (Petty & Cacioppo, 1986), message recipients engage in extensive elaboration only to the extent that they are motivated *and able* to do so. When ability is compromised by message complexity or ambiguity, recipients fall back on reliance on peripheral cues (Chaiken & Maheswaran, 1994). Experts make this an easy option in that they themselves, in their status as expert sources, have cue value. Several trial simulation studies have observed this complexity effect. For example, Cooper, Bennett, and Sukel (1996) found that, in a civil case involving a corporate lawsuit, a scientific expert witness's credentials had little impact on verdicts when the expert testimony was low in complexity. But when the testimony was highly complex, a highly credentialed expert witness was more persuasive than an expert witness with more modest credentials. A conceptually analogous finding was observed by Schuller, Terry, and McKimmie (2005), also in a civil trial. In the trial, the expertise domain (price-fixing in the construction industry) was stereotypically gender-related, such that male experts would be considered more expert. As predicted from this, when presenting complex testimony, but not when presenting less complex testimony, a male expert was more persuasive than a female expert.

It is not clear how these findings might relate to eyewitness expert testimony. For one thing, such testimony typically is not, or need not be, all that complex and difficult to understand. Eyewitness experts typically take pains to use accessible examples and to define psychological constructs and processes in everyday language. But jurors could be driven to fall back on the peripheral cue of expertise by more than just message complexity. It could be the result of tedium and boredom in combination with a message that is accessible but not easy to follow. If jurors do decide to tune out the content and tune in to credentials, they may tend to accept whatever conclusion or implications they glean from superficial attention to the expert's testimony. The conclusion is most likely to be that the eyewitness evidence has problems. On this, indiscriminate skepticism effects may ride.

Source

Message complexity may indeed lead recipients to rely more on source cues and less on message-derived information. But it is also the case that source cues, by themselves, can reduce reliance on message information. Laboring under high information load, jurors might see the expert's very expertise as sufficient to accept the apparent conclusion or general thrust of the expert testimony with little scrutiny or careful elaboration. This may well contribute to a skepticism effect, if jurors take from their superficial processing an overall expert conclusion that eyewitnesses are prone to error. As noted previously, this essentially is Cutler and colleagues' (1990) interpretation of their finding that, compared to an adversarial eyewitness expert called by the defense, an expert called by the court created a skepticism effect even when the eyewitness had experienced good witnessing conditions. Expert enough to be called by the court, and unconnected to adversarial interests that could compromise trustworthiness, mock jurors deferred to the expert with minimal, noncritical message processing.

It is more typical, however, for eyewitness experts to be called by the defense, and hence risk being perceived as biased and untrustworthy, as "hired guns" for one side (cf. Cooper & Neuhaus, 2000). In more than two dozen court appearances as an eyewitness expert, the first author cannot recall a single instance in which he was not asked by the prosecuting attorney whether he is being paid, who hired him, and whether he had ever testified for the prosecution and not the defense. Clearly, prosecutors attempt to instill doubt about the trustworthiness of experts for the other side in the minds of jurors. And for good reason. Persuasion research indicates that recipients more critically scrutinize the messages of sources deemed untrustworthy, and are primed to counterargue them right from the start (Hass, 1981; Pratkanis, Greenwald, Leippe, & Baumgardner, 1988). Although this could certainly be a hurdle for the eyewitness expert if the opposing side is successful in its undermining efforts, it seems unlikely that the undermining often does succeed. Surveys indicate that jurors understand how the adversarial system works (Vidmar, 2005) and can discount such adversarial tactics. Surveys also indicate that, in general, jurors and prospective jurors have positive regard for courtroom experts (Griffith, Hart, Frigo, Hosecheck, & Harkins, 2005), including eyewitness experts (Lindsay, MacDonald, & McGarry, 1990).

Message and Context

Provided they receive appropriate attention and processing, messages with strong arguments are more persuasive than those with weak arguments. But what makes for a strong eyewitness expert message? We would argue that clarity and simplicity in explaining the science and the findings are paramount. The use of examples to which recipient jurors can personally relate should also enhance both comprehension and acceptance, by promoting processing through familiar self-schemas and encouraging self-referencing (e.g., Cacioppo, Petty, & Sidera, 1982). Such examples, and accessible arguments about how intuition can mislead all of us, may be necessary to overcome the resistance to changing beliefs about human nature that was noted previously. Relevance to the case at hand should also heighten persuasive impact. Even general testimony should be framed in ways that connect to the case. The stronger effects of specific (vs. general) testimony found by Geiselman and co-workers (2002), and the absence of effects of the very general, unconnected expert testimony in most conditions of Leippe and associates' (2004) experiments might be understood in terms of the perceived relevance factor. Finally, perhaps the most important message strength component may be dictated by the quality of eyewitness evidence in the case at hand. Again, however, acceptance of the expert's message should not normally be measured in terms of verdict preferences or even level of belief in the eyewitness. Primarily, the persuasive impact of the expert's message involves learning of and acceptance of new information about eyewitness memory and a belief that the information *applies* to the current eyewitness evidence. It is up to the attorneys, and a function of the nature and amount of other evidence, to make specific linkages and arguments that connect what the expert says about memory to the case.

Conclusions

This final analysis of eyewitness expert testimony in terms of persuasion provides some indication of how expert testimony may impact jurors and the factors that should moderate that impact. The analysis points up avenues of new research that need to be pursued before we have a full understanding of how and when eyewitness expert testimony meaningfully influences the thinking and decisions made by factfinders. In particular, more attention needs to be paid to belief change and the integration and application of new or changed beliefs to judgments of the eyewitness and eyewitness situation in the case at hand.

Perhaps most importantly, the analysis points up the obstacles to persuasive impact. Message material that may be difficult to understand and apply, jury audiences with entrenched prior beliefs about human psychology, challenges to source credibility and message relevance that are certain to arise, message strength that depends critically on the nature and quality of a much greater amount of other messages and trial information—most or all of these persuasion-unfriendly factors, among others, are likely to characterize the communication setting of the eyewitness expert. Given these obstacles, the relatively limited influence of eyewitness expert testimony—especially on the trial outcome variables like verdicts to which it can almost never directly speak—makes much sense. Yet, at the same time, our review of the research and consideration of theory suggest that eyewitness expert testimony is more likely than not to have influence—to increase knowledge of eyewitness psychology and skepticism about the eyewitness at trial—when it is needed most as a rectifying, safeguard force in cases dominated by questionable but confident eyewitness testimony.

References

Benton, T. R., Ross, D. F., Bradshaw, E., Thomas, W. N., & Bradshaw, G. S. (2005). Eyewitness memory is still not common sense: Comparing jurors, judges and law enforcement to eyewitness experts. *Applied Cognitive Psychology, 20,* 115–129.

Brigham, J. C., & Bothwell, R. K. (1983). The ability of prospective jurors to estimate the accuracy of eyewitness identifications. *Law and Human Behavior, 7,* 19–30.

Boyce, M., Beaudry, J., & Linsay, R. C. L. (2007). Belief of eyewitness identification evidence. In R. C. L. Lindsay, D. F. Ross, J. D. Read, & M. P. Toglia (Eds.), *The handbook of eyewitness psychology,* Vol. II: Memory for people (pp. 501–525). Mahwah, NJ: Erlbaum.

Bothwell, R. K., Deffenbacher, K. A., & Brigham, J. C. (1987). Correlation of eyewitness accuracy and confidence: Optimality hypothesis revisited. *Journal of Applied Psychology, 72,* 691–695.

Cacioppo, J. T., Petty, R. E., & Sidera, J. A. (1982). The effects of a salient self-schema on the evaluation of proattitudinal editorials: Top-down versus bottom-up message processing. *Journal of Experimental Social Psychology, 18,* 324–338.

Chaiken, S., & Eagly, A. H. (1976). Communication modality as a determinant of message persuasiveness and message comprehensibility. *Journal of Personality and Social Psychology, 34,* 605–614.

Chaiken, S., Liberman, A., & Eagly, A. H. (1989). Heuristic and systematic processing within and beyond the persuasion context. In J. S. Uleman & J. A. Bargh (Eds.), *Unintended thought* (pp. 212–252). New York: Guilford Press.

Chaiken, S., & Maheswaran, D. (1994). Heuristic processing can bias systematic processing: Effects of source credibility, argument ambiguity, and task importance on attitude judgment. *Journal of Personality and Social Psychology, 66,* 460–473.

Cooper, J., Bennett, E. A., & Sukel, H. L. (1996). Complex scientific testimony: How do jurors make decisions. *Law and Human Behavior, 20,* 379–394.

Cooper, J., & Hall, J. (2000). Reactions of mock-jurors to testimony of a court-appointed expert. *Behavioral Sciences and the Law, 18,* 719–729.

Cooper, J., & Neuhaus, I, M. (2000). The "hired gun" effect: Assessing the effect of pay, frequency of testifying, and credentials on the perception of expert testimony. *Law and Human Behavior, 24,* 149–171.

Cutler, B. L., Dexter, H. R., & Penrod, S. D. (1990). Nonadversarial methods for sensitizing jurors to eyewitness evidence. *Journal of Applied Social Psychology, 20,* 1197–1207.

Cutler, B. L., Penrod, S. D., & Dexter, H. R. (1989). The eyewitness, the expert psychologist, and the jury. *Law and Human Behavior, 13*, 311–332.

Deffenbacher, K. A., & Loftus, E. F. (1982). Do jurors share a common understanding concerning eyewitness behavior? *Law and Human Behavior, 6*, 15–30.

Devenport, J. L., & Cutler, B. L. (2004). Impact of defense-only and opposing eyewitness experts on juror judgments. *Law and Human Behavior, 28*, 569–576.

Devenport, J. L., Penrod, S. D., & Cutler, B. L. (1997). Eyewitness identification evidence: Evaluating commonsense evaluations. *Psychology, Public Policy, and Law, 3*, 338–361.

Devenport, J. L., Stinson, V., Cutler, B. L., & Kravitz, D. A. (2002). How effective are cross-examination and expert testimony safeguards? Jurors' perceptions of the suggestiveness and fairness of biased lineup procedures. *Journal of Applied Psychology, 87*, 1042–1054.

Devlin, Hon. Lord Patrick. (1976). Report to the Secretary of State for the Home Department Of the Departmental Committee on Evidence and Identification in Criminal Cases. London: Her Majesty's Stationery Office.

Eagly, A. H. (1974). Comprehensibility of persuasive arguments as a determinant of persuasion. *Journal of Personality and Social Psychology, 29*, 758–773.

Fazio, R. H. (1979). Motives for social comparison: The construction-validation distinction. *Journal of Personality and Social Psychology, 37*, 1683–1698.

Fox, S. G., & Walters, H. A. (1986). The impact of general vs. specific expert testimony and eyewitness confidence upon mock juror judgment. *Law and Human Behavior, 10*, 215–228.

Geiselman, R. E., & Mendez, B. A. (2005). Assistance to the fact finder: Eyewitness expert testimony versus attorney's closing arguments. *American Journal of Forensic Psychology, 23*, 5–15.

Geiselman, R. E., Putman, C., Korte, R., Shahriary, M., Jachimowicz, G., & Irzhevsky, V. (2002). Eyewitness expert testimony and juror decisions. *American Journal of Forensic Psychology, 20*, 21–36.

Griffith, J. D., Hart, C. L., Frigo, C., Hoscheck, D., Householder, K., & Harkins, J. (2005). Expert witnesses: Perceptions of eligible jurors. *American Journal of Forensic Psychology, 23*, 23–39.

Hass, R. G. (1981). Effects of source characteristics on cognitive responses and persuasion. In R. E. Petty, T. M. Ostrom, & T. C. Brock (Eds.), Cognitive responses in persuasion (pp. 141–172). Hillsdale, NJ: Erlbaum.

Horowitz, I. A., Bordens, K. S., Victor, E., Bourgeois, M. J., & ForsterLee, M. J. (2001). The effects of complexity on jurors' verdicts and construction of evidence. *Journal of Applied Psychology, 86*, 641–652.

Jones, E. E. (1990). *Interpersonal perception.* New York: Freeman.

Jones, E. E., & Harris, V. A. (1967). The attribution of attitudes. *Journal of Experimental Social Psychology, 3*, 2–24.

Kaplan, M. F., & Kemmerick, G. D. (1974). Juror judgment as information integration: Combining evidential and nonevidential information. *Journal of Personality and Social Psychology, 30*, 493–499.

Kassin, S. M., & Barndollar, K. A. (1992). The psychology of eyewitness testimony: A comparison of experts and prospective jurors. *Journal of Applied Social Psychology, 22*, 1241–1249.

Kassin, S. M., Ellsworth, P. C., & Smith, V. L. (1989). The "general acceptance" of psychological research on eyewitness testimony: A survey of the experts. *American Psychologist, 44,* 1089–1098.

Kassin, S. M., Tubb, V. Z., Hosch, H. M., & Memon, A. (2001). On the "general acceptance" of eyewitness testimony research: A new survey of the experts. *American Psychologist, 56,* 405–416.

Kovera, M. B., Gresham, A. W., Borgida, E., Gray, E., & Regan, P. C. (1997). Does expert psychological testimony inform or influence juror decision making? A social cognitive analysis. *Journal of Applied Psychology, 82,* 178–191.

Leippe, M. R. (1991). A self-image analysis of persuasion and attitude involvement. In R. C. Curtis (Ed.), *The relational self: Theoretical convergences in psychoanalysis and social psychology* (pp. 37–63). New York: Guilford.

Leippe, M. R. (1994). The appraisal of eyewitness testimony. In D. F. Ross, J. D. Read, & M. P. Toglia (Eds.), Adult eyewitness testimony: Current trends and developments (pp. 385–417). New York: Cambridge University Press.

Leippe, M. R. (1995). The case for expert testimony about eyewitness memory. *Psychology, Public Policy, and Law, 1,* 909–959.

Leippe, M. R., & Eisenstadt, D. (2007). Eyewitness confidence and the confidence-accuracy relationship in memory for people. In R. C. L. Lindsay, D. F. Ross, J. D. Read, & M. P. Toglia (Eds.), Handbook of eyewitness psychology, Vol. 2: Memory for people (pp. 377–425). Mahwah, NJ: Erlbaum.

Leippe, M. R., Eisenstadt, D., & Kiddoo, K. (2005, March). Eyewitness expert testimony and instructions about reasonable doubt: Independent influences on perceptions of trial evidence. Paper presented at the annual meeting of the American Psychology-Law Society, La Jolla, CA.

Leippe, M. R., Eisenstadt, D. E., Rauch, S. M., & Seib, H. (2004). Timing of eyewitness expert testimony, jurors' need for cognition, and case strength as determinants of trial verdicts. *Journal of Applied Psychology, 89,* 524–541.

Leippe, M. R., Eisenstadt, D., Rauch, S. M., & Stambush, M. (2006). Effects of social-comparative memory feedback on eyewitnesses' identification confidence, suggestibility, and retrospective memory reports. *Basic and Applied Social Psychology, 28,* 201–220.

Leippe, M. R., & Elkin, R. A. (1987). When motives clash: Issue involvement and response Involvement as determinants of persuasion. *Journal of Personality and Social Psychology, 52,* 269–278.

Lindsay, R. C. L. (1994). Expectations of eyewitness performance: Jurors' verdicts do not follow from their beliefs. In D. F. Ross, J. D. Read, & M. P. Toglia (Eds.), *Adult eyewitness memory: Current trends and developments* (pp. 362–384). New York: Cambridge University Press.

Lindsay, R. C. L., MacDonald, P., & McGarry, S. (1990). Perspectives on the role of the expert witness. *Behavioral Sciences and the Law, 8,* 457–464.

Lindsay, R. C. L., Ross, D. F. Read, J. D., & Toglia, M. P. (Eds.), *Handbook of eyewitness psychology, Vol. 2: Memory for people.* Mahwah, NJ: Erlbaum.

Lindsay, R. C. L., Wells, G. L., & Rumpel, C. (1981). Can people detect eyewitness identification accuracy within and between situations?. *Journal of Applied Psychology, 66,* 79–89.

Loftus, E. F. (1974, December). The incredible eyewitness. *Psychology Today, 8(7),* 116–119.

Martire, K. A., & Kemp, R. I. (2009). The impact of eyewitness expert evidence and judicial instruction on juror ability to evaluate eyewitness testimony. *Law and Human Behavior*, in press.

Moore, P. J., & Gump, B. B. (1995). Information integration in juror decision making. *Journal of Applied Social Psychology, 25*, 2158–2179.

Patterson, B. W. (2004). The "tyranny of the eyewitness." *Law & Psychology Review, 28*, 195–203.

Penrod, S. D., & Cutler, B. (1995). Witness confidence and witness accuracy: Assessing their forensic relation. *Psychology, Public, Policy, and Law, 1*, 817–845.

Petty, R. E., & Cacioppo, J. T. (1984). The effects of involvement on responses to argument quantity and quality: Central and peripheral routes to persuasion. *Journal of Personality and Social Psychology, 46*, 69–81.

Petty, R. E., & Cacioppo, J. A. (1986). *Communication and persuasion: Central and peripheral routes to attitude change.* New York: Springer-Verlag.

Petty, R. E., Ostrom, T. M., & Brock, T. C. (Eds.). (1981). *Cognitive responses in persuasion.* Hillsdale, NJ: Erlbaum.

Petty, R. E., & Wegener, D. T. (1998). Attitude change: Multiple roles for persuasion variables. In D. T. Gilbert, S. T. Fiske, & G. Lindzey (Eds.), *The handbook of social psychology* (4th edition, Vol. 1, pp. 323–390). New York: McGraw-Hill.

Pezdek, K. (2007). Expert testimony on eyewitness memory and identification. In M. Costanz, D. Krauss, & K. Pezdek (Eds.), *Expert psychological testimony for the courts.* Mahwah, NJ: Erlbaum.

Pratkanis, A. R., Greenwald, A. G., Leippe, M. R., & Baumgardner, M. H. (1988). In search of Reliable persuasion effects: III. The sleeper effect is dead. Long live the sleeper effect. *Journal of Personality and Social Psychology, 54*, 203–218.

Ramirez, G., Zemba, D., & Geiselman, R. E., Jr. (1996). Judges' cautionary instructions on Eyewitness testimony. *American Journal of Forensic Psychology, 14*, 31–66.

Ross, L. (1977). The intuitive psychologist and his shortcomings. In L. Berkowitz (Ed.), Advances in experimental social psychology (Vol. 10, pp. 173–220). New York: Academic Press.

Scheck, B., & Neufeld, P. (2008). *The innocence project.* Retrieved January 15, 2008 from The Innocence Project Homepage: http://www.innocenceproject.org/.

Schmechel, R. S., O'Toole, T. P., Easterly, C., & Loftus, E. F. (2006). Beyond the ken? Testing jurors' understanding of eyewitness reliability evidence. *Jurimetrics, 46*, 177–214.

Schuller, R. A., Terry, D., & McKimmie, B. (2005). The impact of expert testimony on jurors' Decisions: Gender of the expert and testimony complexity. *Journal of Applied Social Psychology, 35*, 1266–1280.

Sigler, J. N., & Couch, J. V. (2002). Eyewitness testimony and the jury verdict. *North American Journal of Psychology, 4*, 143–148.

Vidmar, N. (2005). Expert evidence, the adversary system, and the jury. *American Journal of Public Health, 95* (Supplement 1), S137–S143.

Wegener, D. T., & Petty, R. E. (1997). The flexible correction model: The role of naive theories of bias in bias correction. In M. P. Zanna (Ed.), Advances in experimental social psychology (Vol. 29, pp.141–208). San Diego: Academic Press.

Wells, G. L. (1986). Expert psychological testimony: Empirical and conceptual analysis of effects [Special issue: The ethics of expert testimony]. *Law and Human Behavior, 10,* 83–95.

Wells, G. L. (1993). What do we know about eyewitness identification? *American Psychologist, 48,* 553-571.

Wells, G. L., Ferguson, T. J., & Lindsay, R. C. L. (1981). The tractability of eyewitness confidence and its implications for triers of fact. *Journal of Applied Psychology, 66,* 688–696.

Wells, G. L., & Leippe, M. R. (1981). How do triers of fact infer the accuracy of eyewitness identification? Using memory for detail can be misleading. *Journal of Applied Psychology, 66,* 682–687.

Wells, G. L., Lindsay, R. C. L., & Ferguson, T. J. (1979). Accuracy, confidence, and juror perceptions in eyewitness identification. *Journal of Applied Psychology, 64,* 440–448.

Wells, G. L., Lindsay, R. C. L., & Tousignant, J. P. (1980). Effects of expert psychological advice on human performance in judging the validity of eyewitness testimony. *Law and Human Behavior, 4,* 275–285.

Wells, G. L., & Wright, E. F. (1983). *Unpublished raw data.*

Whitley, B. E., Jr., & Greenberg, M. S. (1986). The role of eyewitness confidence in juror perceptions of credibility. Journal of Applied Social Psychology, *16,* 387–409.

Yarmey, A. D., & Jones, H. P. T. (1983). Is the psychology of eyewitness identification a matter of common sense? In S. M. A. Lloyd-Bostock & B. R. Clifford (Eds.), Evaluating witness evidence: Recent psychological research and new perspectives (pp. 13–40). Chichester, England: Wiley.

9

Limitations of Expert Psychology Testimony on Eyewitness Identification

Heather D. Flowe, Kristin M. Finklea, and Ebbe B. Ebbesen

Psychologists are being called upon more than ever to evaluate the reliability of eyewitness testimony. This state of affairs is novel because the legal system's reception of psychological research was cold early on, stemming in part from the contention that the research was lacking in legal verisimilitude (Yarmey, 2001; also see Epstein, Chapter 4). The frustration felt by psychologists regarding the initial unwillingness on the part of legal officials to apply psychological research findings in the courtroom and in the police station is well-exemplified by Wells, Memon, and Penrod (2006), who write, "psychologists were able to use experiments to identify eyewitness problems long before the legal system was smacked in the face with DNA exonerations" (p. 46).

The external validity of eyewitness testimony research has also been debated within the field of psychology (see the 1986 special issue of *Law and Human Behavior*, McCloskey, Egeth, & McKenna). Some have argued that the conditions (the witnessing, testing, and/or measurement contexts) experienced by laboratory research participants may not be representative of the conditions faced by actual witnesses (e.g., Clifford and Lloyd-Bostock, 1983; Ebbesen & Konečni, 1997; Elliott, 1993; Konečni & Ebbesen, 1986; McCloskey & Egeth, 1983; Yuille, 1993), and others have argued that the methods and subject samples employed by researchers are diverse enough (e.g., Deffenbacher, 1984; Haber & Haber, 2000; Loftus, 1983; Yarmey, 1997; Yarmey, 2001) and the body of research evidence extensive enough (see

Pezdek, Chapter 2) to warrant the generality of the findings. We revisit some of these issues in this chapter, and argue in the main that the methods by which research findings are translated to legal cases by expert consultants raise important issues that require careful consideration.

In the sections that follow, we will argue that in generalizing from laboratory research to actual cases we must consider (a) the extent to which the procedures or psychological processes that instantiate variables in the laboratory occur outside of the laboratory; (b) whether the background conditions of laboratory studies are diverse enough to warrant gross application; (c) whether testifying about a given factor (e.g., weapon presence, cross-race witnesses, post-identification confidence) provides incremental validity over traditional safeguards; and (d) the extent to which the process by which the legal system selects witnesses to testify affects the generalizability of laboratory research to a criminal case. Experts also have been known to argue to the court that the DNA exoneration cases provide evidence that eyewitness memory is unreliable (e.g., *People v. Adams*, 2008; *People v. Copeland*, 2007; *People v. Davis*, 2004; *People v. Ellison*, 2008; *People v. Garcia*, 2008; *United States v. Burton*, 1998). In this chapter, we will comment on the limited generalizability of the DNA exoneration cases (for other examples of criminal cases in which DNA exonerations were discussed in relation to eyewitness identification reliability see *People v. Dubose*, 2005; *People v. Herrera*, 2006; *People v. Lawrence*, 2007; *People v. Lewis*, 2008; *People v. Romero*, 2007; *People v. Williams*, 2006; and *People v. Woolcock*, 2005). Finally, we will argue that by acting as case consultants in an adversarial role, we possibly hamper our future ability to work with the legal system as scientists in developing procedural safeguards to improve the reliability of eyewitness testimony.

At the outset, it is important to point out that expert testimony on eyewitness identification can influence the disposition of criminal cases in a number of ways. Typically, one thinks of an eyewitness expert as someone who educates the jury with respect to the factors that can influence eyewitness memory. Expert opinion, however, can influence the disposition of a criminal case at other stages. In our interactions with the legal system, we have learned that expert opinion can be influential in plea bargaining a case, in deciding whether to admit the testimony of a particular witness, and in preparing a case for appeal. (Unfortunately, no systematic data exist on these issues.) In the sections that follow, our discussion applies to not only expert testimony proffered to juries, but also to eyewitness expert opinions offered in specific cases at other processing stages.

Laboratory Versus Real-World Procedures and Psychological Processes

How do expert witnesses on eyewitness memory generalize from laboratory research to a real-world case? They do so by comparing the similarity of attributes found in a specific case to the conditions simulated in laboratory studies:

> To the extent that a particular variable or set of variables was present at the time of the witnessing, and those variables are known through scientific research to have a particular effect or set of effects, then it is possible that expert testimony on those witnessing conditions could be relevant and of assistance to the jury in evaluating particular points at issue. (Yarmey, 2001, p. 94)

This statement makes the assumption that research variables themselves are causal entities, rather than components tied to specific laboratory procedures. Danziger and Dzinas (1997) traced the historical use of the term "variable" in psychological research by empirically analyzing the context in which it appeared in psychology papers. They found that the term was first imported into psychological research in the 1920s to describe statistical procedures. Subsequently, variables began appearing in papers as methodological entities to describe the procedural aspects of experiments. Variables eventually graduated into theoretical and substantive entities in discussions of research findings. In explaining this transformation, they propose, "That may point to a fairly widespread, though implicit and unexamined, belief that, any psychologically relevant part of reality was already prestructured in the form of distinct variables, and that psychological research techniques merely held up a mirror to this structure" (Danziger & Dzinas, 1997, p. 46).

If the procedures that give rise to a construct in the laboratory differ from the procedures that give rise to a construct in the real world, then simply matching variables found in the scientific literature to the variables found in a criminal case based on prima facie resemblance may be inappropriate. To illustrate, *stress* as a construct may manifest differently in the real world than it does in the laboratory. Stress may be heightened by perceived danger, which could vary depending on the proximity of the eyewitness to the perpetrator in the real world (Civilini & Flowe, 2008; Yuille & Cutshall, 1986). It is plausible that being in closer proximity to the perpetrator may offset any negative impact of stress on a given witness' memory. Additionally, the onset of stress in relation to when the perpetrator is first seen by the eyewitness may also be important, and research has not addressed this issue. More than a third of witnesses in our field research saw the perpetrator for a period of time prior to being victimized (Civilini & Flowe, 2008). Additionally, the procedure that is used to instantiate eyewitness recall in the laboratory may also be an important determinant of whether stress has a negative effect on memory reports. Deffenbacher and colleagues (2004) reviewed the laboratory literature on the impact of stress on the accuracy of eyewitness memory. Their meta-analysis indicated a statistically significant increase in errors in the stress compared to the control conditions for descriptions that were given under *interrogative recall*. The error rates in the stress and control conditions did not differ under conditions of *free recall*. These results indicate that the effect of stress on description accuracy may be tied to other psychological variables (e.g., inter-ference, fatigue) that are affected by the type of interview procedure used. Although the procedure police use to interview witnesses may vary across jurisdictions, field research suggests that witnesses typically provide testimony in conditions that are more similar to free recall than interrogative recall (Civilini & Flowe, 2008; Fahsing, Ask, & Granhag, 2004; Lindsay, Martin, & Webber, 1994; Sporer, 1996). The extent to which the effects of stress reported by laboratory studies occur in real-world cases may depend on the extent to which the interview conditions found in real-world cases matches those of the laboratory. The Deffenbacher and colleagues' (2004) meta-analysis also indi-cated that, in the stress compared to the control conditions, an increase occurred in filler identifications in *target-present* lineups. No effects were found in *target-absent* lineups. Wells, Memon, and Penrod (2006) discuss the importance of including perpetrator-absent lineups in laboratory investiga-tions, as "target-absent lineups simulate the real-world situation in which police have focused their suspicion on an innocent suspect" (p. 50). The vari-ables that control the error rate in target-present and target-absent lineups may differ; therefore, testimony about factors that lead to errors in target-present lineups might be completely irrelevant in cases in which the issue is whether the witness has mistakenly identified an innocent suspect.

As another example, research has found that misleading post-event infor-mation has a negative impact on memory reports (Ayers & Reder, 1998). An expert may be inclined to draw broadly from this research literature and tes-tify that eyewitnesses who encounter misleading information are more likely to have inaccurate memory reports. Laboratory research has indicated, how-ever, that the misinformation effect is affected by the procedures that are used to introduce the misleading post-event information, including the timing of the presentation of the misinformation (e.g., Loftus, Miller, & Burns, 1978), the retention interval between misinformation presentation and the final memory test (e.g., Loftus, Miller, & Burns, 1978; Windschitl, 1996), whether the misleading information is about central versus peripheral details (e.g., Wright & Stroud, 1998), the format of the questions on the final memory test (e.g., McCloskey & Zaragoza, 1985), and the type of source providing the mis-information (e.g., Hope, Ost, Gabbert, Healey, & Lenton, 2008). Whether these effects manifest in a real-world case depends on the totality of circum-stances involved, and broad generalizations (e.g., testifying that "research generally finds that exposure to misleading information can reduce the accu-racy of memory reports") may be misleading.

A related issue is whether psychological construal of a given laboratory procedure can be broadly applied to the legal system (see Berkowitz & Donnerstein, 1982, for a discussion of psychological construal as it relates to the external validity of social psychology experiments). To illustrate, the *cross-race (own-race) bias* describes the finding that the rate of making a correct identification is lower if the to-be-remembered face is of a different race than the participant eyewitness (e.g. Brigham & Malpass, 1985; Feingold, 1914;

Meissner & Brigham, 2001; Sporer, 2001). The name of the effect alludes to the causal mechanism being tied to a difference in race between the witness and perpetrator. Currently, the most widely supported explanation of the effect suggests that a low level of cross-race contact leads to an impoverished ability to differentiate, using the appropriate cues, the faces of other-race individuals (e.g., Meissner & Brigham, 2001; Sporer, 2001). Given this theoretical position, at least one key issue might be the psychological construal of other-race faces, which might be affected by the amount of contact the witness has had with other-race faces. An expert, of course, is not able to test the eyewitness in an actual case to know the level of experience the witness has had with other-race faces. Still further, no research is available to tell us what degree of experience a witness should have with other-race faces before accuracy is expected to improve, nor do we have any empirical basis for recommending how "other-race face experience" ought to be reliably measured in actual witnesses.

A final point we wish to touch on is that in testifying in the courtroom, the possibility exists that an expert will confound constructs with levels of constructs. As an example, assume that an expert testifies that eyewitnesses have more difficulty remembering stressful than nonstressful events. More aptly put, research finds that memory (as studied in a particular context, measured in a particular way, and with a particular type of participant) performance (as measured with a particular type of memory test) decreases given a certain level (and type) of exposure to stress compared to some certain baseline level of nonstress. Exposure to stress per se does not change memory, but rather some degree (or quality) of stress changes behavior, which in turn may affect memory. For instance, we would not automatically conclude that a student will perform well on an exam because he has studied, or that bombarding a plutonium atom will cause a nuclear explosion. In all cases, we have to take into account the dosage level of the precipitating factor and the other variables that may have been present at the time of witnessing in order to postdict whether the factor may have negatively impacted memory.

Background Conditions May Affect Causal Relationships

Meta-analyses of lab studies (e.g., Bradfield-Douglas & Steblay, 2006; Steblay, 1992) are often done with an eye toward making a particular research area more amenable to courtroom presentation. A typical conclusion reached from this work is that a variable is important and reliable enough for generalization to the legal system if its effect is statistically significant in the majority of the studies that have investigated the phenomenon. To illustrate, Bradfield-Douglas and Steblay (2006) performed a meta-analysis of the post-identification feedback effect and concluded based on their findings: "For experts who testify in court, this meta-analysis will facilitate admittance of testimony on this topic. . . . The consistency in outcomes demonstrated in this review lends credence to the argument that post-identification feedback effects should be 'generally accepted'" (pp. 865–866). The range of conditions in which an effect has been investigated, however, may have a direct relationship to the range of population characteristics to which generalization is possible (Meehl, 1989). The closer a researcher's enterprise is to a domain of application, the more important it is to raise questions regarding external validity. This point is made well by Mook (1983): "Of course there are also those cases in which one does want to predict real-life behavior directly from research findings. Survey research and most experiments in applied settings such as the factory or classroom have that end in view. Predicting real-life behavior is a perfectly legitimate and honorable way to use research. When we engage in it, we do confront the problem of E[xternal] V[alidity]" (p. 386).

One might contend that sufficient variability is present across studies in the operationalization of key variables and in the background conditions employed (i.e., the variables that are held constant across the experimental and control conditions, such as duration of exposure to the culprit, the lineup employed, the to-be-remembered event), and as such, we have explored a sufficient range of conditions for many variables (e.g., weapon exposure, cross-race witnesses, stress) to be able to broadly generalize the cause-and-effect relationships observed across laboratory studies to specific cases in the legal system. In this section, we compare the similarity of laboratory and field eyewitness contexts, and the results suggest that we have charted only a part of the distance.

Table 9.1 presents the background conditions of papers summarized by well-known meta-analyses (Meissner & Brigham, 2001; Steblay, 1992; Steblay, Dysart, Fulero, & Lindsay, 2001). Of particular interest here are the background conditions employed by these studies that affect memory strength; namely, the length of the critical event exposure duration and the length of the retention interval between the to-be-remembered event and the identification task. If the meta-analysis study authors did not provide summary information about memory strength, we obtained the information from the original published reports that were part of the meta-analysis (i.e., "gray literature," or unpublished work, was not included our analysis). In Table 9.2 we present the average duration of exposure and retention interval found in our analysis of 721 cases (rape, robbery, and assault) involving lineup identifications that were randomly selected from files that were submitted by the San Diego Police Department to the San Diego District Attorney's Office for review. As a comparison of Tables 9.1 and 9.2 indicates, the background conditions in the laboratory studies differ from the conditions experienced by archival eyewitnesses making identifications. The duration of exposure to the culprit and the identification retention interval typically employed by the laboratory studies are short relative to the archives.

Our analysis of duration of exposure to the culprit was the result of estimating the duration on the basis of the information reported in the case file (including witness statements in the majority of the cases, police incident

Table 9.1 Critical Event Exposure Duration and Identification Retention Interval by Research Literature

	Critical Event Exposure Duration		Retention Interval	
	Median	Range	Median	Range
Weapon focus effect	45 s	18 s–240 s	20 min	Immediate–36 days
Cross-race effect	3 s	.12 s–4 min	2 min	Immediate–21 days
Simultaneous and sequential	1.25 min	4.5 s–6 min	15 min	Immediate–7 days

Table 9.2 Archival Results for Critical Event Exposure Duration and Identification Retention Interval by Case Type

	Critical Event Exposure Duration		Retention Interval	
	Median	Range	Median	Range
Assault	10 min	4.8 sec–9 hours	18 days	1–90 days
Rape	10 min	30 sec–120 hours	2.97 days	1–72 days
Robbery	5 min	15 sec–7.5 hours	5.31 days	1–44 days

reports, etc.). Therefore, because the validity of our estimates can be questioned, we also analyzed a field study (Woolnough & MacLeod, 2001) that examined the accuracy of testimony given by witnesses in real-world cases by comparing the contents of the witness reports to closed-circuit television videorecordings of the witnessed crime. The average duration of exposure to the culprit (based on our analysis of the raw data presented in the report) was 1 minute, 27 seconds (median: 1 minute, 20 seconds; range: 20 seconds to 3 minutes, 45 seconds), which again is relatively long compared to the laboratory studies.

Yet another crucial difference between the laboratory research and the field is that eyewitnesses in the field may be questioned on multiple occasions, whereas laboratory witnesses are typically questioned once (Ebbesen & Rienick, 1998). Accuracy is expected to be lower for eyewitnesses who render testimony after a long compared to a short delay (e.g., Shapiro & Penrod, 1986). Real-world eyewitnesses, however, experience retention intervals differently than eyewitnesses in the lab if they provide testimony at several points in time; usually, they are questioned immediately after the event, and then yet again at other points in time (Civilini & Flowe, 2008). Ebbesen and Rienick (1998) demonstrated, by comparing memory loss functions within and between subjects, that forgetting did not occur if participants were questioned repeatedly within the retention interval. This work illustrates that it is crucial to time experimental procedures in a manner that is comparable with how police question and test eyewitnesses. Experts testifying in the courtroom assume that the effects obtained in the laboratory generalize across memory strength conditions. It is highly plausible, however, that many of the effects that experts testify about are moderated by memory strength.

Even if we did have comparable levels of memory strength in the lab and in the real world, we still might wonder whether the real-world and laboratory contexts are comparable in other respects. We located 290 published experiments on lineup/showup identification (conducted from 1975–2006) from the PsychInfo database. Of the studies, 44% presented the target in a video, 17% live in a lab, 13% live in an auditorium or a classroom, 11% in a photograph, 8% live in a natural setting, and 7% in a slide sequence. The target was portrayed under conditions that were not criminal in 41% of the studies (e.g., laboratory participants memorized a photograph, or field participants were asked to identify a customer or a researcher with whom they had previously interacted), and the target committed theft in 32%, robbery in 20%, other types of crimes in 4%, assault in 1%, and committed rape in less than 1% of the studies. Additionally, the majority of studies involved college students (68% of the studies recruited exclusively college students, 23% were from other adult populations, and 9% were children). These results indicate that the eyewitness memory studies most commonly study (based on the modes presented earlier) noncriminal activities presented in videotapes to college students. The research context employed may of course vary across the domain of investigation (e.g., lineup research, misinformation effect research, stress research). However, one might still wonder whether differences between the contexts in which the research is carried and the contexts in which eye witnessing occurs are important considerations for determining whether an experimental effect generalizes.

One response to our contention that laboratory and real-world contexts may not be comparable is the argument that memory for real-world crime events is bound to be worse compared to memory for laboratory events. This point is often raised in arguing that the laboratory studies are generalizable because they represent the best-case scenario: "The results showed that participants who watched the videos reported more details and with higher accuracy than those who saw the live events, suggesting that laboratory experiments may actually overestimate memory performance" (Loftus, 2003, p. 868). Although this could be true, we simply do not know. How background factors (such as memory strength, or eyewitness vs. student witness/lab participant motivation and intelligence) might interact with primary eyewitness variables (such as weapon focus, race of the eyewitness and perpetrator, or stress) is an empirical issue that necessitates further investigation. Additionally, the results of field studies raise the possibility that variables (such as memory strength) within the eyewitness context might moderate the effects of primary eyewitness variables. For instance, field studies examining the weapon focus effect did not find significant differences in suspect identification rates depending on whether a weapon was present (Behrman & Davey, 2001; Valentine, Pickering, & Darling, 2003; Wright & McDaid, 1996), or depending on whether the witness was subjected to violence (Wright & McDaid, 1996). Additionally, field studies have found mixed results regarding the cross-race effect (Behrman & Davey, 2001; Valentine, Pickering, & Darling, 2003). As another example, Yuille and Cutshall (1986) found that stress and accuracy were not associated in their case study of statements made by actual eyewitnesses to a shootout. They further found that witnesses who reported higher levels of stress were closer in proximity to the perpetrator than witnesses reporting lower levels of stress. In other words, in actual cases, stress and vantage point of the witness are likely confounded. Even though archival studies are correlational and cause-and-effect relationships cannot be educed from the results, they draw our attention to the complexity of circumstances that exist outside of the laboratory that may serve to moderate the main effects of variables on accuracy that are found in the laboratory.

Incremental Validity of Error-Detection Factors Versus Effect Size of Variable

A key issue addressed in other domains of applied psychology (e.g., organizational psychology, clinical psychology, health psychology, personality psychology) is *incremental validity*, which refers to the extent to which a particular selection procedure improves on decision making in the context of application. Incremental validity is important because the validity of a selection test can vary depending upon the context of application (see Hunsley & Meyer, 2003, for further commentary on issues concerning incremental validity in applied psychology). Selection tests can be costly, both financially and in human terms; hence, it is important to assess whether the goal behind using a particular selection test is achieved in a particular context.

In testifying in the courtroom, we are assuming that expert testimony on the issue of eyewitness memory, which is a selection procedure for identifying cases that are possibly problematic, has incremental validity over not having the testimony. Traditional safeguards, such as police and prosecutor case screening procedures and cautionary instructions to the jury regarding the factors that can affect the reliability of eyewitness testimony (see Devenport, Kimbrough, & Cutler, Chapter 3, for a review), have been argued to be ineffective in preventing erroneous convictions based on erroneous eyewitness testimony. As such, expert testimony about risk factors that decrease the accuracy of eyewitness testimony may be advisable.

The size of the effect, or the validity coefficient for the construct about which the expert is testifying (r) (see Pezdek, Chapter 2, for discussion of the content of expert testimony), is but one factor to consider in determining whether expert testimony is warranted. Meta-analytic results indicate that the effect size estimate for weapon focus in lineups ($r = .09$) (Steblay, 1992), for instance, is smaller than the effect size estimate for biased instructions in target-absent lineups ($r = .38$) (Cutler & Penrod, 1995). We could conclude, based on this comparison, that the biased instruction effect is relatively more robust than the weapon focus effect, and therefore, is a factor about which we should testify more often. However, other factors must be taken into account as well in determining what is gained by providing the expert testimony to the courts. Incremental validity in applied psychology is examined by taking into account the effect size of the predictor, the base rate of the outcome, the selection ratio, or the number of cases that will be examined in the applied context, as well as the definition of the construct in question. In the eyewitness memory domain, the incremental validity of utilizing testimony in a given jurisdiction would be assessed by determining:

- The effect size of the predictor
- The base rate of innocent versus guilty defendants
- The selection ratio, or the proportion of cases in which the expert testifies
- The applied definition of the construct (i.e., the type of scenarios that the expert qualifies as meeting the definition of a construct, such as what types of scenarios would qualify as involving weapon focus or mugshot-induced bias)

To illustrate, consider a scenario in which the effect size for a risk factor is $r = .40$ and the selection ratio is 20%. We can examine the *true-positive rate*, or the proportion of cases in which the expert would testify when the defendant is in fact innocent. We can also examine in relation to the base rate of innocence the *false-positive rate*, or the proportion of cases in which the expert would testify when the defendant is in fact guilty. Holding the effect size and selection ratio constant, we can compute the true-positive rate and the false-positive rate as a function of different base rates of innocence.[1] The results of the analysis are shown in Figure 9.1. As can be seen, if 15% of defendants appearing in the courtroom are in fact innocent, then the true-positive rate will be 3% and the false-positive rate will be 17%. In other words, in a population of 100 cases in which 15 defendants are actually innocent, the expert would provide testimony in 3 cases. For the remaining 85 defendants who are actually guilty, the expert would testify in 17 cases. Under the conditions described, the true-positive rate will equal or exceed the false-positive rate only when the base rate of innocence is equal to or greater than 50%. This analysis makes clear that the risk of false-positives exists when expert testimony is utilized.

Although not central to the discussion, the false-negative and true-negative rates refer to occasions when the expert does not testify. The *true-negative rate* (the proportion of cases in which the expert does not testify and the defendant is guilty) and the *false-negative rate* (the proportion of cases in which the expert does not testify and defendant is innocent) are also provided in Figure 9.1. As can be seen, if the base rate of innocence is 15% and the selection ratio is 20%, out of 100 cases there will be 68 in which the defendant is guilty (true-positive rate), and 12 in which the defendant is innocent

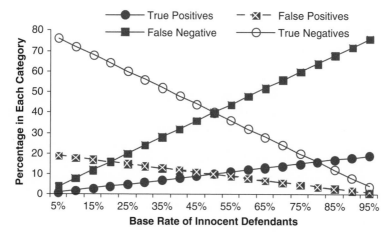

Figure 9.1 Hypothetical example illustrating the effects of base rates of defendant innocence and expert testimony on case outcomes. The example assumes that the effect size for the risk factor about which the expert testifies is $r = .40$, and the rate at which the expert testifies in cases (i.e., the selection ratio) is .20. The *true-positive rate* reflects the proportion of cases in which the expert testifies when the defendant is innocent. The *false-positive rate* is the proportion of cases in which the expert testifies and the defendant is guilty. The *false-negative rate* indicates the proportion of cases in which the expert does not testify and the defendant is innocent, and the *true-negative rate* indicates the proportion of cases in which the expert does not testify and the defendant is guilty.

(false-negative rate). One might think that the expert should testify more often to decrease the false-negative rate. Doing so, however, would simultaneously increase the false-positive rate.

Last, the type of scenarios that the expert qualifies as weapon focus is also important. The size of the effect can be expected to vary depending on the standards employed. For instance, what type of instrument (e.g., gun, knife, screwdriver) qualifies as a weapon (see Pickel, 1998), and for how long should the witness be exposed to the perpetrator in order for the weapon focus effect to hold? (See Steblay, 1992, for meta-analysis of moderators of weapon focus effect in mostly target-present lineups.)

As a means for further discussing some of the difficulties an expert might encounter in mapping laboratory variables onto real-world scenarios, consider the case of 19-year-old Adam Noriega, who was accused of shooting a rival gang member to death (*People v. Noriega*, 2003). Eyewitness identifications of Noriega served as the primary evidence and were made by his companion, who was present during the shooting and by D.S., a 14-year-old witness who saw the shooting take place from across the street. The expert in the case presented a written motion to the court regarding the possible negative effects of "photobiasing" on eyewitness identification accuracy. The eyewitness expert explained to the court that "photobiasing" is a priming effect whereby a witness identifies a suspect from the lineup because she had been previously exposed to the suspect's photograph. D.S. had been presented with 30 photographs of local area gang members, one of which was a photograph of Noriega taken at a younger age, and she did not identify anyone. Six weeks later, she positively identified a recent photograph of Noriega in a lineup test. The expert was ultimately not allowed to testify because the photograph of Noriega taken at a younger age bore little resemblance to him at the time of the shooting, an observation to which the defense conceded. The exclusion of the expert testimony was later raised on appeal, however, after Noriega was found guilty of premeditated murder. For our present purposes, this case raises interesting issues concerning how to translate effects found in laboratory studies to actual cases. The term given in the research literature to the biasing effect of previously having been exposed to mugshots on lineup identification accuracy is called *mugshot-induced bias* (see Kassin et al., 2001 survey). Some of the questions that arise in mapping mugshot bias research onto the Noriega case include: If a witness does not identify a suspect from a photo that does not look like him, and later the witness identifies the suspect from a photo that does look like him, is the positive identification an example of mugshot-induced bias? Does mugshot-induced bias arise in the absence of a positive identification from the mugshots? (Research by Dysart and colleagues (2001), which may not have been available at the time of Noriega's trial, suggests that it does not.) What is the relationship between the age of a suspect in a photograph and the suspect's current age with respect to eyewitness identification accuracy, a topic about which no research exists?

The foregoing example illustrates that there is considerable room for judgment on the part of the expert in deciding whether a particular effect found in a laboratory study applies to a real-world scenario. Expert judgment in this translation has a direct effect on the incremental validity of expert testimony. It is unknown how often the issues we raise present difficulty for experts. To be sure, we do not know how often some of the translational difficulties found in the *People v. Noriega* (2003) case arise in the cases that experts retain, as systematic research has not been done on the issue. If these difficulties commonly occur, then it would be interesting to find out how experts go about solving them. Considerable agreement may exist among experts that certain variables have reliable effects in the laboratory and that the effects are reliable enough on which to testify (Kassin et al., 2001). But whether agreement among experts exists in the application of the definitions of these variables in real-world cases is an empirical issue that remains to be addressed.

Field Eyewitness Selection Biases May Limit Comparability of Real-life and Laboratory Eyewitnesses

Some who advocate applying laboratory research in the courtroom might argue that laboratory eyewitnesses have better memories, better visual acuity, and are more alert than are other adult populations (e.g., Wells, 2004). A conclusion that could be reached based on this supposition is that accuracy rates are bound to be higher for laboratory compared to real-world eyewitnesses (e.g., Loftus, 2003).

Although factors such as memory ability surely affect memory accuracy, we simply do not know whether the eyewitnesses selected by the police to testify differ in memory ability and motivation compared to laboratory eyewitnesses. We know based on our analysis of police cases forwarded to the Prosecutor's Office in San Diego that, on average, only about 50% of the witnesses in a case are given a lineup test. In contrast, laboratory studies administer a lineup test to every participant, without regard to motivation, vantage point, or memory strength of the participant. If witnesses in real-world cases are selected on the basis of these factors—and these factors moderate cause-and-effect relationships demonstrated in the lab, then generalizations from the laboratory to the courtroom are questionable. Moreover, witnesses may self-select into identification groups and decline to take an identification test if their memory is weak: "A true weapon-focus effect could be obscured if witnesses to crimes involving weapons believe that their memory is weak and are therefore less inclined to attend lineups. The result could be a reduction in the number of weapon-focus–impaired witnesses presented with lineups and thus a reduced number of cases of weapon focus" (Wells, Memon, & Penrod, 2006, p. 53). Still further, a weapon focus effect may not be obtained in field studies because witnesses exposed to weapons agree (or are asked by the police) to take a lineup test only if they attended to the perpetrator's appearance, whereas witnesses who did not attend to the perpetrator's appearance, decline (or are not asked to attempt an identification). In short, if such selection biases operate in the legal system, research participants may be unrepresentative of the characteristics of witnesses in actual criminal cases.

Experts Should Not Generalize from DNA Exoneration Cases

Eyewitness identification evidence plays a crucial role in apprehending the guilty. The following example attests to the power and accuracy of human memory:

> On October 2nd, 1975, three eyewitnesses positively identified Theodore Robert Bundy from a seven-person lineup. One of the eyewitnesses was Carol DaRonch, who indicated that Bundy had kidnapped her, threatened her with a handgun, and attempted to smash her head in with a crowbar before she managed to fight him off and escape his clutches. Although Bundy repeatedly professed his innocence, the police launched a full-blown investigation after Bundy was positively identified.

Of course, this example does not prove the aforementioned premise. This anecdote says nothing at all regarding the rate at which eyewitnesses correctly identify guilty suspects, nor does it tell us why the witnesses in the case might have been correct. Still further, this example draws our attention away from the fact that witnesses can also fail to identify a guilty perpetrator, who in turn kills other people, or that witnesses can mistakenly identify an innocent person, who in turn languishes in prison while the guilty perpetrator is left free to kill.

Despite the inherit limitations of anecdotal evidence, researchers in the eyewitness memory domain often introduce their work by referring to actual cases of mistaken identification. In fact, in a sample of eyewitness research articles published in 2007, nearly a third of the published research papers on eyewitness identification utilize anecdotes of mistaken identification cases to introduce their topic of inquiry (Busey & Loftus, 2007; Haw, Dickinson, & Meissner, 2007; Keast, Brewer, & Wells, 2007; Krug, 2007; Lindsay, 2007; MacLin & Phelan, 2007; Neuschatz et al., 2007; Remijn & Crombag, 2007; Wells & Hasel, 2007). Additionally, DNA exoneration cases in relation to the issue of mistaken eyewitness identification are also cited in cases in which eyewitness memory experts have been involved (e.g., *People v. Adams*, 2008; *People v. Copeland*, 2007; *United States v. Burton*, 1998). One problem with drawing conclusions from a specific case regarding the factors that may increase the likelihood of mistaken identification is that the characteristics of the case may be unrepresentative of false identifications in general. For instance, the fact that the majority of DNA exoneration cases involve sexual assault does not mean that eyewitness memories are particularly weak in sexual assault cases; rather, sexual assault cases have DNA evidence available for analysis, whereas other cases do not. Therefore, potential eyewitness errors may be identified in sexual assault cases but not in other cases like robbery (Wells, Memon, & Penrod, 2006). Nevertheless, despite the fact that DNA exoneration cases are not randomly sampled, and hence unrepresentative of false identifications in general, experts providing information to the court may draw a parallel between eyewitness factors present in the DNA exoneration cases and similar factors that were present in the case at hand. The intention in so doing is to argue that eyewitnesses who are exposed to factors like those found in DNA exoneration cases tend to be inaccurate. However, to determine whether a given factor is influential, the sample should also include cases in which eyewitnesses made correct identifications (see Finklea and Ebbesen, 2007, for such an analysis).

The DNA exoneration cases appear to have had a profound influence on the admission of expert testimony on eyewitness identification. Because the DNA exoneration cases seem to often arise in court discussions (*People v. Dubose*, 2005; *People v. Herrera*, 2006; *People v. Lawrence*, 2007; *People v. Lewis*, 2008; *People v. Romero*, 2007; *People v. Williams*, 2006; *People v. Woolcock*, 2005), we feel that it is worth going into a bit more detail about the extent to which these cases are informative, with regard to using them in other cases to weigh the potential for eyewitness inaccuracy. Predicting the contexts in which mistaken identifications are likely to occur requires analyzing a broad spectrum of cases, not just the cases in which eyewitnesses have made "known" errors. Observing a common feature among exoneration cases does not necessarily mean that the feature caused the mistaken identifications to occur. The observed feature might be common even among cases in which the eyewitness identifications were accurate. Additionally, the frequency of the causal feature in question, such as cross-race eyewitnesses, may fluctuate across the different levels of the criminal justice system. To illustrate, Gross and colleagues (2005) argued that cross-race identifications played a major role in the DNA exoneration cases. This proposition is difficult to evaluate, however, in the absence of knowledge regarding the distribution of cross-race cases across the various levels of the criminal justice system (e.g., arrest, prosecution, convictions levels). Gross and colleagues (2005) found that, in 69 DNA exoneration cases in which Black males had been convicted of raping a stranger, just about 50% involved White victims. They reasoned that the number of White victims among the Black exoneration cases should have instead been on the order of 5–6%, because victim surveys indicate that most perpetrators are White men (90%), that most rapes are committed within race (88%), and that the rate of being a survivor of rape is equal for Black and White women. Thus, since systematic research finds that people are prone to making cross-race identification errors, they concluded that the overrepresentation of Black defendants among the exoneration rape cases suggests that mistaken identifications were caused by the cross-race effect.

One might conclude on the basis of Gross and colleagues' (2005) analysis that the DNA exoneration cases demonstrate that cross-race identifications are more likely to result in eyewitness error. However, there is another alternative explanation for their findings that derives from an analysis of case flow in the criminal justice system. The base rate of interracial rape varies across the different levels of the criminal justice system. The base rate of Black on White victimizations is 27% among stranger cases reported to the police (U.S. Department of Justice, 1992–2004). Gross and colleagues (2005) derived their estimate of interracial rape based on the characteristics of National Crime Victimization Survey respondents who reported having experienced rape, and these respondents may not be representative of the characteristics of the victims/defendants in rape cases reported to the police, or in rape cases that are prosecuted, or in rape cases in which a conviction is obtained. The vast majority of women indicating on victim surveys that they were raped do not report the rape to law enforcement, especially rape perpetrated by acquaintances. Additionally, in stranger rapes, both Black and White victims are more likely to report rape to the police when the assailant is Black. This contention is supported by the fact that although victim surveys indicate that 90% of the assailants are White men, the percentage of Black (35%) and White (37%) men in prison for rape is approximately equal (U.S. Department of Justice, 2005). Still further, even though rape is more likely to occur within race, Black males might be more likely convicted for raping White compared to Black women. Research with mock jurors has found that the probability of a guilty verdict is reduced in cases that involve Black women as complainants (Klein & Creech, 1982). Therefore, the percentage of stranger rape convictions involving Black defendants and White victims most certainly exceeds 27% (i.e., the rate of reporting Black on White stranger rape to the authorities). As a result, when Black men are convicted of raping strangers, a large number of cases will involve White women. Thus, Gross and colleagues' (2005) contention that the disproportionate number of Black on White rape exoneration cases is highly suggestive that cross-race identification errors led to the wrongful convictions can be alternatively explained by differential rape reporting and prosecution rates stemming from the race of the victim and defendant. Indeed, in the random sample of rape cases that were referred by the police for prosecution in San Diego, across rape survivors who were previously unacquainted with the perpetrator, 47% were cross-race.

By the foregoing analysis, we are not arguing that the cross-race effect plays no role in wrongful convictions. Rather, our point is that the expected frequency of the feature in question might not be equal across the different levels of the criminal justice system, due to case selection effects. Therefore, we have to be cautious in drawing conclusions if we find that certain factors are common in exoneration cases. The common factors may not be necessarily causal with regard to mistaken identification.

Conclusion: Moving Forward

In this chapter, we have argued that generalizing from the eyewitness identification literature to specific cases in the legal system by simply matching variables across laboratory and real-world contexts may be invalid. Variables in the laboratory are inextricably tied to the totality of the specific procedures that were used to instantiate the variable. If the procedures that were used to instantiate the variable in the laboratory differ from the operations that give rise to the variable in the context of the legal system, then the nomological network (Cronbach & Meehl, 1955) in the lab and in the real world may very well be different. In other words, if a variable has a causal effect on behavior in the laboratory, a similar-looking construct that presents in a real-world case may not have the same effect on behavior in the real world as it does in the laboratory. We also reasoned in this chapter that the unqualified application of main effects research to a particular case in the legal system may also be invalid. The dimensions on which laboratory and real-world contexts differ is important because of the fact that factors may be present in real-world cases, such as memory strength, that serve to moderate the negative impact of a variable that adversely affects memory in the laboratory. We also argued that courtroom testimony that includes discussion of DNA exoneration cases is invalid because we cannot infer anything whatsoever from DNA exoneration cases alone regarding the factors that cause mistaken identifications.

We believe that the best application of our science to the legal system is field tests that enable us to compare procedures for collecting and preserving eyewitness identification evidence. Our science does not permit us to make predictions regarding whether a given factor has affected a particular eyewitness' testimony. We can, however, determine how a particular procedure, implemented in a particular manner, in a particular context, influences suspect identification rates in the long run. We cannot expect that courtroom testimony in the long run will prevent more errors than not, due to the difficulties inherent in having an expert map laboratory factors onto a given case. (See Dawes, 1994, for a discussion of clinical vs. actuarial prediction.) Still further, as illustrated in this chapter, the incremental validity of expert testimony will vary depending on the base rate of defendant innocence. We run the risk of presenting to factfinders information regarding the factors that negatively impact eyewitnesses in cases in which the defendant is actually guilty. Moreover, by analyzing the natural context in which eyewitnesses render testimony, we can improve the representativeness (see Hammond & Stewart, 2001, for an in-depth treatment of Egon Brunswik's conception of representative design) of our experimental designs and thereby increase their applicability.

The external validity of our research is an important empirical issue, much too important to leave to chance; it is not enough to assume that, after 20 years of conducting research in a particular field, the background conditions will vary widely enough across studies to permit the generality of the findings, or to assume, without empirical evidence from the field, that real-world conditions are more likely to produce inaccurate identifications than laboratory studies (e.g., Loftus, 2003).We hope that the points we have raised in this chapter will invigorate interest in describing the natural context in which eyewitness identifications are carried out and stimulate researchers to empirically delineate the real-world contexts to which a theory applies. Finally, prospective field studies are needed to test within context those procedural recommendations that have been proposed for increasing the reliability of eyewitness testimony.

References

Agresti, A. (2002). *Categorical data analysis*. New York: Wiley.

Ayers, M. S., & Reder, L. M. (1998). A theoretical review of the misinformation effect: Predictions from an activation-based memory model. *Psychonomic Bulletin & Review*, 5(1), 1–21.

Behrman, B. W., & Davey, S. L. (2001). Eyewitness identification in actual criminal cases: An archival analysis. *Law and Human Behavior*, 25(5), 475–491.

Berkowitz, L., & Donnerstein, E. (1982). External validity is more than skin deep: Some answers to criticisms of laboratory experiments. *American Psychologist*, 37(3), 245–257.

Bradfield-Douglass, A. B., & Steblay, N. (2006). Memory distortion in eyewitnesses: A meta-analysis of the post-identification feedback effect. *Applied Cognitive Psychology,20*(7), 859–869.

Brigham, J. C., & Malpass, R. S. (1985). The role of experience and contact in the recognition of faces of own- and other-race persons. *Journal of Social Issues, 41*(3), 139–155.

Busey, T. A., & Loftus, G. R. (2007). Cognitive science and the law. *Trends in Cognitive Sciences, 11*(3), 111–117.

Civilini M. C., & Flowe, H. D. (2008). *An archival analysis of the factors that affect the completeness of eyewitness statements.* Poster presentation at the Western Psychological Association meeting, Irvine, CA.

Clifford, B. R., & Lloyd-Bostock, S. M. A. (1983). Witness evidence: Conclusions and prospect. In S. M. A. Lloyd-Bostock, & B. R. Clifford (Eds.), *Evaluating witness evidence: Recent psychological research and new perspectives.* New York: Wiley.

Cronbach, L. J., & Meehl, P. E. (1955). Construct validity in psychological tests. *Psychological Bulletin, 52*(4), 281–302.

Cutler, B. L., & Penrod, S. D. (1995). *Mistaken identification: The eyewitness, psychology and law.* New York: Cambridge University Press.

Danziger, K., & Dzinas, K. (1997). How psychology got its variables, *Canadian Psychology, 38*, 43–48.

Dawes, R. M. (1994). House of cards: Psychology and psychotherapy built on myth. New York: The Free Press.

Deffenbacher, K. A. (1984). Experimental psychology actually can assist triers of fact. *American Psychologist. 39*(9), 1066–1068.

Deffenbacher, K. A., Bornstein, B. H., Penrod, S. D, & McGorty, E. K. (2004). A meta-analytic review of the effects of high stress on eyewitness memory. *Law and Human Behavior, 28*, 687–706.

Dysart, J. E., Lindsay, R. C. L., Hammond, R., & Dupuis, P. (2001). Mug shot exposure prior to lineup identification: Interference, transference, and commitment effects. *Journal of Applied Psychology, 86*, 1280-1284.

Ebbesen, E. B., & Konečni, V. J. (1997). Eyewitness memory research: Probative v. prejudicial value. *Expert Evidence: The International Digest of Human Behaviour, Science, and the Law, 5*, 2–28.

Ebbesen, E. B., & Rienick, C. B. (1998). Retention interval and eyewitness memory for events and personal identifying attributes. *Journal of Applied Psychology, 83*(5), 745–762.

Elliott, R. (1993). Expert testimony about eyewitness identification: A critique. *Law and Human Behavior, 17*(4), 423–437.

Fahsing, I. A., Ask, K. & Granhag, P. A. (2004). The man behind the mask: Accuracy and predictors of eyewitness offender descriptions. *Journal of Applied Psychology, 89*, 722–729.

Feingold, G. A. (1914). The influence of environment on identification of persons and things. *Journal of Criminal Law & Criminology, 5*, 39–51.

Finklea, K. M., & Ebbesen, E. B. (2007). Eyewitness accuracy in the real world: DNA evidence as "ground truth" for eyewitness accuracy rates. Unpublished manuscript.

Gross, S. R., Jacoby, K., Matheson, D. J., Montgomery, N., & Patel, S. (2005). Exonerations in the United States, 1989–2004. *The Journal of Criminal Law & Criminology, 95*(2), 523–560.

Haber, R. N., & Haber, L. (2000). Experiencing, remembering, and reporting events. *Psychology, Public Policy, and Law, 6*(4), 1057–1097.

Hammond, K. R., & Stewart, T. R. (Eds.). (2001). *The essential Brunswik: Beginnings, explications, applications.* New York: Oxford University Press.

Haw, R. M., Dickinson, J. J., & Meissner, C. A. (2007). The phenomenology of carryover effects between show-up and line-up identification. *Memory, 15*(1), 117–127.

Hope, L., Ost, J., Gabbert, F., Healey, S., & Lenton, F. (2008). "With a little help from my friends . . .": The role of co-witness relationship in susceptibility to misinformation. *Acta Psychologica 127*(2): 476–484.

Hunsley, J., & Meyer, G.J. (2003). The incremental validity of psychological testing and assessment: Conceptual, methodological, and statistical issues. *Psychological Assessment, 15*, 446–455.

Keast, A., Brewer, N., & Wells, G. L. (2007). Children's metacognitive judgments in an eyewitness identification task. *Journal of Experimental Child Psychology, 97*(4), 286–314.

Klein, K., & Creech, B. (1982). Race, rape, and bias: Distortion of prior odds and meaning changes. *Basic and Applied Social Psychology, 3*(1), 21–33.

Konečni, V. J., & Ebbesen, E. B. (1986). Courtroom testimony by psychologists on eyewitness identification issues: Critical notes and reflections. Special Issue: The ethics of expert testimony. *Law and Human Behavior, 10*(1–2), 117–126.

Krug, K. (2007). The relationship between confidence and accuracy: Current thoughts of the literature and a new area of research. *Applied Psychology in Criminal Justice, 3*(1), 7–41.

Lindsay, D. S. (2007). Autobiographical memory, eyewitness reports, and public policy. *Canadian Psychology, 48*(2), 57–66.

Lindsay, R. C. L., Martin, R., & Webber, L. (1994). Default values in eyewitness descriptions: A problem for the match-to-description lineup foil selection strategy. *Law and Human Behavior, 18*, 527–541.

Loftus, E. F. (1983). Silence is not golden. *American Psychologist, 38*, 564–572.

Loftus, E. F. (2003). Make-believe memories. *American Psychologist, 58*(11), 867–873.

Loftus, E. F., Miller, D. G., & Burns, H. J. (1978). Semantic integration of verbal information into a visual memory. *Journal of Experimental Psychology: Human Learning & Memory, 4*(1), 19–31.

MacLin, O. H., & Phelan, C. M. (2007). PC_eyewitness: Evaluating the New Jersey method. *Behavior Research Methods, 39*(2), 242–247.

McCloskey, M., & Egeth, H. E. (1983). Eyewitness identification: What can a psychologist tell a jury? *American Psychologist, 38*(5), 550–563.

McCloskey, M., Egeth, H., & McKenna, J. (1986). The experimental psychologist in court: The ethics of expert testimony. Special Issue: The ethics of expert testimony. *Law and Human Behavior, 10*(1–2), 1–13.

McCloskey, M., & Zaragoza, M. (1985). Misleading postevent information and memory for events: Arguments and evidence against memory impairment hypotheses. *Journal of Experimental Psychology: General, 114*(1), 1–16.

Meehl, P. E. (1989). Law and the fireside inductions (with Postscript): Some reflections of a clinical psychologist. *Behavioral Sciences and the Law, 7*, 521–550.

Meissner, C. A., & Brigham, J. C. (2001). Thirty years of investigating the own-race bias in memory for faces: A meta-analytic review. *Psychology, Public Policy, and Law, 7*(1), 3–35.

Mook, D. G. (1983). In defense of external invalidity. *American Psychologist, 38*(4), 379–387.

Neuschatz, J. S., Lawson, D. S., Fairless, A. H., Powers, R. A., Neuschatz, J. S., & Goodsell, C., *et al.* (2007). The mitigating effects of suspicion on post-identification feedback and on retrospective eyewitness memory. *Law and Human Behavior, 31*(3), 231–247.

People v. Adams, No. A-103, N.J. LEXIS 144 (2008).

People v. Copeland, No. E2002-01123-SC-DDT-DD, Tenn. LEXIS 502 (2007).

People v. Davis, No. D042297, C.A. LEXIS 4369 (2004).

People v. Dubose, No. 2003AP1690-CR, W.I. LEXIS 400 (2005).

People v. Ellison, No. D048918, C.A. LEXIS 1292 (2008).

People v. Garcia, B195201, C.A., LEXIS 6665 (2008).

People v. Herrera, 187 N.J. 493; 902 A.2d 177; N.J. LEXIS 1047 (2006).

People v. Lawrence, SC 17452, Conn., LEXIS 172 (2007).

People v. Lewis, N.Y. Slip Op. 51747U; 20 Misc. 3d 1136A; N.Y. Misc. LEXIS 4873 (2008).

People v. Noriega, B152427; C.A. LEXIS 9087 (2003).

People v. Romero, 191 N.J. 59; 922 A.2d 693; N.J. LEXIS 585 (2007).

People v. Williams, Slip Op. 26469; 14 Misc. 3d 571; 830 N.Y.S.2d 452; N.Y. Misc. LEXIS 3429 (2006).

People v. Woolcock, N.Y. Slip Op. 25045; 7 Misc. 3d 203; 792 N.Y.S.2d 804; N.Y. Misc. LEXIS 157 (2005).

Pickel, K.L. (1998). Unusualness and threat as possible causes of "weapon focus." *Memory, 6*, 277–295.

Remijn, C. A. C., & Crombag, H. F. M. (2007). Heuristics in causal reasoning and their influence on eyewitness testimony. *Psychology, Crime & Law, 13*(2), 201–211.

Shapiro, P. N., & Penrod, S. (1986). Meta-analysis of facial identification studies. *Psychological Bulletin, 100*, 139–156.

Sporer, S. L. (1996). Describing others: Psychological issues. In S. L. Sporer, R. S. Malpass, & G. Koehnken (Eds.), *Psychological issues in eyewitness identification* (pp. 53–86). Hillsdale, NJ: Lawrence Erlbaum.

Sporer, S. L. (2001). Recognizing faces of other ethnic groups: An integration of theories. *Psychology, Public Policy, and Law, 7*(1), 36–97.

Steblay, N. M. (1992). A meta-analytic review of the weapon focus effect. *Law and Human Behavior, 16*(4), 413–424.

Steblay, N., Dysart, J., Fulero, S., & Lindsay, R. C. L. (2001). Eyewitness accuracy rates in sequential and simultaneous lineup presentations: A meta-analytic comparison. *Law and Human Behavior, 25*(5), 459–473.

United States v. Burton, No. 3:97-cr-154, U.S. Dist. LEXIS 18730 (1998).

U. S. Department of Justice (1992–2004). *National crime victimization survey.* Washington, D.C.: U.S. Department of Justice.

U. S. Department of Justice (2005). *Uniform crime reports.* Washington, D.C.: U.S. Department of Justice.

Valentine, T., Pickering, A., & Darling, S. (2003). Characteristics of eyewitness identification that predict the outcome of real lineups. *Applied Cognitive Psychology, 17*(8), 969–993.

Windschitl, P. D. (1996). Memory for faces: Evidence of retrieval-based impairment. *Journal of Experimental Psychology-Learning Memory and Cognition, 22*(5), 1101–1122.

Wells, G. L., & *Primer on eyewitness ID research*. Retrieved April 14, 2008 from http://www.nlada.org/Defender/forensics/for_lib/Index/ Eyewitness%20ID/Eyewitness%20ID%20Defense%20Expert%20Materials/ Prof/%20Gray%20Wells/Index_html#Prof.%20Gray%20Wells.

Wells, G. L., & Hasel, L. E. (2007). Facial composite production by eyewitnesses. *Current Directions in Psychological Science, 16*(1), 6–10.

Wells, G. L., Memon, A., & Penrod, S. D. (2006). Eyewitness evidence: Improving its probative value. *Psychological Science in the Public Interest, 7*(2), 45–75.

Woolnough, P. S., & MacLeod, M. D. (2001). Watching the birdie watching you: Eyewitness memory for actions using CCTV recording of actual crimes. *Applied Cognitive Psychology, 15*(4), 395–411.

Wright, D. B., & McDaid, A. T. (1996). Comparing system and estimator variables using data from real line-ups. *Applied Cognitive Psychology, 10*(1), 75–84.

Wright, D. B., & Stroud, J. N. (1998). Memory quality and misinformation for peripheral and central objects. *Legal and Criminological Psychology, 3*, 273–286.

Yarmey, A. D. (1997). Probative v. prejudicial value of eyewitness memory research. *Expert Evidence, 5*(3), 89–97.

Yarmey, A. D. (2001). Expert testimony: Does eyewitness memory research have probative value for the courts? *Canadian Psychology, 42*(2), 92–100.

Yuille, J. C. (1993). We must study forensic eyewitnesses to know about them. *American Psychologist, 48*(5), 572–573.

Yuille, J. C., & Cutshall, J. L. (1986). A case study of eyewitness memory of a crime. *Journal of Applied Psychology, 71*(2), 291–301.

Notes

1. The values in Figure 9.1 were calculated by assuming a 2×2 contingency table, where a = true positives, b = false positives, c = false negatives, and d = true negatives. The following formulae were used to solve for these values (following Agresti, 2002, and advice obtained in personal communication with James H. Derzon, from The Centers for Public Health Research and Evaluation, Battelle):

$$a = N(p_{r1}p_{c1} + r\sqrt{p_{r1}r_{ci}(1-p_{r1})(1-p_{c1})})$$
$$b = Np_{r1} - a$$
$$c = Np_{c1} - a$$
$$d = N - (a + b + c)$$

where r = the correlation coefficient for a 2×2 contingency table, N = total sample size, pr_1 = the selection rate for the predictor, and pc_1 is the base rate for the outcome.

10

The Prosecutor's Perspective on Eyewitness Experts in the Courtroom

Patricia J. Bailey and Sheri H. Mecklenburg

Has Eyewitness Identification Been Proven Inherently Unreliable?

> The [prosecuting] Attorney is the representative not of an ordinary party to a controversy, but of a sovereignty whose obligation to govern impartially is as compelling as its obligation to govern at all; and whose interest, therefore, in a criminal prosecution is not that it shall win a case, but that justice shall be done. As such, he is in a peculiar and very definite sense the servant of the law, the twofold aim of which is that guilt shall not escape or innocence suffer.
> (*Berger v. United States* (1935)

The advent of DNA marked a milestone in prosecutors' ability to ensure that "justice shall be done." DNA has ensured convictions of the guilty and has set free the innocent, both before and after charging. The effects of DNA, however, have been far wider than the cases in which probative DNA exists: DNA also has called into question the reliability of a host of other evidence, including eyewitness identification.[1] As a result, prosecutors are more and more frequently encountering eyewitness research experts called to testify about the unreliability of eyewitness identification. In light of the duty to

---

The views expressed in the chapter are those of the authors and do not necessarily represent the opinions of their respective Offices.

ensure justice, the prosecutor should bear in mind that the DNA exonerations teach us that experts in the courtroom, including eyewitness experts, must be subject to the rigors of reliability and relevancy required by *Daubert v. Merrill Dow Pharmaceuticals, Inc.* (1993).

In *Daubert*, the Supreme Court ordained the trial judge as the gatekeeper of expert testimony under Federal Rule of Evidence 702; requiring a two-prong analysis when assessing the admissibility of expert opinion: first, whether the expert is offering scientifically reliable and valid opinions; and second, whether such opinions are relevant and will assist the trier of fact in understanding or determining a fact in issue.[2] The Court recognized that this gatekeeping function "on occasion will prevent the jury from learning of authentic insights and innovations . . . [t]hat, nevertheless, is the balance that is struck by the Rules of Evidence, designed not for the exhaustive search for cosmic understanding but for the particularized resolution of legal disputes" (*Daubert v. Merrill Dow*, 1993). Keenly aware that "there are important differences between the quest for truth in the courtroom and the quest for truth in the laboratory," the Court explained:

> Scientific conclusions are subject to perpetual revision. Law, on the other hand, must resolve disputes finally and quickly. The scientific project is advanced by broad and wide-ranging consideration of a multitude of hypotheses, for those that are incorrect will eventually be shown to be so, and that in itself is an advance. Conjectures that are probably wrong are of little use, however, in the project of reaching a quick, final, and binding legal judgment—often of great consequence—about a particular set of events in the past. (*Daubert v. Merrill Dow*, 1993)

When analyzing both the relevance and reliability of eyewitness expert opinions, it is clear that proffered testimony by an eyewitness expert often does not meet the admissibility standards of *Daubert*. In this chapter, we discuss why this type of research to date may not meet the standard of admissibility.

Is the Eyewitness Expert Testimony Scientifically Reliable?

Prosecutors often concede the reliability prong of *Daubert* when challenging the admissibility of an eyewitness memory expert, perhaps because the courts have been more receptive to excluding such testimony based upon the second prong, relevance. Consequently, judicial opinions frequently assume that the proffered testimony is scientifically reliable, typically on the basis that the science is "well-tested" and "accepted in the scientific community" (*United States v. Libby*, 2006; see also Chapter 4 by Epstein, for a historical overview of admissibility of eyewitness memory experts). But replicating studies by conducting methodologically similar experiments, and even publishing the results in the trade journals, does not establish that those experiments constitute a reliably scientific basis for offering opinions on real witnesses in real cases. As the Supreme Court taught us in *General Electric Co. v. Joiner* (1997), an expert's opinion may be excluded from the courtroom even when it is based upon an acceptable or reliable methodology, if the opinion is not rationally supported by the methodology.[3] In other words:

> Nothing in either *Daubert* or the Federal Rules of Evidence requires a district court to admit opinion evidence that is connected to existing data only by the *ipse dixit* of the expert. A court may conclude that there is simply too great an analytical gap between the data and the opinion proffered. (*United States v. Libby*, 2006)

The laboratory methodologies underlying the eyewitness expert opinions and, for a number of factors, the level of dissent in the research community resulting from the use of those methodologies demonstrate that often the proffered expert opinion falls squarely within the *Joiner* definition of unreliable expert testimony.

Has the Eyewitness Expert's Opinion Been Sufficiently Tested and Proven?

Eyewitness experts have based their opinions upon laboratory experiments of staged events seen by research participants, often university students or paid volunteers. These staged events lack important elements that hinder the conclusions experts draw from the research experiments from being reliably applied, or generalized, to the assessment of eyewitness testimony about real crimes.

To begin, the laboratory experiments simply do not approximate either real crimes or real witnesses. For example, research participants usually view a staged event, often on a videotape and, sometimes, in a classroom setting. The participants are neither involved in, nor experience the videotaped event in the way a real victim, or even a bystander, is involved in or experiences a real crime. They are, essentially, watching a 'YouTube' video. The participant rarely, if ever, undergoes the same level of stimulation, arousal, or excitement occasioned by witnessing an actual robbery, assault, or homicide. While watching a video or classroom disruption may, at most, occasion some sense of discomfort, it does not raise emotions such as fear or horror, or result in depression or the loss of sleep, appetite, and sense of security that actual witnesses to real crimes describe on a daily basis.[4]

Also, in the real world, witnesses who are unreliable because they did not see or remember enough, or who had poor viewing conditions or have some bias, are weeded out. This does not occur in the lab, where all participants are included in the recall or recognition phase of the experiment, regardless of whether they paid attention or saw or even remember anything of value. Thus, the lab participants are not representative of the witnesses who testify in court.[5]

In addition, whereas real-world witnesses have the option of making no identification (by saying "I don't see him" or "I don't know"), research participants are often required to make an identification choice. Research participants, of course, realize that there are no consequences to making, or even guessing at, an identification. The research participant, unlike the real witness, knows that the person selected will not be charged with a crime; the participant knows that he will not be subject to a battery of police interviews about either his identification or his factual recall, followed by prosecutor interviews, followed by sworn testimony before a court and jury and sub- jected to cross-examination, with grave consequences attendant to every stage of the proceedings. (In Chapter 9, Flowe and colleagues provide a compre- hensive discussion of how the laboratory experiments fail to approximate the real-world conditions that jurors are tasked with assessing; see also, Mecklenburg, Bailey & Larson [2008]; Ebbesen & Konečni [1997].) Some experts have long recognized the questionable relevance or application of laboratory experiments to certain real-world crimes. As one has noted some time ago:

> Real-world crimes, and their aftermath, of course, create motives (e.g., avoidance, retribution, motivation to get one's attackers "locked-up") and psychological states (e.g., trauma, fear, resent- ment) that cannot be studied experimentally. Not much is known about how such factors influence memory itself, and when one or more of them are dominant witness qualities, the eyewitness experts should probably admit that the research addresses eyewitness memory that is "untainted" by exceptional witness motives or emotions and that caution is warranted regarding generalization to cases in which these qualities are suspected. (Leippe, 1995)

Given the differences in witnessing conditions in the experiments, as well as the lack of consequences to and potential motivations of the research par- ticipant, compared to the circumstances facing a real crime witness, Leippe's point should be well taken. At a minimum, the court should understand that the expert's general opinions about eyewitness reliability or accuracy rates may not apply to the particular case before that court, or for that matter, to any criminal case whose facts are not representative of the methodologies used in the lab. Clear support exists for such caution. For example, in an archival review of actual crimes caught on security cameras in England, which showed that the witnesses performed at "ceiling or near ceiling levels (96% accuracy)," the researchers observed:

> When witnesses are personally involved they are likely to engage in increased monitoring or scanning of the situation in order to understand what is going on and to ensure that the behavioral response selected is most efficient . . . maintaining a state of aware- ness and readiness is likely to be essential from a survival or evolutionary perspective, and better memory for dangerous

situations may be adoptive in the sense that if such events can be clearly remembered, they can be avoided in the future. (Woolnough & MacLeod, 2001)

Yuille and Cutshall (1986) also studied real-world witnesses to a robbery, and they, too, concluded that the difference between the real crime witnesses and the research participants "was the degree to which the witnesses were actively involved in the event . . . significantly higher accuracy rates [for recall] among the five witnesses directly involved in the event suggest that details may be retained more vividly by those who participate in an event."[6]

Aside from the issues associated with the use of some of the experimental methodologies, the laboratory results do not always support some of the specific opinions offered by eyewitness experts. Although these opinions may be presented as if based upon consistent and generally accepted laboratory results, even a brief examination of a few areas in which eyewitness experts frequently proffer opinions illustrates that this is not always the case.

Confidence and Accuracy

Eyewitness experts most often cite the "counterintuitive" relationship between confidence and accuracy (CA) found in the research experiments as the reason why expert opinions are necessary. However, the laboratory experiments do not produce a consistently "counterintuitive" CA relationship; instead, the studies show varying degrees of the correlation, depending upon varying factors including the learning conditions and how the relationship is assessed. For instance, some research has shown that highly confident witnesses are likely to be accurate (Behrman & Davey, 2001; Brewer, Keast, & Rishworth, 2002a, 2002b; Ebbesen, 2000). Research also has shown that as the learning or witnessing conditions surrounding the crime improve, so too does the accuracy and confidence rate, and that the resulting CA correlation is, again, quite substantial.[7] Thus, an opinion that the confidence of a witness does not correlate to, or is a poor predictor of, accuracy may be inapplicable and even misleading in a case in which jurors are assessing the reliability of a highly confident witness or the effects of excellent viewing conditions.

The research literature raises other reliability questions about the CA relationship, beginning with the differences between how the laboratory and the real world measure confidence. For example, the vast majority of laboratory experiments define confidence using numeric scales (Sporer, Penrod, Read, & Cutler, 1995). However, the majority of real-world witnesses are not limited to using numeric scales as the sole expression of their confidence, but rather may express their confidence in a variety of ways that a jury can understand and, thus, assess. Laboratory experiments are unable to capture the range of emotional and verbal responses seen in real-world confidence measures, such as an immediate "That's him!" or "I am absolutely certain that is him!"[8] Also, jurors do not just hear about an identification and a numerical value of confidence; rather, they learn about and use the witness's response at time of the out-of-court identification procedure, the witness's response at the time of any in-court identification, and the witness's testimony about what the witness saw, smelled, felt, heard, and thought, as well as what the conditions were at the time of the incident. As such, the researchers' reliance on numerical scales to accurately assess a witness's confidence fails to reflect the real-world assessments of confidence that jurors hear, see, and utilize to evaluate eyewitness reliability.

Another significant issue raised by the literature is that the CA relationship is calculated in different ways in different experiments, and the strength of the relationship depends upon the method of measurement chosen for an individual experiment. The question, then, is which method most closely matches the issues before the jurors. Laboratory experiments do not typically report the accuracy rate for each level or numerical scale of confidence, but instead report the average, or mean, relationship for the entire group across all levels of confidence, including those who report very low levels of confidence or were even guessing. These results do not reliably address the issue before a jury (Deffenbacher, 1980; Sporer et al., 1995). Jurors are typically tasked with assessing the reliability of highly confident witnesses, not those who say that they guessed or are unsure. Providing juries with an opinion based upon the average CA correlation of all subjects, from the guessers to the absolutely sure, tells the jury little, if anything, about the witness in the courtroom. Recently, experts have begun to question the validity of averaging all confidence levels as the "correlation measure can be severely misleading and may often fail to disclose a forensically useful confidence–accuracy relation . . . [and thus] does not provide the court with the kind of information that is needed. This information is provided by the calibration analysis" (Juslin, Olson, & Winman, 1996). The calibration analysis "suggests that, contrary to the conclusion generally drawn from CA correlation studies, confidence is informative about accuracy" (Brewer & Wells, 2006; Brigham, 1990).

If the CA relation is to have any forensic meaning, we argue that researchers should at least report the accuracy rate separately for each numerical level of confidence given by the participants. Such information, along with a report of the learning conditions of the experiment, may provide more reliable information for a juror. In any event, prosecutors should be requiring that any expert's opinion on the CA relationship necessarily include how that measurement was calculated, so that courts can assess the reliability as well as the relevance of the opinion to the facts of the case.

As prosecutors know, a witness's confidence and accuracy, both at the time of the identification and at trial, can be affected by any number of factors, such as fear, dislike for law enforcement, a code of private retaliation, and bias. These factors simply cannot be captured in the laboratory experiments in any systematic way (*People v. Smith*, 2004).[9] This interaction of factors, coupled with the disparate laboratory methods for calculating the CA relationship and the fact that the size of the relationship changes depending upon the method used, along with the differences in the viewing conditions used in the laboratory, renders it is difficult to understand how an expert opinion about the relationship between confidence and accuracy, based upon these very laboratory experiments, can be considered reliable, let alone applicable to most real-world witnesses.[10]

Unconscious Transference

Either because the testimony was confusing or because experts appear to have different "generally accepted" opinions about the topic, courts have differently understood what the experts mean by *unconscious transference* (UT). For example, one court found that the expert's opinion was that UT broadly refers to the notion that people can "get confused about the context in which they have seen people and misidentify them as coming from the wrong situation or context, *either before, during or after the event*" (*People v. Smith*, emphasis added*)*. Yet another court understood the expert to describe UT as when a witness becomes confused and identifies a person as the perpetrator of a crime simply because he saw the person *at the crime scene* (*United States v. Haynes*, 1999). And yet another understood the expert to opine that UT refers to the notion that "it is easier for a person to remember a face than to remember the circumstances under which the person saw the face" (*McMullen v. Florida*, 1998).

Regardless of the definition of the phenomenon, research studies on UT have provided inconsistent data on the subject. For example, in a 1990 study, researchers attempted but repeatedly failed to produce the UT effect, prompting the authors to opine that "the concept's empirical and theoretical foundation requires considerable additional support before it may be broadly applied to courts of law" (Read, Tollestrup, Hammersley, McFadszen, & Christensen, 1990). Since then, additional research has continued to provide inconsistent data about any unconscious transference effect (Read, 1994; Ross, Ceci, Dunning, & Toglia, 1994; Geiselman, Haghighi, & Stown, 1996; Phillips, McAuliff, Kovera, & Cutler, 1999. Such conflicting results prompted one court, in denying admission of the expert's opinion, to note that the expert, in conceding the "limited external validity" of the research, stated at the admissibility hearing that "the literature provides mixed and somewhat weak support for unconscious transference, and the empirical evidence for the [theory's] existence is rather meager" (*United States v. Langan*, 2001). Again, with such inconsistent data, as well as a lack of clarity as to what exactly the UT phenomenon is, the reliability of any opinion based on the research data must be questioned.

Weapon Focus

Experts are often proffered for the opinion that a witness will focus attention on a weapon used during a crime and, therefore, is less likely to accurately remember the perpetrator (*United States v. Lester*, 2003). Here, again, the research data are not consistent. For instance, in a review of 19 weapon focus studies, 13 studies showed no significant effect for the presence of a weapon (Steblay, 1992).[11]

Studies have shown that a witness's ability to remember the perpetrator does not worsen when the perpetrator "threatens" another individual (Pickel, 1998), or when the witness is "threatened with a painful stimuli" (Maas & Kohnken, 1989).[12] Findings such as these support Steblay's observation that "it may be argued that real-life crime events include so many stimuli that the weapon focus effect becomes irrelevant or insignificant in magnitude" (Steblay, 1992, p. 422). This observation is well placed in light of an archival review of actual witnesses to an armed robbery, which found that those witnesses recalled significantly more details of the perpetrator's description than witnesses to crimes that did not involve a weapon (Tollestrup, Turtle, & Yuille, 1994; see also Kensinger, 2007; Woolnough & MacLeod, 2001).[13] Given the results of these studies and the confounding nature of the real-world crime, it is difficult to render a reliable opinion on how the presence of a weapon alone affects an eyewitness identification or factual recall.

Post-event Information

Experts who opine that the post-event information (PEI) influenced the eyewitness's testimony often rely upon experiments that suggest that witnesses accept inaccurate information after the event, or theoretically the crime, and incorporate that suggested misinformation into their memory. The laboratory results concerning PEI highlight the importance of understanding how interaction between various factors (or stimuli) may affect eyewitness reliability and reveal that a reliable and relevant expert opinion on this subject is limited to few, if any, circumstances. For example, studies show that it is easier to create an erroneous memory for *peripheral* as opposed to central details of an event, and for unfamiliar as opposed to familiar events (Elliot, 1998). Studies also show that the effect of PEI depends upon the credibility or expertise of the source providing the misleading information (Okamoto & Sugahara, 1986; Ceci, Ross, & Toglia, 1987). Thus, it may not be scientifically valid for an expert to opine that PEI from a law enforcement officer or elsewhere influenced the accuracy of an eyewitness who has no trust in or respect for the source of that information. Other factors impacting the effect of PEI are the level of the witness's participation (Rudy & Goodman, 1991), the degree to which the participant is able to discriminate between the source of the original information and the source of misinformation (Lindsey, 2002), and the retention interval (Belli, Windschitl, & McCarthy, 1992). Still other studies show post-event suggestion errors result not from memory distortion, but from guessing on the part of the subject (Highhouse & Bottrill, 1995). Given the various factors that need to be present to achieve an effect from PEI, it is clear that the generalized statement that "eyewitness testimony about an event often reflects not only what they actually saw but information they obtained later on" (Kassin, Tubb, Hosch, & Memon, 2001) would not be reliable unless the expert provided jurors with all the qualifiers discussed earlier, not the least of which is that the PEI must be inaccurate.

Has the Proffered Opinion Gained General Acceptance?

Since the early days of *Frye v. United States* (1923), the standard for general acceptance has caused hesitancy in courts, for fear that science would enter the courtroom via "a popularity contest" (*Daubert v. Merrill Dow*, 1993, p. 587).[14] Still, the *Daubert* Court acknowledged that, "general acceptance of the scientific theory can have a bearing in determining the admissibility of expert testimony," and that a lack of widespread acceptance of a theory may properly weigh against admissibility (*Daubert v. Merrill Dow*, 1993, p. 594).

Even under the more liberal approach advocated by *Daubert,* general acceptance continues to mean more than proponents of testimony counting their own votes in favor of general acceptance. Nevertheless, some experts have developed and participated in surveys designed specifically to document the "general acceptance" necessary for allowing such testimony (Kassin, Ellsworth, & Smith, 1989; Kassin et al., 2001). These surveys do not reflect the opinions of the broader relevant scientific community and, more significantly, reveal dissent over general acceptance even within the limited research community surveyed.[15]

Courts should be skeptical of these seemingly self-serving surveys to establish either the "relevant scientific community" or "general acceptance."[16] Certain aspects about the surveys cast doubt upon whether they objectively establish general acceptance necessary for courtroom testimony. First, the authors of the 2001 (Kassin et al., 2001) survey measured general acceptance by pooling together the respondents who believed that the research "tends to prove," is "generally reliable," and is "very reliable," for specific propositions, such as "very high levels of stress impair the accuracy of eyewitness testimony" (Kassin et al., 2001, Table 3). Certainly, in this post-DNA, *Daubert* world of expert scientific testimony, acceptance of scientific evidence as "reliable," and not, "tends to prove" or "generally reliable," is the standard that applies to scientific evidence in the courtroom.

The 2001 survey by Kassin and his co-authors further claimed that the percentage of experts who responded that they were willing to testify on a particular proposition demonstrates that the proposition is generally accepted for purposes of courtroom admission. However, a critical component of the actual question asked was: *Under the right circumstances* would you be willing to testify (Kassin et al., 2001)? The authors did not define, nor were the respondents given an opportunity to explain, what "right circumstances" had to be present before the respondent would be willing to testify. Such a definition would be crucial to a court's determination of both reliability and relevance, and, indeed, may be relevant to issues of the expert's bias and credibility. Without an understanding of the "right circumstances" for each of the respondents, courts should be hesitant to blindly accept the survey as amounting to general acceptance.

In conclusion, the experts seek to proffer opinions to courts on many different facets of eyewitness memory research, far more than space here permits us to address. Each facet has its own unique set of studies that relate to the reliability of the expert's opinion. It is incumbent upon the prosecutor to carefully examine all studies relevant to the specific opinions proffered in order to develop arguments, where appropriate, regarding the reliability of those opinions.

Is the Eyewitness Expert Testimony Relevant?

The court's inquiry does not end after reliability. Rather, *Daubert* further imposes a duty upon the trial judge to determine, before opening the gate to any expert testimony, whether the testimony will "assist the trier of fact to understand or determine a fact in issue" (*Daubert v. Merrill Dow*, 1993, pp. 579, 592). Likely because prosecutors have often failed to object under the reliability prong, courts excluding eyewitness experts frequently have done so under the relevancy prong, holding that such an expert would not assist the trier of fact. When assessing whether the expert would assist the trier of fact, the court looks to whether the testimony falls within the common knowledge, or "ken" of the jury, and if so, then determining that the testimony would not be necessary to assist the jurors in understanding issues concerning eyewitness reliability. Whether the jury can fairly assess the eyewitness without expert testimony also depends upon whether other means, such as cross-examination, argument, and instructions, are sufficient to alert a jury as to factors which should be considered in assessing the eyewitness testimony at issue (*Daubert v. Merrill Dow*, 1993, pp. 591–592). (Devenport and colleagues, in Chapter 3, discuss the research concerning the traditional safeguards afforded by the judicial system.) Courts also look to whether the testimony fits the facts of the particular case (*Daubert v. Merrill Dow*, 1993, pp. 591–592). Finally, courts must balance the potential helpfulness of the expert testimony against the potential confusion caused by such expert testimony, including whether it usurps the jurors' role of evaluating a witness's credibility.

Beyond the Ken: Are Factors Influencing Eyewitness Testimony Within the Understanding of Ordinary Jurors?

Expert testimony is limited to information that is not within an ordinary juror's knowledge or ken: If an ordinary juror can understand an issue without expert assistance, then the expert testimony is neither necessary nor helpful (*United States v. Libby*, 2006; *United States v. Hudson*, 1989).[17] Courts widely recognize that jurors have an understanding of the factors affecting eyewitness identification, and that they do not need an expert to explain that an eyewitness identification can be unreliable under certain circumstances (*United States v. Carter*, 2005).[18]

Proponents of eyewitness expert testimony argue that jurors do not understand the factors that impact eyewitness testimony.[19] These claims that jurors unquestioningly accept eyewitness identification rely upon outdated information. For instance, advocates of eyewitness experts often cite a well-known 1974 study in which mock jurors placed substantial weight on an eyewitness identification of a robber/murderer, even when told that the eyewitness had poor vision, was not wearing his eyeglasses, and viewed the robber only from a distance (Loftus, 1974). The perception of eyewitness reliability in the popular culture has changed dramatically since DNA, so that studies from even a decade ago hardly reflect the common experience and beliefs of jurors today (Cutler & Penrod, 1995).[20] Every prosecutor knows the "CSI effect" on the expectations of today's jurors. Although Justice Brennan pointed out in 1981 (*Watkins v. Sowders*, 1981) that "there is almost nothing more convincing than a live human being who takes the stand, points a finger at the defendant and says 'that's the one!,'" prosecutors today are faced with jurors who then want to know: "Where is the DNA?"; "Where are the fingerprints?"; "Where are the fancy forensics that we see on television?"

Increasingly today, the perils of eyewitness reliability have been discussed in the popular media. Eyewitness blogs abound, television news shows and fictional dramas regularly feature stories about mistaken eyewitness identification, and, significantly, widespread media coverage often highlights for the public the role of mistaken eyewitness identification in DNA exonerations. The subject of eyewitness reliability, and particularly criticism of eyewitness identification, has permeated our culture, so that, unlike the juror of decades ago, today's average juror has been exposed to and has an understanding of the potential weaknesses of eyewitness reliability.

Ironically, a survey undertaken to pave the way for eyewitness experts in the court has demonstrated that jurors are well aware of the perils of eyewitness identification, perhaps to a greater degree than scientifically justified (Schmechel, O'Toole, Easterly, & Loftus, 2006).[21] Proponents of expert testimony have relied upon the fact that 46% of the survey respondents, potential jurors in the Washington, D.C. area, agreed that "the act of remembering a traumatic event is like a video recording in that one can recall details as if they had been imprinted or burned into one's brain" (*United States v. Libby*, 2006, p. 17). However, a careful reading of the survey results reveals that an overwhelming percentage of the jurors understand, quite well, that any concept of a "videorecording" is subject to substantial editing. For example, 89% of the respondents understood that "an eyewitness who identifies the same culprit in a number of identification procedures can still be mistaken." Nearly 80% of the respondents agreed that even multiple eyewitnesses making the same identification can be wrong. An extraordinarily high percentage of the respondents understood that an eyewitness's confidence can be affected by factors other than accuracy, in that 86% agreed that "before an eyewitness testifies at trial, if they learn that someone else has also identified the defendant as the culprit, that eyewitness is more likely to express greater confidence in their identification when they testify in front of the jury." Only 10% of the respondents disagreed with this proposition. Eighty-five percent of the respondents acknowledged the effect of feedback on an eyewitness's confidence, agreeing that post-event information provided by the police could cause an eyewitness to express a greater level of confidence in their identification than the eyewitness initially expressed. Likewise, 80% of the respondents believed that post-event information could affect an eyewitness's recollection of details of a crime. Fewer than 40% of the respondents believed that confidence of an eyewitness was "an excellent indicator of that eyewitness's reliability." More than 70% of the respondents accepted the proposition of "unconscious transference," that "an eyewitness will sometimes identify a person as the culprit because they have seen that person somewhere before, and the face is familiar, even though the person was not who they actually saw committing the crime." And only 27% of the respondents agreed that witnesses are equally accurate in identifying those of a different race and those of their own race (Schmechel et al 2006).

This survey belies any misconception that the average juror accepts eyewitness identification unconditionally. (See Read and Desmarais, Chapter 6, for an in-depth discussion of the various methods researchers use to assess laypersons' knowledge of eyewitness issues. The results vary by jurisdiction, method of assessment, and date of the research. All of which point to the importance of using voir dire to assess the specific jury that will be examining the particular witnessing issues in any given criminal case.)

Simply because the common juror does not know the psychological terms used by the experts does not mean that he does not understand the concepts. As the court in *United States v. Welch* (2004) observed:

> Although the average person may not know what the term "clothing bias" means, it is common knowledge that one may mistake a person for someone else who is similarly dressed. Moreover, the typical juror would know that two people who are structurally similar are more likely to be confused for each other than are dissimilar individuals. Finally, it does not require an expert witness to point out that memory decreases over time. Where expert testimony "addresses an issue of which the jury is already generally . . . aware," such testimony does not assist the jury.

This survey demonstrates, too, the importance of voir dire in learning what is or is not within the ken of the jury. During voir dire, the trial court and the lawyers need to take the time necessary to ferret out the prospective jurors' perceptions of eyewitness reliability, just as the voir dire is used to explore jurors' perceptions of other issues relevant to the case.

To the extent that voir dire or other aspects of the trial show that the jurors need guidance in assessing eyewitness testimony, courts commonly recognize that issues affecting the reliability of the eyewitness can be addressed through cross-examination of the particular eyewitness, as well as the law enforcement officers, and through argument and jury instructions (*United States v. Rodriguez-Felix*, 2006; *United States v. Langan*, 2001; *United States v. Hall*, 1999; *United States v. Rincon*, 1994), all of which address the specific facts of the case. There is no evidence that jurors, when subjected to such cross-examination, argument, and instructions, in the context of a trial as a whole, do not understand how to assess eyewitness testimony. As the *Libby* court recognized:

> None of the studies provided to the Court shows whether the rigors of the normal trial process provide jurors with the knowledge they need to critically assess the merits of the positions presented to them concerning the accuracy of one's memory, even if it is true that the average juror lacks an understanding of the frailties of memory at the outset of a trial. And, Dr. Loftus testified that she knows of no such studies. These surveys are designed to ask respondents hypothetical questions, presented in multiple choice format over the telephone, to ascertain how the respondents would interpret a particular piece of evidence. These hypothetical situations make no assessment of whether the respondent's answers might change if exposed to, for example, probing voir dire questions, vigorous cross-examination and closing arguments, and instructions that advise the jury of the factors that may impact on the accuracy of memory. Nor do these studies account for the effect of the deliberation process. . . and because these studies examined responses to questions posed in the abstract, and not through the lens of the actual trial process, their usefulness in establishing that jurors need assistance from an expert witness to understand the fallibility of memory is extremely limited, at best. (*United States v. Libby*, 2006, pp. 13–14)

Unlike in a survey, jurors in a trial are presented with an entire context in which to evaluate the eyewitness identification, including the presence or absence of corroborating information (*United States v. Hall*, 1999).[22] Jurors now come to the courtroom with an understanding of the factors that may impact an eyewitness identification, and such an understanding readily can be refined through cross-examination, argument, and instructions.

Does the Expert Testimony "Fit" the Facts of the Particular Case?

In many cases, the proffered testimony is simply a broad, academic exploration of psychological concepts, bearing little relation to the facts of the particular case. Expert testimony should not be admitted simply to inform the jury that eyewitness testimony in general is unreliable, because such a general opinion will not aid the jury in assessing the factual issues in a particular case (*United States v. Brien*, 1995; *United States v. Rincon*, 1994; *United States v. Larkin*, 1992; *United States v. Blade*, 1987; *State v. Coley*, 2000). Experts also should not be permitted to testify where the facts of a case involve variables outside the research experiments, such as where an eyewitness had prior familiarity with the culprit (*United States v. Welch*, 2004),[23] where the defendant was videotaped leaving the scene of the crime (*United States v. Rodriguez-Felix*, 2006),[24] or where there is sufficient corroborative evidence against the defendant (*United States v. Smith*, 1977).[25] Prosecutors also should seek to bar general testimony about "wrongful convictions," a highly prejudicial subject that is no more probative of the specific case at bar than all the convictions that have been corroborated by DNA or other forensics.[26]

Expert Opinions On Eyewitness Reliability May Confuse, Mislead, or Unduly Influence Juries

Eyewitness expert testimony, even when relevant to the facts of case, must be balanced against the costs of confusing or misleading the jury. "Expert evidence can be both powerful and quite misleading because of the difficulty in evaluating it" (*Daubert v. Merrill Dow*, 1993, p. 595).[27] Although it is improper for an expert to comment on whether the actual eyewitness in a specific trial has made an accurate identification (*United States v. Hall*, 1999),[28] the eyewitness expert's opinions often do just that. For instance, expert testimony advising jurors that a witness's confident demeanor does not translate into accuracy constitutes a direct and impermissible invasion of the juror's sole right to assess the credibility of a witness. As one court noted, "to admit such testimony in effect would permit the proponent's witness to comment on the weight and credibility of opponents' witnesses and open a door to a barrage of marginally relevant psychological evidence" (*United States v. Smith*, 1997, pp. 1355, 1357). Likewise, expert testimony on a witness's focus during the crime or level of stress, offered under the weapon focus theory, essentially comments on what the witness observed, which constitutes impermissible comment on the credibility of that witness. It can be confusing for jurors to separate the expert's testimony from their own role as sole evaluators of the witness's credibility, if the purpose of the expert is not, in fact, to comment on the eyewitness's credibility.

Allowing expert testimony that touches on a witness's credibility is particularly troublesome because it can lend an unwarranted appearance of authority on the subject of credibility and, as a result, carries a risk of supplanting the jurors' determination of credibility (*United States v. Lester*, 2003).[29] The risk of a juror being unduly swayed by credibility testimony offered with the imprimatur of scientific expertise is significant, particularly when the more traditional methods of exploring credibility— cross-examination, jury instructions, and closing argument—do not carry that risk and are directly relevant to the actual witness (*United States vs. Smith*, 1997; *United States v. Hicks*, 1996; *Moore v. Tate*, 1989).[30]

Even more significant is that juries may well be confused as to how to apply the eyewitness expert's opinion. For instance, a reported expert opinion that weapon focus effect results in a "10% difference in accuracy" (*United States v. Lester*, 2003) does not tell a jury if that means that the 10% of the witnesses facing a weapon will make an erroneous identification, that the witness's identification will be wrong 10% of the time, or that the witness will recall 10% fewer details when a weapon is present. Likewise, a reported expert opinion that "it's two to three times *as likely* that the identification in the photo montage was made based on seeing the photograph four weeks earlier than it was based on seeing the [perpetrator]" is meaningless to jurors (*United States v. Mathis*, 2001).

Similarly, experts' opinions about cross-race identifications serve to confuse jurors. "Same-race bias" does not necessarily translate into false identifications in cross-race identifications in the real world. In laboratory experiments, where the research participants are required to make a choice, cross-racial identifications result in a higher rate of errors than in same-race identifications. But field data indicates that cross-race crimes have a higher rate of "no identifications," rather than known errors (Report to the Illinois Legislature, 2006; Behrman & Davey, 2001). Archival study found that real witnesses are less likely to make any identification in a cross-race crime. The ability to opt for no identification in the real world may eliminate many of the forced errors in the cross-racial identifications generated by the laboratory experiments. Thus, an opinion based upon errors seen in the laboratory does not shed any light on the accuracy of those real witnesses who are actually able and willing to make an identification across racial lines (*United States v. Lester*, 2003). (Noting the confusing nature of testimony proffered on cross-race identification, the Lester Court stated that "an average juror hearing the testimony likely would not understand the statistical significance and might even conclude that the task of a cross-race identification is hopeless.")

As a cautionary note to prosecutors, the individualized inquiry advocated by the *Daubert* Court may result in cases in which the considerable risks of a particular expert opinion, in terms of reliability, relevancy, and potential confusion, still are outweighed by "exceptional circumstances" (*People v. McDonald*, 1984).[31] These are the cases in which the prosecutor should not rely upon the courts' obligation to undertake an individualized inquiry as to whether expert testimony should be admitted; rather, the special role of the prosecutor to do justice mandates a duty to examine whether certain identification cases, in particular those with conflicting evidence and no corroboration, should be prosecuted at all. The fact that an expert opinion challenging the eyewitness testimony may not meet the rigorous standards for admissibility in the courtroom does not excuse the prosecutor from the duty to undertake a careful and educated analysis of the eyewitness identification at the charging stage, and continuing throughout the proceedings.

Conclusion: What Does This Mean for the Justice System?

The concern over eyewitness reliability generated by the DNA exonerations should not cause courts to eliminate the rigorous examination required by *Daubert* for eyewitness or other expert opinions. Any lowering of standards for admissibility of eyewitness experts undoubtedly can open the courtroom doors to other expert opinions of questionable reliability and relevancy, including those that may contribute to convictions. Members of the justice system must be diligent in applying the legal standards for any expert opinion entering the courtroom, in equal measure, whether it increases or decreases the likelihood of a conviction.

The science of eyewitness reliability continues to develop, with field studies just beginning to be undertaken. As solid and consistent data are collected from real cases, experts may have a truer understanding of the strengths and weaknesses of real-world eyewitness memory to impart to both law enforcement and the justice system. However, based upon the current experimental status of the science, we advocate guarding against lowering the *Daubert* standards by which expert testimony on eyewitness identification, or any science, is admitted into the courtroom.

The Exoneration of Kirk Bloodsworth: An Eyewitness Identification Lesson

The case of Kirk Bloodsworth, exonerated by DNA in 1993, is often cited as a prime example of the inherent fallibility of eyewitness identification: multiple eyewitnesses identified Bloodsworth for the rape and murder of a 9-year-old girl, sending him to death row for a crime that he did not commit. The facts of the case, however, show a very different scenario than seemingly reliable eyewitnesses making an erroneous identification (Junkin, 2004).[32]

In the summer of 1984, two boys observed the victim walking into the woods with the offender, shortly before she was found sexually assaulted and dead. The first, a 10-year-old boy, described a white male; 6'5" tall; slim to medium build; dirty blond, curly hair, with a light brown mustache. Despite the boy's difficulty picking the hair, eyes, and moustache from composite choices, police still produced a sketch with this boy's assistance. The second boy, 7 years old, gave a description that varied from that of the 10-year-old. He was too uncertain to cooperate with a composite, so an officer simply showed him the composite that the 10-year-old had helped create, even though this violated police protocol.

The police distributed the sketch, even though the 10-year-old boy was not satisfied that it accurately depicted the offender. As expected, the sketch generated numerous tips, one leading to the arrest of Kirk Bloodsworth. One tip was about a man, 5'8" with blond curly hair, who was already wanted for child rapes in the area. DNA later proved he had committed the crime for which Bloodsworth was convicted.

Bloodsworth had a thick build and was just under 6' tall, with red hair and mutton chop sideburns, distinctive characteristics not described by any witness. Police also noted that Bloodsworth fit the "psychological profile" of the killer, which boiled down to an offender who was familiar with the area, lived and worked nearby, and had an older or domineering wife. Police discounted the fact that the size of a shoe impression taken from the crime scene did not match Bloodsworth.

The two young boys were shown a photo array containing the photo of Bloodsworth (but not containing a photo of the real offender). Of the six photos, only three had the curly hair and moustache described by the boys—one photo depicted a clean-shaven man, and another photo depicted a man with a full beard. Several of the photos were suspects, so that, essentially, there was more than one "right" answer. Still, the 7-year-old correctly stated that the offender was not in the photo array. The 10-year-old picked Bloodsworth, with the proviso that the offender's hair was not as red.

After a highly suggestive interrogation led to Bloodsworth making statements that were deemed incriminating, the police arrested Bloodsworth on a Friday, and paraded him, shackled, in front of the media. Concerned over the effect the media show might have on the lineups scheduled for the following Monday, police contacted key witnesses and cautioned them not to watch television over the weekend because the offender would be shown on television. Video of the shackled Bloodsworth ran repeatedly on television all that weekend preceding the lineups and, of course, the witnesses watched.

At the live lineups, three witnesses who had seen someone in the area who may or may not have been the offender identified Bloodsworth as the person whom they had seen. Other witnesses who excluded Bloodsworth as the man whom they had seen in the area on the morning the little girl was killed were discounted by police as unreliable. The 7-year-old picked a filler from the lineup, but weeks later, after Bloodsworth had been charged, the child's mother told the police that her son had recognized Bloodsworth as the offender, thus allowing her to receive a share of the reward.

At trial in 1985, one woman who initially reported that the sketch depicted a friend of hers, but then picked Bloodsworth out of the lineup after seeing him on television, testified that she had seen Bloodsworth the morning of the murder. Another woman who was on drugs the

(*Continued*)

morning of the murder and initially reported that she had heard, but had never seen, the offender, now identified Bloodsworth as the offender, claiming that she "got a good look at him." Bloodsworth sought to introduce eyewitness expert testimony, but his request was denied (*Bloodsworth v. State*, 1986). On the basis of the clearly unreliable eyewitness identifications and Bloodsworth's own allegedly incriminating statements, Bloodsworth was convicted. Whether an expert would have changed the outcome in such an emotionally charged case in 1985 is subject to speculation, but the unreliability of the eyewitness identifications certainly would not be beyond the ken of a jury today, nor would it be beyond the ken of a conscientious prosecutor.

References

Behrman, B. W., & Davey, S. L. (2001). Eyewitness identification in actual criminal cases: An archival analysis. *Law and Human Behavior, 25*(5), 475–491.

Behrman, B. W. & Richards, R. E. (2005). Suspect/foil identification in actual crimes and in the laboratory: A reality monitoring analysis. *Law and Human Behavior, 29*, 279–301.

Belli, R. F., Windschitl, P. D., & McCarthy, T. T. (1992). Detecting memory impairment with a modified test procedure: Manipulating retention interval with centrally presented event items. *Journal of Experimental Psychology: Learning, Memory, and Cognition, 18*, 356–367.

Berger v. United States, 295 United States 78 (1935).

Bloodsworth v. State, 512 A.2d 1056 (Md. 1986).

Brewer, N., & Wells, G. L. (2006). The confidence-accuracy relationship in eyewitness identification: Effects of lineup instructions, foil similarity and target-absent base rates. *Journal of Experimental Psychology: Applied, 12*, 11–30.

Brewer, N., Keast, A., & Rishworth, A. (2002a). Improving the confidence-accuracy relation in eyewitness identification: Evidence from correlation and calibration. *Journal of Experimental Psychology: Applied, 8*, 44–56.

Brewer, N., Keast, A., & Rishworth, A. (2002b). The confidence-accuracy relationship in eyewitness identification: The effects of reflection and disconfirmation on correlation and calibration. *Journal of Experimental Psychology: Applied, 8*, 46–58.

Brigham, J. C. (1990). Target person distinctiveness and attractiveness as moderator variables in the confidence-accuracy relationship in facial identification. *Basic and Applied Social Psychology, 11*, 111–112.

Ceci, S. J., Ross, D. F., & Toglia, M. P. (1987). Suggestibility of children's memory: Psycho legal implications. *Journal of Experimental Psychology General, 116*(1) 38–49.

Commonwealth v. Johnson, 420 Mass. 458, 467 (1995).

Cutler, B. L., & Penrod, S. D. (1995). *Mistaken identification: The eyewitness, psychology and law.* pp. 171–209. New York: Cambridge University Press.

Daubert v. *Merrill Dow Pharmaceuticals, Inc.*, 509 United States 579 (1993).

Deffenbacher, K. (1980). Eyewitness accuracy and confidence: Can we infer anything about their relationship? *Law and Human Behavior, 4,* 243–260.

Ebbesen, E. B., & Konečni, V. J. (1997). Eyewitness memory research: Probative v. prejudicial value. Expert Evidence: The International Digest of Human Behaviour, *Science, and the Law, 5,* 2–28.

Ebbesen (2000). *Some Thoughts About Generalizing the Role that Confidence Plays in the Accuracy of Eyewitness Memory.* hhp://www.psy.ucsd.edu/~eeebbesen/ Confidence.htm.

Elliot (1998). Expert testimony about eyewitness identification: A critique. *Law and Human Behavior, 17*(4) 423–437.

Frye v. United States, 293 F. 1013 (D.C. Cir. 1923).

Geiselman, R. E., Haghighi, D., & Stown, R. (1996). Unconscious transference and characteristics of accurate and inaccurate eyewitnesses. *Psychology, Crime, and Law, 2,* 197–209.

General Electric Co. v. *Joiner*, 522 United States 136 (1997).

Highhouse, S., & Bottrill, K. V. (1995). *Organizational behavior and human decision processes.* New York: Elsevier, 220–229.

Illinois v. Tisdel, 316 Ill. App.3d 1143, 1144 (2000).

Junkin, T. (2004). Bloodsworth: The True Story of the First Death Row Inmate Exonerated by DNA. New York: Shannon Ravenel.

Garden v. Delaware, 815 A.2d 327, 338 (Sup. Ct. Del. 2003).

Juslin, P., Olson, N., & Winman, A. (1996). Calibration and diagnosticity of confidence in eyewitness identification: Comments on what can and cannot be inferred from a low confidence-accuracy correlation. *Journal of Experimental Psychology: Learning, Memory, and Cognition, 5,* 1304–1316.

Kassin, S. M., Ellsworth, P. C., & Smith, V. L. (1989). The "general acceptance" of psychological research on eyewitness testimony: A survey of the experts. *American Psychologist, 44,* 1089–1098.

Kassin, S. M., Tubb, V. Z., Hosch, H. M., & Memon, A. (2001). On the "general acceptance" of eyewitness testimony research: A new survey of the experts. *American Psychologist, 56,* 405–416.

Kensinger, E. (2007). Negative emotion enhances memory accuracy. *Current Directions in Psychological Science, 16*(4), 213–218.

Koch, R. (2003) Note, process v. outcome: The proper role of corroborative evidence in due process analysis of eyewitness identification testimony. *Cornell Law Review 88,* 1097.

Klobuchar *et al.* (2006). Improving eyewitness identifications: Hennepin County's Blind Sequential Lineup Project. *Cardozo Public Law, Policy, and Ethics Journal.* April, 381–407.

Kurosawa, K. (1996). System variables in eyewitness identification: control experiments and photospread evaluation. *Japanese Psychological Research, 38*(1), 25–38.

Leippe, M. R. (1995). The case for expert testimony about eyewitness memory. *Psychology, Public Policy, and Law, 1,* 919.

Lenoir v. State, 77 Ark. App. 250 (Ct. App. Div. 4, 2002).

Lindsey, D., Read, J., & Sharma, K. (1998). Accuracy and confidence in person identification: The relationship is strong when witnessing conditions vary widely. *American Psychological Society, 9*(3), 215–218.

Lindsey, D.S., (2002). Misleading suggestion can impair eyewitnesses' ability to remember event details. *Journal of Experimental Psychology: Learning, Memory and Cognition, 16*, 1077–83.

Loftus, E. F. (1974, December). The incredible eyewitness. *Psychology Today, 8*(7), 116–119.

Maas, A., & Kohnken, G. (1989). Eyewitness identification: Simulating the weapon effect. *Law and Human Behavior, 13*(4), 397–408.

MacLin, O., MacLine, K., & Malpass, R. (2001). Race, arousal, attention, exposure and delay: An examination of factors moderating face recognition. *Psychology, Public Policy and Law, 7*(1), 134–152.

McMullen v. Florida, 714 S0.2d 268, 269 (Sup. Ct. Fla. 1998).

Mecklenburg, S. H., Bailey, P. J., & Larson, M. R. (2008). The Illinois Field Study: A significant contribution to understanding real world eyewitness identification issues. *Law & Human Behavior, 32*, 22–27.

Moore v. Tate, 882 F.2d 1107, 1110–11 (6th Cir. 1989).

Okamoto, S., & Sugahara, Y. (1986). Effects of postevent information on eyewitness testimony. *Japanese Psychological Research, 28*, 196-201.

People v. Kelly, 17 Ca1.3d 24, 38 (1976).

People v. McDonald, 37 Ca1.3d 351, 208 Cal. Rptr. 236, 690 P.2d 709 (1984).

People v. Smith, Misc. LEXIS 255 (N.Y. 2004).

People v. Wesley, 83 NY2d 417 (1994).

Phillips, M. R., McAuliff, B. D., Kovera, M. B., & Cutler, B. L. (1999). Double-blind photoarray administration as a safeguard against investigator bias. *Journal of Applied Psychology, 34*, 940–951.

Pickel, K. L. (1998). Unusualness and threat as possible causes of "weapon focus." *Memory, 6*, 277–295.

Read, J. D. (1994). Understanding bystander misidentifications: The role of familiarity and contextual knowledge. In D. F. Ross, J. D. Read, & M. P. Toglia (Eds.), *Adult eyewitness testimony: Current trends and developments* (pp.56–79). New York: Cambridge University Press.

Read, J. D., Tollestrup, P., Hammersley, R. H., McFadzen, V, & Christensen, A. (1990). The unconscious transference effect: Are innocent bystanders ever misidentified? *Applied Cognitive Psychology, 4*, 29.

Read, D. J., Lindsay, S. D., & Nicholls, T. (1997). The relation between confidence and accuracy in eyewitness identification studies: Is the conclusion changing?, In Thompson, Herrman, Read et al. (Eds.), *Eyewitness memory: Theoretical and applied perspectives* (pp. 107–130). New Jersey: Lawrence Earblaum Associates.

Report to the Illinois Legislature (2006); Illinois Pilot Program on Double-Blind Sequential Procedures. (2006). Retrieved March 21, 2006, from http://www.chicagopolice.org/IL%20Pilot%20on%20Eyewitness%20ID.pdf

Riske, M. L., Wallace, B., & Allen, P. A. (2000). Imaging ability and eyewitness accuracy. *Journal of Mental Imagery, 24*,(1), 137–148.

Ross, D. F., Ceci, S. J., Dunning, D., & Toglia, M. P. (1994). Unconscious transference and lineup identification: Toward a memory blending approach. In D. F. Ross, J. D. Read, & M. P. Toglia (Eds.), *Adult eyewitness testimony: Current trends and developments* (pp. 80–100). New York: Cambridge University Press.

Rudy, L., & Goodman, G. S. (1991). Effects of participation on children's reports: implications for children's testimony. *Developmental Psychology, 27*, 527–538.

Schmechel, R. S., O'Toole, T. P., Easterly, C., & Loftus, E. F. (2006). Beyond the ken? Testing jurors' understanding of eyewitness reliability evidence. *Jurimetrics, 46*, 177–214.

Sporer, S. L., Penrod, S., Read, D., & Cutler, B. (1995). Choosing, confidence, and accuracy: A meta-analysis of the confidence-accuracy relation in eyewitness identification status. *Psychological Bulletin, 118*, 315–327.

State v. Coley, 32 S.W.3d 831 (Tenn. 2000).

Steblay, N. M. (1992). A meta-analytic review of the weapon focus effect. *Law and Human Behavior, 16*, 413–424.

Tollestrup, P. A., Turtle, J. W., & Yuille, J. C. (1994). Actual witnesses to robbery and fraud: An archival analysis. In D. F. Ross, J. D. Read, & M. P. Toglia (Eds.), *Adult eyewitness testimony: Current trends and developments* (pp. 144–162). New York: Cambridge University Press.

United States v. Blade, 811 F.2d 461 (8th Cir. 1987).

United States v. Brien, 59 F.3d 274 (1st Cir. 1995).

United States v. Brownlee, 454 F.3d 131, 142 (3rd Cir. 2006).

United States v. Carter, 410 F.3d 942 (7th Cir. 2005).

United States v. Christophe, 833 F.2d 1296, 1299 (9th Cir. 1985).

United States v. Curry, 977 F.2d 1042 (7th Cir. 1992).

United States v. Hall, 165 F.3d 1095, 1107–08 (7th Cir. 1999).

United States v. Haynes, 172 F.3d 54 (7th Cir. 1999).

United States v. Hicks, 103 F.3d 837, 847 (9th Cir. 1996).

United States v. Hudson, 884 F.2d 1016, 1024 (7th Cir. 1989).

United States v. Kime, 99 F.3d at 884 (8th Cir. 1996) cert. denied 519 U.S. 1141 (1997).

United States v. Langan, 263 F.3d 613, 619 (6th Cir. 2001).

United States v. Larkin, 978 F.2d 964 (7th Cir. 1992).

United States v. Lester, 254 F.Supp. 2d 602, 609 (E.D.Va. 2003).

United States v. Libby, 406 F.Supp. 2d 3 13–14 (D.C. Cir. 2006).

United States v. Lockhart, 476 U.S. 162, 170–72 (1986).

United States v. Mathis, 264 F.3d 321, 334 (3rd Cir. 2001).

United States v. McGinnis, 201 Fed. Appx. 246, 248 (5th Cir. 2006).

United States v. Moonda, 2007 WL 1875861 (N.D. Ohio 2007).

United States v. Rincon, 28 F.3d 921, 925–26 (9th Cir. 1994).

United States v. *Rodriguez-Felix*, 450 F.3d 1117 (10th Cir. 2006).

United States v. Smith, 122 F.3d 1355, 1357–59 (11th Cir. 1997).

United States v. Welch, 368 F.3d 970, 974 (7th Cir. 2004).

United States v. Williams, 583 F.2d 1194, 1198 (2d Cir. 1978).

Wagstaff, G. et al. (2003). Can laboratory findings on eyewitness testimony be generalized to the real world? An archival analysis of the influence of violence, weapon presence and age on eyewitness accuracy. *Journal of Psychology, 137*(1), 17–28.

Watkins v. Sowders, 449 United States 341, 352 (1981) (Brennan, J., dissenting).

Woolnough, P. S., & MacLeod, M. D. (2001). Watching the birdie watching you: Eyewitness memory for actions using CCTV recording of actual crimes. *Applied Cognitive Psychology, 15*(4), 395–411.

Yuille, J.C. (1993). We must study forensic eyewitnesses to know about them. *American Psychologist, 48*(3), 572–573.

Yuille, J. C., & Cutshall, J. L. (1986). A case study of eyewitness memory of a crime. *Journal of Applied Psychology, 71*(2), 291–301.

Notes

1. See for example, *United States v. Brownlee,* 454 F.3d 131, 142 (3rd Cir. 2006), and *Commonwealth v. Johnson,* 420 Mass. 458, 467 (1995): "eyewitness testimony is often hopelessly unreliable."

2. Given that the origins of *Daubert* stem from Federal Rule of Evidence 702, state courts are not bound by it; however, most have adopted a similar analysis. Even those states that still follow the pre-*Daubert* approach set forth in *Frye v. United States,* 293 F. 1013 (D.C.D.C. 1923), will find *Frye's* "general acceptance" standard encompassed in *Daubert's* first prong. See *Daubert,* 509 U.S. 593–594 (1993).

3. In *Joiner,* the plaintiff's expert offered testimony about experiments involving baby mice exposed to PCBs, in order to support the claim that the plaintiff's exposure to PCBs caused his cancer. The Supreme Court held that the trial court did not abuse its discretion in keeping out such testimony where there was no basis to extrapolate to the issue before the jury. As discussed herein, the laboratory experiments relied upon by the eyewitness experts lack a sufficient basis to extrapolate onto assessing real eyewitness identifications presented to the jury.

4. Yuille and Cutshall (1986) reported that witnesses most directly involved in an actual robbery, where the perpetrator was shot and killed, all reported sleeping and other emotional difficulties.

5. Kurosawa (1996) found that 33% of the students present for a lecture hall staged event could not recall seeing the staged event, and 40–50% of the students were unable to say what the perpetrator did. Riske, M.L. et al. (2000) found that only 34 of 147 students in a lecture hall during a staged theft had actually observed the incident.

6. Flowe and colleagues (under review) compared 720 closed felony cases from San Diego, California to the conditions manufactured in the laboratory, leading these authors to conclude that many of the laboratory conditions, such as exposure time and filler similarity, do not approximate conditions in real crimes. MacLin and colleagues (2001) reported that "no matter how well executed or elegant our studies are, they will be of questionable relevance at best without a knowledge of the differences between eye witnessing in real situations compared with research situations." See also Behrman, B. & Davey, S. (2001); Tollestrop, P., et al. (1994); and Yuille, J.C. (1993). The limited field data reported also demonstrates a difference between real witnesses and research participants. See Kobuchar et al., 2006; Report to the Illinois Legislature (2006; which provides field data collected in Queens, New York).

7. Read and colleagues (1997) report that "it is clear that the C/A relationship can be very strong . . . and it provides for reliable predictions of accuracy from rated confidence.") See also Lindsay, D., et al., 1998.

8. Behrman and Richards (2005) present a review of 183 real criminal cases involving 461 viewings, which showed that *confidence was the most effective*

discriminator of accuracy, leading the authors to conclude that, "witnesses who display high levels of certainty or witnesses who make their identifications rapidly without eliminative processes are *unlikely* to choose innocent persons from lineups" (p. 297, emphasis added). The authors also list some of the common identification and confidence statements found in real world cases (p. 284, Table 1).

9. As aptly noted by one court, "common sense suggests that a myriad of factors may interact to affect the validity of actual crime scene identification. The [CA] correlation may or may not vary dependent on the age, race, or visual acuity of the observer, the level of stress, the presence of a weapon, the level of cognitive input at the point of observation (e.g., loud noises, strong smells, related distractions such as approaching vehicles, etc.), the historical observation skills and memory of the observer, and the duration of observation. Similar concerns affect confidence malleability, weapon focus, post-event influence on testimony, and even unconscious transference. Yet, eyewitness memory research fails to examine the extent that the relationship of any given variable or hypothesis will be affected by such other variables and their interaction at a given crime scene."

10. Reported expert opinions on this subject also reflect the lack of a consistent opinion on the CA relationship. See for example, *Illinois v. Tisdel,* 316 Ill.App.3d 1143, 1144 (2000), reporting that the expert opined that there is *no* correlation between confidence and accuracy; and *Garden v. Delaware,* 815 A.2d 327, 338 (Sup. Ct. Del. 2003), reporting that the expert opined *both* that there is no correlation and that there is a low correlation. That same expert apparently opined in *United States v. Mathis,* 264 F.3d 321, 334 (3d Cir. 2001) that the correlation was "at best, 25%" and that the witness's confidence in that case would have "essentially zero" correlation to accuracy. Other cases have reported expert opinions claiming a *weak* correlation between confidence and accuracy, *United States v. Hall,* 165 F.3d 1095, 1101 (7th Cir. 1999); and a *reverse correlation* between confidence and accuracy, *Lenoir v. State,* 77 Ark. App. 250 (Ct. App. Div. 4, 2002). In *Lenoir v. State,* it was opined that confidence is not a good predictor of accuracy; in *People v. Lewis* 2002 WL 31656204 (Cal. App. 2nd Dist.) and *People v. Smith,* 2004 N.Y. Misc. LEXIS 255, it was opined that confidence is a moderately good predictor of accuracy under pristine conditions (the transcript is on file with first author).

11. Although this meta-analysis, by pooling results across all studies, arrived at a mean effect of .13 for recognition as a result of weapon presence, not one of the studies actually produced an effect of .13. Moreover, although the effect size is significant, when the majority of tests showed no weapon focus effect, the mean cannot be truly representative of the group of studies included in the meta-analysis, let alone be reliably applied to real-world cases.

12. Wagstaff and colleagues (2003) found no significant effects for the presence of a weapon and age on accuracy and found that the highest levels of violence increased accuracy for description of hair color.

13. In a report to the Illinois Legislature (2006), two experts who separately analyzed field data on the presence of weapons each found, independently, that the identification rates did not differ in the real world between crimes in which a weapon was present and cases in which no weapon was present.

14. In *United States v. Williams,* 583 F.2d 1194, 1198 (2d Cir. 1978), using *Frye's* "general acceptance" rule, the court stated that "whatever the scientific 'voting'

pattern may be, the courts cannot in any event surrender to scientists the responsibility for determining the reliability of that evidence."

15. In the 1989 Kassin survey, only 63 of 119 identified experts responded. The authors of the survey acknowledged that the respondents included both researchers who accepted that the research findings "are reliable enough to present to the court," and researchers from the relevant community who were "equally vehement [and] argue that the research is inconclusive or inapplicable," but curiously characterized the latter as "obstructionists" (p. 1090). In 2001, due to additional research in the eyewitness area, Kassin and colleagues conducted a second survey regarding "general acceptance." Although the targeted population of experts had grown, the survey produced a response rate of only 34.4% of the scientific community as defined by the authors of the survey. This survey was able to eliminate any problem caused by the "obstructionists," as those who had expressed opposition to courtroom testimony in the prior survey, in published works or otherwise, were not included in the 2001 survey. *People v. Smith* and Hosch and colleagues (in Chapter 7 of this volume) provide a discussion of general acceptance.

16. When assessing general acceptance, courts have examined a number of different factors, including the professional and commercial interests of those who developed or support the proffered claim. See *People v. Wesley,* 83 NY2d 417 (1994); *People v. Kelly,* 17 Cal.3d 24, 38 (1976), in which the court questioned if a leading proponent of the technique proffered could "fairly and impartially . . . assess the position of the scientific community."

17. See *United States v. Libby,* 406 F.Supp. 2d 3 (D.C. Cir. 2006); and *United States v. Hudson,* 884 F.2d 1016, 1024 (7th Cir. 1989), in which eyewitness expert opinions were not admitted "because it addresses an issue of which the jury is already generally aware, and it will not contribute to their understanding of the particular dispute". See Chapter 6, by Read and co-workers, for a further discussion of issues concerning the common knowledge of today's jurors.

18. See for example, *United States v. Carter,* 410 F.3d 942 (7th Cir. 2005): "jurors understand that memory can be less than perfect . . . the hazards of eyewitness identification are 'well within the ken of most lay jurors . . ." (citations omitted); *United States v. Brien,* 59 F.3d 274, 276 (1st Cir. 1995): "the expert testimony [on eyewitness] involved a credibility determination within the ken of the ordinary judge and juror—unlike, say, DNA identification"; *United States v. Christophe,* 833 F.2d 1296, 1299 (9th Cir. 1985): "there is virtually no empirical evidence that [jurors] are unaware of the problems with eyewitness testimony."

19. See, for example, the article by Rudolph Koch (2003), taking the position that jurors rarely have the commonsense understanding that eyewitnesses make mistakes.

20. See, generally, Cutler & Penrod, (1995, pp. 171–209) for a discussion of other pre-DNA jury studies often relied upon by experts to support the need for their testimony. The studies consist of surveys in which students respond to short factual scenarios, are asked to predict the outcome of a completed experimental study, or undergo simulated cross-examination; mock jurors then make judgments about the "witness." In other studies, students read a transcript of 800–1500 words and render a verdict, or participants view videotaped simulated trials and then render a verdict by answering questions. See also *United States v. Lockhart,* 476 U.S. 162, 170–72 (1986); in critiquing mock-jury studies, the Court stated,

"we have serious doubts about the value of these studies in predicting the behavior of actual jurors."

21. From Schmechel et al. (2006). Despite the commentary claiming that the study supports the need for eyewitness expert testimony, and the ambiguity of some of the survey questions, the survey results, particularly those reported in response to question 11 (p. 211), show that potential jurors are well aware of the vagaries of eyewitness identification. See also *United States v. Libby,* 406 F.Supp. 2d 3 at fn 9 (D.C. Cir. 2006), for a full critique of both the survey and the Schmechel et al. (2006) commentary: "the authors stretch the results and reach conclusions that are neither supported by the data or even questions asked of prospective jurors."

22. See *United States v. Hall,* 165 F.3d1095, 1107–08 (7th Cir. 1999); "the existence of corroborating evidence undercuts the need, except in the most compelling cases, for expert testimony on eyewitness identifications."

23. See *United States v. Welch,* 368 F.3d 970, 974 (7th Cir. 2004), in which eyewitnesses knew the defendant prior to the crime, and the proposed testimony did not "fit" the facts of the case; and *United States v. McGinnis,* 201 Fed. Appx. 246, 248 (5th Cir. 2006), in which the science did not "fit" the facts of a recognition case. But see *United States v. Moonda,* 2007 WL 1875861(N.D. Ohio 2007), in which the expert testified, without scientific support, that "the same factors apply whether the witness claims that it's somebody they know or someone they didn't know."

24. See *United States v. Rodriguez-Felix,* 450 F.3d 1117 (10th Cir. 2006), in which an undercover officer relayed the defendant's license plate number to other officers, resulting in the videotaped traffic stop of defendant.

25. See *United States v. Smith,* 122 F.3d 1355 (11th Cir. 1977), in which the bank robber used a silver automatic firearm and fled in an orange Mustang, and the defendant had purchased such a firearm and car days prior to the robbery, was identified through the surveillance video by someone who knew him, and had rented

a hotel room in which a co-offender, who had used bait bills from the bank robbery, was located.

26. For instance, the wrongful conviction of Kirk Bloodsworth is often cited as a powerful example of how DNA has demonstrated the unreliability of eyewitness identification; yet, the facts of the case do not show seemingly reliable eyewitness identifications that were inexplicably proven wrong. Instead, the facts show how a disregard for the evidence results in unreliable identifications. The factors that caused the wrongful conviction in the Bloodsworth case should be apparent even to the nonexpert, which is precisely why the case so shocks the conscience of police, prosecutors, and the public alike. *See* Sidebar: *The Exoneration of Kirk Bloodsworth: An Eyewitness Identification Lesson.*

27. See *Daubert,* 509 U.S. at 595 (internal citation omitted). See also *United States v. Rincon,* 28 F.3d 921, 926 (9th Cir. 1994), recognizing "the powerful nature of expert testimony, coupled with its potential to mislead the jury; *United States v. Brien,* 59 F.3d 274, 277 (1st Dist. 1993); and *United States v. Curry,* 977 F.2d 1042 (7th Cir. 1992). See generally Federal Rules of Evidence 403: "although relevant, evidence may be excluded if its probative value is substantially outweighed by the danger of unfair prejudice, confusion of the issues, or misleading the jury . . ."

28. See *United States v. Hall,* 165 F.3d 1095, 1107 (7th Cir. 1999): "the credibility of eyewitness testimony is generally not an appropriate subject matter for expert

testimony because it influences a critical function of the jury—determining the credibility of the witnesses"; and *United States v. Kime,* 99 F.3d at 884 (8th Cir. 1996) *cert. denied* 519 U.S. 1141 (1997), holding that it is the exclusive province of the jury to determine the credibility of a witness, and an expert is not permitted to offer an opinion as to the credibility of a witness. A prosecutor should bring a specific motion in limine to avoid any such testimony.

29. See *United States v. Lester,* 254 F.Supp.2d 602 (E.D.Va. 2003): "the added caution is necessary because expert testimony often carries a certain aura that might lead a jury to attach more significance to the testimony than is reasonably warranted . . . a trial judge, therefore, may exclude reliable scientific evidence if the court concludes that the risk of confusing the jury is too great"). See note 27 above.

30. See, for example, *United States v. Smith,* 122 F.3d 1355, 1358–59 (11th Cir. 1997); *United States v. Hicks,* 103 F.3d 837, 847 (9th Cir. 1996); and *Moore v. Tate,* 882 F.2d 1107, 1110–11 (6th Cir. 1989). The risk is of unduly swaying the jury is particularly dangerous when the eyewitness expert takes on the role of an advocate. See also *United States v. Rincon,* 28 F.3d 921, 923 (9th Cir. 1994): "the proposed expert eyewitness identification testimony is being offered by the defense more in the role of an advocate and not as a scientifically valid opinion."

31. See, for example, *People v. McDonald,* 37 Cal.3d 351, 208 Cal. Rptr. 236, 690 P.2d 709 (1984), in which four of the eyewitnesses had identified the defendant for murder, three eyewitnesses could only say that the defendant resembled the murderer, and one eyewitness excluded the defendant from having committed the crime, there was no corroborating evidence, and the defendant presented six alibi witnesses.

32. These facts are summarized from Junkin, T. (2004).

11

A New Approach to Litigating an Old Problem: Getting the Identification Expert into the Defense Case

Suzanne K. Drouet and Patrick E. Kent

On July 6, 1982, a 47-year-old schoolteacher was raped in her apartment. The police quickly focused on a possible suspect, Bernard Webster. At the time, Mr. Webster was a 20-year-old African-American male who had been arrested previously on a minor theft charge in the same neighborhood.

As a result of the unrelated arrest, Mr. Webster's picture was placed into a photo array, which was presented to two potential witnesses within a week of the rape. The female manager of the victim's apartment complex told police that she had spoken with an African-American male who was hanging around the apartment complex and acting suspiciously shortly before the rape occurred. She identified Mr. Webster as the individual to whom she had spoken. The apartment complex groundskeeper was also shown the array, and he, too, identified Mr. Webster as the individual he had seen on the complex grounds around the time of the rape. These two witnesses subsequently selected Mr. Webster from a five-person lineup. The victim, who had not been shown the photo array, identified Mr. Webster as the rapist at the lineup.

During Mr. Webster's trial, all of the witnesses testified without hesitation as to the accuracy of their identifications. Indeed, the likelihood that the witnesses were mistaken in their identifications was so remote that the prosecutor confidently told the jurors in closing:

> Now, the defense is going to get up here and explain to you, probably
> in very convincing terms, that these identifications are essentially
> ones of mistaken identification, that all three people are mistaken. . . .
> And I submit to you that's an insult to your intelligence . . .

Members of the jury, it's not often that you get a case where you
have three solid identifications like this, and the question here is,
how many do you need? How many people have to come in here
and say this is the man? I submit to you that those identifications,
alone . . . that evidence alone warrants a conviction of this
defendant and shows beyond any question that he's the person who
perpetrated this offense (*State v. Bernard Webster*, 1983).

The jury agreed with the prosecutor's assessment that three mistaken identifications were highly unlikely, and they convicted Mr. Webster of rape and related crimes. He was sentenced to 30 years' incarceration.

Twenty years later, DNA testing on sperm fortuitously preserved by a hospital's pathology staff showed that all three witnesses were indeed mistaken. Mr. Webster was not the man who had broken into the victim's apartment and raped her. He was released from prison on November 7, 2002. Through the DNA profile, another individual was identified as the culprit, and he subsequently pled guilty.

Regrettably, similar stories are all too common. The assurance of prosecutors that identifications by witnesses are inherently reliable, the belief by witnesses that they can make positive identifications, and the faith of jurors that confident witnesses are accurate have combined to create situations in which innocent persons can be convicted without anyone having violated a single rule or code of conduct. In a letter she wrote to Mr. Webster after his release, the victim expressed her deep regret concerning his wrongful incarceration but noted that she had been completely sincere when she identified him in court, as she believed he was the man who attacked her. This is the heart of an old and challenging problem faced by defense counsel—how to handle the honest, but completely mistaken, identification witness.

Although the DNA revolution has crystallized the problem for the general public, the suspicion that eyewitnesses could be mistaken has been around for as long as systems for accusing people of committing crimes have existed, with the belief in the possibility of error varying depending on which side—accuser or accused—one was on. Decades before DNA testing came to fruition, the Supreme Court noted, "the vagaries of eyewitness identification are well-known; the annals of criminal law are rife with instances of mistaken identification . . . The identification of strangers is proverbially untrustworthy" (*United States v. Wade*, 1967).

In the last 20 years, though, scientific research has caught up with the anecdotal evidence: "The research strongly supports the conclusion that eyewitness misidentification is now the single greatest source of wrongful convictions in the United States, and responsible for more wrongful convictions than all other causes combined" (*State v. Dubose*, 2005). And it is this research that, at long last, brings hope for significant changes in the criminal justice system with respect to eyewitness identification, both in the police station and in the courtroom.

With the social science research in hand, defense attorneys must forge a path beyond the traditional methods of litigating identification cases. Cross-examination may be known as the "greatest legal engine ever invented for the discovery of truth," but it cannot always carry the load of showing that a sincere and confident witness is mistaken. Our clients cannot afford the limitations of the status quo.

We do not pretend to have a perfect set of cross-examination questions that will devastate the honest but mistaken eyewitness. The purpose of this chapter is assist defense counsel in using social science research in the litigation of eyewitness identification cases, with a particular focus on the use of experts. Although no single chapter in a book can cover all the issues that present themselves during the litigation of eyewitness identification issues, the goal of this chapter is to outline a general and sophisticated approach to modern eyewitness litigation and to preview areas for which the litigator should be cognizant and prepared.

The decision to conduct an attack on the reliability of eyewitness identifications using scientific research and experts should be made carefully with full knowledge of the difficulties that lie ahead. Properly conducted litigation can be expensive and requires extensive preparation time by the lawyer. The litigation undertaken may represent the first of its kind in any given locale. The lawyer may practice in an area where the last significant milestone was the local court's acceptance of the requirements in *Miranda v. Arizona*. Nonetheless, neither "my judge will never buy this" nor "I won't win" are acceptable excuses for not attempting the litigation, *in an otherwise appropriate case.*

Selecting the Appropriate Case

Determining whether the case at hand is "appropriate" can be a vexing and difficult decision, as bad cases make bad case law. Like George Orwell's farm animals, some cases are "more equal than others" when it comes to deciding whether the use of an identification expert is appropriate. Many cases can be eliminated easily, such as those in which witnesses have made the identification because they know and are familiar with the defendant. The heart of the analysis is to determine what factors are present in the case that lend themselves to expert testimony. No court of which the authors are aware has permitted an expert to testify that the eyewitness is mistaken. One or more factors must be present for which expert testimony will assist the trier of fact. These factors include:

- Cross-race identification
- Presence of a weapon (weapon focus)
- Duration of event
- Confidence–accuracy relationship

- Confidence malleability
- Mugshot transference
- Multiple identification procedures
- Post-event feedback
- Passage of time between the incident and the identification procedure (memory decline)
- Stress

Examination of the published case law shows that the factors most likely to gain court acceptance for the use of the expert include cross-race identifications, confidence–accuracy relationship, weapon focus, and stress.

A working familiarity with identification issues as developed by social science research is important for every defense counsel in much the same way as a working familiarity with the general rules of evidence is important for every litigator. Several good online resources deal with eyewitness identification issues, including EyeID.org and the Web site for the National Association of Criminal Defense Lawyers. Both resources contain useful guides for an attorney making the initial screening decision, as well as conducting the early stages of investigation and litigation.

A second consideration is financial. This is a part of the reality that is modern criminal law practice and to pretend otherwise would simply be ignoring a fact of life for most defense attorneys and their clients. While identification cases involving clients who can afford the expert fees involved may occasionally present themselves, lawyers usually will have to deal with the reality of trying to obtain court financing for the expert. This may add another layer of litigation to an already difficult course. Nonetheless, even if the routine practice in the jurisdiction is to deny requests for defense experts, the attorney must make a record that the denial of funds for an identification expert will preclude the defendant from receiving a fair trial. Too often, attorneys accept the status quo and fail to request expert funds or fail to make a proper record regarding the necessity for the expert.

The quantity and quality of the other evidence in the case are important factors in the analysis. The time and expense of obtaining and working with an expert may not be well-spent if, at the end of the trial, the jury is considering not just the identification witness but also strong, unimpeached scientific evidence. At the same time, the presence of other circumstantial evidence does not necessarily preclude the use of an expert given that the strength of the other evidence may diminish substantially if the jury has doubts about the accuracy of the identification. In other words, no exact tipping point exists. The attorney must carefully analyze all of the evidence to make a sound decision about the use of an expert.

Defense counsel should not necessarily be deterred by the presence of more than one eyewitness. No "magic" number of witnesses guarantees witness accuracy or automatically precludes the use of an identification expert. In a famous Maryland case, five eyewitnesses positively identified Kirk

Bloodsworth as the last man seen with a young girl shortly before her murder. All were mistaken.

Expert Selection

Once the lawyer decides that a case may be an appropriate one for expert testimony, the next step is to select the expert. A search through the relevant case law will identify experts who are presently testifying on behalf of defendants. EyeID maintains a comprehensive list of identification experts. In addition, the psychology departments of local universities may be staffed with professors versed in the eyewitness identification research.

Experts, like defense attorneys, come in varying degrees of proficiency. Counsel should obtain prior transcripts of the potential expert in order to assess his efficacy in the courtroom, as well as to evaluate potential deficiencies. A witness who is well versed in the scholarly literature may not be able to translate this information well to a jury. Finally, like any other litigation endeavor, counsel should consult with attorneys regarding their prior experiences with the potential expert.

The first issue to be addressed is whether the expert's credentials are appropriate to the matter at hand. Does the expert have significant experience with the relevant issue? A general expertise in psychology does not make the individual a worthwhile expert for identification issues. Although attorneys are sometimes reluctant to approach potentially embarrassing topics for fear of harming a developing relationship, difficult questions concerning the expert's credentials need to be asked before the expert has expended substantial time on the case. The last place that a lawyer should be finding out embarrassing facts about his own expert is during that expert's testimony. An Internet search of the expert's name should be completed, but the expert should be asked directly about topics that might be fatal to his credibility. Has the individual ever been rejected as an expert by a court? Has any court ever opined that the expert was not credible? Has he been rejected as a member of an association in any field? Has the expert been convicted of a crime?

Retention as an expert by a law enforcement entity may be helpful to establish that the expert is not simply a defense hack, but this may also raise a potential pitfall. If the expert has testified for the "other side," on what topic did the expert opine and was the opinion inconsistent in any way with the opinion that he is now providing?

The attorney must discover any potential shortcomings in the expert's credentials or history at an early stage, so that a rational decision can be made regarding the expert's use. This is an instance in which ignorance is not bliss but rather will inevitably lead to embarrassment for the lawyer and devastating results for the client.

Initial Consultation

The expert should rely not just on the lawyer's version of the facts but, to the extent they exist, the relevant records. The lawyer must obtain the relevant police reports, scene photographs, transcripts of witness testimony, 911 recordings, hospital records, toxicology records, and any other relevant discovery that relates to the identification, which may include defense investigation. If possible, have an investigator document the scene as close in time to the event as possible. An attorney who has adequately researched the topic himself is in a better position to focus the expert on issues that may not be apparent from the documentary record, such as the race of the defendant and the witnesses.

The first contact with the expert is usually critical to developing a successful relationship. The expert is making an assessment as to whether the relationship will be productive or one destined to harm his reputation by an ill-prepared attorney. Although some lawyers believe that payment is enough to secure any opinion from an expert, credible experts resist attempts to strong-arm them into a favorable opinion regardless of the facts. Like any relationship, it depends on trust between the respective parties. Identification experts are scarce, and establishing a professional relationship that will extend beyond the instant case is usually helpful in the long term.

After the first consultation, the attorney may realize that more items of discovery are needed by the expert or that the case requires more investigation as a result of insights provided by the expert. A follow-up appointment should be set within a reasonable time period, so that both parties remain focused on the salient issues.

The expert must be informed of facts that are inculpatory but relevant to the expert's opinion, even if the "facts" at issue are contested. Some attorneys feel that these bad facts may harm the relationship with the expert or cause him to not want to "help" the defendant. One can assume, however, that the prosecutor will bring these issues out on cross-examination, so the attorney should know at a fairly early stage whether the information, if true, would cause the expert's opinion to change rather than face that revelation when the expert is testifying. For an extended discussion of the typical content of expert testimony and case selection from the expert's perspective, see Chapter 2.

Expert Disclosure

Advising the prosecutor that the defense intends to call an identification expert should occur as soon as practical. Judges are often keen on excluding experts, and lack of timely disclosure provides a simple but efficient mechanism for exclusion. Nonetheless, the disclosure should not occur before the expert has had a full opportunity to review and incorporate all relevant material. The client is not helped when an expert disclosure must be changed or modified because the attorney has not provided all relevant material in a timely manner.

The disclosure should summarize the qualifications of the expert and his conclusions. The exact format of the disclosure is a matter of strategy and jurisdictional practice. A letter may suffice; a report is not required and may not be the most desirable mechanism. Whether to have the expert draft an affidavit is a discretionary call. An affidavit involves additional time and expense and, unless mandated by local rule, is not a necessity. If an affidavit is required, experts usually appreciate attorneys who prepare the affidavit so that the expert can devote his limited resources to other cases and responsibilities.

Never file an expert disclosure without first having the expert review the document to confirm that it is accurate, comprehensive, and consistent with the expert's opinion. No matter how many oral conversations the attorney and expert have had regarding the opinion, viewing the opinion in writing tends to focus the mind. Heeding this simple rule will save both the expert and the attorney from the many future problems that can be caused by a poorly drafted disclosure. Similarly, if the expert drafts an affidavit, the attorney must carefully review it with an eye toward ensuring that any facts or assumptions underlying the opinion are accurate and that the opinions and conclusions are clearly worded.

Opposition and Response

The mere mention of expert testimony about eyewitness memory issues elicits strong reactions from both the judiciary and prosecutors. The defense attorney can expect a vigorous opposition and usually a request that the proposed defense expert be precluded without a hearing.

Often, the State's objection to the admissibility of the proffered testimony arrives on the eve of trial. Consequently, the defense attorney must prepare for trial with the presumption that an admissibility hearing will occur at some point. Otherwise, the attorney risks having to prepare a critical part of the process "on the fly" and at the same time that other parts of the trial are being handled.

In its objection, the prosecution will invariably assert some permutation of the following: the proposed testimony invades the province of the jury; the conclusions are nothing more than common sense; the conclusions lack a sufficient scientific basis; and the testimony risks juror confusion or is more prejudicial than probative.

Defense counsel must be aware, at every stage in the process, that she is making the record for appeal. The odds are great that some or all of the expert's proposed testimony will be excluded by the trial judge. Therefore, the lawyer must plan every pleading, objection, proffer, and argument with an eye toward the appellate record. The lawyer must thoroughly understand the error preservation requirements in her jurisdiction.

The written response to the prosecutor's motion to exclude testimony is the first volley in that battle. The response should, of course, cite the numerous cases in which identification testimony has been allowed. The response should emphasize that analyses of wrongful convictions have demonstrated that eyewitness identification is the leading cause of wrongful convictions. This is an opportunity to fully and carefully educate the judge regarding the exponential increase in empirical research over the last two decades that has resulted in an incontrovertible consensus among the relevant scientific community regarding the factors that lead to mistaken identifications (see Chapter 7). The response should also delineate the specific areas of testimony expected, so that the judge does not reach the erroneous conclusion that the expert will be opining that the witness' identification is mistaken—a sure road to exclusion.

Admissibility Hearing

Admissibility challenges are rare events in both criminal and civil proceedings. This unfamiliarity makes for a potentially treacherous path to navigate. Consequently, there are no shortcuts in preparing for an admissibility hearing. The lawyer is in charge of the litigation and remains so even after the expert is retained. The expert's job is to analyze the facts of the particular case in light of his scientific knowledge and understanding regarding the identification process as it pertains to the instant case; the lawyer's job is to litigate. Too often, lawyers assume that an expert will "know what to do" once on the witness stand and consequently fail to prepare either themselves or the expert adequately. This is a severe disservice to the client and the expert, as well as to all the cases that will suffer in the wake of the bad case law that inevitably develops from cases presenting poor records on appeal.

At issue in the admissibility hearing is whether the expert's conclusions are based on reliable scientific research. To effectively argue the client's position, the litigator must be conversant in: (a) the case law regarding admissibility of expert testimony in general in that jurisdiction; (b) case law concerning the admissibility of eyewitness identification testimony in the relevant jurisdiction and case law in all jurisdictions, including unfavorable precedent that may need to be distinguished; and (c) the relevant scientific literature. The expert can help to identify the critical journal articles and often can supply copies of the research that cannot be easily accessed through the internet. After reading the scientific literature, consultation with the expert will be needed to make sure that the material has been correctly synthesized and understood. After an initial steep learning curve, most litigators quickly become acquainted with the relevant concepts and terminology.

The judge may be unfamiliar with how to oversee an admissibility challenge and may preclude the expert without any additional information beyond what was submitted with the already filed pleadings. In this instance, the attorney must insist on providing a detailed proffer of the proposed expert's intended testimony at the hearing and trial. The litigator should have a written proffer approved in advance by the proposed expert as to substance to read into the record. Because the proffer is likely to be complex, covering many distinct factors, this step should not be relegated to "winging it" at the hearing. The proffer should clearly articulate all identification issues present in the case and the research basis supporting admission, along with submission of all relevant journal articles. The written proffer should be marked as an exhibit and entered into evidence.

If an admissibility hearing is granted, the attorney must work closely with the expert to ensure that the appropriate areas needed for the admissibility challenge are covered. Preparation and organization are critical parts of a successful admissibility hearing. The litigator must be cognizant of the legal standards for admissibility of expert testimony in his jurisdiction; that is, whether it is a *Daubert* or *Frye* state. The factors emphasized by the appellate courts differ from jurisdiction to jurisdiction, and the expert should know where the focus will be placed. Understanding the case law is key to preparing the direct examination of the expert.

The witness stand is not the appropriate place for the expert to learn how the attorney plans to proceed with the direct examination. Prehearing preparation involves educating the expert regarding the topics to be presented, the order in which they will be approached, and the documents about which the expert will be queried. Prehearing preparation also involves careful organization of exhibits, which may be extensive due to the focus on research.

The essential goal of the hearing is to establish that the field of eyewitness identification is accepted within the relevant scientific community. The attorney cannot place the burden of reading and understanding the scientific literature exclusively on the shoulders of the expert. If the prosecutor mischaracterizes the findings of the research, the attorney will be unable to conduct an effective redirect unless he, too, is well versed in the literature.

Generally, with respect to the actual testimony, the first and easiest step is establishing that the expert, by virtue of knowledge, training, and experience, is an expert in the field of eyewitness identification. The starting point for the more substantive testimony can be a general introduction to the principle that erroneous identifications exist, that honest witnesses can nonetheless be inaccurate, and that mistaken identifications are the chief reason for wrongful convictions. The litigator should not assume that the court has necessarily been following the extent of the DNA exonerations that have occurred in the past decade or the reasons for them.

In the next phase of the admissibility hearing, the attorney will demonstrate the existence of a consensus among eyewitness identification researchers as to what factors impact the accuracy of eyewitness identifications.

Because the proponent of the evidence bears the burden of proof with respect to its reliability, the primary emphasis of the direct questioning will be to elicit the scientific underpinnings of the expert's conclusions. The last 20 years have seen a dramatic burst of activity in research in areas related to identification. Hundreds of published peer-reviewed journal articles predicated on the scientific model of experimental research have been written regarding the systemic issues known to impact the accuracy of an identification. The testimony, however, is not a general discussion about the various problems with identifications. The litigator must know which areas are at issue, the research related to that issue, and how that research meets the *Frye* or *Daubert* standards. While some areas are universally applicable—such as the memory process—most factors are case specific. The attorney and the expert waste time and lose credibility if the expert testifies about problems in cross-race identifications when the defendant and the witnesses are of the same race.

The governmental response is usually a mix of criticisms that the research does not meet *Frye/Daubert* standards and is not a proper subject for expert testimony because the findings are nothing more than "commonsense" principles known to the jurors. With respect to the first criticism, the defense attorney can expect two areas of attack in particular: (a) the research does not accurately reflect the "real world" because "real" witnesses act differently than "laboratory witnesses"; and (b) the existence of opposing views proves that no consensus exists in the relevant scientific community. Responses to all of these attacks and criticisms can be developed, but the attorney must give thought to the answers and prepare the expert to meet the anticipated challenges.

The two general categories of research that have been conducted are: (1) experimental; that is, simulations of crimes by persons working with the researchers or by having subjects view a tape of a simulated offense, and (2) archival; that is, analyses of the accuracy of identifications made by actual witnesses reporting actual crimes. The overwhelming amount of research that has been conducted has been peer-reviewed experimental research in which the researchers know who committed the "offense," so that the researcher knows to an absolute certainty whether the "witness" identified the correct suspect. As a result, prosecutors repeatedly assert that the entire field of study is irrelevant because the research does not concern identifications made by actual eyewitnesses following actual crimes. Ethical considerations, of course, prevent researchers from staging actual crimes in order to test the reliability of eyewitnesses. Nonetheless, the scientific community overwhelmingly endorses experimental research as it provides control of the salient variables in order to systematically study the factors that impact eyewitness identification.

If properly prepared, the expert should be able to explain to the court the scientific basis that permits researchers to conclude that experimental research is representative of actual identifications. A comparison of archival and experimental research demonstrates concordance as to foil selection rates, in that foils are selected in both types of research approximately one-third of the time. In other words, both "laboratory witnesses" and "real witnesses" pick the wrong person at about the same rates. (Valentine, Pickering, & Darling, 2003).

The similarity of foil selection rates in experimental and archival research is one argument countering the claim that victims of crime exercise more care and caution than do subjects in an experimental research project.

The existence of opposing views in the expert community is often cited as evidence that (a) the conclusions claimed by the defense expert are invalid, and (b) there is no "consensus" among experts regarding the proper interpretation of the research. Opponents to the admission of expert testimony point to conflicting conclusions within the hundreds of studies that have been performed to date. Science is built on conflicting opinions that ultimately coalesce into a consensus. The legal question has never been whether unanimity exists, but whether consensus has been achieved within the relevant scientific community. Furthermore, two well-designed and comprehensive studies show that scientific consensus does indeed exist (Kassin, Ellsworth, & Smith, 1989; Kassin, Tubb, Hosch, & Memon, 2001). For more discussion of the status of consensus, see Chapters 7 and 10.

Although judges often preclude expert testimony due to a perception that the research to be discussed is little more than "common knowledge," the evidence actually shows that jurors are not universally familiar with any of the common principles established by identification research. A survey of potential jurors found, for example, that significant percentages believed that remembering a traumatic event was "like a videorecording" and that cross-race identifications were as reliable as same-race identifications. (Schmechel, O'Toole, Easterly, & Loftus, 2006). The research on lay knowledge of eyewitness factors is reviewed more comprehensively by Read and Desmarais (Chapter 6). The expert should be able to provide research to counter the claim that the expert's testimony is nothing more than common sense. For more discussion of the admissibility of expert testimony, see Chapters 4 (by Epstein), 5 (by Groscup and Fulero), and 10 (by Bailey and Mecklenburg).

Trial Presentation

The transition from pretrial admissibility hearing to trial can be difficult, because the objectives are different. In the admissibility hearing, the major priorities are to educate the judge and to make a record in case of an adverse ruling. Admissibility hearings are long and protracted affairs, and as the proponent, defense counsel must create a voluminous record. In contrast, for the trial, counsel must simplify and reduce the subject matter, so that jurors clearly understand the concepts presented.

The cross-examination of the prosecution witnesses should be tailored to those issues that the expert is expected to address. With respect to many of the relevant issues, the witness may be quite willing to provide helpful details even though completely unwilling to concede that he could be in any way mistaken. For example, witnesses are likely to acknowledge that the incident was frightening and traumatic, a beneficial concession if the expert will be discussing the effects of stress on identification accuracy. If memory decline is relevant, the attorney must ensure that the exact dates on which witnesses were presented with photo arrays or lineups are presented in testimony.

Even though the litigator may be fortunate enough to be presenting expert testimony at trial, some portion of the proffered testimony may have been excluded. Again, the litigator must preserve the record for appeal, which, in most jurisdictions, requires an objection to the exclusion of the requested testimony when the expert is presented as a trial witness. One cannot emphasize enough the need to preserve objections. Many excellent appellate issues have fallen by the wayside because of a failure to preserve the issue.

The attorney will need to critically review the planned direct examination after the admissibility hearing, as specific topics may have been deemed inadmissible and the expert may be precluded from discussing one or more substantive topics. Various topics may overlap, so that retooling the direct is often not as easy as simply deleting sections. Not surprisingly, the judge, prosecutor, and defense attorney often will have divergent views as to the contours of the exclusion. Therefore, the litigator should anticipate objections and be prepared to forge ahead with an alternative direct should the objections be sustained.

Litigators must avoid the common trap of failing to make the material accessible to the most important entity—the jury. Eyewitness testimony is similar to any other complex evidence tendered at trial. Defense counsel is asking a jury, the members of which may have very disparate educational levels, to understand a whole new language and subject matter in a very short time frame. The litigator must work with the expert to ensure that the entire panel can understand all the relevant technical terms and complex concepts.

A mock direct and cross-examination with colleagues or friends who have had no prior contact with the subject matter is a helpful tool. This simple process often falls by the wayside during the inevitable pretrial preparation crush, but it should not be readily abandoned. If the litigator fails to simplify the material so that the jury can readily understand it, the result will be a large expenditure of energy with little accomplished.

Instructions

The art of formulating jury instructions has fallen into disuse as attorneys more and more rely exclusively on pattern instructions. This can be a mistake with respect to many areas of the case but particularly with respect to identification issues. Defense counsel should use instructions to (a) enhance the expert's testimony, if an expert was permitted; (b) present identification issues if an expert was not permitted or not requested; and (c) prevent concepts that are not supported by scientific research from reaching the jury.

Although judges often are skeptical of proposed instructions that have not been sanctioned by a court, many jurisdictions have case law supporting a defense request for instructions pertaining to specific issues. The Court in State *v.* Long (1986), for example, succinctly articulated why comprehensive jury instructions must be tendered upon request:

> We are convinced that, at a minimum, additional judicial guidance to the jury in evaluating such testimony is warranted. We therefore today abandon our discretionary approach to cautionary jury instructions and direct that in cases tried from this date forward, trial courts shall give such an instruction whenever eyewitness identification is a central issue in a case and such an instruction is requested by the defense. Given the great weight jurors are likely to give eyewitness testimony, and the deep and generally unperceived flaws in it, to convict a defendant on such evidence without advising the jury of the factors that should be considered in evaluating it could well deny the defendant due process of law under article I, section 7 of the Utah Constitution.

The Court's holding in *Long* resulted in the adoption of Utah Model Jury Instruction CR404, which states:

> An important question in this case is the identification of the defendant as the person who committed the crime. The prosecution has the burden of proving beyond a reasonable doubt that the crime was committed AND that the defendant was the person who committed the crime. If you are not convinced beyond a reasonable doubt that the defendant is the person who committed the crime, you must find the defendant not guilty.
>
> The testimony you have heard concerning identification represents the witness's expression of (his) (her) belief or impression. You don't have to believe that the identification witness was lying or not sincere to find the defendant not guilty. It is enough that you conclude that the witness was mistaken in (his) (her) belief or impression.
>
> Many factors affect the accuracy of identification. In considering whether the prosecution has proven beyond a reasonable doubt that the defendant is the person who committed the crime, you should consider the following:
>
> (1) Did the witness have an adequate opportunity to observe the person who committed the crime? In answering this question, you should consider:
>   (a) the length of time the witness observed that person;
>   (b) the distance between the witness and that person;
>   (c) the extent to which that person's features were visible and undisguised;
>   (d) the lighting conditions at the time of observation;

(e) whether there were any distractions occurring during the observation;

(f) any other circumstance that affected the witness's opportunity to observe the person committing the crime.

(2) Did the witness have the capacity to observe the person committing the crime? In answering this question, you should consider whether the capacity of the witness was impaired by:

(a) stress or fright at the time of observation;

(b) personal motivations, biases or prejudices;

(c) uncorrected visual defects;

(d) fatigue or injury;

(e) drugs or alcohol.

[You should also consider whether the witness is of a different race than the person identified. Identification by a person of a different race may be less reliable than identification by a person of the same race.]

(3) Even if the witness had adequate opportunity and capacity to observe the person who committed the crime, the witness may not have focused on that person unless the witness was aware that a crime was being committed. In that instance, you should consider whether the witness was sufficiently attentive to that person at the time the crime occurred. In answering this question you should consider whether the witness knew that a crime was taking place during the time (he) (she) observed the person's actions.

(4) Was the witness's identification of the defendant completely the product of the witness's own memory? In answering this question, you should consider:

(a) the length of time that passed between the witness's original observation and the time the witness identified the defendant;

(b) the witness's mental capacity and state of mind at the time of the identification;

(c) the exposure of the witness to opinions, to photographs, or to any other information or influence that may have affected the independence of the identification of the defendant by the witness;

(d) any instances when the witness either identified or failed to identify the defendant;

(e) any instances when the witness gave a description of the person that was either consistent or inconsistent with the defendant's appearance;

(f) the circumstances under which the defendant was presented to the witness for identification.

[You may take into account that an identification made by picking the defendant from a group of similar individuals is generally more reliable than an identification made from the defendant being presented alone to the witness.]

[You may also take into account that identifications made from seeing the person are generally more reliable than identifications made from a photograph.]

[A witness's level of confidence in (his) (her) identification of the perpetrator is one of many factors that you may consider in evaluating whether the witness correctly identified the perpetrator. However, a witness who is confident that (he) (she) correctly identified the perpetrator may be mistaken.]

Again, I emphasize that it is the prosecution's burden to prove beyond a reasonable doubt that the defendant is the person who committed the crime.

Although the Utah instruction is not perfect, it provides a foundation from which a case-specific instruction can be drafted. The website EyeID has a comprehensive collection of jury instructions that can be utilized in conjunction with the Utah instruction. Even limited research will turn up cases with supporting language useful for drafting an instruction substantially more favorable than the typical pattern-identification instruction.[1]

Finally, if any requested identification testimony has been precluded on the basis of common sense or general jury knowledge, the attorney should request that the judge incorporate this "fact" into an instruction. Memory decline is an example. Judges typically conclude that the rapid decline in memory is a matter of common knowledge and not a proper subject for expert testimony. If the court has made such a finding, the attorney should request that the instruction state that the jury shall consider the time between the offense and the actual identification as a factor affecting the reliability of the identification.

Even if all else has failed, defense counsel may still be able to prevent concepts based on faulty or inaccurate science from reaching the jury through the guise of jury instructions. In many jurisdictions, a standard eyewitness jury instruction is given that often includes numerous factors for the jury to consider in evaluating the eyewitness' testimony. One common factor that frequently appears in these lists is witness "confidence." Social science research has established that the relation between witness confidence and accuracy is not necessarily strong, but rather complex and dependent on other factors. In some circumstances, no relation may exist between confidence and accuracy. Therefore, including "confidence" in a list of factors to be considered by the jury is as reasonable as telling the jurors to consider the witness' eye color. The attorney must ensure that jury instructions comport with scientific research and should request the striking of any reference that witness confidence can be considered as a factor indicating reliability.[2]

Closing Argument

Closing argument is not the time to either relax or lose focus. Defense counsel must be particularly alert to prosecutorial comments relating to identification issues that are not based in evidence, not based in science, and could have been rebutted if expert testimony had been permitted. For example, a common but erroneous statement is that memory improves when a witness has experienced trauma because the witness is focusing more intently. The following prosecutorial comment, made in the *Webster* case, is typical:

> Your senses become very keen, and your visual perception becomes
> keen, and they photograph, literally, the individual . . . the more
> traumatic, the more reliable, the more clear the memory becomes . . .
> It's amazing what the mind can do under stress, and one of the
> things that it can do is record the impression, the face is etched into
> the mind like it's in stone forever. That is why [the witness']
> identification is extremely reliable and there was no question in her
> mind when she got up on this witness stand that this was the man.

Prosecutors often claim that memory is like a videorecording that can simply be played back at will. The attorney should object to all such statements and clearly note that counsel's proposed expert would have rebutted such comments.

In many ways, Utah Model Jury Instruction CR404 provides a checklist for the issues to be argued in the defense closing. The concept that must be conveyed to the jury is that the witness, who often is a sympathetic victim, may be completely honest but nonetheless mistaken in his identification. The attorney's job is to integrate the litany of eyewitness identification issues present in the case, so that the jury is not deciding whether the witness is lying or worthy of sympathy but whether the witness could have made an accurate identification under the conditions present at the time of the offense. Even if an expert was not permitted, counsel should be alert during trial for court rulings (the "common knowledge" findings) or even witness testimony that creates opportunities for the defense attorney to present identification research principles during closing argument.[3]

Conclusion

Lawyers must change with the times if they are to effectively serve the interests of their clients. Although attorneys have long known that even a witness who assuredly states that he is "100 percent confident" in his identification can be 100 percent wrong, they had little to work with other than the tool of cross-examination, a tool that too often proved futile when used against an honest but mistaken witness. The advances in social science research, combined with the DNA testing exonerations, provide opportunities to educate courts and juries about the fallacies of eyewitness identification. But the education will not happen unless attorneys initiate the litigation that will bring this research into the courtroom.

References

Daubert v. Merrell Dow Pharmaceuticals, Inc., 509 U.S. 579 (1993).

Frye v. United States, 293 F. 1013 (D.C. Cir. 1923).

Kassin, S. M., Ellsworth, P. C., & Smith, V. L. (1989). The "general acceptance" of psychological research on eyewitness testimony: A survey of experts. *American Psychologist, 44*, 1089–1098

Kassin, S. M., Tubb, V. A., Hosch, H. M., & Memon, A. (2001). On the "general acceptance" of eyewitness testimony research: A new survey of the experts. *American Psychologist, 56*, 405–416.

Schmechel, R. S., O'Toole, T. P., Easterly, C., & Loftus, E. F. (2006). Beyond the Ken: Testing juror's understanding of eyewitness reliability evidence. *Jurimetrics Journal, 46*, 177–214.

State v. Dubose, 699 N.W.2d 582, 592 (Wis. 2005).

State v. Long, 721 P.2d 483, 495 (Utah 1986).

State v. Bernard Webster, Circuit Court for Baltimore County, 82 CR 2847, March 11, 1983.

Steele, L. (2004). Trying identification cases: An outline for raising eyewitness id issues. *Champion Magazine* . Retrieved February 4, 2009 from: http://www.nacdl.org/public.nsf/0/9973f3ec244ba99685256f6a00558f39?opendocument.

United States v. Wade, 388 U.S. 218, 228 (1967).

Valentine, T., Pickering, A., & Darling, S. (2003). Characteristics of eyewitness identification that predict the outcome of real lineups. *Applied Cognitive Psychology, 17*, 969–983.

Notes

1. See *United States v. Burrous*, 934 F.Supp. 525 (E.D.N.Y. 1996), on incorporating principles based on scientific research into instruction.

2. See *Brodes v. State*, 614 S.E.2d 766, 769 (Ga. 2005).

3. See *Smith v. State*, 880 A.2d 288 (Md. 2005), in which defense counsel should have been permitted to argue problems with cross-race identifications given witness testimony.

Afterword

Brian L. Cutler, Editor

The aim of this volume is to provide a thorough update and expansion of the topics addressed in the 1986 special issue of *Law and Human Behavior*. Toward this end, the contributors to this volume reviewed basics of eyewitness science; the effectiveness of alternative safeguards against wrongful conviction; the content, form, and ethics of expert testimony; trial and appeal court decisions concerning its admissibility; the research on expert consensus; lay knowledge of eyewitness matters and the effects of expert testimony; and the research on whether the methods of eyewitness research generalize to actual cases. Teams of attorneys reviewed issues associated with expert testimony from the prosecution and defense perspectives.

When the 1986 special issue of *Law and Human Behavior* was published, the body of research on eyewitness identification was at a nascent stage. The research base has grown dramatically, as illustrated by the chapters in these volumes. The chapters provide the most thorough reviews to date, identifying research conclusions that are well-accepted, others for which the verdict is still out, and gaps in the literature that would benefit from further investigation. In this afterward, I organize a few thoughts by actor rather than topic, focusing on the question: What are the implications of this research for eyewitness researchers, expert witnesses, and lawyers and judges whose work includes cases involving eyewitness identification?

Eyewitness Researchers

Some of the chapters provide research directions on issues such as lay knowledge (Read & Desmarais; Chapter 6), consensus (Hosch, Jolly, Schmersal, & Smith; Chapter 7), and the effects of expert testimony (Leippe & Eisenstadt; Chapter 8). This volume was not intended as a review of the eyewitness research per se, and researchers cannot expect to find guidance regarding critical gaps in the literature concerning specific eyewitness factors and their interactions. Nevertheless, at least one important concern came to light. Several of the chapters address the issue of external validity of eyewitness research, asking the question of whether the eyewitness research base generalizes to actual crimes. Serious challenges are raised, for example, by Bailey and Mecklenburg (Chapter 10) and by Flowe, Finklea, and Ebbesen (Chapter 9). A call is made for more field research to test whether laboratory research generalizes to actual crimes. Indeed, the call for field validation is becoming a common refrain in published research on eyewitness identification. Although it would be ideal if we could examine the effects of factors such as weapon focus, extreme stress by the witness, sequential presentation, double-blind lineups, and filler selection methods in actual cases, it is unlikely to happen. Research on actual crimes can have serious methodological limitations, including lack of control of extraneous variables, inability to randomly assign cases, and uncertainty over the accuracy of identification decisions. These limitations are evident in the few field studies that have been published. They are not very informative with respect to determining whether an eyewitness factor has a causal influence on identification accuracy. This does not mean, however, that we should simply assume external validity and otherwise ignore the matter. We need to find other ways to test the external validity of our research and to increase the likelihood of generalization. The chapters here provide some clues. Bailey and Mecklenburg (Chapter 10) and Flowe and colleagues (Chapter 9) remind us, for example, that theory has an important role in generalization, and that we can do a better job of ensuring that the conditions that we investigate in the lab resemble conditions that occur in actual crimes. Bailey and Mecklenburg remind us that until we address the issue of external validity more fully, the appropriateness of expert testimony will remain in question.

Eyewitness Experts

Scholars who serve as expert witnesses or are considering such service will find a wealth of guidance in these pages. Attorneys are typically well-versed in the case law and rules for admissibility, but the expert bears responsibility for educating the attorney about eyewitness research and the research on admissibility factors such as lay knowledge, consensus, and the effects of expert testimony. In this respect, the chapters by Read and Desmarais (Chapter 6),

Hosch and colleagues (Chapter 7), and Leippe and Eisenstadt (Chapter 8) provide the relevant research summaries and details. The expert will benefit from understanding the admissibility challenges facing attorneys, as reviewed by Epstein (Chpater 4) and Groscup and Penrod (Chapter 5). Expert witnesses interested in improving their skills and prospective experts wishing to acquire the relevant skills will benefit from the experience and perspective of another highly experienced expert (Pezdek; Chapter 2). The Leippe and Eisenstadt chapter should cause experts to reflect upon the impact of their testimony. This chapter provides new perspectives on how to conceptualize and perhaps improve the impact of expert testimony. Experts will benefit from learning the approaches to and challenges faced by defense attorneys in their routine work with experts, as explained by Drouet and Kent in Chapter 11, and they will get a good sense from Bailey and Mecklenburg (Chapter 10) of what they will face when their opinions about the research are seriously challenged.

Attorneys and Judges

One of the primary benefits of this volume to practicing attorneys and judges is its state-of-the-knowledge review of most of the issues surrounding this form of expert testimony presented between two covers, but there is more to offer. Just as researchers learn from the perspectives of attorneys and judges about the challenges that they face, attorneys and judges who read this volume will gain insight into the challenges that researchers face in their attempts to provide empirical research that is directly relevant to the justice system. Attorneys should benefit directly from the advice of their very experienced peers (Drouet and Kent, in Chapter 11 and Bailey and Mecklenburg, in Chapter 10) who represent both the prosecution and defense in criminal cases. Those who are not familiar with how eyewitness experts approach their tasks will learn from the Pezdek chapter (Chapter 2). There is much to be gleaned from these chapters to sharpen advocacy skills and to increase one's confidence in deciding the appropriateness of expert testimony in a specific case.

Last, having witnessed and contributed to the development and growth of the literature on expert testimony about eyewitness identification, I wish to offer a few observations. In what other forensic, scientific, or other expert field have researchers attempted to empirically assess lay knowledge, expert consensus, and the effects of their expert testimony? I know of none. And no one should make the mistake of dismissing this research on the basis of conflict of interest (i.e., expert witnesses trying to justify their work and bring in more business), for many if not most of the researchers engaged in this research are not expert witnesses. When this research began, no model or best practices existed for how to conduct research on lay knowledge or legal concepts, consensus among experts as it related to expert testimony, and effects of expert testimony, and this shows in the research literature. Methodologies and standards vary, some studies are more informative than others, and some sets of findings are open to multiple interpretations. The research literature has matured and is now very informative. Future research on lay knowledge, consensus, and effects of expert testimony in other forensic domains will benefit from the groundwork laid by the research reviewed in these chapters.

Index